Lavery Library

St. John Fisher
College

Rochester, New York

Successful Gaijin in Japan

HOW FOREIGN COMPANIES ARE MAKING IT IN JAPAN

NAGAMI KISHI

DAVID RUSSELL

Printed on recyclable paper

NTC Business Books

a division of *NTC Publishing Group* • Lincolnwood, Illinois USA

Acknowledgments

Sincere thanks are gratefully extended
to Ms. Minako Kichiraku for her help
in preparing this manuscript.

Library of Congress Cataloging-in-Publication Data

Kishi, Nagami, 1945–
    Successful gaijin in Japan: how companies are making it in Japan /
    Nagami Kishi, David W. Russell.
        p.   cm.
    Includes bibliographical references and index.
    ISBN 0-8442-3549-0
    1. International business enterprises—Japan—Management.
    2. Corporations, Foreign—Japan—Management.   3. Success in
    business—Case studies.   I. Russell, David, 1952–   .   II. Title.
    HD62.4.K56   1995
    658'.049'0952—dc20   95-11302
                                                                              CIP

Published by NTC Business Books, a division of NTC Publishing Group
4255 West Touhy Avenue
Lincolnwood (Chicago), Illinois 60646-1975, U.S.A.
© 1996 by NTC Publishing Group. All rights reserved.
No part of this book may be reproduced, stored in a retrieval
system, or transmitted in any form or by any means,
electronic, mechanical, photocopying, recording or otherwise,
without the prior permission of NTC Publishing Group.
Manufactured in the United States of America.

5 6 7 8 9 BC 9 8 7 6 5 4 3 2 1

Contents

Preface   ix

**Chapter 1   Foreign Firms *Can* Succeed in the
Japanese Market**   1

Image   3
Corporate Identity   5
Good Management   6
On Hiring Japanese Managers   14
The Importance of *Jinmyaku*   15
The Unimportance of MBAs and English Skills   18
Jinmyaki in Action   21
You *Can* Acquire *Jinmyaku*   22
Study Your Market   25
Master Distribution Channels   27
No Models to Copy, Only Hints at How to Succeed   29

Chapter 2   East of Eden: *Levi Strauss*   31

Beginnings: Holes in the Floor   32
Dead on Arrival   34
Heroes Wanted: Dead or Alive   35
Hit List   38
Aging Baby Boomers   40
Made in the U.S.A.   42

Distribution Savvy   44
LSJ Today   46
Executive Profile   47
Conclusions   49

Chapter 3   Breaking the Rules: *Louis Vuitton*   **51**
The Bubble Years   52
Background   54
Enter the Consultants   57
Loyalty to Vuitton Comes First   59
No Discounts—Ever   62
Two More Critical Points   64
Were Japanese Sales Too Successful?   66
Conclusion   67

Chapter 4   The Road Not Taken: *BMW*   **69**
From Kawasaki to BMW   71
From Airplanes to Motorcycles to Luxury Cars   75
Learning the System   77
Be Smart—Do It Our Way   79
Putting the Swing in Marketing   80
You Only *Think* You Can't Afford It   81
What? A $40,000 Used Car?   82
A *Gaishi* Needs a Visible Headquarters   84
Changing of the Guard   85
Safe, Environmentally Friendly Luxury Cars   86
Conclusions   87

Chapter 5   Becoming a Household Name:
Procter & Gamble   **89**
A Joint Venture Born of a Joint Venture   90
Oil Crisis Management   91
The Pampers Fiasco   94
Building Strategy and Image   95
The Whisper Success   97
Expanding the Corporation   100
Conclusion   102

Chapter 6   Hard Work Is the Real Thing: *Coca-Cola*   **105**

The Father of Coca-Cola   106
Obstacles from the Start   108
Not Diet Coke—Coke in the Diet   111
Gaiatsu   113
Just a Few Conditions . . .   116
The Last Hurdle   118
Route of the Problem   120
Missing: The Pepsi Generation   121
Speed Bumps   124
Too Much Success?   126
Conclusions   128

Chapter 7   The Impossible Dream: *AFLAC*   **129**

A Local Firm Goes International   130
The Right Person for the Job   133
Taking Up the Challenge   135
Sleepless Nights   137
Regulation, MOF-Style   139
A Waiting Game   141
A Man Who Couldn't Quit   143
Looking for Agents   144
Selling the Product   146
Monopoly   148
New Products, New Home   151
How Do You Spell Success?   154

Chapter 8   Door-to-Door Success: *Amway*   **157**

Becoming a Distributor   158
American Dreams   160
The Early Years in Japan   160
Crisis Management   164
How to Process a Few Million Orders   167
Durables + Consumables = Long-term Profit Picture   169
Creating a High Profile   170
Overcoming Internal Communication Problems   171

An Inspired Idea   172
Can They Keep It Up?   173

Chapter 9   Writing Its Name Large:
Parker Pen   **177**

The Word Processor of the Ancients   178
Juggling Presidents   180
Up and Down With Wella   182
Changing the Natural Order of Things   185
Human Relations   187
The Duofold Image   189
Image-Building   190
New Marketing Strategies   192
Becoming Number 1   195

Chapter 10   Investing in Tokyo:
Salomon Bros.   **199**

Some Recent History   200
Ping-Pong and *Bonenkai*   201
Small Town Saloon-Keeper   204
Crazy Like a Fox   208
Economists and Researchers   210
M&A   212
The Look of a Survivor   215
Post-Bubble Strategy   216
Conclusions   217

Chapter 11   "When in Rome . . .":
Nippon Olivetti   **219**

Dealing with the *Tonya*   219
Localization   222
Banking on New Demand   224
Matsushita Man   226
The Key to Restructuring: Personnel Policies   229
Oriental Desk   231
Scoring Big with Sports Equipment   233
Communicating with the Head Office   234
Conclusion   235

Chapter 12 A Success Story in the Making: *Nobelpharma Japan* 237

A Million Patients 238
Selling the System 239
Attracting the Dentists 241
Revolving Presidents 244
Problems with Female Workers 245
The Electrolux Story 248
Time to Move 251
Afterword: Some Notes from the Top 253

Chapter 13 If at First You Don't Succeed: *Nestlé* 255

A Long History 256
Tonya Power 258
Learning about the Local Market—the Hard Way 259
Winning and Losing a Market 262
Three Misses: It's All in the Timing 264
Going Native 266
Cold Coffee 267
Diversification 269
Feline Gourmets 271
Changing Organizational Strategy and More 272

Chapter 14 An Eye for Opportunity: *Alcon* 275

America Beckons 276
An Impressive Career 278
From JV to Independence 279
Growing Pains 281
There Are Going to Be a Few Changes Around Here 283
Teaching the Home Office about Japan 286
Bureaucratic Myopia 288
Smoke Doesn't Get in Your Eyes 291
Conclusions 293

Chapter 15 Drinking in Success: *United Distillers* 295

Protecting Domestic Drinkers from Imported Liquor 296

Foreign Studies 300
Career Moves 302
Number Two Blues 303
Radical Surgery 304
Time to Rethink Strategy 306
Two Jobs 309
Aiming for Number 1 310
The Family Relationship 311
Weathering the Recession 312
Conclusion 313

Chapter 16 Delivering on Its Promise: *DHL* 315
One-Man Show 316
Leaving Home Without It 319
The Emperor's New Clothes 322
Most Executives Have Never Used a Computer 325
Motivation Makes the Difference 328
Profit Center 331
Conclusion 332

Afterword   A Few Notes to Firms Hoping to Find Success 335
On Dealing with the Bureaucracy 335
A Touch of Humility Doesn't Hurt 337
Beware of Consultants 339
. . . And While You're at It, Beware of Headhunters 342
A Tip for Structuring Top Management at a *Gaishi* 343
Conclusion 345

Index 347

About the Authors 353

Preface

Despite its unimpressive geographical size, in economic terms Japan is already close to three-quarters the size of the United States. That alone makes it one of the two most important markets in the world. Add to that Japan's strategic position in Asia, the only area of the world that will sustain high growth rates over the next decade, and one could easily argue that for any company to under-commit to the Japanese market is a sure sign of myopic management.

And yet the statistics regarding foreign investment in Japan provide eloquent testimony to the difficulties of setting up operations here. Furthermore, the countless tales of bureaucratic roadblocks, incomprehensible business practices, and innumerable other obstacles encountered by foreign executives in Tokyo are more than enough to give any responsible CEO pause to reconsider the wisdom of pouring money and personnel into a Japanese operation.

Without either ignoring or denying this state of affairs, our recommendation to any company thinking about starting up or increasing business in Japan is simple: Do it and do it now. The bureaucratic climate for allowing foreign firms to come into Japan, either to set up 100 percent-owned subsidiaries or joint ventures with Japanese partners, is better than ever. Changes in Japanese society and the corporate community stemming from the end of the "bubble era" of the late 1980s and the subsequent long recession have made buying foreign products and doing business with foreign firms more attractive than ever. In addition, the economy is just beginning to pull out of the recession and looks on course to chart solid (if unspectacular) long-term growth.

Firms that miss this window of opportunity will have to wait at least another decade, possibly two, to find rents on the decline and a large, highly educated (arguably the world's most highly educated) labor pool lined up and looking for work. In short, the latter 1990s will not be a golden age for Japan, but they *can be* a golden age for foreign companies looking to expand in or into Japan and to position themselves for the coming decade of growth in Asia.

What about all the horror stories of doing business here? Believe a lot of them. Many probably were true (although many were not, and some were simply convenient excuses for failures, both personal and corporate). But what of the other stories, the ones that don't make the papers very often? The success stories of hundreds upon hundreds of foreign firms that came to Japan and stuck it out and ultimately produced good profits? Tokyo chambers of commerce are full of success stories, not only from America but also Britain, France, Germany, Spain, Sweden, Italy, Switzerland, Australia, and several other nations. Their stories are seldom told for two reasons: first, they aren't as sensational as the negative stories, and second, the companies that did stick it out here, who did become "insiders" in this admittedly clubby market, often discovered that their profits were the kind they'd rather not draw too much attention to (the most oft-cited case being Coca-Cola, which for years made more profit in Japan than it did in the United States). As an American executive of another *Fortune* 500 company confided years ago, "Now we understand why the Japanese fought so hard to keep this market to themselves for so long. Once you finally figure out how to make the system work for you, it's a gold mine."

It is not difficult to understand such enthusiasm once you see things from the "inside" as this local president now does. It is true that Japan has a bureaucratic labyrinth as complex as any in the world, and regulations piled on top of regulations. It also has cartels ("industry associations") and price rigging, and shady connections between politicians, industry, and organized crime, and all the other scandalous arrangements that surface in the papers from time to time. Yet what corporation has ever done business overseas and not run into at least some of these problems? A few of the challenges Japan throws at a foreign company trying to do business here may be unique, but most of them are just variations on a theme they've already learned to dance to in Europe, or Latin America, or elsewhere in Asia. New rules? Certainly. A new game? Perhaps. Impossible to figure out or to win? Don't be ridiculous.

The bottom line is this: Japan is nowhere near as difficult a market as some people would have you believe, nor as simple a market as many foreigners would *like* to believe.

Before we look at some of the foreign companies that have made it in Japan, we need to make an important distinction between institutional markets and consumer markets. If you want to sell products to an institutional market—supercomputers to a government-affiliated research center, for example—you will probably find that the Japanese market is every bit as tough as you've heard. To a large extent it has changed very little in the past several years. Institutional markets, especially those concerning products which the government considers in some way strategic to Japan's economic growth, will continue to be wrapped in bureaucratic red tape, in-group (*keiretsu*) purchasing biases, and so on.

However, for the many companies involved in the consumer sector, Japan has "opened up" dramatically over the past few years. More than anything having to do with government policy, this is an effect of the recession and what it has done to the attitudes of Japanese consumers.

In other words, if you are trying to sell semiconductors to Japan, you can certainly do it, but you'll have your work cut out for you. But if you're trying to sell consumer-use end products, such as computers, peripherals, software, etc., the market is wide open. The huge success of Apple Computer and the very significant inroads of companies such as Compaq on the local PC market— which until recently was no more welcome to foreign makers than the local auto market—are proof that things are changing.

In this book we will look at the operations of the Japanese subsidiaries or affiliates of a small sampling of consumer products, service, and financial firms. We will often refer to these Japanese companies, owned wholly or in part by foreign parents, by the common term *gaishi*, taken from the Japanese *gaishikei kigyo*, meaning foreign-capital companies. As you will see in these chapters, *gaishi* firms that set up in Japan with good products and good management, then added good local marketing and distribution, sooner or later found a rich market ready to reward them. In some cases it was a long, difficult road—often due to the xenophobic regulatory climate in decades past—but in every case, the companies have found their efforts worth the investment.

The firms portrayed here make up only a tiny percentage of the many that have already succeeded in Japan, and an even smaller fraction of the many more that will succeed here in the next several years.

Nagami Kishi
David Russell
Tokyo

CHAPTER 1

Foreign Firms *Can* Succeed in the Japanese Market

Buying foreign brands is nothing new for the Japanese: Japan has been a net importer for the greater part of its history. It has imported not only foreign products, but also foreign culture for much of the past 1,500 years or so—writing, printing, art, religion . . . the list goes on and on. Even things that the Japanese think of as especially unique to their culture, things like green tea and *miso* (soy), were originally imported from abroad. The nation "closed" for a time during the rule of the shoguns, but a little over a century ago the modern era dawned and Japan was reopened to the world. Its new leaders wanted to catch up to the West in many fields, so the government spent vast sums in a frantic effort to *encourage* the importation of ideas, technology, and skills. Along with this opening to the world came a flood of new products, new clothing, new music, new literature, and so on. The country "closed" once again during the militarist period in this century, but began reopening after the war. And sure enough, there was a new flood of Western ideas, Western technology, and Western products. In some cases, the government severely limited the influx of certain products in order to support domestic industries as they struggled

1

to get back on their feet, but as the decades went by and the world's economic and political situation changed, that policy has become less and less tenable. Among the masses there has always been demand for foreign goods, and that has only increased in the past few decades.

Since the end of the war, almost anything that was American was seen as good, and anything European was almost as good. Japanese have long felt that "foreign" indicates "superior," and that image is largely intact today. It is interesting to note that the Japanese language has two parallel alphabets, and the one called *katakana* is mostly used for foreign words, such as foreign brand names, company names, etc. But these days *katakana* denotes something special, unusual, often attractive. Names in *katakana* are felt to be "with it." Everything from the names of new software companies to stereos, cameras, and even Japanese cars are generally written in *katakana*. The "*katakana* image" is one of currency, of quality. Even the company name Sony is written in *katakana*. All this points to the attractiveness of things that have a "foreign" or "international" feel.

Even in Japanese TV commercials, you are likely to see many foreign faces. Simply having foreigners appear together with an otherwise ordinary product makes it look better. And if the foreigner happens to be famous, so much the better. Why on earth would a company that makes instant noodles, one of the most popular foods in Japan, want to show Arnold Schwarzenegger slurping its noodles? Because Arnold's image alone indicates foreign "acceptance" of a traditional Japanese product. Japanese companies are so in tune with this trend that they regularly license foreign brand names, produce famous foreign goods locally, and cash in on the caché of the foreign name (many of the most popular "imported" beers in Japanese bars and restaurants are actually imported from breweries a few miles outside of Tokyo).

What all this means is that Japan is not a "closed" market in the sense that people don't want to buy what outsiders have to sell. Yes, there have been many areas in which government regulations kept foreign products out, but that situation has been changing for some time. Yes, Japan is famous for its complex, sometimes Byzantine distribution system. But many foreign companies have succeeded in going around the distribution system and many others have succeeded by taking advantage of its strengths. For most products, neither the government nor the distribution system should be regarded as a formidable obstacle to doing business in Japan.

The fact is, there is no big secret to doing business in Japan nor to becoming successful here. The real mystery is why so many firms fail. Companies that have done their homework and have prepared an appropriate strategy for this market have at least as good a chance of succeeding as they do in any other country, and in some cases a much better chance. There are three important points to keep in mind:

- Establish a positive corporate image, and preserve that image at all costs.

- Have a clear product identity in Japan.

- Structure your management and create your marketing strategy in accordance with the local market.

Image

Every company says it is concerned about its image, but taking care of your image is something special in Japan. For example, think about what happens when a consumer feels he or she has been taken advantage of; that is, bought something that proved to be a lot less than it was advertised to be. The Western attitude to this situation is summed up by the old principle *caveat emptor*, "let the buyer beware." But from the Japanese perspective, this is unacceptable. As the Japanese consumer sees it, a manufacturer or a distributor—both of whose responsibilities include helping to provide for the common good—have tricked unsuspecting shoppers out of hard-earned cash. Regardless of how people in the West may view this, the fact remains that it engenders a very strong negative reaction in Japan. If Japanese buy something that they are led to believe is high quality, and it turns out to be otherwise, the company that sold it will suffer a tremendous decline in image. This is one of the reasons that Japanese firms offer such extensive "after-care" policies, providing free or inexpensive repair services for years after a product is sold. A firm that does not support its products in a way that Japanese consumers feel is appropriate may find that other products in its line-up will no longer sell because of this image problem. In short, Japanese consumers are not forgiving. Once your image hits the skids, it is almost impossible to rebuild it.

Many *gaishi* firms start with a very positive image, only to let it erode through lack of care. Despite the similarity in taste, color, packaging, etc., Coke still has Pepsi-Cola on the ropes in Japan. Why hasn't Pepsi grabbed more than a small fraction of the market? It has been haunted by mistakes made in its early days and is still trying to catch up in the image department. For a time, Borden was the best-known premium-quality ice cream in Japan, enjoying an overwhelming market share. But it had trouble with its Japanese partner, terminated its joint venture, and thus cut off its sales channels. In no time at all Borden products were being discounted and its image fell in the marketplace. Today, although it has tried licensing its brand name to another Japanese firm, the company has for all practical purposes withdrawn from Japan.

The message is simple: If you have a good product image and allow it to suffer for almost any reason, it is nearly impossible to resurrect. This is not only true for *gaishi*, but for Japanese companies as well.

There are rare exceptions, of course—Apple Computer had a terrific image in Japan in its very early days, but then let bad marketing policies ruin that image so badly that many dealers didn't want to carry the Macintosh computer when it came out. Finally, after much effort, Apple turned its image around remarkably, but even so, it took years to get back on track, and during that time countless sales were lost. No manager should allow this to happen. Apple was extremely lucky; other companies have not been.

Keep in mind that Japanese always rank everything. This seems natural to them, and rankings become very important, often too important. People want to know what university a person went to and what company he or she works for. A person from a famous university is assumed to be intelligent, hardworking, and honest, but may be none of these things. On the other hand, Japanese expect little of those from unknown universities and don't give them a chance to perform. The same is true with products. No matter how good a product or service is, if it is unknown, it has a very difficult time getting into the consumer market. If it has a good image (and remember, foreign products start off with a generally high-quality image), Japanese are far more willing to listen to a sales pitch, look at the product, buy it, taste it, drive it, etc. In short, nothing is as important as creating and then preserving a good image.

Corporate Identity

Identity means having a special something that sets your company and/or your products apart from all the rest. Brand-name goods are an easy example: Louis Vuitton bags are unique; they have a design, a logo, a variety of patterns that set them apart from rival products. BMW only came to Japan in the 1980s, but immediately set about establishing an identity as an exclusive vehicle maker. Rather than play up the common features of its cars and compete with other auto makers on a point-for-point basis, the company presented its products as special, not for just any buyer. L.L. Bean's outdoor goods have a special identity because for decades they were available from only a single mail-order outlet in the U.S. When retail shops sporting the Bean logo opened in Tokyo, they were an instant hit because the company's identity was already well known to young shoppers before the stores opened.

Companies like Procter & Gamble (P & G), whose products are not so very different from those of their competitors, are also highly successful in Japan. Part of that success is due to good management, and part to good marketing and strategy, but part stems from the strong identity they have built for their products.

What about companies that have come to Japan with good images, often good management, and possibly good strategies, but no clear market identity? Consider the dozens of banks and securities firms that rushed into Tokyo in the 1980s, looking for a piece of the action during the boom years. They didn't know anything about the Japanese market, and many didn't work very hard to learn. As a result, there are dozens of foreign banks and brokers barely breaking even today or already operating in the red. Many will be gone within a year or two. They may have a clear identity in their home markets, but they failed to communicate that identity in an understandable way to Japanese investors and institutions, and they failed to provide services that differentiated themselves sufficiently from their rivals.

Other foreign houses worked overtime to make a name for themselves. Salomon Bros., one of the firms we will look at here, offered Japanese investors not only information on Japanese stocks, bonds, real estate, and so on, but also real comparisons with the same investments in America, Europe, and other markets, and provided more detailed information about investing both at home and abroad than any Japanese broker had yet provided. The quality and depth of Salomon's information, together with its aggressive stance and ability to move markets, became its identity. A few firms like Salomon and Morgan Stanley enjoyed good business results—in fact, much better than almost any of their Japanese rivals, even in the midst of a painful recession.

Good Management

Obviously, it takes more than identity. Other quality brands came to Japan before Louis Vuitton and offered similar goods with a recognizable identity, but where are those companies now? P&G became highly successful in Japan, but other large foreign firms have tried to sell household goods here and failed. There are hundreds upon hundreds of cases where one *gaishi* succeeds but half a dozen in the same field do not. And it has nothing to do with the size or financial clout of the parent company (a relatively small firm like BMW was selling cars as fast as they could import them while GM was still trying to convince customers to look for its showrooms). Even world-famous companies with lots of capital to invest in building up their local operations are not guaranteed a place in the winners' circle in Tokyo.

The bottom line in many cases is not money or number of years in Japan, but something more fundamental: good management. However, what constitutes good management at the parent firm may not always, in and of itself, be good at the Japan subsidiary. *Gaishi* firms are often stigmatized by Japanese rivals as having good products but bad management, a combination that scares off many local companies that would otherwise be willing to do business with them.

Too many books that attempt to explain success in the Japanese market stress the importance of adopting Japanese-style management throughout a local organization. As we will see shortly, that is seldom the best approach. For the moment, however, note that when we refer to good management as a factor in a company's success, we are talking about a company with a strong leader or leaders and clear, consistent lines of administration, a company that hires and trains good staff, and develops a solid, unified corporate culture. The same holds true whether the firm is large or small. It is no exaggeration to say that the one thing your clients, your bankers, and even your rivals will view as most important in predicting the future of your business is the quality of your local management. They believe that good management can overcome any obstacle the local market (or your home office) may have set in your path—and we would have to agree. Let's take a more careful look at the problems of managing a *gaishi* company.

The Myths of Japanese Management

One of the biggest problems for any firm operating in a foreign country is localization: "To what extent should we adapt our way of running our business to suit the local market?" For example, *gaishi* firms in Japan worry about things like how to deal with hiring and firing local staff, pay scales, and promotions. For decades now, some of the top foreign business consultants in Tokyo have been reciting the same litany—"Japan is a special place with a special culture. You cannot try to change its lifetime employment system; you cannot tinker with its seniority system or age-linked pay scales. These are traditional elements of Japanese corporate culture and are inextricably connected with the bonds that hold Japanese society together."

While the fundamental spirit underlying this approach is right on target—to succeed in Japan you must adapt to the Japanese environment—the conclusions drawn are very misleading. Many years ago they were somewhat closer to the truth than they are today, but in the world of contemporary Japanese business they are nonsense. What is perhaps most remarkable is that despite the radical and ongoing changes in Japanese business, the same corporate advisers are still reciting the same slogans that they did in the 1970s and 1980s, and foreign companies are still listening. Such well intentioned but inaccurate advice has caused untold problems at scores of companies that should be rolling in profit today instead of making annual trips back to the head office to explain why they need a little more time to get things running smoothly in Tokyo. Neither the parent company nor the Japanese subsidiary can figure out why things are so slow; they attribute it to the recession, to the difficulties of a new market, to government regulations, to anything but the real problem: management of the Japanese office is out of touch with reality.

Let's look at some specifics. First, pay scales. At the average large Japanese company, if you look at the salaries of men in their 40s, that is, people who have been working for the same company for 20-odd years, there is a variation of as much as 30–40 percent in their pay scales. That may be less than in the United States, but it is far from the old myth that "all Japanese workers of the same age receive the same pay." Middle-aged Japanese salaried employees have known for years that the idea that everyone gets paid the same is a big lie.

What about lifetime employment? A study of Japanese workers several years ago (before the big recession began) found that only around 20 percent of them had anything even resembling lifetime employment. It is a safe bet that during the recession that figure dropped considerably.

For the most part, lifetime employment and the seniority system came about right after World War II as companies struggled to catch up with their Western rivals. These were practical measures for a poor nation with a war-ravaged population that prized long-term security above all else and weakened industries that needed a loyal, stable workforce. But they were temporary measures. As Japanese companies grew and these systems began to have less and less applicability to the new corporate realities, many big firms quietly dropped them and began moving to something more flexible. The first oil crisis provided the perfect opportunity. Many workers had to be let go in order for companies to survive that difficult period. Lifetime employment became a cosmetic fiction that was maintained at all big companies, at least during good times, to attract new workers.

In the recession of the early 1990s, thousands of middle-aged employees have discovered the true nature of "lifetime" employment: when times get bad, the company will ask you to leave; if you don't quit voluntarily, the company will make your life so miserable you will soon want to quit. The newspapers and magazines have played up stories of men in their fifties being suddenly transferred to branch offices hundreds of miles away from their families, or given a desk in the dark basement of a huge office building. Some men who have been with their companies for thirty years come to work one morning to find no phones on their desks. When they say that they can't do their jobs without telephones, the boss says, "You don't have any real work to do. Why don't you do us all a favor and quit?" This is their reward for decades of service. While such cases are extreme, the rapid spread of the "slash the payroll" mentality at Japan's big corporations has shown lifetime employment to be another big lie.

Until the oil crisis, the average retirement age was set at 55 throughout most of Japanese industry. But after the oil crisis and up until the early 1980s, it was extended to 60. However, the companies realized that if salaries kept rising and promotions were automatic for those extra five years, they would be taking on a huge additional financial burden. So the big firms decided that during those extra five years (except for a very few special employees) salaries would not rise. In fact, in many cases pay rates would actually drop by up to 30 percent, and status in the company would likewise decline. Many senior employees who found themselves in this position left the companies they had worked for all their lives to join client firms or other affiliated companies.

The Museum of Antiquated Personnel Policies

It is ironic but true that *gaishi* are actually more concerned with lifetime employment and seniority system-based personnel policies than are many Japanese firms. Part of this is a result of their past experience. Many of the firms that came to Japan years ago had labor problems, often stemming from what the Japanese term a "dry" management style (being insensitive to employees' feelings, abruptly firing staff, etc.). To deal with this problem, many *gaishi* began hiring Japanese personnel managers away from local firms. As intended, these personnel managers brought the current management practices of those days (the 1960s and 1970s) with them to their new firms. This was all right at first, because Japanese firms were not changing very much, and it could have been a very successful strategy for years to come if the Japanese economy had not hit a few speed bumps in the following years.

Of course, there were the two oil shocks of the 1970s which had powerful effects on big business. But there was another big shock, one that, unlike OPEC, would not go away. In the aftermath of the Plaza Accord of 1985, the yen took off like a hot-air balloon. It was blown sideways many times over the next few years, and sometimes even pushed down temporarily, but everyone with eyes could see that it was destined to rise.

Following the oil shocks and the post-Plaza "yen shock," many large Japanese firms realized it was time to change their personnel systems. Seniority-based pay scales were hit hard. In the years immediately following the Plaza Accord, Japanese companies began a process of adjusting pay rates. Both these trends slowed down a bit during the easygoing bubble years, but intensified once again during the recession of the 1990s.

Despite all these changes, most Japanese personnel managers who had transferred to *gaishi* firms had little idea what was going on inside their old companies. And many of those who heard about changes at other companies had already convinced executives at their new firms that old-fashioned Japanese-style management was the only way to go. So, as Japanese corporate society began to change, the *gaishi* were often left behind, trying desperately to preserve a system that they believed was essential to successful operations in Japan (and trying to persuade their head offices of this fact as well).

In some ways, it is hard to blame the top management of these firms, for they relied on their own Japanese personnel managers to guide them. But in addition, they retained outside professionals whose job it was to observe and analyze important trends in the Japanese markets and alert management to problems in the offing. Many of these business consultants proved to be highly knowledgeable about the macro side of Japanese business, but very few knew what was going on with the micro side—such as the changes inside Japanese personnel departments. This problem was not limited to *gaijin* consultants: even some of the most famous Japanese consultants, some of whom regularly advise *Fortune* 500 firms, have been totally out of touch with Japanese business at the micro level for 20 years or more. We will come back to this problem at the end of the book.

The result is that the *gaishi* began with a good idea—adapt their policies to the local business environment—but then fell out of step as that environment continued to change. Trusted advisers, both Japanese and foreign, told them essentially to "do as the Japanese do," and so they tried to copy the Japanese approach. The problem was that no one was watching carefully to see if "what the Japanese do" was changing. Both the *gaishi* firms' personnel managers and the outsiders who were paid to keep an eye on Japanese business for them were in many cases badly informed.

If we look at major Japanese companies today, we find that about half of them adhere to the old, Japanese-style seniority-system approach and about half have already turned to a more Western-style merit-system approach. The ongoing trend is definitely toward the latter. Yet many *gaishi* firms are still locked into some version of the traditional Japanese system and are having a painful time trying to become more Western.

The maxim for foreign firms in adapting to the Japanese market should be: *Don't just say "Do It the Japanese Way" —find out what Japanese companies are actually doing, and then act accordingly.*

Motivating Employees, Maintaining Internal Communication

Foreign firms usually have very clear-cut job descriptions. The basic idea is that if everyone does as they are supposed to and works diligently, the company will operate efficiently, and hopefully attain its goals. This idea is alien to most Japanese firms, and if you try to apply that same approach to Japanese workers, it may even backfire.

Many Japanese workers don't want the same kind of individual responsibility. Instead, they want to know what their group's goals are, and then find a way to reach those goals together with their coworkers. On an assembly line this can be done in simple, concrete terms, but few *gaishi* offices look like assembly lines. Thus, one of the questions management consultants most often hear from *gaishi* managers is, "How do I motivate my Japanese workers?"

And one of the key answers is surprisingly simple. Managers need to give workers a view of the "big picture" and then let them see how their work fits into that picture. Show them how their work contributes to the company's overall success. Most people, when they see how significant their role is in achieving the company's long-term goals, will work very hard, many of them putting in overtime without being asked. Japanese employees want to be part of a team, they want to feel that they are contributing to a bigger effort, not merely fulfilling a job description and going home as soon as the clock strikes five. In the broadest sense, they want to belong to an organization with a *mission*. Your company's mission may simply be to sell more ballpoint pens or hot dogs in Japan than anyone else. That's fine. But make sure your employees understand it as your mission, not some arbitrary sales target. Hold regular meetings, explain the company's strategy to all your staff, and make sure that each one understands how important his or her role is in helping the company to achieve its goals. The concept of teamwork is important in the West, but it is many times more important in Japan.

If you don't keep your employees informed about your business (and many *gaishi* don't), some of them will begin to worry about the company's long-term stability or commitment to the market. Some of your staff will spend a lot of time and energy trying to find out about the company's business picture, and they will start rumors based on what they find out, regardless of its accuracy. Some employees at the other end of the spectrum will stop thinking about the company entirely and start thinking only of themselves. Once the company has let them fall "out of the loop," what the firm does is no longer important; their jobs are no longer important. They become just like your worst employees back home, planning to do the minimum amount necessary to keep from getting fired and nothing more. Others who adopt this "look out for number 1" approach feel it's all right to make their coworkers look bad if it serves to make themselves look good. All of this spells trouble for *gaishi* management.

Another pitfall has nothing to do with bad decision making in Japan. Often, *gaishi* find themselves victims of policy changes at the head office. What was company policy until yesterday will have to be turned around 180 degrees today. This may be confusing enough to your native staff, but it is incomprehensible to Japanese staff and it will quickly give your firm a reputation as a company on the skids.

These same kinds of problems have happened to so many "good" firms here, firms with worldwide reputations, that one wonders what kind of preparation their managers had before coming to Japan.

Good management means having open communication (not just open lines of communication) between the home office, the Japanese subsidiary, and your local staff. It means giving employees a feeling of participation and an individual role in company business, and a unified sense of the company's identity. Where pay scales seem erratic, there must be a system, an understandable formula to rationalize what exists, because everyone will know what is what sooner or later.

It is also very important for the top executives of a *gaishi* firm to do more than report to their home office; they must constantly work to inform the headquarters of the situation in Japan, the needs of the Japanese market, and so on. The local CEO must always be willing to argue on behalf of the Japan operation, and this should be understood throughout the company. Such an attitude is fundamentally good for the head office (any parent company that wants "yes men" as CEOs of its subsidiaries had better stay out of Japan), but it is especially important in building morale inside the local subsidiary.

Good management also means building strong, long-term relations with distributors, wholesalers, stores, etc. The American approach to marketing—advertise your product on TV, consumers see the ads, and then rush to the store to ask for the product—is nowhere near as successful in Japan. Japanese consumers like to shop, and they like to shop face-to-face when it is practical to do so. Consequently, people in the distribution chain, such as the nation's thousands of small shopowners, have tremendous power over consumer decisions. Many a housewife goes to the drug store or the housewares shop or the do-it-yourself store and asks the owner's advice on what to buy. If she's heard about it on TV, she may recognize a product name when the store owner mentions it, and she may want to try it, but the key is often the local store owner's recommendation. And where do store owners get their information? From their distributors. Thus, how much time a firm spends working with and educating its distributors can have a great deal to do with its success.

On Hiring Japanese Managers

After many years of observing foreign companies in Japan, looking at CEOs and other senior executives, it is striking how often we see Japanese managers and have to wonder, "How did that guy ever wind up in that job?" This says a lot about hiring policies at *gaishi* companies.

Whatever their failings, at least most of the middle managers in a Japanese company look and act like middle managers. One may argue about their level of responsibility or training compared to a manager in a Western firm, but there is no arguing that they are usually competent within the context of the Japanese corporate system. In other words, when you see a *bucho* or *kacho* (department head or section chief), he looks like a *bucho* or *kacho*, and after talking to him for five minutes you know just what he does for his company. If only this could be said for Japanese managers with similar titles at foreign firms.

It is not difficult to see why there are problems. Consider these men, most in their 40s and early 50s. At the time they graduated from university no one wanted to work for a *gaishi*. Even today foreign firms have a stigma among Japanese workers: join a *gaishi*, it is thought, and you can be fired at any moment, human relations are terrible, company policies change like the weather, depending on the whims of the head office, and there is seldom anything meaningful in the way of pension plans. Thus, if someone is looking for work at a *gaishi*, it's pretty obvious that he or she is after the one thing that all *gaishi* offer: money. You can imagine what kind of image this creates among more serious Japanese workers.

In fact, if you look at the Japanese men over 60 in a *gaishi*, many worked for the Occupation forces or in some way picked up English long ago. A fair number of those in their 40s and 50s are men who couldn't get jobs in the better Japanese companies and thus opted for *gaishi*, where the pay is at least better and their lack of competence is assumed by their foreign managers to be the norm for Japanese workers.

In the past several years some top-notch Japanese managers have jumped to *gaishi* to become CEOs and directors, but until they did so, there was a general feeling among Japanese businessmen that anyone working for a *gaishi* was just a third-rate manager with some English skills. More than one incompetent Japanese manager has found that beefing up his English (or French or German) ability is the fastest ticket to a good job and better pay. This image still lingers on today among many Japanese executives.

The Importance of *Jinmyaku*

One thing that *gaishi* executives don't seem to understand until it is too late is the typical Japanese way of evaluating up-and-coming management personnel. For example, because every Western manager is assumed to hold an MBA, *gaijin* executives never fail to be impressed by a young Japanese with an MBA from a "name" university. Certainly, they think, this young man (it is almost inevitably a man) is on the fast track to the top; he should make quite a catch for any company.

In fact, nothing could be further from the truth. But to understand why, you must first understand how Japanese companies work and how they evaluate their staff.

The first thing to remember is that until quite recently being sent overseas was not a good career move. Even men from Japan's top universities who join the very best companies must compete with dozens, sometimes hundreds of people just like themselves for promotions. Incomprehensible though it may seem to foreign firms, job performance is almost never the real criterion at Japanese companies. Rather, emphasis is placed on what is called "human relations." Part of this is merely getting along, at least superficially, with everyone in a company, but another part is what non-Japanese managers think of as networking.

A man from a top university who has been in a company for 15 or 20 years is not looking to be the best manager in his division. Instead, he is looking to get along well with his colleagues and to have the best connections, both inside and outside the company. That means not only connections with people of his own age in other divisions, with his superiors, and with directors of the company, but also with clients, suppliers, banks, government officials, even the media, and so on. The importance of these connections cannot be overemphasized. In Japan, this network of personal connections that one works hard to build up year after year has a special name: *jinmyaku*.

One of the criteria for promotion to a company's upper ranks and one of the keys to real success as an executive is *jinmyaku*. The problem is that it takes years of work and lots of effort, and, needless to say, everyone else is trying to do exactly the same thing. If you want to succeed, you can't waste time; you have to start early. Japanese who are really on what Westerners would call the "fast track" started building their *jinmyaku* in high school or earlier. They most certainly do so when they enter the elite universities.

As we said before, in Japan everyone is ranked. Thus, there is an acknowledged No. 1 school (Todai, as the University of Tokyo is called) and within that school there is even a No. 1 department (the law faculty). No one cares much whether a student learns anything in that faculty or not. Simply having passed through its portals assures one of a substantial *jinmyaku* of professors, lecturers, and *sempai* and *kohai* (those ahead of and behind you in school). Ten or twenty years after graduating, every Todai grad has an awesome store of *jinmyaku* (although whether they know how to use it or not is another matter entirely).

In the best cases, with just a phone call an executive who graduated from a top university can influence key people in a ministry that regulates his company's activities, a bank that is considering a loan, a politician who is lobbying for something that affects his firm, and so on. (We will look at a specific example in just a moment.) It is for this reason more than any other that Japanese companies hunt Todai grads with a passion. Likewise, graduates of Kyodai (Kyoto University), Waseda, Keio, Hitotsubashi, and a few other schools are assumed to have the kind of *jinmyaku*— not managerial training—that will make them valuable to any company.

If we could somehow see the invisible lines of power that tie together the corporate, bureaucratic, and political worlds in modern Japan, and trace how policies and decisions are actually formulated and carried out, we would see that Japan is nothing but layer upon layer of these human networks, like axons in the human nervous system. Actions that appear to originate and be executed through a single organization, a company or a ministry, for example, usually involve a multitude of signals going in and out of that organization at dozens of different levels. The bigger the organization and the more important the decisions involved, the more complex this process becomes.

In this organizational nervous system, information and opinions are sent and received, ideas are sounded out, prices are discussed, political implications are examined, relevant authorities are queried, and often permission is actually sought from outside the organization before any important new policy is carried out. This subject is worthy of a book in and of itself, but the important thing to understand here is that this concept of networking, of *jinmyaku*, is not simply a collection of powerful people who can help an individual rise to the top of a corporate ladder, but a vast human network linked to other human networks without which no executive can operate efficiently in the Japanese context. To put it bluntly, without *jinmyaku*, a senior executive is worth little to a corporation.

When a Japanese enters a company, he has about 30 years to build up his *jinmyaku*, before he may be tapped to enter the upper echelons of company management. Every year is important, and every other employee who hopes someday to be named a director is thinking the same thing. Thus, until very recently, the idea of being sent overseas for anything longer than a few months was anathema. A two-year posting, whether in New York or Antarctica, meant a two-year absence from this all-important network-building activity back at the head office. Now that more and more Japanese firms are beginning to think globally, there is a glimmer of hope for those posted overseas. It is possible that one can develop some *jinmyaku* abroad, and in certain businesses, such as those that do a great deal of international trade, this may turn into a valuable asset. A few of the banks and even some manufacturers are beginning to look favorably upon employees who have some knowledge of international business. Of course, the giant trading houses have always prized international skills, but for most Japanese companies this trend has only just begun.

For the large majority of companies, the feeling is still strong that anyone who has spent more than a year or two abroad has effectively lost out on the promotion ladder to his peers who put that time to good use back home.

The Unimportance of MBAs and English Skills

This sense of the importance of staying close to the politics of the head office is the background to the problem of the Japanese MBA. Until recently, no Japanese was sent overseas for an MBA because his company wanted him to learn what was taught in a Western business school. They were sent to improve their English (or some other foreign language), to master foreign customs and business practices, and to make contacts with useful people overseas. Even today very few Japanese companies hold the MBA in high regard, and it is assumed that most Japanese employees who went overseas for two years to obtain one have missed out on advancement within the company. (It is interesting to note how many Japanese firms send bright, talented young men to top foreign business schools for *one* year. Professors often ask these students, "Why not stay another year and get your MBA?" but the companies know what they're doing. One year is plenty of time to get a feeling for life overseas; then it's time to bring the potential executive back home where he belongs.)

Consequently, Japanese who have spent several years overseas are often regarded as lagging behind their peers in some important respect, and those who stayed longer or (perish the thought) really enjoyed it are sometimes viewed as outside the company mainstream. These are people who no longer "fit in" in a Japanese company; they have lost the most valuable assets for management—the ability to get along with everyone, the years of drinking and playing golf and going on company outings together. Some unfortunates come back from abroad and actually criticize company policies or talk at length about how much better things are at the foreign firms they have seen firsthand. Such people are going nowhere in a Japanese firm. If they were talented to begin with, they may be good prospects for a *gaishi* firm to headhunt away, although they are still far too young to understand what Japanese business is all about, and most importantly, they haven't had time to build up the necessary *jinmyaku*. What they have, and what attracts *gaishi* managers more than the MBA, are language skills. And this is the biggest trap into which almost every *gaishi* falls.

Here is a simple question, a no-brainer that any manager of any age should be able to answer instantly: Which is more important in hiring a top executive for your firm, good language skills or good management skills?

The answer is obvious, you say. But if so, why do so many *gaishi* make the wrong choice year after year? These days there are growing numbers of people in their 20s and 30s who combine both skills, but they are still far too young to be considered executive material in the Japanese context. Among men in their 40s there are very few, and over 50—the real starting point for senior executives—almost none. And if you were fortunate enough to find a person with experience (age), managerial ability, and language skills, his salary demands would be outrageous. You would be better off hiring two people instead.

As we noted earlier, a number of big Japanese companies are asking staff to retire early these days, and voluntary retirements are running at relatively high levels. It is tempting to think that those who were asked to leave are the less capable and that those who remain are the more competent, but it isn't so. Those who are asked to leave are often very talented. They simply don't "fit in." Perhaps they speak their minds a little too often, criticize when they should simply go along, or insist on some level of quality in projects that everyone else is content just to pass from one desk to another. These are the proverbial nails that stick up, and, in Japan, if they're not hammered down, they're pulled out. Some of these people, regardless of their lack of language ability, are excellent managers and can be useful (and probably much happier) in a foreign firm.

Gaishi that look for managers from Japanese firms should not worry if the best-looking candidates come from unrelated business sectors. Specialized information about a certain line of business is much less important than whether the candidate has had extensive training at his or her previous company and what kind of human network he or she has built up. Even less should you worry about whether or not the prospective candidate is fluent in your native language. As we have tried to show, those who have taken the time to live overseas and master foreign languages have usually done so at the expense of gaining experience inside a Japanese company and at the expense of extending their *jinmyaku*. The younger the person is, the more this is true, for an older manager may have had ten or fifteen years in his firm prior to spending time overseas.

Why do foreign companies place so much emphasis on language skills? Most likely because the top management of both the Japan subsidiary and the parent company are insecure about communication. Talk to any headhunter in Tokyo and you will find that they all have an almost identical profile for executive-level Japanese personnel: middle-aged, highly presentable, dresses fairly well, and speaks English (or the parent company language) at least passably. If the candidate is going to be interviewing for a CEO spot at a *gaishi* firm, the language requirement is often raised to "speaks English well." Parent firms want Japanese executives who can not only discuss business over the telephone but who can join in executive meetings at the head office occasionally and present themselves reasonably well to the board of directors if necessary.

The sentiments underlying this approach are quite understandable, but in the context of operating effectively in an increasingly competitive global environment it is surprisingly short-sighted. As noted, the number of Japanese who meet all these qualifications is very limited, and many if not most of those who do are sadly lacking in real management skills. Yet *gaishi* continue to look for Japanese executives with nice suits and good English pronunciation. What they *should* be doing is hiring the same kind of people Japanese corporations value: people with many years of experience, preferably at good companies (and this can include some experience overseas), people with good school backgrounds, and people who show evidence of real managerial talent. Does a candidate speak English well? Probably not. Does it matter? Not at all. Hire an English-speaking secretary or a full-time interpreter, either one at a fraction of the executive's salary. The point is simple: in Japanese society as a whole English is a relatively common skill, something like being able to play the piano. If you need people with that particular skill (e.g., to improve communications with your home office), you can hire them fairly cheaply. Managing a company is, as you know very well, a difficult skill, one not easily acquired. Finding a good manager with the requisite background and *jinmyaku* is tough enough. Looking for one who also speaks good English is asking for too much.

Of course, there are those who feel that English is an international language and that everyone in business should speak it. Perhaps so. But Japan is the second largest economy in the world and will be for some time to come, and 99 percent of the good managers in Japan don't speak English well enough to answer the phone. It is not much of an exaggeration to say that a man's abilities as a manager are usually in inverse proportion to his ability in foreign languages. What are you going to do? Complain about the way things should be or hire the right person for the job?

Jinmyaku in Action

Let's take a break from all this theoretical discussion for a moment and consider what *jinmyaku* and management know-how can really mean to a company.

One of our favorite examples of *jinmyaku* in action at a foreign firm concerns a gentleman named Manpo Komatsu, who became the chairman of the Japan subsidiary of American medical-equipment maker Baxter International. Komatsu was at Sony for years and rose to the post of *bucho* (division head), and then was seconded to an affiliated company as a director. At that time he was headhunted by Baxter to take over as their new president in Japan.

Until that time, Baxter's Japan operation had been run by a very bright young man in his 30s with an MBA from a prestigious foreign university. But due to his age (more than 20 years too young to be a top executive by Japanese standards) and his years spent overseas, he lacked the kind of human network that a *shacho* (company president) is expected to have. When his firm took applications to the Ministry of Health and Welfare (MHW) for approval, the bureaucrats looked over the paperwork carefully and said "Thank you. We'll study them in detail." And that's all. Despite having some excellent technology, the company couldn't make real progress in Japan because its applications were sitting in a file at MHW, and no amount of begging or cajoling from the applicant can move a ministry when bureaucratic inertia sets in. The unfortunate young president had no idea how to solve the problem; this was out of his range of experience and he lacked the contacts to find out what to do.

At this juncture the new *shacho*, Komatsu, arrived on the scene. He took one look at the situation and knew immediately what was wrong: Baxter was doing everything by the book— in other words, incorrectly. If you simply submit important applications to some minor official at a ministry and don't follow up appropriately, you're going to be waiting a long, long time for an answer. Komatsu knew he had to go over the MHW section chief's head. First he called a department head at the ministry, and then he rang one of the vice ministers who, it turned out, was an old classmate from his own university days. He explained the company's situation and asked if there wasn't some way the ministry could take a fresh look at Baxter's applications.

Of course the upper-level people in any ministry know little about details; they called the junior official in charge of the Baxter applications and asked him what was going on. There was nothing wrong, he said, the ministry was just being careful. The senior bureaucrat instructed his subordinate on the spot to issue an approval to Baxter's applications. From the very next day Baxter discovered that the attitude of the official in charge had changed completely and he approved their applications just as fast as he could stamp the paperwork.

You *Can* Acquire *Jinmyaku*

It is easy to see why *jinmyaku* is one of the most important qualities a Japanese company looks for in a senior executive. While it is theoretically possible to acquire executives with a powerful network of contacts simply by hiring men from the top ranks of Japan's best corporations, in reality, very few of them would ever consider leaving a big-name company where they have worked for more than 30 years in order to switch allegiance to a foreign firm.

There is another avenue open to *gaishi* firms, however. In some cases it is possible to hire an individual who has considerable *jinmyaku* but no allegiance to any specific company — that is, an ex-official from one of the ministries. Bureaucrats normally retire from their posts through a system called *amakudari* (lit., "descent from heaven"), which means they "descend" from the "pure" realm of tireless and altruistic work for the good of the nation to the sullied world of raw commercialism. Another way of looking at it (the bureaucrats' favorite way of looking at it) is that after decades of selfless service and low pay, these officials are entitled to market their intimate knowledge of industry and the government, to create, in effect, their own "pension plan."

Ex-bureaucrats become advisors to industry (quite often the same industries they used to regulate) and are paid handsome salaries for little more than using a telephone and making key introductions.

The law does not allow bureaucrats simply to descend from, say, the Ministry of Finance onto the board of directors of Mitsubishi Bank. That would be a bit *too* obvious. Instead, there is a "cooling off" period of two years before a retiring official can join a private sector firm in the same area that he used to regulate. Thus, officials usually spend two years in another post, perhaps at one of Japan's scores of public corporations or some other intermediary agency, or perhaps they join a company unconnected with the operations of their old ministry.

Needless to say, it is very difficult for *gaishi* to acquire ex-bureaucrats. For one thing, every company in Japan wants them, and for another, they are all of an age where *gaishi* have been traditionally considered interlopers in the Japanese market, and unstable ones at that; a *gaishi* firm by definition has management shake-ups, policy changes, orders from the home office, and when all is said and done is still fundamentally *foreign*, not a place where one would expect to find happiness in an advisory role.

But two interesting trends have changed the old situation. One is the proliferation of *amakudari* bureaucrats. As the ministries have continued to grow, so has the number of retirees. Today most big Japanese companies already have one or more ex-government officials on their boards of directors. Most firms don't need or want any more. To make matters worse (for the bureaucrats, that is), there are growing calls to slim down the government and eliminate or privatize many of the public corporations. So, as new retirements come up, there seem to be fewer places for these retirees to go. No one wants to go to work for some medium-sized manufacturing firm out in the provinces; it wouldn't be fitting for a man who has stepped down from an influential ministry, and besides, the pay wouldn't be sufficient. The bottom line is a dwindling number of suitable positions for officials to descend into.

The second trend is the steady growth of *gaishi*, both in terms of performance and respectability. More *gaishi* are being run largely by Japanese executives, more of them are adapting their management styles to the needs of this market (which also means a need for people with *jinmyaku*), and more of them are becoming major players in their respective industries. In other words, it is no longer out of the question for a retiring official to consider working for large, well-established *gaishi*. This is an opportunity that foreign firms cannot afford to pass up. Let's look at one example of how a *gaishi* company can take advantage of this situation.

Some years ago the number 2 man at the Ministry of International Trade and Industry (MITI) came up for retirement. He needed two years to "cool off" before taking up a position on the board of some major Japanese industry. Salomon Bros. agreed to take him on for two years as an advisor, and paid him about $300,000 a year (roughly double what he was making on his government paycheck). Since MITI does not regulate the financial sector, there was no legal problem in having this very influential ex-official work for an investment bank. His only responsibility was to telephone executives at big Japanese firms and let them know that he was currently advising a certain foreign investment firm called Salomon Brothers.

At that time, the merger and acquisition part of the business was growing and was fiercely competitive. To succeed in M&A it was vital to be able to create viable takeover scenarios and present them convincingly to top executives of Japanese corporations. Salomon had the skills to do the first part easily, but just like its foreign rivals, it ran into difficulties when it tried to get in to see the presidents of major firms on short notice. In fact, Salomon's staff often had trouble arranging meetings with mere division managers at many of those firms.

In Japan the normal practice is not to meet with, not even to take calls from, people or organizations you don't know; the Western practice of cold-calling is usually ineffective or, if partially successful, a guaranteed way to get off on the wrong foot. Even consultant Kenichi Omae, the former chairman of McKinsey & Co. in Japan, found he couldn't get an appointment with many company section chiefs when he started in business. Today, thanks in large part to Omae's efforts, McKinsey is famous, but ten years ago it was unknown in Japan, and unknown means unwelcome. Omae roamed all over Tokyo going from one company to another. He was kept waiting for hours at various companies, and when finally someone would meet with him, it was usually a very young employee who had no say in executive decisions.

Thus Salomon's strategy was to stop acting like all the other *gaishi* and do things the Japanese way. The ex-MITI official they hired had but one job: use the phone and make sure that the firm's M&A people could get in to see someone with clout at the big Japanese firms they were targeting. Being one of the most important figures in MITI only a short while ago, his name was familiar to most of Japanese industry—certainly far better known than Salomon's. He was able to speak directly with the presidents and senior directors of target companies and arranged for visits from Salomon's M&A team. After that the sales job was their own responsibility, but at least they had a foot in the door. This "advisor" proved highly effective and the company felt its money was well spent. By the time his two years were up, the Salomon name was already well known throughout Japanese industry.

Ex-bureaucrats can perform other important function as well. The most common one is not interfacing with Japanese industry but with the bureaucracy itself. For any *gaishi* that wants to smooth relations with various ministries, improve communication with its main banks, or open a number of otherwise closed doors throughout the business world, there are few means as effective as employing a retired bureaucrat who has some clout. This, too, is part of networking in Japan, and—if your company can arrange it—a very smart strategic move for management.

Study Your Market

There are all sorts of problems that await a foreign firm trying to break into this market. We have touched on the problems of developing and maintaining a good corporate image, of hiring talented managers, of using *jinmyaku*, and so on. We will also discuss the problems of dealing with the Japanese bureaucracy at some length in the following chapters. But one of the biggest problems comes from another source, one that most firms see as an ally rather than an obstacle: the Japanese consumer.

The difficulties of dealing with Japanese consumers have become the stuff of legend in the international marketing world. In other countries you can sell canned goods or bottled goods with labels that are slightly wrinkled or torn, but not in Japan;

stores will refuse to carry the merchandise. To the Japanese way of thinking, "If there's a problem with the packaging, there's a good chance something is wrong with the contents."

It should be obvious that *gaishi* in particular need to study the local market inside out before making some foolish (and often expensive) blunder, and yet there are countless stories of fundamental marketing mistakes that were all easily avoidable. Even the experts make mistakes. George Fields, the chairman of ASI Market Research (Japan) and an old "Japan hand," has often told the tale of trying to sell a new-style cake mix that could be baked in the Japanese family's rice cooker. It seemed like a great idea and technically feasible, but failed to take into account the near-sacred attitude which the average Japanese housewife accords her humble rice cooker—no cake mixes, bread mixes, potted plants, or anything else were going in there. But even this kind of marketing error is relatively mild. Too many *gaishi* have made far more idiotic mistakes. One giant U.S. toothpaste maker (who shall remain mercifully anonymous) launched a big marketing push years ago, running a series of TV commercials and dropping thousands of free tubes of its toothpaste through the mail slots of Japanese homes. The only thing the firm hadn't bothered to investigate was whether or not Japanese actually *liked* the taste of their product. As it turned out, they didn't. And so, the more samples the company handed out, the worse its reputation became.

Clearly, researching and understanding the Japanese market is of paramount importance to any company's success. Sometimes just a little good advice can save millions of dollars in wasted investment and a black eye in the marketplace. A Japanese executive was asked to help a *gaishi* that planned to import frozen cakes from Australia. After one look at the product she said they could not be sold as is. Why not? the company asked. She pointed out that their product, a round cake, had been pre-cut into several pieces, but the pieces were not all the same size. "If the size of the pieces is not uniform, it won't sell," she explained to an obviously baffled executive audience. When Buitoni tried selling spaghetti in Japan it ran into the same problem: the spaghetti sent from Italy was of slightly different lengths. The firm's Japanese distributor said to make all the pieces even or they wouldn't sell. In the end, Buitoni devoted one entire production line to producing spaghetti for the Japanese market with each piece cut to exactly the same length. Also, Japanese eat much less spaghetti at a sitting than Westerners do. The firm caught on, and made smaller packages of the product specifically for the Japanese market. This also helped to differentiate it from rival brands, and today you can find Buitoni's product in any supermarket.

In addition to researching your potential market and delivering attractive products that are packaged properly, remember that a very high level of service is taken for granted in Japan. And service includes everything imaginable, not just taking care of consumers who have bought your product. For example, deliveries: shipments to clients, whether a giant corporation or a chain of retail stores, must be made on time. In Japan there is no acceptable excuse for failure to deliver what a customer expects when he expects it. No one will buy "The plane was late," "There was a strike at the dock," "There was a 50-km. pile-up on the highway," or anything of the kind. All these things are supposed to be taken into account in advance as a matter of course. There is no reason for anyone to miss a delivery date.

A Western telecom company delivered a very sophisticated, high-tech phone system to a Japanese client. The Japanese firm liked it and ordered an extra unit. The foreign firm's reply was "We'll send to our head office for it. You should have it in about 2–3 months." That was the last order the foreign firm ever saw from that client. If you can't provide the goods you've advertised in a timely fashion, Japanese customers wonder about your company's business practices even if your firm happens to be one of the largest in the world. Bad service reflects on your company's attitude toward customers in general, or toward the Japanese market. People say to themselves, "If this firm can't take care of me now when everything is going well, what will happen if I have a problem with this equipment? If they can't provide complete service here in the local market, perhaps I should be talking to somebody else."

Master Distribution Channels

One thing that makes or breaks foreign manufacturers in Japan is distribution. Everyone—companies and foreign governments alike—complains that Japan's distribution system is complex and difficult to enter. Indeed, if you start from scratch and try to work your way into the system, it is extremely difficult. But there are all sorts of ways to take advantage of the system, and with a little research and a little effort, many *gaishi* are admirably rewarded.

Look at rivals Schick and Gillette. The latter never managed to develop a first-rate distribution network; as a result, its products are available at many stores, but seldom as a full line, and are often accorded only about a third the space of Schick's merchandise. Why are Schick's products available everywhere? Because the firm tied up with Hattori Seiko and used Seiko's established distribution channels to move their goods.

In the following chapters we will look at case studies of companies like Levi Strauss that took good advantage of the Japanese wholesalers called *tonya*, a tactic that more *gaishi* should try before giving up on the local distribution system as impossibly complex. We will also look at firms like Coca-Cola and Electrolux that bypassed all established distribution routes and succeeded by setting up their own, independent systems. Neither approach is correct: the right approach varies depending on what kind of product you have, what kind of competition already exists, and what kind of distribution networks are available to help you.

One approach to handling a product in this market is to turn over all responsibility to a general agent. Sometimes this works well, sometimes not. Again, the decision involves a number of factors, including the quality of the prospective agent, his business experience, reputation, etc. But simply trying to bypass the agent and handle business directly is not the panacea that many *gaishi* assume. BMW and UDJ bypassed the agent system, sold directly through their own sales networks, and became very successful. But other companies have tried the same thing and failed.

For example, Volkswagen had a sales agent contract with a well-known foreign car import firm called Yanase, but later cancelled the contract and tried to sell on its own. Result: sales dropped to one-third of their previous level. VW didn't understand Yanase's marketing clout.

Foreign firms also forget that a good sales agent not only markets a product, but represents it. That is, a really good agent will help to position or even redesign a foreign product so that it will better suit Japanese consumers. In addition, the agent should provide the kind of after-purchase support that Japanese expect from any respectable company. A good example is Mont Blanc, the German fountain pen company, which cancelled a long-standing contract with its Japanese agent, Daiya Sangyo. It so happens that older Japanese (the main market for fountain pens) prefer pens with a very soft touch (a holdover from writing with a brush, perhaps). Consequently, Daiya Sangyo polished and prepared the Mont Blanc pen nibs so as to make them better suited to Japanese preferences. If Japanese travelled overseas and bought a Mont Blanc pen abroad, then found they weren't happy with it when they got home, the agent would process the nib just as if it had been bought from them in Japan. The Mont Blanc executives sent from the company headquarters in Germany insisted that the firm's representatives in Japan adopt a strategy that worked well in Europe but wasn't suited to Japan. When the firm cancelled the contract with Daiya Sangyo, it also lost access to the special processing the agent was using to make the pens more attractive to Japanese buyers. Before long Mont Blanc lost its number 1 position in the fountain-pen market to rival Parker Pen (whose success we will examine shortly).

No Models to Copy, Only Hints at How to Succeed

We could go on and on about various facets of *jinmyaku*, hiring staff, dealing with joint ventures, positioning products, researching markets, etc., but that would fill another volume. Instead, we will leave a few words of general advice about the bureaucracy, consultants, management structure, and so on for the end of this book. Let us move on to the stories of more than a dozen companies from different nations and different fields that have managed to become successful here in Japan. It is interesting to note that most of these firms, even those with big names and well-known products, found the going very tough when they first started up here. Each firm won not by virtue of its huge market clout or famous product line, but more often by learning from its mistakes in Japan, refusing to give up, and picking up a few tricks for doing business as it went along. Other companies can learn from these earlier mistakes, too, and perhaps find some tricks of their own in the chapters that follow. No company's success story is a model for other firms to copy, but many can serve as useful guides to help later entrants avoid well-plumbed pitfalls and find their way to the proper paths in a shorter time. We hope that will be the case for readers who take to heart the examples that follow.

CHAPTER 2

East of Eden

Levi Strauss

The year was 1993. As the worst recession in half a century
dragged on, almost every retail company in Japan braced for a succession of bad news. Monthly sales figures at department stores
had been falling steadily for almost two years, and once-flush
Japanese consumers seemed to have locked away their wallets for
the duration. Yet even as many retail firms were slashing costs in
an effort to stem the rising tide of red ink, one company stunned
the industry with its best-ever earnings report. In November,
jeans maker Levi Strauss Japan K.K. announced that it had
topped ¥40 billion (about $400 million) in sales for the first time.
Revenue was up, profits were up, and after a long struggle, Levi's
had finally become the top jeans company in Japan.

   To most Americans, indeed, to most consumers worldwide,
this would seem less than earthshaking news. Considering the
century-old reputation and powerful market position of Levi
Strauss & Co., the U.S.-based parent company, it seems only
natural that the number 1 in America should also be number 1 in
Japan. However, the Japanese markets are famous for ignoring
what is "natural" elsewhere.

   The truth is it took a tremendous amount of effort over more
than twenty years for Levi Strauss to become number 1 in its field

in Japan. Most outside observers would probably attribute the firm's success to one or another of its presidents over the years. But the real "hero" of the Levi's story was a young American who knew nothing about management or international business or marketing. He also knew nothing of Japanese culture and never so much as set foot in Japan. Yet this one American was responsible for selling more jeans in Japan than all the marketing professionals in all the jeans companies combined—which is quite a feat considering that he died in 1955.

Beginnings: Holes in the Floor

Levi's came to Japan in 1971. At that time the parent company's Far East regional office was in Hong Kong, and Japan was set up as a small branch company. Heisuke Wada, who now runs the firm's extensive Hirazuka Distribution Center, remembers those days clearly. Wada was managing a small plant for a different firm back then when a friend called and told him that a company called Levi Strauss had started up a business in Japan. The friend invited him to join. At first Wada had no desire to join a small branch of an unknown American firm selling a product he knew nothing about. "I'd never even worn a pair of jeans. I only went to their office to turn down the offer," he says.

Back then, Levi Strauss Japan (LSJ) was renting a part of an old, dilapidated building from a Japanese trading company. The caretaker of the building lived on the premises with his wife and two young children. The wife must have either liked the new tenants or felt sorry for them (probably both), because she regularly made lunch for the LSJ staff. Wada came for his interview in time to see the wife handing out homemade lunches to all the men. He saw the family-like setting and the relaxed atmosphere at the firm (the caretaker's kids were playing Ping-Pong in the empty warehouse), which stood in sharp contrast to most Japanese companies, and before he knew what he was doing he had signed up.

What was it like working for the world's top company in the blue jean industry? "I'd never heard of the company," Wada says. "They didn't even have a brochure or anything, so what did I know? When I asked if I should submit a resumé, the answer was, 'We don't need it.' It was only a while after I joined that I realized how big the company is globally."

It wasn't just the lack of brand recognition or the lack of a company brochure in Japanese or even the Ping-Pong in the warehouse. Nothing about LSJ inspired confidence in the firm's future. Take the building itself: it was very old, with a tired wooden floor pockmarked with holes. There wasn't a single forklift in the place, only handcarts to move inventory around. Nor was there space to store a truck-sized container, so everything had to be stored in the boxes in which they arrived. Because of the holes in the floor, the handcarts would often get stuck, sometimes tipping over and spilling the clean merchandise all over the floor. If this was an international giant in the world apparel business, it sure didn't feel like one.

At the time Wada joined, LSJ had just been established. Shipments from Levi Strauss's Asian factory in Hong Kong were irregular. His main work consisted of tagging new stock as it came in and checking to make sure that none of the merchandise was damaged. Without a real inventory control system, no one knew exactly what was stored where or how much of it there was. Wada remembers that the stock control methods of the day were punctuated by expressions like "I think it must be over here" and "It's gotta be around here somewhere."

As befits such an operation, sales were abysmal. "If we ever saw someone actually wearing Levi's on the street, we were overjoyed," Wada remembers with a smile.

It got worse. Because the U.S. parent saw itself as a world leader, he says, it assumed that its products would sell like hotcakes around the globe. "The American side just kept sending more and more stock. But in Japan the jeans weren't selling at all. So the stock just piled up. We couldn't put any more in the warehouse, so we stacked the boxes outside. And during the rainy season the merchandise in the warehouse got so damp and mildewed that we had to stretch ropes outside whenever there was a clear day and hang the stuff out in the sun to dry. Birds and mice made nests in the piles of jeans, which then attracted snakes looking for food. It was an unbelievable mess."

As a result, jeans sent to Japan became dead stock; inventories piled up and had to be re-exported to Africa and Southeast Asia. This was not the way to build a number 1 company.

Dead on Arrival

One mistake that the parent company made in the early days was not paying enough attention to local market needs. Employees who remember the start-up days say that everything was done by trying to imitate the success of the American parent. One problem was that since Levi Strauss was a market force to contend with in the United States, it acted as if this was also the case around the world. It ran its overseas offices very tightly, usually under rather strict conditions. For example, the entire Japanese clothing indus-try (like most other businesses) pays its accounts by 90-day bills, and 4-month bills are not uncommon. But Levi Strauss insisted that its Japanese subsidiary operate on a 20-day cash payment system. Also, in Japan exchanges and returns are common, but for Levi's, unless there was a defect in the merchandise, returns and exchanges were prohibited.

There was nothing intrinsically wrong with these policies, but they almost guaranteed that stores would prefer to do business with someone else. It took years to overcome this problem.

Of course, Levi Strauss was not blind to differences in foreign markets. It redesigned the jeans made in its Hong Kong factory for the "Asian" market. But it created only one pattern designed to fit people from Japan to India; it did not recognize any differences in physiognomy or preferences among the dozens of countries in Asia. Consequently, no effort was made to adapt the American fashions to Japanese tastes or to the needs of the Japanese apparel industry.

The one thing that Japanese shoppers found indisputably good about the parent company's product was that it was identified as 100 percent American, and for decades after the war anything American was assumed to be top quality. This should have been a big plus for LSJ. The problem was that the company was under the control of the Hong Kong regional office and had to buy its stock from the Hong Kong factory. This meant that the pants sold in Japan were neither original American Levi's jeans nor were they specially designed for Japanese buyers. The latter problem would have been mitigated in part by the prestigious "Made in America" label telling Japanese that the article, though it might not fit them perfectly, was The Real Thing. But jeans that didn't fit well and were labelled "Made in Hong Kong" were dead on arrival. To make matters worse, there were some parallel imports from the United States. A few batches of "real" Levi's jeans were reaching Japan, but under the company's global marketing plan LSJ was not permitted to sell anything but the Hong Kong product.

The management of Levi Strauss Japan knew that this was commercial suicide. Their business was like one of those over-loaded handcarts stuck in a hole in the warehouse floor. It would go nowhere without some new strategies, and especially some Japan-oriented strategies.

In the mid-1970s LSJ began negotiating with its head office in San Francisco to be able to import merchandise directly from the U.S. The head office gave the OK, and soon "real" American-made Levi's were arriving in bulk on Japanese shores. The shipments included the company's standard-bearer for the past hundred years, the model 501 jeans, a symbol to Japanese of the America they knew from seeing off-duty soldiers lounging around in tough blue denim pants. At last the company had a product it was confident it could sell. It still wasn't tailored to the Japanese market, but at least it was the Real McCoy. The problem was how to make local consumers aware that this new, authentic product had arrived in Japan. Without some drastic marketing efforts, this precious stock they had talked the head office into shipping to Tokyo would soon be piling up outside the warehouse just like its predecessors. The answer was a bold advertising campaign and a new, some-what unlikely "hero" in the century-old Levi Strauss story.

Heroes Wanted: Dead or Alive

Until 1978 LSJ had never run any kind of serious ad campaign. But that year the company acquired a new executive: Masafumi Ohki (now senior managing director and national sales manager) left a local ad agency to become the little company's marketing manager. He found the situation at LSJ even more dire than he had thought: the company had not given him an assistant or any staff; he was, in effect, running a one-man show.

What the firm had done was to pick an ad agency and a market research firm. So Ohki began by commissioning some market research. First, the company needed to find out what kind of a base it had to build upon. For instance, how well was its name known in Japan? The studies found the answer all too quickly: not at all. Less than 10 percent of those surveyed recognized the Levi name. In another survey, LSJ asked shoppers, "When you hear the word 'jeans,' which brand do you think of first?" That one was also not very good for morale: Levi's placed dead last. Ohki knew he had his work cut out for him.

The next step was more constructive. The marketing team set out to learn something that neither the parent company nor the Japanese subsidiary really understood: what did the Japanese buyer want in a pair of jeans? This would be the basis for its first real ad campaign. Ohki explains:

"Back then the big names in Japan were labels like *Edwin* and *Big John*. *Wrangler*, a big name in the U.S. market, was licensed to a JV (joint venture) between Mitsubishi Corp. (the giant trading house) and Toyobo (a huge textile firm), which was both producing and selling them in Japan. *Lee*, the other big name in the U.S. market, was also being imported. We had to do some market research to find out how to sell against this kind of competition. What we found was that young people identified jeans with America and their idea of an American lifestyle. They wanted jeans that said 'America' to them. So we decided to make the most of our heritage and advertise not just that Levi's were 100 percent American, but that they were America's original jeans."

As a result, in December of 1978 a little, almost unknown firm called Levi Strauss Japan launched what was to become one of the most successful and long-running ad campaigns in Japanese retail history.

What LSJ called the "Hero Campaign" was a series of TV commercials aimed at 15- to 25-year-old shoppers, both male and female, in the population corridor from Greater Tokyo to the central Nagoya region (an area that accounts for roughly 60 percent of all sales in Japan). The commercials featured America's best-known cultural icons wearing jeans. The campaign started with James Dean, then expanded to include John Wayne, Steve McQueen, and others. The campaign slogan was "Heroes wear Levi's," and the subtext ran "Since 1850, in America, jeans meant Levi's." It was more than a simple "testimonial" type ad; it was a direct association of Hollywood's post-war "heroes" with the image of a tough, no-nonsense product made in America for a hundred years, and now available in Japan.

The ads were done in one-month batches, saturating the networks with film clips such as James Dean in *Giant*, John Wayne in *Stagecoach*, and Marilyn Monroe in *The Misfits*. Wait a minute—Marilyn Monroe in a jeans ad? Who would put the glitziest of Hollywood stars in an ad for plain old blue denim? The Japanese would, of course. With an eye toward the female market, they dug up clips from Monroe's last film, a contemporary cowboy drama in which she plays opposite a 60-year-old Clark Gable (also his last film), and sure enough, she wore jeans for the part.

Still photos, posters, and stand-up panels of these "heroes" (and "heroines") were sent to jeans shops catering to the youth market. It was a big gamble for the little firm, but it worked. The image of Levi's as an all-American tradition suddenly burst forth in Japan and the product began to disappear from store shelves for the first time.

A year after the "hero campaign" kicked off, the firm retested its market position. Brand recognition had jumped from under 10 percent to 86 percent. Shoppers who were asked, "When you hear the word 'jeans,' which brand do you think of first?" began to respond with a name they didn't know just a short while before, and within another two years the answer "Levi's" was a solid No. 1 in the mind of young shoppers.

This single ad campaign is credited with boosting Levi's image from nothing to first place in just a few years. It took a little longer for the sales figures to catch up, but ultimately Levi's jeans became the top seller as well. Everyone agreed that the ads were a stroke of genius. All Japanese, and certainly all *young* Japanese, knew James Dean and John Wayne and Marilyn Monroe. They represented America around the world. Moreover, everyone knew that they were no longer alive, which meant they were not people Levi Strauss had paid to wear its products; they wore them because they liked them.

Within a short time, it became apparent that the basic thrust of the ad campaign was right on target, but that it was too much of a good thing. The kids weren't lining up to look at posters of John Wayne or Marilyn Monroe or Steve McQueen. One young vulnerable face, one image in that series seemed to reach out to Japanese youth and speak to them directly, crossing any language barrier. James Dean symbolized something that the others could not—the outsider, the rebel, the loner, someone who wanted so badly to fit in but just didn't seem able to. This image somehow struck a chord in the adolescent Japanese psyche. Kids identified with him and they were drawn to him—and to the jeans shops with his picture in the window.

It is doubtful any American ad executive would have chosen Dean to be the company's image-builder in Japan, but LSJ could not have found a better symbol.

"Of course, James Dean is still popular in America, but nothing like he is in Japan," says Masaki Watanabe, manager of LSJ's marketing department. "Using his image was a very big factor in the success of our ad campaign."

So Dean became not merely a one-season marketing tool to be used and then discarded, but the symbol of America, the symbol of youth, and the symbol of Levi's. The company didn't realize it, but it had struck a gold mine, one that would keep producing brand loyalty in Japanese fans for an incredible 14 years.

Of course, there were other, less obvious advantages to the whole idea behind this ad campaign. One was the savings it meant for a young company without a huge ad budget. Hollywood stars (the live variety) do not come cheap. In 1989 Toyota hired Eddie Murphy to do its new Celica ads for a fee reported to be in the neighborhood of $5 million. Other Japanese companies have used the likes of Bruce Willis, Sylvester Stallone, Harrison Ford, Sean Connery, Jodie Foster, Demi Moore, even Sting and Jerry Garcia to promote their wares, and the outlays are usually substantial. LSJ's ad campaign was every bit as effective, in fact more so, but the cost of paying royalties to a dead star's estate for the use of a name and image was a tiny fraction of what contemporary box-office "heroes" would charge.

Hit List

Of course LSJ's success was due to much more than the selection of a popular actor for its image. Part of the story lies in good timing. Levi's did not initiate the "jeans boom" in Japan, but rather came in on the tail end of it. Jeans sold well in the early 1970s, as the post-war baby boomer generation grew up. But Levi's started its hero campaign as this boom was fading out. The baby boomers were already in their mid-30s and gradually moving away from wearing jeans. But LSJ was happy about their new campaign coinciding with the end of the old boom, because it meant that its rivals were sharply cutting back their ad outlays, leaving the field wide open for a new entrant.

Shortly after starting its advertising offensive, Levi's accounted for 50 percent of total ad outlays in the industry. In other words, LSJ was spending as much on advertising as all the other jeans firms combined.

In the 1980s, a new trend began to appear in the jeans market, but LSJ was not quite ready for it. The buying public decided it wanted more than just "authentic" American-made Levi's 501 jeans and other styles. It wanted something fashionable, softer, more in tune with the changing times. In the industry it was said that the mood was shifting from basic jeans to "fashion jeans." LSJ was very strong in basics, of course, but weak in anything that might be called fashion jeans. Besides, the heady profit increases of the past few years had the company reeling. In a sense its strategy had become static in this period, and from 1982 to 84 sales and profits stagnated.

"Lots of customers come into a jeans shop," says General Merchandising Manager Hajime Tanaka. "About 20 percent of them are just there because jeans are the thing to buy. They want the basics. But the other 80 percent is real consumer demand, just like in any other business, and it's necessary to listen to what your customers want, not tell them what they want. Even if you say that these jeans are 100 percent American or that this style is a classic, these customers won't wear something that doesn't fit the way they like."

So, awakened by the call to get back in touch with its market, LSJ began a new campaign to capture both basic and fashion jeans. It carefully analyzed other products that were selling well in Japan to see what its rivals were doing right and it was doing wrong: The firm also did exhaustive consumer testing. In one test, dozens of people were asked to try on brand new Levi's jeans and give their honest reactions. Designers and developers who were present were told to keep quiet (not the common way to do things at the time) and let the consumers talk. The result was that Levi Strauss Japan quickly grasped what the shopping public wanted.

The next step was to design jeans to fit Japanese bodies. The company designed from scratch, forgetting about what were supposed to be Levi's trademark features, and created pants to respond to the immediate needs of the Japanese market. This was a bold step since up until that point, even though the company was doing some of its own manufacturing in Japan, all of its new product ideas came from America. The result of its first major domestic design efforts was a line that came to be called "new generation fashion jeans."

They did not get off to a good start. When the new fashion jeans were first shown inside the company, there was considerable opposition. Many salespeople didn't like the new look, others said they weren't really Levi's, and more than a few in the company said they just wouldn't sell. There was a feeling for a short time that perhaps the firm was about to make a big mistake.

However, LSJ was confident of its research and confident that the market knew what it wanted, so it went ahead and introduced the new jeans anyway. Just as many of the experts had warned, they were not popular. They were explosively popular. In no time at all the factories couldn't keep up with demand. Jeans shops began telling the Levi's reps, "We can't keep 'em in stock; couldn't you just stop advertising for a while!" The company finally agreed and tried to cool the sales rush for a little while by announcing that some stores were already out of stock. This only fanned the flames of demand and cleared warehouses to the walls. Levi Strauss had done it again.

The U.S. parent did not complain about LSJ's development of this new, Japan-specific product line, but let them go their own way. In fact, the parent firm soon picked up on the fashion jeans idea, and it turned into a multi-million dollar market in the United States as well.

Aging Baby Boomers

Another reason that Japanese demand for jeans had been on the decline prior to this new product development was a demographic factor: the baby boomers who had pioneered wearing jeans in Japan were all aging. This group, which had really opened up the market, was in their mid-30s by this time and had gradually moved away from wearing jeans. Simply aiming sales at the under-25 crowd could not make up for the loss of these monied baby boomers.

National Sales Manager Ohki explains: "There were two reasons why the middle-aged crowd stopped wearing jeans. First,
because they were aging, the jeans didn't fit as well as they used
to; and second, they didn't feel comfortable walking into the urban
jeans shops crowded with teenagers."

But things changed. More comfortable jeans designed especially for Japanese bodies began to appear. And the urban jeans
shops, which catered to teenagers and people in their early
twenties gradually spread out to the suburbs, where the ex-rebels
now lived with their families. Suburban stores with thousands
of square feet of floor space appeared, carrying a huge stock of
different styles of jeans. Soon whole families were going there to
buy clothes.

At the beginning of the 1980s, jeans shops held nearly 100
percent of the retail market for jeans. By the end of the decade,
however, their share had fallen to about 60 percent as department
stores and super stores chewed into their sales. Even buyer pro-
files changed, as older people and more women over 30 started
wearing jeans.

During the famous "bubble era" of the late 1980s many
Japanese suddenly became wealthy and many more felt that way.
The basic trend was to buy anything that was top-class, name-brand
merchandise, whether it said Rolex or Pebble Beach. Status
labels like Giorgio Armani and Ralph Lauren eclipsed the high
visibility of Levi Strauss, yet thanks to the new generation jeans
and the expanding consumer demographics, sales continued to
grow at a blistering 20–30 percent a year on average.

Then at the beginning of the 1990s the economic bubble burst
and the expensive name-brand boom came crashing to a halt.
Levi's, too, was caught in this sudden collapse of consumer spending. But during the bubble days Japanese consumers had developed a new appreciation of quality. With the economy in a
tailspin, consumers did not switch from fancy European labels to
cheap Hong Kong throw-away clothes, but rather to dependable,
long-wearing goods. Status labels gave way to "recession fashion,"
reasonably-priced goods that were made to last. Within a couple
of years labels like L.L. Bean were replacing Armani on the
streets of Tokyo. And that could only mean good news for Levi's.

In this context yet another jeans fad began in Harajuku, the
trendy gathering place for hip Tokyo teenagers (and a radar screen

for retailers nationwide). Here, Levi Strauss' old, reliable main-stay, the 501 jeans, suddenly acquired a new following. Although basic designs like the 501 have existed for many decades, there have been slight changes in the style and pattern over the years. For some reason people seemed to like the old style better. Thus it was the classic 1950s-model 501s that suddenly became popular. One pair could sell for $2,000 or more. This should have set off alarm bells at LSJ, but the company admits it was a little slow to catch on at first. After all, when jeans start selling for that kind of money, it means either that buyers are suddenly losing their minds or that a major new fashion wave is about to break.

At about the same time, LSJ had been receiving a number of inquiries about its old-style jeans from other quarters. So the firm decided to begin production of versions of its 1940s-style and 1950s-style jeans. There was no easy way to make them in Japan, so LSJ asked its parent company in San Francisco to locate original equipment facilities to produce them in the United States. The company found a denim mill in North Carolina that had pioneered the denim used in the 501 jeans and still had plenty of old equipment on hand. It began turning out the old-style fabric, which was then made into classic-style Levi's jeans in San Francisco. Of course these "old" jeans were to be sold in the Japanese market, which meant they had to be absolutely top qual-ity, without defects or blemishes. Still, they handsomely repaid the expense of special development, manufacture, and shipping: they sold in Japan for about $150 a pair, roughly double the price of a pair of plain 501s. And once again, the company had a hit on its hands.

Made in the U.S.A.

It is often said that Japanese consumers have the highest standards in the world. They generally insist on top quality, not only in the goods themselves, but in design, in packaging, and so on. Part of this stems from the Japanese reputation for fastidiousness in everything from food preparation to auto manufacturing. Japanese corporations became world famous years ago for their fanatical quality control operations (copied, they readily admit, from the United States). As a result, Japanese-made versions of Western products are often highly prized overseas. For example, IBM computers made in Japan are reported to be better than those produced elsewhere, and American pilots have been known to claim that an F–16 made in Japan is "tighter" and better built than its bolt-for-bolt identical American counterpart. Clearly, even when the brand name is the same and the materials are the same, the manufacturing process is not.

Thus where there is a choice between a product made in Japan and an identical product made overseas, Japanese should logically prefer the former.

But when it comes to fashion, logic goes out the window. Many customers, and young people in particular, prefer labels that say "Made in America" and they are willing to pay a premium for such goods. Even if there is a slight difference in quality, this means nothing to the Japanese buyer who wants to acquire a symbol or a sample of American culture. Nowadays licensing is common. Even world-famous brand-name items are made in Japan and throughout Asia. But many Japanese shoppers eschew goods that say "Made in Japan" or "Made in Taiwan," and so on. Japanese kids know that jeans originated in America. So jeans from anywhere else are just a copy. It is ironic, perhaps, that the Japanese, who became world famous by producing good copies, discovered that they want to own originals.

To respond to this trend, LSJ increased the percentage of its American-made jeans. In the early years, most of its merchandise was made in Asia, but (in an interesting reversal of the trend at most other manufacturers) that production has gradually shifted to the United States. Today only about 20 percent of Levi's products sold in Japan are made in Asia, while about 30 percent come from the United States, and roughly half of its total goods are still made in Japan. The firm could increase the U.S. portion even more simply by importing standard American-style Levi's for all its sales. However, despite the obvious demand for "authentic" jeans, the Japanese also want jeans that match their tastes in fabrics and colors. So these authentic U.S.-made Levi's have to be made specially for the Japanese market.

For the large part of its manufacturing that is done in Japan, the company is naturally very tough about standards. Almost all licensed manufacturing in the Japanese garment industry is done by subcontractors. The normal practice is to commission work from a number of factories; then if the goods sell well, the firm simply adds new factories. This keeps manufacturing costs flexible (subcontractors can normally be hired and fired at will), but it offers minimal control over the factories themselves and therefore often leads to a decline in quality.

LSJ used a limited number of factories and it demanded that they all undergo special training. The company noted that sewing machines from different makers are all slightly different. Levi's insisted its factories all use identical machines. It was also very picky about materials and production techniques. Quality inspectors were sent around from LSJ to check the work in the factories, a practice almost unheard of in the Japanese apparel industry.

Distribution Savvy

Two other factors played a big role in Levi's success in Japan, and they are both connected with the firm's approach to distribution problems.

Much has been written in the Western media about Japan's Byzantine distribution system. This intricate, multi-layered system of first-level wholesalers, second-level wholesalers, distributors, and various other unnecessary middlemen has been branded a non-tariff trade barrier by many foreign firms. LSJ took a different approach: instead of griping about the problem, they tackled it head on. Levi's actually got inside this allegedly impenetrable system, and turned its obstacles to the firm's advantage.

At a very early stage in its growth, LSJ decided that it would directly control sales and distribution of its products in the large urban centers that hold the bulk of the Japanese population. For the rest of the country, it turned to regional *tonya* (wholesalers), allowing them to act as agents outside the big cities. When the label was still hardly known, these regional agents bought into the Levi's dream and used their marketing muscle to move the goods in the smaller cities and towns. LSJ is still the only major jeans company in Japan to do business with the regional *tonya*. Even today, about 12 regional wholesale agents account for about 50 percent of the firm's sales.

The second key to LSJ's distribution operations is the development of its own high-tech distribution system from the late

1980s to early 1990s. As the firm watched its annual growth rate begin to contract from the intoxicating 20–30 percent bubble days to the hungover recession days, it had to think more seriously about how to respond to changing market trends and changing growth patterns. A major problem was how to supply stock to match actual demand as closely as possible.

So, when the decision was made to expand the firm's distribution center, the problem was not simply how to make it bigger, but how to make it more efficient. The firm set out to build a modern, automated, information-intensive operations center to coordinate demand from retailers and supply from factories both at home and abroad. The scope of this investment can be grasped from the fact that the firm listed its shares on the OTC market to raise capital for the project.

In the United States, retail stores commonly place orders six months in advance, with a specific breakdown for each month's expected sales. The stores are required to keep any unsold stock, so there is no burden on the maker. While this has obvious advantages for the maker, it also distances the firm from its customers. Because stores order in bulk twice a year and stock is never returned, the maker has no way of knowing how closely those orders match customers' needs. The system assumes that the stores will stay on top of changing trends and not be too far off target in their orders. That kind of imprecision drives Japanese managers crazy.

LSJ also decided that it wanted to be closer to its customers. So it developed a point-of-sales (POS) system that feeds data on individual store sales directly to the distribution center. Not every Levi's store has it. As yet only about 10 percent of total sales nationwide are connected to the system, but big national chain stores, super stores, and the bigger jeans shops are online, and many more are signing up.

With this system, an online store places an order one day, stock is unloaded from the warehouse that same night, and the next day the merchandise is on its way to the retailer. Of course, this puts a huge extra burden on the supply end, but the advantages to the company in knowing what its largest sales points are moving on a day-to-day basis are tremendous.

Because of this system, the role of the distribution center grew rapidly. It was no longer simply shipping goods from warehouses to shops, but actually predicting sales trends and advising about new product development. The head of the distribution center became, in effect, a senior manager in the company.

LSJ Today

By the early 1990s, LSJ's market researchers began to turn up young buyers who said things like, "How long are you going to stick with this James Dean thing?" In the midst of its almost non-stop success, the firm had not seriously considered putting the main symbol of Levi's out to pasture. After lots of discussion, however, management decided that the company was becoming too closely associated with this one figure. Perhaps it was time to freshen up the company image. So in 1993 Levi's ended the unbelievably successful James Dean ad campaign it had begun back in 1978.

The new Levi's commercials broke away from the old silver screen hero approach and began using average Americans. The basic message was still the same, but without the Hollywood touch. Now, instead of simply borrowing old film clips, the company could afford to create its own. The new ad series was directed by David Fincher (*Alien 3*), and the sound tracks were provided by rock star Lennie Kravitz. No one expected the new ads or any subsequent ones to have the social impact that the old James Dean mania triggered, but the results speak for themselves. Levi's is number 1 in Japan and looks set to stay there. (It is interesting to note that even though the firm said *sayonara* to its number 1 symbol in terms of television and poster advertising, Levi's can't seem to break off such a good relationship so easily: the company's 1994 jeans catalog had a plain white cover with just a single black-and-white photo on both front and back, and both were pictures of James Dean.)

In October of 1993 one of the big department stores on Tokyo's fashionable west side opened a "Levi's Only" corner. The Odakyu store that sits above the nation's busiest railroad terminus put the whole Levi's lineup on display. This marked yet another breakthrough for the company, as Japanese department stores always like to show a variety of goods from several makers. As a rule, stores don't have special "boutiques" devoted to only a single maker since dedicating so much sales space to one product line entails a big risk. The only exceptions are unusually popular name brands, such as Louis Vuitton. For Levi's to be featured in this way in a major department store was proof that in a little over twenty years the company had risen from nothing to the same level of name recognition as the most exclusive brands in the world.

Executive Profile

In 1991 when the recession dashed hopes of ongoing bubble-era profits for thousands of firms, LSJ took on a new president, John Chappell. A New Zealander by birth, after becoming a director in charge of marketing at the U.S. parent, he spent time as vice-president of Levi Strauss Canada before coming to Japan. Chappell understands that ways of doing business are different in different countries. Since arriving in Tokyo he has devoted a great deal of time to learning about Japanese working habits, distribution structures, retailing, etc. His observations on Japanese business go far beyond the scope of Levi's activities, though.

For example, Chappell says that despite all he read about Japanese diligence, he was surprised by how long people work every day. "It's not at all unusual to see staff working until 9 or 10 at night," he says, "yet when you look at it carefully, office productivity is rather low." He notes that whereas American workers tend to act first and think about it later, Japanese study every conceivable possibility before undertaking any new project. Of course, there is much to be said for not being rash, but he concludes that Japanese workers spend too much time trying to avoid failure. "They're too afraid of taking risks; they hate risk so they move very slowly to be sure they're getting it right. A lot of time is wasted in the process."

Chappell sees a number of advantages to the Japanese system, however. Because everyone works together in a team venture, everyone faces the same goals and is conscious of them. Consequently, he says, companies avoid the Western problem of one executive trying to make another look bad so that he or she will look good. The Japanese setting provides a "very secure feeling" which allows both employees and management to take a long-term view.

How has Chappell dealt with the downside of Japanese work habits at Levi's? First he instituted a leadership training program for managers in an effort to build faster decision making without losing the firm's cooperative atmosphere. He has also implemented a human resources development program, trying to improve the quality of all LSJ employees.

Another big problem in Japanese firms is static, 1940s-style lines of corporate communication. Noting that mail even among the company's own offices was being sent via the post office, Chappell encouraged the use of E−mail inside the company and is pushing development of online integrated systems. He admits it's a big jump, like moving from a horse-drawn cart to a sports car, but it is necessary.

"Times are changing, markets are changing," he says, "We have to speed up the way we operate. Japanese traditionally work in a way so that each employee overlaps the next guy's responsibilities. We're making people become more efficient. Where two people do a job, we're trying to see if one person can take control of it."

What about the future? "Levi's has become a big success in Japan. Our employees are generally happy and years of success have led to complacency. Right now there isn't enough urgency or mental toughness. To respond to the coming changes in the market, we must strengthen our attitude. We're in a low-growth economy now; there won't be any more 20–30 percent growth years for Levi's as in years past. Our big problems will be how to control costs and how to cope with rapid changes in the market, in distribution systems, and in price structures."

Chappell believes that some degree of biculturalism is necessary for anyone to run a company in a foreign country, especially Japan. "In a foreign-based company, it is very important that the president is someone with experience living and working in at least two other countries. In addition, communications with the head office are critical. Of course, dealing with the local language problem is also important, but if someone understands the language but doesn't understand the business, you'll never get anywhere. A good executive can accomplish a lot even through an interpreter."

Although Chappell doesn't say it, it is clear that Levi Strauss Japan is in better shape today than just a few years ago, not because of sales increases, but because ideas such as his are making the firm increasingly competitive. The firm fought hard to become number 1 and it plans to stay there.

Conclusions

The Levi's story is a good example of how to build a powerhouse brand in Japan through good marketing. The product was not unique, so the sales approach had to be.

One fundamental reason behind Levi's success is that it captured for Japanese youth the essence of American culture. The company cleverly established a link between its products and the aspects of American culture that young Japanese shoppers found most attractive. The result was a simple equation: Levi's = America. For foreign manufacturers who often hear tales of how much the Japanese prefer domestic goods and how proud they are of Japanese quality, there is an important lesson here. At the same time, Levi Strauss combined its all-American image with special attention to the needs of the Japanese market, modifying styles, colors, and materials when necessary. Moreover, the firm put special emphasis on its distribution network, both co-opting the regional wholesalers and using a sophisticated POS system to keep tabs on day-to-day sales trends.

LSJ's early years were under-capitalized and the head office in the United States had more on its mind than just the Japanese market. But as is so often the case, the parent firm found that Japan is not just another market and that Japanese sales can be a huge pillar to support consolidated earnings. As the Tokyo subsidiary grew, Levi Strauss came to respect its Japan operation more, and because the parent agreed to allow direct imports and assist with manufacturing specific products in the United States aimed at the Japanese market, both companies prospered. The message for firms with Tokyo subsidiaries or JVs is clear: Japan is the largest potential market in the world (based on current disposable income); the more the head office supports efforts to tap into this market, the greater the rewards will be.

CHAPTER 3

Breaking the Rules

Louis Vuitton

People who say that consumers are not spending during the recession don't know what they're talking about. We've never been so busy. We're running like crazy just to meet customer demand. In 1993 our annual unit sales jumped an unprecedented 20 percent. Don't tell me that consumers are sitting on their wallets.

Gojiro Hata, President of Louis Vuitton Japan

The fabled *bubble* economy that grew up in Japan in the late-1980s has been called the greatest asset boom in world history. For a time, Japanese companies all seemed to have forgotten their main businesses in favor of speculation in the high-flying stock and real estate markets. Most firms recorded unusually high profits during that period, which led to higher paychecks and higher bonuses for their employees year after year. Individuals caught the fever, too, and used their earnings to buy stocks, land, or golf club memberships, and almost all of these investors also profited from the astronomical rise of asset values. Two-thirds of the Japanese population owns their own homes, and many of those average homeowners became paper millionaires overnight. Thousands became multimillionaires.

Not surprisingly, this had a profound effect on spending patterns. Within a very short time, the traditionally frugal Japanese were seeking out the best-known, most expensive brands in the world. Companies bought Van Gogh paintings to hang in their lobbies and ordinary businessmen bought Mercedes to leave in their garages. Thanks both to expanding asset values and extremely easy credit, it was not at all uncommon to see 21-year-old secretaries in Tokyo wearing a combination of watches, jewelry, and fashion accessories worth several tens of thousands of dollars. Of course, this was on weekdays—on weekends they dressed up.

The Bubble Years

As a result, foreign firms, and especially European firms, that were perceived as producing the world's highest quality and most fashionable goods found themselves riding a wave of seemingly unlimited demand. And one of the premier companies that came to symbolize this "money is no object" consumerism of the bubble years was French luggage-maker Louis Vuitton.

Only a few years later the whole situation turned upside down. As the bubble deflated, sales of brand-name goods collapsed, and the big-name foreign companies that were doing so well in Japan suddenly saw their oceans of profit evaporate. In many cases, CEOs of the Japan units were forced to take responsibility for these reversals, and quite a number of heads rolled as a result. The problem was not simply poor performance in an overseas market: that would not normally result in so many recalls of top execs from Tokyo. The real problem was that in just a few years the Japanese market had come to represent 30–50 percent of many firms' aggregate worldwide sales. Thus the collapse of consumer spending in Tokyo did more than damage the Japan subsidiaries; it sent shock waves through corporate structures from Geneva to New York to Sydney.

For those firms that stayed on and tried to keep their sales afloat in the wake of the recession, the competition turned even more severe. One of the few companies that has not only survived but is positively thriving in this brutal environment is Louis

Vuitton, the symbol of a vanished era. How the company managed to jump from success during the wild-spending boom days to even bigger success during the deepest recession in fifty years is a superb study in marketing strategy.

All too often the business press likes to credit some great corporate achievement to a single top executive when in fact the company's growth resulted just as much from the work of dozens of less visible managers. However, in Louis Vuitton's case it is no exaggeration to say that one man's vision not only created the Japanese subsidiary and turned it into a recession-proof profit machine, but was literally the architect of the parent company's global expansion. That man is Gojiro Hata, president of Louis Vuitton Japan (LVJ).

Hata's comments on the company's current fortunes provide good advice for any firm trying to sell in Japan: "It is very true that since the recession started the discount shops have been doing good business. But that doesn't mean that consumers are only looking for cheap goods. In the bubble days, people bought expensive goods as a kind of personal asset; today they look for value in everything they buy. People want to avoid wasting money at all costs. So, for daily necessities, they buy the cheapest goods they can find. But for more important items, they look for quality, which translates into long-term value even if the price is much higher. And when they find real quality, they buy it without hesitation. The *average* level of household savings in Japan right now is about $130,000. That means that good products, things which are seen to have real value, can still sell well. The best *quality* products can always sell in this market regardless of the state of the economy."

Louis Vuitton Japan's Director of Sales and Operations, Takeshi Oishi, says the company succeeds because it has a very different outlook than its rivals: "We don't think of Louis Vuitton merchandise as 'brand-name goods,' that is, items which are expensive simply because they have a fancy name attached. People like to wear brand-name goods when they go out; they're for show. We see Louis Vuitton goods as very different. They're high-quality commodities, things people use every day. So you pay for the quality, not the brand name."

The problem with brand-name goods, he explains, is that the value lies principally in the name, that is, in the high-priced image, not in the merchandise itself. Thus, when the economy turns sour and the maker begins slashing prices to bolster sales, it has killed the primary value of the item. Once the goods lose their status value, sales will decline rapidly. There were numerous examples of this phenomenon in Japan long before the recession, but the recession intensified it considerably.

With expensive but high-quality goods such as Vuitton bags, buyers are happy if their purchase also conveys status, but what they really want is the merchandise. They are willing to pay a high price because they have no doubt of the quality they are buying. If the price comes down, they are delighted, and sales will rise rather than fall. Case in point: LVJ lowered its retail prices by a total of 15 percent in 1993 and its unit sales rose by 20 percent.

Discounting at Louis Vuitton? Not so, says President Hata. "We didn't lower our prices because the goods weren't selling. We lowered them because of the rising yen. We always try to keep our Japan prices at no more than 45 percent above the price of the same goods in France. In the decade and a half that we've been in business here the yen has appreciated steadily, so we've had to lower prices repeatedly. For example, when we started, a certain 30 cm. bag sold for ¥52,000 (about $520 today); considering inflation over that period of time, it would be normal for the price of that item to rise substantially. Yet today the same bag costs less, about ¥45,000 ($450). That's a big difference."

Background

There is nothing unusual about American or European companies, especially in the fashion business, making hefty profits in the Japanese market. But Louis Vuitton is one of the very few companies that actually became a global enterprise due to Japanese demand.

French founder Louis Vuitton developed a reputation among the carriage trade of Paris for making very high quality, durable luggage in the middle of the nineteenth century. His boxes were made of wood, not leather, decorated with the best hardware, and covered with good cloth.

As more people began to travel internationally, and modes of transportation changed from coaches and carriages to railroads and steamships, large wardrobe-style trunks became fashionable. Here, Vuitton's experience in making sturdy luggage paid off.

In 1896 Louis's son Georges developed what is now a world-famous logo, his father's initials inscribed in chestnut-brown cloth with beige flowers and stars. Artistic though it may seem to shoppers today, the original purpose of the logo was to positively identify Louis Vuitton originals, for even a hundred years ago the firm's goods were being copied illegally. But the mark did much more: it established a brand-name image for Louis Vuitton goods among the elite of Europe's culture capital.

The post-war economy changed the world (and world travel) forever. People jumped in cars and went away for the weekend or boarded planes and casually flew across the ocean for a week's holiday. This spurred demand for soft luggage rather than big, boxy trunks, bags that could be tossed in the back of a car, then checked in at an airport. But the cloth the company had been using for more than 50 years on its trunks was not well suited to soft-sided luggage. Making a new material for modern bags was a challenge. So in 1959 Georges' son Gaston developed the new cloth that is still in use on Louis Vuitton bags. It is a combination of cotton and linen, coated with vinyl. Using this soft but extremely durable material, Gaston designed one series of "soft bags" after another.

Although the company's products were carried all over the world and the Louis Vuitton logo became famous from London to Singapore, the company remained a small, family-run enterprise with only two stores right up until the mid-1970s when a surge of demand from Japanese customers forced the firm to reexamine its business.

The Japanese love affair with Louis Vuitton bags did not happen all at once. There are dozens of stories, some going back 20 or 30 years, of Japanese executives discovering the Vuitton reputation and passing the word to friends and business acquaintances. One of the old stories involves a European tour taken by a group of leading Japanese industrialists and their wives. For some reason, the wives' luggage was separated in transit and then left behind on a dock when the party moved on. Before the luggage could be identified and forwarded it was thoroughly drenched outdoors. Needless to say, the women's clothes—expensive dresses, hats, shoes, and all—were completely soaked. Only one woman opened her trunk to find her things exactly as she had packed them. Not a drop of water had seeped inside. Of course it was a Louis Vuitton trunk. Now this would have turned into good word-of-mouth publicity had the woman been any Japanese on holiday with her friends. But it so happened that the woman whose watertight trunk saved her vacation was the wife of the former chairman of Nissan Motors. Her story spread quickly among Japanese business-people, and executives going to Europe began to look for the Vuitton shop in Paris.

Since the company had no single general agent in Tokyo, several Japanese department stores started importing and sell-ing Louis Vuitton bags. But the stores took a typically Japanese approach to imports: keep quantities low and prices as high as possible. Thus as the Japanese economy grew and more Japanese began to travel, they often found that prices in Vuitton's Paris store were only a fraction of the Tokyo price for the same goods. Word got around fast.

Two things happened. Japanese who went abroad thronged the Paris shop, and entrepreneurs in Japan began buying large quantities of Louis Vuitton goods in France and importing them privately. If they sold the bags for a little under the local depart-ment store price, they made a huge profit. By 1976 the Louis Vuitton store in Paris was crowded as never before, largely with Japanese. Some were shoppers and some were dealers. It was hard to tell the difference, since even individual shoppers bought several bags at a time, sometimes a dozen or more. The company, at first pleased, began to see this as a problem. After all, the firm's craftsmen were laboring, just as they had for more than a century, to produce handmade, quality luggage, which they assumed would sell at a dignified pace to discriminating customers. Instead, each day waves of Japanese tourists descended upon the store like swarms of locusts and left it bare to the walls as they departed.

The store finally instituted a "one bag per person" rule, not so much to slow the locusts as to discourage the dealers from buying and reselling in volume. The policy had the opposite effect. It angered the real shoppers (who are now well known for buying gifts by the truckload to haul back to Japan), but it did little to stop the black market dealers. The latter began hiring Japanese exchange students in France to buy for them, and the business continued as before.

Enter the Consultants

Had the matter ended there it would have been just another example of Japanese shoppers moving in herds to a certain European shop. In time the trend might have shifted to a different shop in Paris or in Rome or somewhere else, and life would have gone back to normal at little family-run Louis Vuitton. But what the family management lacked in global marketing experience it more than made up for in open-mindedness and business instinct. In the words of the general manager of the Paris store, "That parade of Japanese shoppers opened our eyes to the hidden potential of Louis Vuitton."

In order to get a better grasp of its financial situation, and to find out why so many Japanese as well as young American buyers were now beating a path to Vuitton's door, the store turned to a U.S. accounting firm to do an audit of the company and then to consult on its potential for expansion.

After some investigation, Peat, Marwick, Mitchell presented its findings to management. Essentially it told the Vuitton family that its quaint, family-run structure was outdated, and that it needed to retain professional managers who could tap the company's real market potential. Audacious as the recommendation may have sounded to the French, it also made sense. Louis Vuitton formed a family holding company to control a new, modern corporation, with both manufacturing and sales divisions.

The family hired a well-known steel company executive to be president of the joint-stock company, then recruited the Paris store manager from France's top children's clothing maker, and picked up a number of other professional managers. But no one had a greater impact on the company's fortunes than a Japanese member of the Peat, Marwick staff, a man who today—though he would deny it—is probably responsible for roughly half of Louis Vuitton's total sales worldwide.

Gojiro Hata was in the management consulting division of PMM's Japan office at the time. He recalls, "In 1976 1 was in Paris on some other business. I happened to have lunch with a French friend who was putting together management ideas for Louis Vuitton. The friend said that the new president of the company wanted to do some research on the Japanese market, and that's how I came in contact with Louis Vuitton."

Hata, it should be noted, was far from a typical Japanese executive. After graduating from Keio University (which is almost a factory for executive talent at Japan's top firms), he went to America. In 1964 he received an MBA from Dartmouth. Nowadays, Japanese with MBAs are a dime a dozen, but in 1964 they were still a rare breed. Upon graduation he joined PMM as a consultant and his reputation grew.

Hata soon began market research in Japan for Louis Vuitton. In addition to the licensed sales agent, he found there were many companies importing LV goods and selling them privately, each one setting prices as it pleased. Hata's report was blunt: "There is tremendous demand for LV goods in the Japanese market, but prices are out of control. If this continues, LV's image will likely suffer . . . The licensed agent approach is an easy way to expand overseas, but it is not necessarily the best. The company now suffers from parallel imports and the lack of a unified image. If the firm wishes to preserve its image as a first-rate manufacturer, direct management of the Japan operation is the only answer."

At that time almost all foreign brands were sold in Japan by representative agents with import licenses or were produced locally via licensing agreements with the foreign maker. Direct management of a Japanese company by a foreign brand was unheard of. Thus, while Hata's report was interesting, in a practical sense it was little more than an unproven theory.

"As a management consultant, I thought the arrangement between a maker and its foreign agent is one of mutual profit with minimal effort. It's a marriage of convenience; but after the honeymoon is over, it's very hard to maintain good relations."

Emulating the founding family's willingness to solicit good advice and then make dramatic changes based on it, the company's newly-hired president adopted the report and its recommendations immediately. At the time the firm had no overseas outlets and was not thinking about expanding overseas. All it had was the word of a Japanese consultant at an American firm that its strategy was all wrong. The company wisely decided that it would be difficult to implement Hata's plan without Hata, and asked PMM to let him run its new Tokyo operation.

Loyalty to Vuitton Comes First

At that time, people who knew retailing in Japan thought Hata's approach was crazy. Common sense dictated that the only effective way to operate a successful retail network in Japan was to find some way to come to terms with the nation's infamous distribution labyrinth, which included its often haughty department stores. Yet at Hata's urging, Louis Vuitton set out to bypass the whole distribution machine. Instead of using wholesalers, it would establish a chain of specialty retail stores and then deal directly with them as part of its own network. In this way it could directly control not only the prices, but the look and the feel and especially the image of its retail shops. Sales techniques, uniforms, the method for responding to customer requests, and just about everything else would follow the pattern of the French parent company. Outside of its own elite group of direct-managed shops in the major urban areas, it would sell only at separate, identifiable Louis Vuitton boutiques inside the top-name department stores, principally outside the big cities. There would be (and to this day there is still) no distribution center to serve department stores: the Paris store would ship directly to department stores in Japan.

This policy put Louis Vuitton on a collision course with the nation's most powerful retailers. Japanese department stores are not like Macy's. The big ones (Mitsukoshi, Takashimaya, Seibu, etc.) are usually members of a *keiretsu,* a large group of diverse but interrelated companies with tremendous industrial and political clout. Many stores (including Seibu, Tokyu, Keio, Odakyu, and Hankyu) sprouted from the retail businesses generated by private railroads of the same name. Some of their directors are seconded from the railroad or from a powerful bank connected with the group. Some of these stores also have a very long history (over two centuries in the case of Mitsukoshi and Takashimaya, for example). All of this adds up to an air of self-importance much greater than Western businesspeople would expect from a department store. Japanese and foreign retailers alike who want shelf space are expected to kowtow to these grand institutions, and if they are lucky, the store may consent to carry their goods—on its own terms, of course. Needless to say, the very idea of a little retail shop giving orders to a department store is absolutely out of the question. No one who wanted to succeed in Japan would contemplate such an insult even for a moment.

No one but Hata, that is. Through him, the French company demanded that any department store that wished to sell its goods must sign a very detailed contract. The store not only had to allot special floor space for retailing Louis Vuitton products, but also had to meet various strict requirements. Moreover, the LV side would invest almost no money in the sales operation; the financial burden was part of the department store's commitment to handling Vuitton merchandise.

Even Hata knew that these demands were outrageous by industry standards, and the firm fully expected to be turned down by most of the stores it approached. The hope inside Louis Vuitton's Tokyo operation was that at least two major stores would say yes. The two they wanted were Takashimaya, a very traditional, high-status store, and Seibu, a chic, modern, high-priced emporium with outlets in most major cities. To everyone's surprise, both stores agreed to LV's terms. But what really shocked them was that four other department stores signed up right from the start. If the little company wanted some sign of its long-term potential to sell in this market, there was no greater proof than this humbling of the nation's top retailers.

This was not the end of the friction with the department stores, however, only the beginning. Louis Vuitton did not merely display its goods at the stores; it took control of the sales operation.

To ensure that all the company's outlets, whether directly managed or part of a giant department store chain, were identical in look and feel, the firm initiated an overseas training program. This was written into the contract with the department stores. One staff member from each store had to go to Paris for a week's training. Overseas trips are naturally a plum that department store management likes to hand out to men it considers headed for executive positions. But Louis Vuitton Japan would have none of that: it chose the person from each store that would go abroad. To add insult to injury, it often chose women. "From the start we selected talented female staff to go to Paris. We know that men in these stores change sections pretty quickly, so we prefer to send women who we feel are more likely to stay with our product line for a longer time. Of course, there were many stores that objected, usually saying that female staff were not allowed to go on overseas study trips for any reason. But we overcame that," recalls Shizue Kuwabara, then Hata's special assistant to the president (now manager of the firm's Veuve Cliquot division).

In France the Japanese trainees would visit the Vuitton factory as well as the stores. They studied the way the stores looked, their atmosphere, and their style, and then they learned more about the merchandise itself. When they returned to Japan, these people naturally felt a special tie to Louis Vuitton, even though they were working for a famous department store. Moreover, all the LV salespeople at the big stores were made to feel like salespeople at shops managed directly by Louis Vuitton: they were living extensions of the Paris store. If this led to some conflicts of loyalty, that is precisely what Vuitton expected.

Hata had wanted to gain complete control of Louis Vuitton's marketing in Japan regardless of where it was done. One story illustrates how effectively he achieved that goal.

Shortly after setting up the business and signing up the department stores, the Paris office shipped 1,500 bags from France to supply its Japan sales network. Somehow the shipment was lost in transit. The real problem was not the monetary loss, which was covered by insurance, but the sudden loss of stock. Since Louis Vuitton goods are not mass-produced, the loss of so many bags meant a severe shortage that could not be compensated for some time, and just at the point when the firm was trying to build up its sales system. The company's response was perfectly logical by Western standards, unthinkable by Japanese standards. It told the department stores, which kept more stock on hand than the company's own retail outlets, to ship some of their merchandise to the LV retail stores that were most desperate for stock.

The staff at the department stores, having been carefully instructed that the way to hang on to a Louis Vuitton sales license was to follow orders to the letter, did as they were told. Only later did stories filter back to the LV Tokyo and Paris offices that many of these salespeople who had followed instructions were bitterly chewed out by their superiors in the department stores. A common theme of the tirades included a line about "Who the hell do you think you're working for anyway—Louis Vuitton or us?" The little company knew its strategy was working.

No Discounts—Ever

Initially the head office realized that sending French executives
who understood little or nothing of the Japanese system to run the
operation in Tokyo would be a colossal mistake. Instead, it asked
Peat, Marwick, Mitchell to keep a hand in the start-up phase of
the business in Japan. When the Louis Vuitton stores were set up
in Japan in 1977, consultant Hata was put in charge of running
them, although he was officially still working for Peat, Marwick.
(One irony of Louis Vuitton's success in Japan was that it was
headed by a Japanese executive who was technically with an
American company.) When the subsidiary, Louis Vuitton Japan
(LVJ), was finally established in 1981, Hata was naturally named
president.

Director of sales and operations Takeshi Oishi came to LVJ
from Takashimaya, one of the country's oldest and most famous
department stores. He knew how they thought and how they felt
about the little foreign company's "do it our way" attitude. He
recalls with a smile, "Hata and some of the others came from
consulting backgrounds. They knew a lot about business, but they
didn't have any firsthand experience in this field. So I had to take
responsibility for dealing with a lot of our sales outlets face-to-face.
It wasn't easy."

The difference in executive backgrounds showed up in various
ways. Oishi was often surprised by things Hata did, like the price
reduction of 1980. Oishi pointed out that the goods were selling
like hotcakes; there was no need to reduce the price at the time.
Hata replied that "The yen has gone up. It is only natural for us to
pass along our foreign exchange gains to the consumer." Oishi's
first reaction was "Only a guy who was not from a retail background could think that way."

The price cuts actually had two objectives: to maintain a fair
price in Tokyo, and to drive parallel imports out of the market. By
taking over direct sales of LV goods, the Japan subsidiary reduced
the disparity in retail prices between Tokyo and Paris from 5:1
to around 1.4:1. At that tight a margin, there is little incentive
for parallel importers to "arbitrage" LV products, especially when
there are so many other name brands whose Tokyo prices are
several times those in their home country.

Of course there has always been a taboo in Japan about lowering prices on brand-name goods. Shoppers invariably think "They can't sell the merchandise, so they have to discount," which means that any high-status image the goods may have had goes right down the drain as soon as the SALE sign appears. Traditionally, Japanese customers have turned up their noses at whatever appeared to be "discount" merchandise. Louis Vuitton challenged this attitude and won. It both lowered prices and increased sales.

The important thing to note about this unusual strategy is that the company carefully controlled these price reductions and never allowed retailers to discount merchandise on their own. Independent discounting of LV products was absolutely forbidden. In short, the official price of LV goods was lowered nationwide, but there was never a "sale" as such.

The problem is that all Japanese department stores give discounts to certain customers, and of course they all run sales from time to time, even on name-brand merchandise. Louis Vuitton said, in effect, "Not with our merchandise." This caused more friction.

Some stores agreed not to include LV merchandise in their discount sales, but wanted LVJ to do something to help promote the goods. LVJ knew the goods didn't need any promotion; it was just the department stores that were looking for something unique to advertise, like a sale—however small—on Louis Vuitton bags. Hata said absolutely not. Stores kept pressing LVJ to let them include Vuitton merchandise in their special mid-summer or year-end sales. Managers pleaded, "This year is different. We're taking a whole new approach to the sales. They'll be done very tastefully. And we won't charge you anything for listing LV goods in our sale flyers. It'll be a big help in boosting your sales figures." Hata replied, "No thanks. We're not all that concerned about increasing our sales."

Sometimes store managers reported that their salespeople had already written up discounts for certain customers who were buying large quantities of merchandise and that some LV goods were included by mistake. A common line was, "The sale has already been input into the computer at the lower price." To which Hata replied, "Fine. If it's in a computer, you can re-input the whole transaction." This did not win him any friends among department store management. But gradually the word got around that Louis

Vuitton goods could not be discounted ever, to anyone, under any circumstances. And everyone came to realize that Hata was not simply being a tough guy, he was working to preserve Vuitton's quality image in a fickle market.

Two More Critical Points

Don't Tolerate Imitations

The problem with working so hard to create a top-notch brand image is that success inevitably brings the wrong kind of admirers. We noted before that Louis Vuitton has had problems with counterfeit bags since the 1800s. And that was in France. In the Orient, where imitation is considered the sincerest form of flattery (and patents and trademarks are often ignored), the problem grew several fold.

At first, fake bags were imported from abroad just like the originals. Then a number of Japanese companies took a close look at the quality of the fakes as well as the perennial popularity of Louis Vuitton goods, and with typical Japanese pride in their manufacturing ability, said to themselves, "We can make these right here and probably make 'em better."

LVJ was not amused. While many firms try to ignore copies and hope the counterfeiters will make a quick buck and move on, Louis Vuitton considers all copies, good and bad, an assault on its image. Every year LVJ alone spends close to $3 million to combat forgeries in Japan. It has five employees and ten outside lawyers dedicated to that task, and when investigations turn up evidence of counterfeiting, the results are turned over to the police. And the Japanese police take these things quite seriously.

For example, in 1981 the police announced the results of an 18-month-long investigation, which netted a total of 250 firms making fake Louis Vuitton bags. The largest of them had a factory outside of Osaka that was turning out several tens of thousands of forgeries every month.

One of the LVJ team responsible for these anti-forgery operations comments, "When we hear that there are fake Louis Vuittons being made in Osaka or Kyushu or wherever, we move on it right away. We're on very good terms with the police officials in charge of the investigation." His colleagues nod in agreement. When their boss got married recently, says one, more than half the wedding guests were from the police department.

As with so many other local industries, though, the homemade counterfeits are losing out to increasing competition from else-where in Asia. These days the Japanese-made fakes are starting to disappear, while those from Korea, Taiwan, and Thailand are increasing.

Take Good Care of Your Employees

Industry observers generally cite two things that have contributed to the firm's success: Hata's strategy of preserving the brand's image at all costs, and the company's internal personnel policies. The company's motto seems to be "Hire good people and hang on to them." That means developing good relations within the firm, and the president of the French parent company sets an example. He travels around the world constantly and visits Japan often. The local staff say that when he is in Tokyo he spends a lot of time with them. They eat meals together and he listens to what everyone has to say; people say he likes to hear their opinions. Thus, unlike many foreign companies in Japan which have become famous as "revolving doors," with this year's staff signing up and last year's hires bailing out at a furious pace, Louis Vuitton is a model of stability. Even during the bubble era when almost every successful company in Japan went on a hiring binge, LVJ refrained. When the recession came and big firms had to trim the extra heads on their payrolls, LVJ was able to keep hiring. In addition, it loses very few people for any reason. According to one foreign headhunter who knows their situation well, staff come into Louis Vuitton Japan at a measured pace and they tend to stay there.

Oishi comments: "At almost every company in Japan it is taken for granted that women will retire when they get married, or at the latest when they have children. At LVJ, having sales staff whom our customers know and trust is very important. We don't want to lose them. That's why we encourage women to stay on even after they have children. Just as one example of how we do things: we have a shop in the Osaka Hilton Hotel, and the company rents a room in the hotel just so our staff will have a place to rest. It's all part of our policy of taking care of our employees."

Were Japanese Sales Too Successful?

As we noted earlier, even the bursting of the economic bubble did not affect LVJ the way it did other firms that were riding high on the wave of consumer spending. While sales of the company's old mainstay line (the "Monogram" series) did not increase, they remained relatively stable, which was a success in itself. But more than that, the firm saw a new line become a major profit earner. The "Epi" line, which it launched in 1986, seemed to grow steadily more popular year after year. "Epi" bags are specially treated to be water-resistant, and unlike the staid "Monogram" bags, come in a selection of colors. The combination of Louis Vuitton's reputation for quality together with this colorful new design proved to be irresistible to Japanese women: today "Epi" bags accounts for 38 percent of LVJ's total annual sales and its popularity is still growing. With a hit like that coming just when it was most needed, it is no surprise that the firm managed to perform so well during the recession even as its rivals watched their sales slide. In 1994, LVJ's sales increased a very healthy 14 percent year-to-year, mostly thanks to the contribution from the "Epi" line.

Today, Louis Vuitton is looking to expand further, using Hata's original plan as the basis for its expansion strategy. In particular it is looking at areas such as the United States which, relative to Japan, is still a largely untapped market. The target is to open 100 stores in the United States (more than three times the number in Japan). Part of this is the company's natural desire to expand, and part stems from the recognition that it has come to depend too much on Japan.

Roughly 44 percent of Louis Vuitton's total sales come from the Far East, principally from Japan and from Japanese travelling overseas, and roughly 60 percent of total international sales come from Japanese shoppers. Everyone expects Japan's love affair with the LV logo to continue well into the future, but at the same time it is unwise to become too dependent on any single market.

It was this same line of thinking which led the parent company to diversify its business as well. In the past few years it has joined with one of Spain's top leather and fashion firms, Loewe, with champagne house Veuve Cliquot, Givenchy perfume, and clothing and accessory maker Christian Lacroix. One strategy common to these businesses is to mine the Japanese market and use the profits to fund global expansion. In Japan, Hata serves as president of Loewe (as well as LVJ). Loewe already has 11 stores in the country and, like LVJ, it sells products from Louis Vuitton, Loewe, Christian Lacroix, and even Veuve Cliquot. The latter operates a direct-managed store in Tokyo's fashionable Aoyama district and has two champagne corners in famous department stores. In short, the LV group is well positioned to leverage off coming growth in the Japanese economy to support future operations.

Conclusion

Less than 20 years ago Louis Vuitton was a tiny, family-run company in France. Despite over a hundred years of manufacturing experience, it had only a two-store network in which to display its goods. Today Louis Vuitton is one of the best-known brand names in the world with dozens of stores around the globe. What is most remarkable—and what should provide a poignant lesson for other makers who are frightened by stories of the complexities of the Japanese market—is that Louis Vuitton's worldwide expansion is largely the result of its success in Japan. In essence, the company created and controlled its own sales network in Japan, forced Japanese retailers to conform to its requirements rather than the other way around, and then levered its monumental success into an expanding global presence.

Most stories that circulate about how to do business in Japan focus on the importance of "doing everything the Japanese way," and the strong implication is that any other approach is doomed to failure. Louis Vuitton proved that, given the right management and the right products, there is another way to do things. The company broke almost every rule in the book except one—it offered the kind of unwavering dedication to quality that Japanese consumers used to think was only possible from a Japanese firm.

CHAPTER 4

The Road Not Taken
BMW

Everyone knows how difficult it was for foreign companies to get into the Japanese market in the years after World War II. More than domestic companies, it was the Japanese government that threw up every possible roadblock to prohibit and encumber foreign entry. Worst of all, recently available historical records now show that the perpetuation of this system was made possible thanks to the U.S. government, which allowed America's own companies to be kept from competing in Japan in the interests of preserving a desired security relationship with that nation. The fact that European companies were also shut out by the same U.S. decision was taken as just "one of those things" that happen in international politics.

With the passing of decades, many firms, both American and European, have been knocking—many pounding—on doors to get into Japan and get a fair shake in its markets. And, to be fair to the Japanese side as well, the situation has changed over the years. Many of the roadblocks that the government put up in the 1950s and 1960s have disappeared, or nearly so, and companies that have the will and the resources to make long-term commitments to the Japanese market are well rewarded (as the examples in this book show very clearly).

However, there are still a few very real roadblocks and thousands of potholes on the road into the Japanese markets. The Japanese themselves are aware of this and they often applaud foreign firms that have the tenacity to beat the system, especially the bureaucratic system that remains one of the largest obstacles to any new business expanding in Japan.

Yet precisely because some roadblocks remain, there are more than a few foreign firms that are quick to cry "Foul" whenever things don't go the way they think they should. Rather than tough it out—as hundreds upon hundreds of foreign firms have done—and earn their rewards, they prefer to cry about unfair government regulations and to pressure politicians at home to bail them out. Not many firms have enough clout to get away with this "we don't want to wait 20 years like everybody else did" strategy, but those that do usually make a big splash in the papers when they succeed.

The classic example of this approach is Detroit's Big 3 auto makers. The Big 3 have long histories in Japan; they were effectively kicked out of the market prior to World War II, and have tried to come back ever since. But rather than come back the hard way—buy land, recruit dealers, start from scratch—they have all tried the backdoor approach: acquiring large stakes in Japan's midsize auto firms (GM's tie-up with Izuzu, Ford with Mazda, and Chrysler with Mitsubishi). Yet in spite of gaining these footholds on Japanese soil in the 1970s, the Big 3, with all their manufacturing muscle and marketing clout, did almost nothing to push their cars in the Japanese market until the beginning of this decade. Instead, they complained loud and long about Japanese regulations, discrimination, and so on. Then after years of ignoring the market, they suddenly awakened and wanted instant sales. At one point they even arm-twisted the President of the United States into escorting them to Japan and pleading their case.

This is not to imply that the Big 3 had an open door to sell in the Japanese market—far from it. Most of their complaints about regulatory obstacles and the rest were accurate. But the idea of three of the biggest and most powerful companies in the world simply giving up and using political pressure tactics instead of marketing savvy to crack the Japanese market provides eloquent testimony to the debilitating advanced stages of "big company disease."

While all the whining from Detroit was in the air, another auto maker came into the Japanese market, a firm with relatively little clout and no heads of state to open doors for it. In just a few years that firm proved that a company with good products and a good marketing strategy can succeed in Japan on its own merits. Germany's BMW (a midget compared to Ford or GM) showed everyone that you can win, and win big, in Japan if you know what you're doing.

From Kawasaki to BMW

The BMW Japan story is largely that of an incredibly dynamic executive who combined a fundamental sales strategy with shrewd marketing and bold financing to create a permanent addition to the Japanese auto industry.

Yoji Hamawaki began as a manager at one of the nation's giant shipbuilders, Kawasaki Heavy Industries. His specialty was exports, but not of ships. Hamawaki handled some of the smaller equipment that Kawasaki Heavy also produced. In 1965 he was exporting engines for tractors and other agricultural equipment to Brazil. Since Brazil had very high duties and high inflation, he decided that to continue doing business there it was necessary to establish a local corporation. He persuaded KHI to set up a firm in Brazil, and soon, as he had predicted, the business began to grow. On his way back to Japan, Hamawaki visited the United States and it was there that he saw one of the early Honda motorbikes that were about to change America's image of two-wheeled travel. Just the sight of a Japanese motorcycle sitting in a show window started a chain reaction in Hamawaki's marketing brain. If Japanese-made bikes could catch on in the world's biggest economy, a country with a huge consumer market and no heavy tariffs or high inflation, there was no limit to the possibilities for expansion.

When Hamawaki returned to Japan, he found Kawasaki Heavy Industries in the process of deciding whether or not to continue production of a motorcycle line it had started some years before. Some said the company should stick to shipbuilding and its other mainstay industries and get out of the bike business. Hamawaki thought otherwise. To the obvious shock of the "yes men" around him, he boldly proposed that the company not only stay in the bike business, but get into exporting in a big way. His recent success in Brazil was no doubt a major factor in his proposal being taken seriously, but his brashness in proposing it in the first place may have helped his superiors make up their minds when he volunteered to go to America and set up the business there personally.

Yoji Hamawaki did go to America, where he established a new motorcycle company, Kawasaki America, and built it up from nothing to one of the top firms in the business. He did that by rejecting the bike Kawasaki Heavy had been selling in Japan (the Meguro, which the firm had produced via a subcontractor) and creating a new product to meet the needs of the American market.

"The Meguro motorcycle simply wouldn't make it in America," he said years later. "We had to design a new bike from the ground up."

Hamawaki oversaw that redesign, and he put together a dealer network in the United States to sell the new product. His success is now legendary. In a market already dominated by Honda and Yamaha, the Kawasaki bikes carved a very big niche. Hamawaki helped to create an identity for Kawasaki, building a strong following among riders who sought the kind of brute power that tamer Japanese bikes couldn't deliver together with the styling and refinements that U.S. bikes ignored. While Japanese manufacturers were gaining a reputation as copycats, Kawasaki became an innovator: the first motorcycle maker to produce a bike with a 1,000cc displacement, the first to introduce electronic ignition, and so on.

Hamawaki's strategy was not to try to stop the flood of Hondas and Yamahas coming into the country, but to differentiate his product line. He insisted that the company's focus should be on quality rather than on quantity and that its products must always stand apart from their rivals.

The principal reason Hamawaki was so successful was that he turned his dealers into market researchers. He used them to funnel consumer reaction back to his headquarters and he asked their opinions about what would sell. He listened to what his dealers told him, then used that information to decide exactly what kind of product was needed for the American market. Then, most importantly, he convinced his head office in Japan to manufacture what the local market required. (We should note here that there is probably no better advice for any foreign executive in Japan today than to use Hamawaki's approach *in reverse*.)

There was a slight problem, however. Kawasaki Heavy Industries, with a proud tradition as one of Japan's oldest shipbuilders, did not think of itself as a motorcycle firm, and so had let Hamawaki pretty much do as he pleased in the United States as long as he kept the operation in the black, which he was certainly doing. But then the shipbuilding industry went into a severe slump, and KHI decided to increase revenue from other divisions and subsidiaries, Kawasaki America among them. Before long the head office was pushing the U.S. side to increase sales. With Tokyo screaming for bigger numbers on the sales reports and Hamawaki worried mainly about quality and product differentiation, a confrontation was just down the road.

It was during this period, while the head office and the president of the American subsidiary were at odds, that BMW first approached Hamawaki with an outrageous idea: How would he like to do the same thing that he had done for Kawasaki—start from nothing and build a solid sales and service network—but do it in more hostile territory? That is, instead of selling Japanese products in America, where there was at least a relatively open market, he would have to do it in Japan, where—as Hamawaki knew very well—the *Welcome* mat was not left out for foreign companies, even those with Japanese presidents.

In addition to the obvious, the timing was terrible. The first oil shock had all but ended Japan's dreams of economic growth, and the second one, in 1979, hit the nation another hard blow. Trying to sell an expensive, imported car in that environment was more foolhardy than adventurous. And the oil shock was only part of the trouble.

At that time almost all foreign cars in Japan were imported by specialized import agents. These agents maintained a very high-class image to attract customers to whom status was everything (and value apparently unimportant). The agents preferred to keep unit sales low and retail prices high, maximizing their margins along the way. Once purchased, service on an expensive foreign car was nowhere near as good as on a much cheaper Japanese car, which was another reason for the low sales.

BMW was not much taken with this approach. The company not only wanted to get away from the agent system, it wanted a single, unified concept of sales, service, and product the world over. It wanted one BMW organization, which looked and felt more or less the same in every country, even Japan. Like Hamawaki's approach to motorcycles in America, the BMW people were big on quality and image. In 1977 the firm launched a corporate identity program to flesh out its concept of "one company, one image." All BMW operations began using the same logo, all dealers had white offices, and everything from the showroom floors to the company stationery was made to look the same.

Hamawaki was intrigued. Why had BMW waited so long to get into Japan, and after waiting, why move now? As it turned out, Japan was the last industrialized nation into which BMW ventured, in large part because everyone in the auto business knew it was a very tough market. Japan has about a dozen car companies, but its own Big Two (Toyota and Nissan) dominate sales so completely that other makers fight tooth and nail for third and fourth place. Traditionally, all the foreign car makers put together have nibbled only a tiny percentage of the Japanese pie. But the Germans were determined. They knew that product standards in Japan were very high, but so were their own. In addition, it seemed that oil shocks or no, the Japanese economy was on a one-way ride, and if it was going to keep going up, sooner or later there would be consumer demand for a kind of car that the domestic makers had not yet dreamed of building. And BMW planned to be there, with dealerships around the country, when that demand came.

Hamawaki asked to be allowed to go back to Japan once to see for himself what the imported car market looked like. When he was there he saw that Mercedes, Volvo, and other foreign cars were beginning to sell, and he decided that BMW had at least as good a chance of succeeding. He said yes, he'd take on the challenge.

Considering the oil shocks, the out-of-reach image of foreign cars propagated by the sales agents, and the recent dip in the economy, BMW probably should have entered the Japanese car market with very modest expectations. Instead, the firm had an extremely ambitious target: Set up a dealer network, open for business, and sell 10,000 cars, all in five years. Many industry insiders said it was totally, absolutely impossible.

Hamawaki did it in three.

From Airplanes to Motorcycles to Luxury Cars

The famous blue-and-white spinning propeller that identifies Bayerische Motoren Werke A.G. around the world harkens back to the company's early days as an aircraft engine maker. During World War I it was one of the top aircraft engine companies in Germany. But after the war the company was forced to change its line of business, so it turned its attention to more down-to-earth flight: motorcycles.

BMW won many races and the firm became well known for its motorcycle line. In 1928 it made a big jump, buying an automobile factory in Eisenach and entering the car business. However, the outbreak of World War II brought BMW back to making aircraft engines in addition to its other lines.

After the war, BMW began to rebuild, first with a single-cylinder motorcycle, and then gradually returning to making automobiles. But the combination of poor management and weak consumer demand in Europe in the 1950s nearly accomplished what Allied bombers had not: putting the company out of business. In 1959 the banks told BMW to swallow its pride and merge with arch-rival Daimler–Benz. The firm was saved at the last minute by the intervention of a rich patron who bought a controlling interest in the company and set it on a course to rebuild.

And rebuild it did. From the ruins of its post-war failures a new BMW was born. The firm's boxy little model 1500 was an instant hit, and from then on BMW became known worldwide for making tough, dependable cars, short on style but long on heart. Yet it aspired to something more. It wanted to create a line of cars that were tough and dependable but also sporty and individual, not merely shoeboxes with good engines.

It achieved that goal in 1972, the year of the Munich Olympics, with the launch of the model 520. With this car BMW felt it had found the concept it had lacked for so long, an identity that would carry it into the future. A new saying became common in Europe: "A man who inherits money buys a Mercedes; a man who makes his own money drives a BMW." From that point on, the firm was ready to position itself globally. After a bitter struggle, it cancelled contracts with its U.S. sales agents in order to make way for a centrally-managed American dealer network. In 1974 BMW set up a 100 percent-owned subsidiary in America. A few years later the company approached Hamawaki about doing the same thing in the Pacific.

After his success in America, Hamawaki must have felt a bit like MacArthur when he arrived in Tokyo, a proven leader overseas, now ready to conquer the hearts and minds of Japan. The difference was that Hamawaki landed alone and there was no army of dealers waiting to greet him. Not only did BMW have nothing in the way of a dealer network, but because foreign cars had already acquired a rather poor image as a result of the sloppy marketing of the import agents, experienced auto dealers wanted to stay with their top-selling Toyotas and Nissans and not sully their image with a low-grade product such as an American or European car. Besides, BMWs were so rare at the time that they were regarded mostly as a curiosity. Who would want to sell them?

Hamawaki must have had some second thoughts on the ride in from the airport. How was he going to find enough dealers to form the kind of organization that could sell 10,000 cars in five years in a country that didn't even like foreign cars?

In Japan when normal personnel channels fail, you generally turn to various university contacts, business contacts, general trading houses, major banks, and so on to set up the necessary introductions to the kind of people you want to meet. In this way it should theoretically be possible to put together a first-class organization in just under a decade. Hamawaki was the impatient type. His stay in America had obviously warped his Japanese common sense, which is the only way his associates could explain his next move. He took out advertisements in the local newspapers: *Car Dealers Wanted. Inquire BMW Japan.*

It was radical; it was direct; it was extremely unorthodox; and it was also quite effective.

"Most of the people in our office said it was embarrassing to do something like that (advertising) and that we should stop immediately," remembers Executive Director Tsutomu Tanegashima, now president of retail outlet BMW Tokyo. "But the truth is, a lot of good people answered those ads, people from all different kinds of businesses, and they became our dealers."

A guy from a shipping company on the outskirts of Tokyo applied; he wanted to try his hand at selling cars. Another guy worked in a small steel company making rails for the national railway; he thought it was time to try something new. A dairy products salesman from up north wanted a change of scenery. Lots of people answered the ads, most of them because they loved cars. They all believed that good cars would sell in Japan and they all wanted to try running a business on their own.

Hamawaki didn't care much that none of them had any experience in running an auto dealership. He didn't expect real car dealers to answer his ad. What he wanted to know from each one of them was if he was successful at whatever he had been doing previously. A man who is a failure at one job may well bring the wrong kind of experiences to a new one, he reasoned. The next criterion was whether the applicants were really compatible with the BMW philosophy, because that philosophy was going to become central to this whole business.

Learning the System

Auto dealers in Japan often work for small regional sales companies that are subsidiaries of larger and larger sales companies. Their loyalties are not so much to the car maker as to their regional sales firm. But BMW was different. Each dealership would be a spoke on a wheel whose hub was the organization Hamawaki was building in Tokyo, and that hub was directly connected to the corporate engine back in Germany. The dealers would not be independent mavericks out to hustle cars; they would be part of a centrally organized system and they would follow Hamawaki's instructions to the letter or say good-bye.

Many of those who answered the ads probably thought they would be selling imported cars and hopefully making big profits in just a few weeks. They were in for a rude awakening. The would-be BMW dealers found that it took between two and three years to complete all the preparations necessary before opening their doors to the public. During that time they were taught the entire BMW concept, from manufacturing to after-sales service. They were taught sales techniques, how to hire salesmen and office staff, how to train them, and how to oversee the business of running a BMW dealership. The company also gave them detailed instructions in how to set up a dealership: what kind of physical

structures they would need, how much space for sales, how much
for offices, how much capital they would need to get started, and
so on.

In addition, the head office in Tokyo established a special dealer
development section to take charge of building and supporting
this new network. For Japanese car makers this was standard
operating procedure: each company has a special section devoted
to hiring and training new dealers, holding seminars, sending out
direct mail to back up the marketing effort, and so on. But no
foreign maker had ever done anything like that in Japan. Nor had
any shelled out millions of dollars to build a local parts center to
back up its dealers. In many ways, BMW's early commitment to
its dealer network was a first.

Even during these early years a few dealers from other makers
heard about what was going on at BMW and decided that it
sounded pretty good. Japanese car dealers usually operate on very
thin margins, so as rumors of the opportunities at BMW began to
leak out, a few dealers "defected" to the foreign maker. After all,
some BMW models cost over 10 million yen, an unbelievable
sum for a car in those days. (You could put that much in the bank
for a year and buy a small Japanese car just with the interest.)
Since BMW was a foreign operation rather than a Japanese
company, they reasoned, there was a better chance that the car
maker had built a good margin into that high price tag as a reward
for its dealers. Even so, many were surprised at how well the
BMW dealers were treated. As one former dealer from a top
Japanese car maker put it, "I never dreamed that selling cars
could be this profitable."

But there was a long way to go before the profits would come
rolling in. As Tanegashima recalls, the first two years (1981–1983)
were just for laying the foundations of the dealer network. Even
the following year the dealers were not considered fully trained
and the dealerships were not quite running smoothly. It was only
from about 1985 that the dealers fully understood and trusted the
BMW corporate philosophy; it was only then that their sales and
service departments had some experience and were beginning to
operate like real professionals. "After about 1985," he says, "sales
just took off."

Be Smart—Do It Our Way

As part of its global policy of keeping a unified image, BMW insisted that all dealerships have the same interior decor worldwide. This didn't bother the new dealers; most of them had to build their dealerships from scratch anyway, so one design was as good as another. But for the people who had switched over from selling Japanese cars to BMW, the costs involved in meeting these corporate identity standards were seen as a waste of money.

Even Hamawaki noted, "There was some pretty strong reaction from former car dealers." In fact, they complained bitterly. Dealers who had carried other brands needed more than 10 million yen ($100,000 in today's terms) to renovate their interiors to match the company's CI strategy. They were furious. Typical comments ran something like: "It's crazy to spend that kind of money just to match paint colors and put down the kind of carpet the head office approves of. If the cars are good, they'll sell no matter what color the showroom carpet is."

They may have had a point, but Hamawaki wasn't listening. If you want to sell BMW, he said, you toe the line and you do things our way. If that's too much trouble, there's probably room for another Toyota dealership in your town . . . .

Another point of contention was the "BMW-only" rule. Company policy stated that dealers could sell only BMWs at their shops. Prior to this, most foreign car dealers carried Mercedes, Volvos, Audis, Porches, Saabs, etc., and let the customers choose whatever they liked. That would not be tolerated in the Hamawaki organization. The new recruits were told that this was simply an unbreakable rule, while the former car dealers were persuaded that it was not only BMW policy but also better business to handle a single line.

"As other foreign car dealers began to hear about BMW's sales and profitability, they contacted us and said they wanted to carry our cars. Some knew about the 'BMW-only' rule and said they would set up a separate company to handle our merchandise. We said, 'No. You sell BMW and only BMW.' We even had a BMW dealer who had leased part of his land to a small trading company and that company wanted to sell another brand, and he called to

ask if it was OK. We said no. Everyone in a small town knows
who owns what land. If Mercedes or Volvos are being sold on
land belonging to a BMW dealer, it's the same thing as the dealer
selling those cars."

Despite all the strict demands from the head office, dealers
who did it the BMW way found that their sales results took the
pain out of following orders. Pretty soon word got around that "if
you do as they say, and follow all their instructions, the company
will back you up 100 percent and sales will take off." Before long
most of the dealers got the message, and the team began to look
like one well-coordinated sales force. Today, about 98 percent of
the company's roughly 150 outlets in Japan carry only BMWs.

Putting the Swing in Marketing

The dealer network grew rapidly. Tanegashima recalls, "In the
beginning we had some dealers who were seriously in the red.
But gradually they improved. Even the ones that were chroni-
cally in the red were turning profits by 1988. Because *gaishi*
companies have an image of being 'dry' (insensitive to human
feelings, especially those of employees) and firing people left and
right, we worked hard to keep our dealers and to keep them
happy." Indeed, as the network grew, BMW lost only one dealership, and that was because the head of the firm died and his
family gave up the business.

Together with setting up the sales network, the firm launched
a carefully orchestrated marketing program. Marketing Manager
Walter Sawallisch emphasized the exclusive, sporty, compact car
concept as he saturated newspapers with ads for a car most Japanese
had never seen. He created unusual ad copy which piqued the
curiosity of readers and sent potential buyers to the new BMW
showrooms to see what the car was all about.

But what of the public's poor reaction to foreign cars? Wasn't
the company's European background a liability? Tanegashima
laughs at the thought: "We didn't worry about any negative image
associated with being 'foreign.' On the contrary, we ran ads featuring European scenery and European faces as if they were all
completely natural. We helped to introduce European style early
on. That's one reason we stood out."

But marketing extended far beyond placing print advertisements. As just one example of the firm's clever adaptation to the Japanese market, in this golf-crazy nation BMW invited its customers to golf tournaments around the country, then rounded up the best golfers from each group and invited them to a BMW Owners' Masters tournament. Golf is almost a prerequisite for corporate communication in Japan, and a large number of BMW buyers were corporate executives. Thus when BMW owners met other owners, many of roughly the same age and social status from around the nation, they did more than talk about cars. They also developed a sense of group identity. And in Japan, where a man's group identity is often stronger than his personal identity, this strategy was right on target.

You Only *Think* You Can't Afford It

BMW needed more than good marketing. It needed to break the hammerlock on the market held by Japanese makers. The first step was to identify the obstacles to buying a foreign car. Here the dealer network helped to feed back consumer reactions. The ads brought people to the showrooms and they obviously liked what they saw, but the bottom line was ultimately the bottom line—the sticker price for a BMW put it out of the reach of a large number of would-be buyers.

In the Japanese auto business, cutting prices is like breathing. Dealers all do it and nobody thinks about it. You make sales by talking discounts. But not at BMW. The company set the retail prices and the dealer who arbitrarily started discounting them would soon find himself out of a job. But without discounts, the cars seemed even further out of the reach of the average buyer.

The company decided that the best way to make the cars more accessible to potential buyers was financing. At the time, most car loans were in the 15–16 percent range, and some as high as 18 percent a year. BMW dropped its loans to 9.25 percent, then down to the 6 percent level. This had a big impact on consumers.

It also had a big impact on dealers: they screamed. For many BMW dealers (as for dealers of Japanese cars) auto loans were a significant source of income. Slashing auto loan revenues bit directly into the dealers' income.

Hamawaki tried to persuade them that this was the right thing to do. "Car dealers make money selling cars, not lending money," he said, but a lot of dealers disagreed. Ultimately, though, it was the ringing cash registers at showrooms around the country that proved him right and quieted the complaints about losing the loan business.

Today the top BMW dealer in Japan has four outlets, sells 1,500 cars a year, and turns over approximately $125 million per year. A number of BMW dealerships in Tokyo operate on a 5-day week (almost unheard-of for Japanese car dealers), and dealers in the Osaka area close for anywhere from a week to ten days during a major national holiday in the spring. Other car dealers grind their teeth in envy: the only reason BMW dealers can afford to live life at a more relaxed pace is that they are making very substantial incomes. And good sales results mean these dealers have the capital to hire good staff. Many of the salesmen at the top BMW dealers make over $100,000 a year, an unbelievable sum for a lowly car salesman, and the dealers, of course, make more. As is often the case, success breeds suiccess.

What? A $40,000 Used Car?

In the late 1980s BMW's first growth phase came to an end, and a second, even more successful phase began. That first stage in the company's growth was led by managers such as Hamawaki, whose background was in the motorcycle business. They were full of enthusiasm and drive, but they were not, at heart, car people. The second phase would require more professional managers with more of a feel for the car business. So the company began scouting highly qualified executives to add to its team. It acquired men from Toyota and other rival auto companies whose experience helped both to boost BMW's sales and to improve its strategy.

One contribution of some of these new managers was to help systematize the company's more random elements. Among other steps, they helped to establish a more rational system of sales and production planning based on monthly reports from the dealers. Another result was the move into used cars, an area where the company had as yet no strategy.

At that time, used cars were generally handled through used car dealers, which meant of course that they controlled the merchandise and fixed their own prices. This strategy might be all right for Toyota or Nissan, but it would ultimately hurt BMW's image. Moreover it was a tremendous loss of potential profit. A quick survey showed him that out of 70 BMW dealers at the time, not even 10 were handling used cars. Management decided it was time to change that.

As with other ideas from the head office that were bound to cost money up front, some of the dealers balked. "Why should we spend valuable time pushing old cars when we're making good money selling new ones?" they said. The resistance to used car sales may seem a bit odd, but in Japan, where land is scarce and always expensive, car dealers do not have large lots, nor do they keep much stock on hand. Many showrooms have only one or two cars and only a half-dozen on the lot. Most of the business is done with sales brochures and pamphlets. Quite often Japanese customers order a car without actually seeing the model they will buy. But with used cars there is no way around it—you have to line them all up on the lot, clean them, wax them, price them, and so on. It takes time, energy, and lots of real estate. From this perspective, the dealers' complaints were understandable.

BMW's response was pragmatic: you don't know what you're missing. With that theme, the company flew a group of dealers to Germany, where they could see used BMWs being cleaned and reconditioned. When they heard the prices for these "used cars," eyes popped out. None of them could believe how much a used BMW was worth. As Hamawaki pointed out later, "In Japan the average BMW sells for around $60,000. But a used one, after it is properly reconditioned, can still go for $40,000. Used cars generally have an image of being $4,000–$6,000 machines, but for the price of a used BMW you could buy a top-of-the-line Toyota back then. We couldn't afford to leave such a lucrative—and important— business to the used car dealers. So we told our dealers to open up a second channel for used cars."

And, as with the other demands from HQ, once the cash registers started ringing, the complaints began to fade.

A *Gaishi* Needs a Visible Headquarters

From its inception, BMW Japan was located in Tokyo's fashionable Azabu district. As the company grew, it rented three nearby offices and split up its operations. Office rents were high and going higher, but the company was doing well, so after a while the decision was made to consolidate all the separate offices into a new company headquarters building—provided that it was outside of downtown Tokyo.

Hamawaki explains, "We sent all the numbers, comparing our rents in four locations in Azabu plus our finance company's office elsewhere in Tokyo, to the home office. We showed them how in the long run it made a lot of sense, both economically and in terms of prestige for the firm, to set up our own building. Of course, it was a very expensive project, but the German HQ was convinced we were right."

The company looked all around the outskirts of the city and as far as Yokohama but couldn't find the right place or the right price. Then purely by luck it found its current location. One day on the way to play golf, Hamawaki spotted an open plot of land in Chiba Prefecture, just east of Tokyo. Today this area is famous, as a number of large developments have gone up in the vicinity, but back then none of them had yet broken ground.

"We went to the prefectural government and started talking. Chiba's image was pretty ordinary to say the least, and they were looking for top-class firms and especially foreign companies to move in and spruce up their image. Our negotiations went so smoothly we couldn't believe it," Hamawaki says. The local government even arranged a lower-than-normal price for the land and a special low-interest loan to cinch the deal. The timing couldn't have been better, as the "bubble" economy was just about to send prices everywhere around Tokyo skyrocketing.

"The contract is with the prefecture," Hamawaki says with a smile that means he wishes he could brag a little bit, "so I can't reveal the price, but let's just say that by the time we finished construction of the (11-story) building, land prices had soared to several times what we paid for it." Even with prices on the decline again, the land alone is still worth far more than the original cost of the site plus the construction of the building.

Changing of the Guard

Hamawaki ultimately turned the president's chair over to his executive managing director (a German) and stepped up to become chairman. The new president was young, sharp, had a Ph.D., and wanted to run BMW Japan like a business-school case study.

Not surprisingly, Hamawaki and the new man did not get along. The former president, who was responsible for building the company's success in Japan, communicated his feelings to Germany and soon enough the young president was flying back to the home office. He was replaced by Dr. Siegfried Richter, whom Hamawaki had recommended for the post.

At that time Hamawaki was 62. In many foreign firms it would not be unusual for him to be making retirement plans, but in Japan (where the *average* male life expectancy is close to 80), passing the 60 mark meant he was just ready to begin an active life on the executive board of a large corporation. Instead, BMW kicked him upstairs to the post of honorary chairman. In a replay of his days at Kawasaki, while he was deciding what to do, an offer came from another firm that was looking for an experienced chief executive. In 1993 Hamawaki took on an even bigger challenge when he became president of Digital Equipment Corp. Japan.

Richter came into office in the depths of the recession, a time when BMW's operations were leaner and even more service-oriented than before. One of the things he has done is to step up the toll-free phone and fax lines whereby customers and potential customers can communicate directly with BMW's top executives. At present, BMW is the only auto company in Japan with toll-free lines for customers to contact the president. Very few of the calls are complaints, and a good number of them are specific inquiries that eventually lead to sales. Thus, the idea of running these customer service phone lines, originally seen as a necessary PR expense, is now generating sales of about 100 cars a year. In other words, operating the toll-free lines is like having an extra dealership run out of the company headquarters at almost no cost.

The company has continued as an innovator. For a reasonable up-front fee, any BMW buyer can have all normal repairs and service covered free for three years. The program has been a big hit.

"The single biggest obstacle to buying a foreign car for a Japanese is maintenance, which is usually poor and very expensive," observes Richter. "We turned that to our advantage."

Safe, Environmentally Friendly Luxury Cars

"After the bubble years we had to take a hard look at our operations. Unit volume was decreasing, prices were still high. What could we offer our customers in the way of extra added value? We decided that the safety and environmental issues could both be a big plus for us," Richter notes. BMW became the first car in Japan to have airbags and an anti-lock braking system as standard equipment. The firm also started up driver training programs, which it runs 10–20 times a year. These programs show how to push a car to its limits, how to panic stop, how to drive safely on snow and ice, how to avoid trouble and how to respond to it. They, too, have been extremely successful (so much so that the Japanese government is asking aloud why a foreign company can do something like this when Japanese firms have not).

At the beginning of 1994 BMW began its "total recycling" effort. Any customer who wants to get rid of his old BMW can call a dealer who will pick it up for free. This is quite an attractive offer in a country where it can cost up to $1,500 simply to junk an old car. Moreover, any local government that finds an abandoned BMW can have it removed for free. The valuable old parts, such as engines and transmissions, are broken down in Japan, then shipped back to Germany for reuse. In its home market BMW is well known for its commitment to the recycling of automobiles. But that environmentally friendly policy is still a novelty in Japan.

Richter explains: "In Germany, people think if you use a car carefully you should be able to turn it in for parts and get money back. That kind of thinking is totally alien to Japan. This is still a throw-away society, even when it comes to cars. Because it costs money to get rid of a car properly, many are simply abandoned on the roadside, which merely adds to the pollution problem. BMW is helping to change attitudes and to limit environmental destruction."

Conclusions

The key to BMW Japan's success was in developing a strong national dealer network, giving the dealers a sense of identity, and supporting their efforts to sell. In addition, a clever marketing strategy and creative input from the firm's top financial officer made a big difference.

BMW Japan was established in 1981. Two years after that, although overall auto import figures continued to decline, BMW's sales figures rose in double digits. In 1983, BMW sales topped 10,000 units, and in 1988 reached about 26,000 cars. The company became so successful that it was largely responsible for igniting Japan's luxury car boom of the late-1980s and has been cited by both Toyota and Nissan as one of the factors that pushed those companies upmarket, giving them the impetus to launch their own highly successful luxury cars, the Lexus and Infinity.

Still, very few success stories are made on strategy and planning alone; there is almost always an element of luck. For BMW it was the bubble economy. The sudden rise of personal assets, the availability of easy credit, and the burning desire among Japanese consumers to own expensive foreign goods all exploded just as BMW was moving into the second phase of its growth. The tidal wave of demand that followed both swelled orders and established the company's reputation from Hokkaido to Okinawa. In one year Japanese buyers drove off with a record 36,000 new BMWs.

As with other foreign products we examine in this book, the bubble collapsed but the company's reputation didn't. In 1993, in the pits of the recession, the firm still sold well over 25,000 cars, and its 260 regular employees produced a total of $1.5 billion in total sales.

When we asked an employee at the firm how most of the staff see the current situation, the reply was immediate: "Most of us feel that the flood of buyers who only wanted a status car is gone, but people who want quality are still buying BMWs . . . and they will keep on buying them."

CHAPTER 5

Becoming a
Household Name
Procter & Gamble

"The [early 1990s] recession has been very difficult. Sales figures at department stores and supermarkets have been on a steady decline, competition has become extremely intense, and prices on all sorts of consumer products are dropping by the week. A number of supermarket chains have begun producing and distributing their own house-brand products. All in all, it's a terrible business environment. And yet, despite all this, our sales and profits in Japan have been the highest in our company's history."

These comments come from Peter Elsing, president of Procter & Gamble Far East, Inc. His firm's products are now visible dozens of times every day on Japanese TV, each commercial spot ending with a large P&G logo. The company's ads run mostly on shows with large female viewing audiences—the same kind of shows supported by P&G's major Japanese rivals, Kao Corp. and Lion Corp. This is one American firm that doesn't flinch from standing toe-to-toe with its Japanese competition. Probably most Japanese housewives know that P&G is a foreign-based company, and most don't care. Unlike life during the boom economy of the

late-1980s, they comparison shop every day and they buy what
they like.

Of course, many Japanese, like many Americans, assume that
because Procter & Gamble is a huge firm in the United States
(ranked number 12 on the *Fortune* 500 in 1994), its success in
Japan was a foregone conclusion. Today it is easy to take that
success for granted, but the company's history in Japan is one of
constant setbacks, red ink, and not a few big mistakes. P&G was
anything but a "natural" success.

A Joint Venture Born of a Joint Venture

The company came to Japan over twenty years ago via an unusual
joint venture (JV). In 1972 the U.S. parent formed a company with
three Japanese partners called P&G Sun Home. The deal was put
together by one of Japan's biggest and most aggressive general
trading companies, Itochu Shoji (better known overseas as C.
Itoh & Co. at that time). The reason for the JV's odd name is a bit
complicated, so let's very briefly summarize how it came into
existence.

Like almost every industry in Japan, the household products
field is dominated by a few overwhelmingly powerful companies
that together account for most of the market, leaving dozens of
smaller firms to scrabble for the remains. In this sector, the two
giants are Kao (now known abroad for its diversification into computer floppy disks) and Lion. To cope with the Kao/Lion control
of the market, three medium-ranked firms formed a JV in 1969.
The partners were Daiichi Kogyo Seiyaku (DKS), Asahi Denka
Kogyo (ADK), and Mitsuwa Soap. DKS was actually fairly large,
the number 3 firm in the business, while ADK and Mitsuwa were
smaller independent companies. Their joint venture was called
Nippon Sun Home.

One day Nippon Sun Home was approached by Itochu Shoji,
which suggested that the JV would never be strong enough to
challenge the domination of the two market leaders, so how about
tying up with a major foreign firm such as P&G to bolster their
strength? Indeed, the companies that made up Nippon Sun Home
were especially weak in new product development. In order to
compete with the two big players it was necessary to obtain new

products, so a tie-up with an overseas partner, especially one as strong as P&G, made a lot of sense.

But for some reason Mitsuwa vetoed the idea, which would have scuttled the plan completely but for a minor tactical error by Mitsuwa's chief executive.

Since Mitsuwa was not happy about a tie-up with P&G, one day executives from DKS and ADK went to talk to Sterling Drug Co. to see if that firm might have any new products that their JV could bring into Japan. Much to their surprise, they were told that the president of Mitsuwa Soap had just been there on his own and had already cut a private deal to introduce Sterling's products to the Japanese market. As a director of the former Nippon Sun Home recalls, "Since the three companies were supposed to be working together, the incident eventually led to a split-up. Mitsuwa Soap pulled out of the partnership, leaving DKS and ADK free to tie up with P&G. Itochu took up the third-man spot that Mitsuwa had vacated, and the JV went ahead."

And so it came about that P&G Sun Home was born. The American firm put up 50 percent of the capital, DKS and ADK together put up 40 percent and Itochu put up the remaining 10 percent.

At the time that Mitsuwa Soap pulled out of Nippon Sun Home, the JV was suffering big losses, so to cover its part of the debt burden when it left, Mitsuwa turned over to the partnership its brand new factory in Takasaki (Gumma Prefecture). As a matter of fact, a few years later Mitsuwa Soap went bankrupt and the new JV, P&G Sun Home, acquired another Mitsuwa factory (in Fuji City, Shizuoka Prefecture), as well as trademark rights to some of Mitsuwa's better-known products, such as "Muse" soap (which is still found on store shelves throughout Japan, but with a P&G logo on the back). Including the factories that DKS and ADK brought to the deal and those acquired from Mitsuwa, P&G Sun Home had a total of five factories under its control, although three of them existed as separate legal entities.

Oil Crisis Management

Through its tie-up, P&G had acquired access to manufacturing facilities, some well-known brand name products, and, especially from DKS, the number 3 player in the business, local employees who knew something about the market. At first things looked pretty good. In March the JV brought in one of P&G's biggest hits in America, "All-Temperature Cheer" detergent. It seemed as if the Japan venture would soon be chalking up some solid profits. Then the oil crisis struck.

Japan, of course, is an island nation, and every year it produces enough oil of its own to lubricate a small Toyota engine for about a week. In October 1973, when the oil shock hit, roughly 75 percent of Japan's energy needs were met by oil and 100 percent of that oil was imported. Thus, the oil shock was more than a shock; it was a panic. While the government quickly set about cozying up to the OPEC nations (leading it into a pro-Arab, anti-Israel stance that lasted for decades), consumers saw years of increasing prosperity suddenly coming to an abrupt end. People rushed to stores and began stockpiling daily commodities, including things like toilet paper, soap, and detergents. The Ministry of International Trade and Industry (MITI) stepped in, as was its habit in those days, and directed a national plan for related industries to supply needed goods to households throughout the country.

One of P&G's greatest strengths in Japan from the very first has been its marketing strategy. The company does not merely dump a new product into the Japanese market and pray; it tests each product again and again in regional markets, observes the results, modifies the product and/or its sales tactics, then test markets in another region, and so on until it is finally ready to move to national sales. This is what it had in mind for the products it had started to market in 1973. But with the oil crisis and MITI's "guidance," the firm had to shift immediately to a national sales program. Worse yet, although retail prices were frozen to eliminate black marketeering, the oil crisis drove up material costs. The result was a painful profit squeeze for P&G's start-up year in Japan.

With operating funds running very low, the JV had no choice but to increase capital. P&G Sun Home was initially capitalized at ¥1 billion, but one year later, in 1974, the capital stood at ¥6 billion. The oil crisis ended, but the joint venture's problems did not. Just to give an idea of how badly things were going, in 1976 the firm's capital was raised again to ¥12 billion, and the following year to ¥24 billion.

In the early 1970s the Japanese government kept a tight rein on flows of foreign capital. If it was determined that foreign capital entry would prove harmful to Japanese industry (in other words, if a foreign company looked like it might take any significant market share away from Japanese competitors and thus bring "confusion" to the market), the foreign firm would simply be told that its request had been denied. The Ministry of Finance (MOF) had a special "Foreign Capital Investigation Committee" which checked each application for capital inflow from abroad, and this ministry, together with MITI, controlled the fate of every foreign firm in Japan.

One of P&G's early staff members, public affairs manager Tokio Ijiri, remembers those days well. "When the company first set up a PR department, I was put in charge. But our PR group didn't deal with the media or with customers—that came later. Instead, my job was to deal directly with the government. I made regular pilgrimages to both MITI and MOF to ask for permission to increase our capital. For a while I was going to Kasumigaseki (the area of Tokyo where most of the ministries are headquartered) about every six months. It was embarrassing. They'd look at me and say, 'Hey, are you here again? Why don't you learn to run your company so it turns a profit instead of jacking up your capital to cover your losses?' Ultimately, we knew they were right and after a while we finally started to cut unprofitable brands from our lineup."

But there was another even bigger problem with the capital increases. Two of P&G Sun Home's Japanese partners were chemical companies badly hurt by the oil crisis and its aftermath, and the third partner was a general trading house which was squeezed even harder when Japanese industry began restructuring after the oil shock. The bottom line was that neither the chemical companies nor the trading house had excess capital to invest in the JV. To keep it afloat, the American side had to come up with the cash. So all these very sizable capital increases were borne by P&G in the U.S. By 1977, the parent company had invested almost 98 percent of the company's paid-in capital. It was obvious that the "partnership" was history. During this time, MOF and MITI had begun to relax the regulations, both official and unofficial, on foreign ownership of Japanese firms, so P&G was able to take over DKS's and ADK's shares in the joint venture. In 1978 it picked up Itochu's shares as well, and at last P&G had a 100 percent-owned company in Japan. But now we're getting a little ahead of our story.

The Pampers Fiasco

P&G in the U.S. had a solid product in another big market area, one relatively undeveloped in Japan: disposable diapers. A few years before, some of the smaller paper companies had tried test-marketing disposable diapers, but the results were not encouraging. The American firm, however, figured that with some good marketing it could turn its Pampers brand into a hit product. P&G Sun Home, which was essentially a soap-and-detergent company, seemed an unlikely base from which to handle the diaper business. Thus in 1976 Nihon P&G was born, and two years later it began selling Pampers in Japan.

P&G was the first firm to attempt to sell paper diapers nationwide. At first it imported Pampers made in the United States, then in 1982 started making them in its Akashi plant. The product caught on quickly, just as the firm had hoped, and P&G quickly grabbed a stunning 90 percent of the market. The company was ecstatic. At last the products it had developed and successfully marketed overseas were proving their worth in Japan. After all, in the United States, Pampers had a lock on the number 1 spot. It was only natural that the Japanese market, as it developed, should follow suit.

But it wasn't the Japanese market that followed suit—it was P&G's much bigger rivals. Japanese firms are notorious for their ability to copy and often improve a successful new product. As soon as Pampers opened up a market for disposable diapers, big-time players such as Kao, Unicharm, Daio Paper, and others jumped in with their own versions. From 1981–83, Nihon P&G found out what it was like to try to hold onto a market with a foreign-designed product not adapted to local needs. Once the big Japanese firms brought their R&D (not to mention their ad budgets and distribution clout) to bear, the outcome was never in doubt.

Gradually, Japanese mothers who had long preferred to use cloth diapers (but were not enamored of washing them) began to switch. The problem was that they were not switching to Pampers. P&G was shocked to discover that it was losing share to one maker after another, falling in only a few years to less than 10 percent of a market it had created, and until recently, dominated.

The United States parent wisely read this as a signal that it was time to reevaluate its approach to the Japanese market. They began to make organizational and management changes and, most important, to study Japanese consumer trends in detail. They found, for example, that Japanese mothers are much more sensitive to even the slightest leaks in diapers than are their American counterparts (some of the rival diapers had introduced more absorbent fabric than Pampers, which was one big reason for P&G losing market share so quickly). Japanese mothers want a diaper that fits snugly and looks clean all the time. So in 1985, P&G switched to using more absorbent materials and redesigned its product to provide a perfect fit. Since then it has slowly regained some of its market appeal and today its national share has climbed to a respectable 20 percent. However, the company will never regain the tremendous lead—nor the profits—it lost in those early years.

The firm realized that its biggest structural problem was the existence of five separate corporate entities in its group—detergent-maker P&G Sun Home, diaper-maker Nihon P&G, and the three factories. Having five different companies was unavoidable considering the firm's history, but it was terribly inefficient and an organizational nightmare. After the diaper fiasco the first big organizational change was to combine these five firms into a single company, P&G Far East, Inc., and to transfer all management control of those former units to the new firm. The ever-patient U.S. parent agreed to absorb all losses up to that point.

Building Strategy and Image

The year 1985 marked a turning point for the operation. It was the company's first three-year management plan, the beginning of a strategy to build a solid reputation in Japan by exhaustively researching the market and then testing products regionally before opening them up to nationwide sales. Until that point, P&G had had little that could be called a strategy. Pampers aside, its approach had been very "Japanese"—that is, it tried to put out me-too versions of hit products already marketed by industry leaders such as Kao and Lion. The Pampers experience taught the firm that the way to win is to strike first, not merely by being first to market, but by being first to put out high-quality, high-value products. The keys would be better market research and better product development.

Another structural problem was the firm's inefficient marketing system. This complex, disorganized "network" included 400 separate wholesalers, many of whom openly competed with one another. Without real coordination or even communication within this network, the members were holding each other back more than spurring new product sales. Management decided it was time to rethink distribution in Japan. The new approach was to cut the total to 100 major wholesalers in important locations spread out geographically to cover the nation. P&G initiated a "strategic alliance" between itself and its wholesalers with the aim of strengthening both sides.

In addition, P&G Far East tightened its own organization, brought in employee training programs, and started corporate identity (CI) activities. The latter had the most visible impact on the company's progress in wooing Japanese consumers. Until early in 1983, the firm sold its goods on the basis of product image alone—the P&G name hardly ever appeared. As the CI program got underway, however, the company name was always prominent in advertising. The idea was to build a strong corporate image in the minds of Japanese customers rather than hoping that a product-by-product association would lead consumers to "discover" P&G.

CI was also important because it sent a message to rivals, to banks, to suppliers and wholesalers, and to related industries that P&G was in the market to stay and that it had full support from the U.S. firm.

One simple but necessary item was a company logo. Many years ago the U.S. parent firm had used a stylized crescent-moon-with-stars logo for its products until the design was attacked by a religious group protesting what it called pagan symbolism. There was even a boycott of P&G products. Rather than fight this non-sensical argument and risk causing adverse publicity, the U.S. firm dropped the logo from its products (although it still remains on various buildings in the company headquarters). The Japan operation decided to adopt some version of the moon-and-stars.

Ijiri says, "Would you believe it? We had meetings for two days to debate whether to put the moon and stars vertically or side-by-side (they opted for the latter). Then we decided as part of our CI effort to run the company name and logo at the end of each TV commercial. Of course, it only takes up about two seconds of each spot, but there were some people who thought we should be using that valuable TV time to promote our products instead of the company itself."

The least dramatic but most important part of the company's first 3-year strategic plan was simply to put out more products and better products. P&G began a strenuous effort to increase the quality of its goods and started putting out new products one after another. In a surprisingly short time consumers began to trust the firm and sales swung into the black.

The results of this mid-term plan were gratifying: sales tripled in three years.

The Whisper Success

P&G learned a great deal from the Pampers fiasco, not only in terms of marketing strategy but also about product development. Pampers was a good product and clearly ahead of its market, but the company did not keep up with the challenges posed by its competition and was not closely attuned to the reactions of local consumers. It would not make the same mistake again.

P&G now prepared to assault a much more difficult market. If keeping baby dry and comfortable worked well in diapers, the company decided, it could apply its American technology and the lessons it had learned about adapting to consumer demands in Japan to another field: sanitary napkins. Unlike disposable diapers, where the U.S. firm could introduce a new product to an untapped market, this was territory already well staked out by two domestic giants, Kao and Unicharm Corp. When people in the industry heard that P&G was going to make a run at the napkin business, the nearly universal reaction was "You'll get burned so badly that Pampers will look like a big success in comparison." Industry experts warned that the company was diversifying its product line too much, that the market was already mature, and that it was impossible to steal more than a tiny share from established Japanese leaders.

P&G proved them all wrong. It successfully combined two unbeatable elements, superior R&D efforts in the United States and extensive market research in Japan, to create and maintain a hit product in Japan.

The American parent company had been researching sanitary napkins for seven years, which gave the firm a huge head start. In 1983 the final product was completed and released in the United States under the name "Always." The head office was so confident of its success that it began to withdraw from the highly competitive tampon market and position itself to compete in napkins instead. This was no small decision, since at the time 90 percent of American women preferred using tampons to napkins. In Japan, however, the preference was just the opposite, so the company's focus on developing and supporting a major new product in this area meant potential big sales for P&G Far East.

The trick was not to repeat the Pampers experience.

Around the time that "Always" hit the stands in the United States, the Japanese firm began to look carefully at how to remake the American product to suit the local market. The company spent an incredible three years testing the new napkin on over 10,000 Japanese women, determined to get a perfect fit and to anticipate every customer need ahead of time. They made it smaller to fit the Japanese physique and more compact in answer to requests from many consumers who wanted something more "discreet." Even the packaging was changed, because Japanese women wanted something that was quieter to open.

Even after all of this fine-tuning of a product that was already selling well in America, the company did not release the Japanese version (dubbed "Whisper") for national consumption. Once again, it moved cautiously. From 1986 to 1988 the firm conducted regional market tests, starting with limited sales in a part of the southern island of Kyushu.

In the first year the company gave out over one million free samples of Whisper and captured 14 percent of the local market. In the following year it expanded the testing area and handed out 1.3 million more samples. By the end of that year, the same P&G which had been warned by experts that it could never get a foothold in the market had a 24 percent share in the region. That was the kind of figure the company was looking for. Fully five years after first testing the product in Japan, it began nationwide distribution, and even then gave away over 20 million samples in that opening campaign.

Why so much emphasis on free samples? The company's philosophy is summed up by an official in one of the regional marketing departments: "We try to reach 60 percent of potential consumers through samples. We want them to know our name and we want them to try our product. Sampling achieves both."

Another important factor is the difficulty of getting women anywhere to change brands. In Japan it is generally assumed that the tampon/napkin market is dominated by a few companies because brand loyalties are so strong. Women pick a product and tend to stay with it. So P&G targeted younger women, especially those in their teens who have had less time to build product loyalty. Company representatives handed out sample packets of Whisper in front of girls' high schools, at junior colleges, 4-year colleges, training schools, even in front of train stations and office buildings where there were large numbers of working women.

The manager of a large retail store in Tokyo explained the success this way: "Whisper is expensive; its retail price is about 20 percent above other brands, and the maker insisted on keeping prices firm. But consumers today want quality goods even if they have to pay a little more for them. They want something that functions well and stands out from its competition, and Whisper fits the bill."

Another big retailer comments: "Until recently, napkins and tampons were all pretty much the same, so they competed only on price. For years there was a discount price war going on. Whisper changed all that. Now, because of Whisper, there is real competition based on function and quality. Whisper made it easy to keep prices stable."

Of course, just as with Pampers, the company's big rivals were quick to bring out their own new products, but they couldn't match P&G's level of research right away. "The others got better but they still weren't as good, not really dry," says the Tokyo store manager. In fact, it took years for the competition to develop products that could match those of P&G. While rivals were releasing copies of Whisper, P&G introduced Whisper Plus. The years it had spent in thoroughly studying the market resulted in much more lead time to stay ahead of the competition and gave the company time to build its own brand loyalty. As a result, the foreign "upstart" today holds a large percentage of this business nationwide and looks well positioned to hang on to it.

Until Whisper, P&G Far East's approach to new products had been to see how they fared in the United States and in Europe first, and then devise a strategy to bring them to Japan. But with Whisper the company did not rely on data from abroad. Instead, it conducted its own tests of Japanese consumers, studying their likes, dislikes, even their habits and customs in order to create a product that matched the Japanese market perfectly. The results more than made up for the time and effort expended in researching product acceptance.

In addition, the American company has also learned a lot from working in the Japanese market. Ed Artzt, chairman of The Procter & Gamble Company in the United States says: "In the early years in Japan we made some mistakes. On top of that there was a vicious price war, government regulations to contend with, complex marketing systems, and the many differences in culture. All of that made doing business in Japan difficult. But the key to the turnaround for us was to better understand Japanese society and Japanese customers.

"For example, Japanese mothers change kids' diapers much more often than American mothers do. What's important to them is a perfect fit, comfort, no leaks. We learned. Japanese women tend to change sanitary napkins twice as often as American women do. They're looking for a very high level of comfort. Understanding things like these made us successful in Japan. We learned that in order to succeed we had to tailor both our products and our marketing to match the needs of individual regions. That lesson, which we learned so well from our experience in Japan, is now helping us all over the world."

Expanding the Corporation

Like many other foreign firms that started small, then expanded somewhat haphazardly, P&G discovered that its internal communications were suffering due to a lack of centralization. One of the company's biggest moves came in 1993 when it consolidated more than nine separate offices into a single Japan headquarters and combined that with a technical center to serve the entire Asia Pacific region.

Almost all major companies, Japanese as well as foreign, are headquartered in Tokyo. P&G is not. The company executives looked at the infamous Narita airport, which is more than an hour from the city and cannot be used at night, as well as the absurd cost of land, the traffic congestion in and around the capital, and other factors. Their decision was to locate the new P&G Far East head office on Rokko Island in Kobe. The office is only a little over half an hour from the New Kansai International Airport, which is open 24 hours.

At the same time the decision to build a new office was underway, the U.S. parent happened to be planning to build a technical center to serve its Asia Pacific operations. Because land is so expensive in Japan and salaries are relatively high, many in the parent firm thought the technical center should be built elsewhere in Asia. But careful studies showed that the level of the engineers and technicians in Japan is also very high, communications are excellent, and market information is readily available. So it was decided to build the tech center in Japan, and to combine it with the new company headquarters.

President Elsing was delighted with the result: "A big advantage of having the technical center inside the head office complex is that our R&D is close to our marketing group. That means that ideas for new products and modifications of existing products that always come out of the technical side can be discussed directly with our marketing people. There's immediate feedback, and the result is more productive applications of our research. For example, the number of new, patentable ideas has nearly doubled since we built the center here."

In 1993 the company instituted a very un-Japanese personnel system, a meritocracy instead of the traditional seniority system. It also undertook a survey of all employees to find out what its staff did and didn't like about the company. The merit system was just one idea springing from the half dozen committees P&G set up to improve its internal structure and make work more rewarding for its workers.

Back in 1991 the parent company in the United States bought the worldwide operations of Max Factor cosmetics, and in 1993 Max Factor's Japan headquarters was consolidated into P&G's

headquarters in Kobe. In the United States, Max Factor is not
such a big player in the cosmetics business, which is one reason
that Revlon was happy to sell it. But in Japan Max Factor is an old,
well-established, and trusted name. In fact, about 60 percent of all
Max Factor's worldwide sales come from Japan. In that sense, the
P&G head office purchased the company with its Japan business
in mind.

Although the Max Factor business in Japan goes back 40 years,
the company did not develop its own line of products; instead,
it turned out goods that were similar to its rivals' products, and
sales grew on the strength of a very large marketing network.
However, when the Japan unit merged with P&G Far East, there
was no need for the cosmetics firm to maintain such a large
regional marketing staff. P&G eased out about 25 percent of the
Max Factor employees who were middle aged or older. In a
country with such a commitment to preserving the image (if not
the reality) of lifetime employment, this could have been the
beginning of a scandal or at least a bout of very negative publicity.
But the continuing recession had forced even Japan's best-known
companies to lay off older, unproductive workers, so P&G appeared
to be simply one of a large crowd of companies tightening their
belts and downsizing.

Conclusion

P&G's success in Japan did not come easily. It took years, some
failed joint venture efforts, and a massive investment from the
head office just to get the local company standing on its own feet.
Then came the Pampers disaster, in which the company was
rejected by consumers and shown up by its rivals. Many a foreign
head office would have pulled the plug at this point, deciding that
Japan was just too complex and expensive a market to continue
the struggle. But instead, the organization—local and parent—
decided to learn from its mistakes and to put that knowledge to
use in the marketplace. Through in-depth studies of Japanese
customers and years of careful market testing, P&G carved out a
substantial market share in a field where wiser heads said they
would get nothing. Once again they found their Japanese rivals
copying them (where only a few years before it was the other way

around), but this time they were ready for it and knew how to stay a step ahead.

P&G's success story is a model of how any foreign firm can start from scratch in Japan and fight its way to the top. More than good connections and famous products, it takes perseverance, lots of patience, and deep pockets.

It is interesting to note that until a few years ago the American firm was part of the chorus saying that the Japanese marketing system and business practices were, in effect, nontariff barriers. Then as the company finally began to see how the system works and moved to take advantage of it, criticism dropped off. When the Clinton administration talked of using the legal trade retaliation provisions known as "Super 301" to punish Japan for not opening its markets faster, P&G actually opposed the move. Cynics would say that the company is merely trying to protect its profits, but that would not explain its stance. The company has discovered that most Japanese markets are not closed, either formally or informally, to foreign firms. They are, however, very "clubby," and so it takes a huge effort for any outsider—domestic or foreign—to break into the circle of top players. As P&G would testify, companies that are willing to invest the time, the manpower, and the capital to achieve that goal will find that the profitability of the Japanese market rewards their efforts many times over.

CHAPTER 6

Hard Work Is the Real Thing

Coca-Cola

No company represents America and American culture to the world like Coca-Cola. Yes, there is Disney and McDonald's, but something about the ubiquity of Coke, its availability in far corners of the globe where no one has ever heard of *Bambi* or a Big Mac, has made this humble soft drink the nation's oldest and best-known ambassador without portfolio. The very image of Coca-Cola says "America," so much so that for years it was a symbol of American decadence to Communist regimes in the former Soviet Union, China, and Vietnam. Thus the blossoming of red-and-white Coke signs in those nations during the past several years has been taken as one of the first visible signs of the beginning of the post-Cold War era.

One place where everything that represents America and American mass culture—from blue jeans to take-out pizza—seems almost guaranteed to succeed is Japan. If there is one nation on earth that was destined to embrace Coca-Cola, it was post-war Japan. In a nation trying to pull itself together after the war, the sight of thousands of all-American GIs munching white-bread sandwiches and drinking bottle after shapely bottle of the strange fizzy cola drink must have seemed at the same time impossibly foreign and yet irresistible. And the government, eager to please the Americans, must have welcomed firms like Coca-Cola with open arms as a sign that the country was indeed under American influence and no longer a potential threat of any kind. The combination of The Coca-Cola Company's massive marketing power, a natural foothold in the untapped Japanese market (thanks to the military occupation), and the government's pro-U.S. stance must have been a marriage made in heaven for the American beverage giant.

Well, not exactly.

The unbelievable fact is that Coca-Cola had an easier time setting up in Russia after the Cold War than setting up in Japan after World War II. Not only could it not get permission to operate in Japan for years, but when the permission was finally granted it was so limited as to have no meaning at all. It is not difficult to understand why certain totalitarian governments have wanted to keep Coca-Cola outside their borders. Yet no Communist government, having finally allowed the company to import and sell its product, has been so adamant about keeping that product out of the hands of its citizens.

However, four decades later, few American companies can boast of such enormous success in the Japanese market, both in terms of sales and profits. Coca-Cola has become a major force in the nation's beverage industry, and its executives say the company has only begun to really develop this market.

In short, Coca-Cola is an archetypal case study, a firm that thought it had everything going for it but couldn't get past Tokyo's bureaucratic door. Then, after years of effort, it finally squeezed through—only to discover that life on the inside was tougher than it had ever imagined. Success ultimately came, as it does for many *gaishi,* by doing whatever was necessary to become an insider and taking advantage of the strengths its domestic rivals had used against it.

The Father of Coca-Cola

The story of Coca-Cola in Japan of course involves many people. But there is one individual who stands out above all the rest. Some years ago The Coca-Cola Company's in-house magazine called him, aptly enough, "The father of Coca-Cola in Japan." He tenaciously fought not only his nation's own bureaucrats, but also powerful ad hoc groups of merchants who allied to keep his product out of Japan.

The fellow's name was Nisaburo Takanashi, and he was one of the great-grandchildren of the founder of soy sauce giant Kikkoman (his older brother went on to become vice president of that famous company). In 1928, after Takanashi graduated from school, he went to work for a food wholesaler (a *tonya*) in the Kikkoman *keiretsu*. That little firm, Koami Shoten, would eventually grow to become a major food company dealing in beer, sake, and a great variety of foods, but when Takanashi joined it was just getting started.

Kikkoman (known as Noda Shoyu in those days) had tremendous clout in the market, and more than ten authorized distributors competed to sell its products. Consequently, life at these *tonya* was always one of slim margins and low salaries. (This relationship of a big manufacturer to its subordinate dealers or subcontractors has continued throughout the century and refuses to die even today.) Takanashi thought it was shameful that the big makers had the wherewithal to invest in new equipment as well as paying good salaries to their staff, but the *tonya* who served them—and who depended on finding and keeping good salesmen to stay in business—could never take care of their employees properly. Life was always difficult, both for managers and staff, and it didn't get any better in 1945, with Tokyo lying in rubble.

It is not surprising, then, that right after the war Takanashi was willing to listen when some people came to sell him what they said was valuable information.

In those hand-to-mouth post-war years when everyone was trying just to stay alive, the black markets thrived, and almost every business deal had a story it preferred to keep quiet. It was not uncommon for people who heard about some upcoming transaction to try to sell the information wherever they could. The biggest lure for any pitch, of course, was access to the cash-rich American Occupation forces. Any deal that involved military spending—official or otherwise—was considered a gold mine.

As it turned out, one of the men who came to talk to Takanashi that day in 1947 worked in a Coca-Cola bottling plant on a U.S. military base on the island of Kyushu. He had picked up some very interesting information, he said. "Everybody knows that the Americans love to drink this sweet, carbonated cola, what they call Coke. Well, the American parent company is thinking of starting up a big operation here in Japan, but they haven't decided just how to go about it."

He was right: it was interesting information, and we may assume that Takanashi was well rewarded for the long journey to Tokyo to pass it along.

Takanashi immediately sent his younger brother to Kyushu to check it out, and his report corroborated the story. Takanashi wasted no time—any story that had leaked as far as his ears had undoubtedly leaked in other directions as well. He set off for Yokohama to meet with Coca-Cola's division manager for Japan. This agent, an American named Spencer, was pleased with Takanashi's interest in the business, and the two chatted at some length about the firm's structure, its sales organization, selling methods, even its long-term management plans. The more Takanashi heard, the more he knew this was what he was looking for. Spencer told him about a franchise system, a form of direct sales called route sales that didn't exist in Japan, a cash business, and other details that made running a *tonya* for Kikkoman seem like a page out of an old history book. The people at Coca-Cola seemed to have it all figured out—marketing, sales, distribution— and a product that seemed to sell itself. Once the Japanese tried Coke, the demand was bound to grow rapidly. The only thing the company didn't seem to have figured out was the most important part: how to get set up in Japan. And that's where Takanashi saw himself fitting into this worldwide success story. He knew a lot about distribution in Japan, especially in the food industry, and he also had the personal drive to get over the inevitable initial hump that every foreign product faces and into widespread market acceptance. With a product like Coke, he thought, how long could it take?

Obstacles from the Start

There were two big obstacles for him to overcome if he hoped to run a Coca-Cola business in Japan. The first was to convince the U.S. parent company's overseas division, a subsidiary called The

Coca-Cola Export Corporation, to grant a production and distribution franchise to a Japanese citizen. The second was to negotiate the maze of the Japanese bureaucracy, since importing Coca-Cola syrup required permission from the agriculture ministry, and paying for it required permission to obtain foreign currency and remit it overseas, a practice that both the Ministry of International Trade and Industry (MITI) and the Ministry of Finance (MOF) regarded as something close to treason.

After the war Japan had almost no foreign currency, so the available supply was, in effect, rationed by the government. Imports were strictly regulated, overseas payments were all but prohibited, and even when Japanese went overseas on business the amount of money they could take with them was severely restricted. (This monetary situation, by the way, was one of the major reasons that Japan worked so hard to become an exporting power in the 1950s—exports brought in millions of U.S. dollars and other currencies that the government desperately needed.)

It soon became clear that neither obstacle was going to be overcome quickly. The U.S. headquarters couldn't decide if the product would really sell in Japan even if they did grant a license to a Japanese. And the bureaucrats didn't want to hear about anyone importing some popular beverage from America and getting Japanese to shell out their earnings for a soft drink when they should be putting every yen in the banks to support local industry. Takanashi knew this was going to take some time, but he also knew somewhere deep inside that it was worth it. He left Koami Shoten and did something quite remarkable for the time—he began travelling around the world to visit Coca-Cola bottling plants. He inspected facilities in the U.S., Europe, and Central America, talking to people as he went, learning everything he could about the business, and preparing himself mentally for the day when he would be able to start up his own business.

As he had suspected, the word that Coca-Cola might want to set up in Japan was the usual kind of closely-guarded Japanese business secret: about a hundred people in the food business were already going to visit Spencer, negotiating with The Coca-Cola Company in the United States, and trying to find a way around the bureaucratic obstacles at home. But with the strict limits on foreign capital outflows, it seemed impossible to make the business work. Moreover, the agriculture ministry was not favorably disposed to grant a license to import Coke syrup, and the banks were not favorably disposed to grant loans to a business not approved by the government. As the competition ran up against the same stone walls that Takanashi had, one by one they began to give up. While he was travelling around the world, studying the Coke business up close, his competitors were throwing in the towel and looking for easier prospects. In the end only Takanashi and his brother remained as serious applicants for a franchise.

None of this went unnoticed by the U.S. firm, and in 1952, in part to reward him for his dogged persistence, the company granted Takanashi a franchise for Tokyo. The first obstacle had finally been overcome—only five years and several pairs of shoes after he first began pursuing the dream of selling Coke in his own land. The next year he submitted a formal application to the Japanese government, asking for permission to import $200,000 worth of Coca-Cola syrup.

Up until that point no formal application had ever been made to the government, by Takanashi or anyone else. Everyone had followed the normal procedure with each of the relevant ministries: They approached each ministry unofficially and asked what its stance would be *if* they were to apply to take some specific action (such as importing Coke syrup). The ministries then replied, also unofficially, what their reaction would be. Merely submitting an application, even a "perfect" one, without testing the waters first almost guaranteed rejection. There were numerous cases in which a company took an application to some ministry only to find that the officials there would not even look at it. They simply refused to receive the paperwork because the applicant had not observed the proper protocol.

This somewhat bizarre system, in which anyone who wanted to open a new business requiring any kind of license or permission from the government (and that covered almost every conceivable new business) essentially had to bow and show respect to the omnipotence of the bureaucracy, was a prominent feature of Japan in the 1950s. And, not surprisingly, it is also a prominent feature of Japan today. The biggest difference is that there are many more regulations than there were in the 1950s.

To be fair, we should note that there is another side to the system. If you approach a ministry unofficially, essentially asking for advice rather than demanding a judgment, the officials can be quite helpful. If they are in a good mood, like the cut of your suit, and all the planets happen to be in conjunction, they might deign to tell you what is wrong with your informal application and recommend changes that will greatly increase your chances of getting a formal application accepted later on. In that sense, the system can be beneficial. However, if you polled the majority of *gaishi* CEOs in Japan about their experiences with the bureaucracy, the number who had stories to tell about how helpful the ministries had been in getting their business started might dine comfortably in a posh *sushi* restaurant in Ginza. The number who had "war tales" to tell would barely squeeze into a stand-up buffet in the ballroom of one of the bigger Tokyo hotels. Takanashi's application fell into the latter category.

Not Diet Coke—Coke in the Diet

In retrospect, the bureaucracy was far from the worst of Takanashi's problems. Noting the nearly addictive appeal of Coca-Cola to American soldiers among others, the Japanese beer companies and various drink makers suspected that it might produce a similar reaction even among stalwart Japanese. So around 1950 these groups began to lobby against the very idea of letting Coke into the country. By 1953 these disparate groups had joined together, forming an organization for the express purpose of keeping any trace of carbonated democracy from landing on Japanese shores.

In retrospect, the idea of an anti-Coca-Cola lobby may seem a bit silly, but at the time it was an extremely serious matter. Even today the four large beer companies completely control their market and have massive power in the beverage sector as a whole. To have these companies, plus a variety of smaller drink makers allied against your efforts to open a business meant that it was time to find a new business. And anyone with any sense would have taken the hint and moved on. But not Takanashi. He waited to hear the results of his application.

At this point the anti-Coke lobby managed to have the matter presented to a committee of the Diet (the national legislature). An outside observer might be forgiven for wondering if the introduction of Coca-Cola was truly such a threat to national security that it was deemed worthy of discussion by the country's leading politicians (many of whom receive large contributions from major industries such as the beer companies). However, as we shall see, there were more political forces at work as well.

When a commercial matter such as this reaches the Diet it becomes more or less public. That means the bureaucracy, which prefers to deal with such things quietly and privately in its own chambers, must stop and explain to normal Japanese what it is that they are doing. The bureaucrats seem less afraid of this prospect than annoyed by it. It is an inconvenience, to be sure, but it can lead to messy complications. Thus, when what should be a private matter involving bureaucratic decision making gets hauled out into the public arena, the ministries' usual response is damage control: They want to contain the issue quickly before it takes on a wider political significance (which may require more of their time and more explanations in front of the Diet). In short, they want to put a lid on whatever the problem is—and fast.

Thus the issue of Takanashi's application was presented to the Diet members in a very negative light. Representatives of MITI and the predecessor of what is now called the Ministry of Agriculture, Forests, and Fisheries (MAFF) both appeared and reminded the legislators of Japan's need to accumulate, not spend, foreign currency. In this sense, Takanashi was portrayed as downright unpatriotic. Then there was the matter of the national beverage industry. The introduction of this American soft drink could have a devastating effect on the local drink makers, and that would cause "confusion" in the marketplace—the bureaucrats' favorite term for unruly competition in a sector that was already nicely cartelized.

The matter was ultimately handled by being referred back to the bureaucrats, who dealt with it in their normal way: they shelved the application and forgot about it. But as a result of his efforts and the things said about him in the Diet, Takanashi's reputation was starting to go down the drain. He had done the unpardonable in Japan, he had tried to be different. He had bucked the system and acted in ways that suggested a desire for personal gain over a respect for the higher interests of the nation. Years later, when the difficulties he encountered in those days were no longer as painful, he noted simply, "I lost most of my friends during that period."

Did running into a dead end with the government regulators, making enemies of most of the domestic beverage industry, and being ostracized by his friends finally bring Takanashi to his senses? Of course not. He renewed his pressure on the bureau-crats and now upon the politicians as well, demanding that his application be acted upon. A couple of times he even seemed to be making some progress, but almost as soon as he did the anti-Coke lobby counterattacked. No less a personage than the minister of agriculture himself appeared in the Diet to state unequivo-cally: "We have no intention of granting permission [to import Coca-Cola]."

Gaiatsu

As if all of this wasn't discouraging enough, the only solid market Takanashi could count on began to drop off, and the whole idea of doing business in Japan came into question.

By the mid-fifties both the U.S. Occupation and the Korean War were over, which meant American military personnel were leaving Japan much faster than they were coming in. That was a good sign to many Japanese, but not a good sign for Coca-Cola. In 1952, there were 2,330,000 cases sold in Japan; by 1955 that number had dropped to only 680,000 and was falling steadily. The Coca-Cola Export Corporation (CCEC) had been running six production plants, but cut the number back to two and began to think seriously about withdrawing from Japan altogether. But the manager of its Japan office at the time opposed a pullout. He saw that the local economy was beginning to build a solid foundation for growth and insisted that there could be a big future for Coca-Cola in the local market. He also said that the company should support this crazy Japanese, Takanashi, who had made selling Coke in Japan his obsession for the past several years. The local manager managed to persuade the company's Northwest Pacific Regional Manager, who had the ear of executives of the parent company back in the States. Finally, Coca-Cola's U.S. corporate headquarters came around to the view that getting into Japan at this stage would be a smart move.

The Coca-Cola organization knew all about the difficulties Takanashi was having with the bureaucracy. Clearly, trying to sell a foreign beverage in Japan must be threatening somebody, because the issue was taking on absurd proportions. Since a Japanese who knew the system quite well couldn't seem to get anywhere playing by local rules, it was time to try something a little less subtle. The Coca-Cola Company took its case to the U.S. government, which then brought the matter up with the Japanese government, and the unequivocal message was "open the door." This approach, using foreign political pressure to open Japanese markets, is still common (and, when done properly, still quite effective) today. The Japanese call it *gaiatsu* (literally "outside pressure") and many Japanese businessmen have called for more of it in the right places.

The reason is simple: There is no higher authority than the bureaucracy in Japan. There is no real system of checks and balances. Even the judiciary often appears to be unusually sensitive to prevailing government policies, which means if you run into a stone wall at a ministry, you're stuck. You can spend a lot of money and get some well-connected politicians to lobby on your behalf with the bureaucrats, but there is no guarantee that this will work, and ultimately you have admitted that you can't go around the ministries, only try to buy their approval. *Gaiatsu* offers an alternative, a force outside the system that—if applied with a scalpel rather than a club—can dramatically change specific policies. The danger in *gaiatsu* is that foreign companies may choose to take the shortcut to market access rather than going through channels and trying to build from the bottom-up. *Gaiatsu* is seen even by its supporters inside Japan as a last resort. Those who try to beat the system without first trying it are given the opprobrium that they deserve.

All the same, *gaiatsu* may not always work. If foreign pressure touches a particularly sensitive nerve in the industrial/bureaucratic mindset, the results may be discouraging. Fortunately for Coca-Cola and for Takanashi, the U.S. government's plea for reconsideration of the Coca-Cola application came at a good time. It was 1956 and the Japanese economy really was starting to get back on its feet. Several economic statistics in that year were actually higher than those before the war, and in an economic white paper the government for the first time officially declared that the economy had surpassed pre-war levels. In other words, the arguments for preserving many of the post-war policies to support Japan's devastated economy were no longer valid.

So as a result of Takanashi's years of effort, American government pressure, and the rapidly changing economy, the situation finally began to improve. In October of 1956 the government asked

Takanashi to submit a new application to import Coca-Cola syrup. This may seem odd, considering that his application from three years earlier was still pending, but this is also part of the bureaucracy's standard operating procedure. To the officials, the old application was shelved for a reason. It was tainted, so to speak, with the political and administrative problems that surrounded it years before, and so was best forgotten. Also, since the decision to shelve it was effectively a negative decision, the idea of reactivating and then approving the old application would appear to be a reversal of position (and even a loss of face) for the ministries involved, and that is something to be avoided at all costs. So the officials' attitude becomes something like, "Let's all pretend that the past never happened. Submit a new application and we'll start all over again."

This may seem infuriating, but it is usually a very positive sign. It certainly was for Coke. The very next month MAFF gave its OK to the new application. For Takanashi it was the culmination of nine years of intense efforts to fulfill his dream of selling American soft drinks. Why, we might wonder, did it take almost a decade and all this political pressure to finally allow such a relatively harmless product—and one with no direct rival whose sales it would be hurting—into the Japanese market?

It is important to remember that at that time there were no supermarkets and only a small range of stores and shops in the majority of towns, even big towns in Japan. Almost all beverages were distributed through liquor stores, and obtaining a liquor license required approval from the government, which was no easy matter. Thus, for other reasons than just selling *sake*, the local liquor store was an extremely important part of the community. The owner of a big liquor store in any town was a man of considerable influence.

The real problem, then, was not so much Takanashi's plan to sell Coca-Cola as to distribute it through different channels. Takanashi had worked for a *tonya* in the food sector; he knew well enough how the system worked, and he knew that there was a better way to distribute soft drinks. His plan was not to rely on the local liquor stores as distributors, but instead to sell directly to restaurants, coffee shops, bread shops, candy shops, and any other small stores where customers might want to pick up a bottle of Coke. Of course, this would greatly expand Takanashi's potential market. It was also a blatant threat to the power of the liquor store owners.

Up until that point, restaurants, coffee shops, and so on bought their beverages wholesale from liquor stores, but now Coca-Cola was saying that there were other routes worth considering. Where would that lead? The liquor store owners felt that Coca-Cola was coming to steal their business out from under them. Needless to say, these owners had a lot of clout in their various communities and they pressured politicians to lobby on their behalf with the bureaucrats. (This, by the way, is a classic illustration of the power relationship between Japanese business, politics, and the bureaucracy that has come to be known as the "iron triangle.")

And so although Takanashi had received the unexpected support of The Coca-Cola Company and the U.S. government, and had finally been allowed to import the product, he knew he was up against a formidable array of enemies. Thousands of liquor store owners, the politicians they were supporting, the big beer companies, and others were all allied against him, and the fact that foreign pressure had led to the ministry granting approval did not make him any more popular. But Takanashi had won. Sort of.

Just a Few Conditions . . .

What the Japanese government had done was something it has long been famous for: When faced with foreign pressure, it had agreed to a demand (let American soft drinks into Japan) and allowed the foreigners to go away smiling to themselves and saying, "You see, sometimes the only way to get anywhere with these Japanese is to get tough." Then the government set about abiding by the letter but not the spirit of the agreement. The Coca-Cola Company may have been shocked some time later on to learn about the conditions that bound its sales in Japan, but Takanashi, who knew what he was up against, was probably only mildly surprised to see how much trouble he had stirred up.

Takanashi's little company, originally called Tokyo Beverage K.K. (later Tokyo Coca-Cola Bottling Co.), had the government-granted right to import Coke syrup and to make the product in Japan. However, in exchange for this right Takanashi had to submit a written document, in effect a contract, to the MAFF minister.

In this contract he had to accept specific regulations as to where he could sell Coke, how he could sell it, how much he could charge for it, how he could advertise it, and so on. Moreover, a portion of his profits had to be paid to the national treasury as a sort of special duty levied on the foreign substance he was selling.

The government probably wasn't counting on financing a space program with the duties it would receive from Takanashi's limited sales. The places where he was permitted to sell Coca-Cola were listed in minute detail: 56 hotels (those frequented by foreigners), 20 golf courses, 1 bowling alley, 8 *gaijin* clubs, 11 schools attended by *gaijin*, the foreign passenger facilities at Haneda Airport (the only international airport at the time), and in certain locations in the port cities of Yokohama and Kobe (both of which have long been foreign enclaves). All in all, Coca-Cola could be freely sold in any of a hundred or so places throughout Japan.

The message was clear: Coke could be made available wherever *gaijin* were likely to congregate, but not in any way sold to Japanese.

That was the good news. Then came price. Each case must be sold for ¥696, of which ¥156 must be paid to the national treasury as a "gift." The minimum price for each bottle was specified, so there could be no discounting to boost sales. Then came advertising. All promotion of Coca-Cola through television, radio, newspapers, or magazines was strictly forbidden. And needless to say, any infraction of these rules would lead to an immediate freeze on the firm's foreign capital transactions and a termination of imports.

What had Takanashi achieved? He could sell Coca-Cola in Japan as long as he sold only to *gaijin*, his prices were controlled, he paid a heavy tax to the government, and he did not advertise. In this way his company could not grow and so would not become a threat to established Japanese businesses. To many in the bureaucracy this must have seemed the ideal solution—they could say publicly that the market had been opened to Coca-Cola while still preserving the status quo of the domestic beverage industry. (It is worth noting that although much has changed in the Japanese bureaucracy since 1956, other things have not changed at all. This same kind of thinking is still quite common. Even today the bureaucrats are very concerned about protecting domestic industries and local special interest groups. Unfortunately the Japanese consumer falls into neither category.)

Takanashi hadn't given up in the previous decade and he wasn't about to give up now that he had a license to import, however hamstrung his firm might be in selling the product. Tokyo Beverage K.K. took over all sales to U.S. military forces from the Coca-Cola Export Corporation as well as its two remaining production plants, equipment, and staff, and officially started business in 1957.

The Last Hurdle

MITI allotted a total of $80,000 in foreign exchange funds to be used for the importation of cola syrup for commercial use. Since Pepsi-Cola had applied for the same rights, Coke and Pepsi were granted $40,000 each. Even then the funds could only be drawn in half-year accounting periods, so the real allotment was a maximum of $20,000 per term per company. We will take up the matter of Coca-Cola's domination of Pepsi in the Japanese market a bit later on, but it is interesting to note at this point that the two companies were granted permission to enter Japan and to start business on a fairly equal footing.

MITI's tight grip on the purse strings seemed like yet another unreasonable stumbling block to success, but in fact it made little difference. In its first term, Tokyo Beverage sold only a little over 20 percent of its $20,000 allotment. With a de facto ban on sales to Japanese, and American forces being withdrawn, the market was already tiny and shrinking. Coca-Cola seemed destined to disappear within a year or two.

Takanashi still wasn't ready to quit. First, he contacted the president of his old firm, Koami Shoten, and convinced him to quit and become the new sales manager for Tokyo Beverage (which must have taken some serious persuasion). Then the two brothers and the new sales manager started a life-or-death campaign to convince the government to relax the restrictions on where Coke could be sold. Ultimately the officials allowed the company to sell its product in restaurants and bars, but not in stores. This seemed like a major victory for the little firm. But again it became clear that the real source of the problem was not the bureaucrats, but the anti-Coca-Cola lobby that was pressuring the bureaucrats.

The whole issue of the propriety of selling Coca-Cola in Japan was brought once again to the Diet for deliberation. The claim was made that Tokyo Beverage had violated its written agreement with the Ministry of Agriculture by trying to sell in stores, and in the subsequent uproar the government had no choice but to retract its offer.

While Takanashi's business was languishing, the Japanese economy was starting to grow impressively. As the economy continued to perk up (in large part due to exports) and Japan began to reenter the world of international politics, the government became a bit more sensitive to its image abroad. The old rules that had effectively banned imports looked like the closed-door policy of the feudal society Japan had been just a century before, which was certainly not the image it was now trying to project. In 1960 the Kishi Cabinet pushed through revisions to the U.S.-Japan Security Treaty, a sign that Japan was viewing itself seriously as a member of the world community rather than as a conquered nation. It was in this climate that a process of meaningful deregulation began.

It is true that the government maintained innumerable hurdles to foreign business and to foreign investment in Japanese business for years to come, but that was particularly the case in industries that were deemed important to the nation's economic growth. Soft drinks did not fall into this category. And so in 1960 Takanashi's ship finally came in. The regulations were changed so that Coca-Cola could be sold anywhere to anyone and could be advertised like any other product. Moreover, the requirement that royalties be paid to the government was also dropped. The only remaining regulation, a formal report that had to be made to the government periodically, was eliminated the following year.

Everyone was happy: Takanashi, his long-suffering family and staff, and even Japanese consumers who had seen the Coke logo and the famous bottles in the big cities and on the silver screen. Coke was part of the American lifestyle, and the American lifestyle was rapidly becoming the model for the Japanese lifestyle. The little company's success was about to skyrocket along with Japan's GNP.

Yes, everyone was happy—everyone except the liquor store owners. Although Coke now appeared on their shelves, it was being handled directly by Coca-Cola distributors. The liquor stores were merely vendors, like any other shop, instead of the powerful wholesalers they wanted to be. The ill will generated by Takanashi's 13 years of effort was not about to evaporate overnight.

Takanashi understood this situation well and also knew that in the long run it would not serve his company's interests to be at war with a nationwide network of liquor dealers. So he began to offer olive branches, first a few and then a bushel and then plane-loads of them. The company arranged seminars for the liquor retailers, it hired consultants to speak and invited liquor shop owners to come and hear about how to modernize their businesses. Takanashi made up special magazines aimed at the liquor stores, he had his salesmen give out a free case of Coke for every 10 cases they sold, and did everything imaginable to win them over.

Ten years later he was still trying. Executive vice president Roy Suzuki recalls, "We worked very, very hard, but relations with the liquor stores didn't improve until the mid-1970s. In 1975 we took a large number of liquor store owners together with their families on 7-day trips to Paris. I think the total came to about 8,000 people, and the Coca-Cola organization picked up a good part of the tab. That had a huge impact on changing relations with the owners."

Route of the Problem

The system that the liquor store owners feared is called route sales. Instead of simply dropping off huge quantities of Coke at a few big distributors, the company's own salesmen trucked it around to thousands of small stores on streets all over Japan. Each truck had an average route of 250 stores and might make 40 to 50 stops in a day. One man on the truck would unload the product while the other checked the store's supply and promotional displays. Salesmen had four duties: to see that the store's stock was refilled, to check that it was properly refrigerated, to make sure the merchandise was in neat, easy-to-buy rows, and to make sure there were Coca-Cola posters and ads easily visible in the store.

For the salesmen on these routes there was a substantial "incentive" bonus every month based on their total sales. Some salesmen earned almost as much in their monthly bonus as in their paychecks. Small shopkeepers liked the direct, personal service, and the salesmen liked the pay. The result was a merchandising system that caught on as fast as the taste for Coke.

To back up the wide distribution of the new product, Coca-Cola appealed to consumers with memorable TV ads. Where Levi Strauss, for example, relied on James Dean in its commercials to establish its American identity, Coke was already associated with the American way of life. With this advantage, the company was able to focus on creating a more Japanese identity. Hideaki Nawa, currently vice president of Coca-Cola (Japan) Co., says, "Coca-Cola was unknown as a product in Japan. The only thing people knew about it was that it was from America. But instead of emphasizing its American origins, we appealed to young consumers by using popular Japanese entertainers in our ads."

Indeed, the company started a whole new type of television advertising in Japan, using popular young singing groups, popular Japanese actors, and others to represent its products. Today it is common to see famous singers and actors in TV ads, but back then it was unknown and a bit surprising. Coca-Cola was also the first company to create color TV ads in Japan.

Nawa adds, "Japanese love American culture, but we decided not to sell the American image. Rather we sold our company image, the image of a company doing business in Japan. Coke became very successful, and there were a bunch of imitators, so we also had to create original advertising to differentiate our product from the me-toos."

Missing: The Pepsi Generation

People who study foreign business in Japan never fail to note that Coke became a huge success here and Pepsi did not. Their market shares in the United States and other countries are not so different; their packaging, advertising, and even (apologies to both firms) their tastes are not so very different. Yet in terms of sales, Coke effectively "owns" Japan. The country has proved to be one of the firm's most profitable markets worldwide (more so than its home market in the United States, in fact). Pepsi, on the other hand, is still knocking at the door with a single-digit share and modest increases. The inevitable question is: Why?

The simple answer is that Pepsi had neither a fanatic like Takanashi, who wouldn't give up until his product was sitting on every store shelf in Japan, nor the same kind of clear-cut strategy of how to win in Japan.

The more complicated answer involves the success of the Coca-Cola organization in getting around the Japanese beverage distribution system. The first success was the introduction of route sales, which, as we have seen, caught on very quickly. The second strategic success was the firm's early move into vending machines, another approach to direct sales.

To American readers, vending machines may not seem like a very serious sales tool. But in Japan vending machines are a major source of retailing. Every city street, every train station, every public place, and almost every corner of every little town is lined with rows of machines. In the West, cigarette and soda machines are common, but in Japan machines dispense a lot more than tobacco. Various machines sell beer, sake, whiskey, wine, canned coffee and tea (hot or iced), soda, soup, CDs, videos, condoms, T-shirts, telephone debit cards, porno magazines, you name it. At last count there were somewhere around 4,100,000 vending machines of all kinds nationwide. About 2.3 million of those are soft drink machines, of which Coca-Cola controls about 35 percent. That comes to a lot of sales, and a lot of sales that don't involve salespeople on the payroll. In addition, the best spots for vending machines have long since been claimed and it is quite difficult to set up new ones in any attractive area. Consequently, a company that holds a high share of the machines currently in operation is very likely to hold onto that share for a long time to come. Pepsi vending machines do exist, but relatively speaking they are few and far between.

A third big reason for Coke's success was the company's establishment of a network of bottlers. Takanashi's original company became Tokyo Coca-Cola Bottling Company, and its primary concern was the huge market around the nation's capital. Then a new company, Coca-Cola (Japan) Co. Ltd., was founded by the parent firm to take charge of strategy and planning for all Coke-related business nationwide. This local subsidiary company then supplied Coca-Cola syrup to the various bottling companies.

There were different ideas about how to set up the bottlers. The American side wanted to create the same local-area bottler system as existed in the United States, where there were about 800 Coca-Cola bottlers. Since Japan has roughly half of America's population, the long-range goal would have been to establish 300–400 bottling companies. As far as Takanashi was concerned, even 30–40 was out of the question. The Japan subsidiary insisted that the number of bottlers be strictly limited, which would make the individual bottling companies accordingly large.

One-time president and current advisor to Coca-Cola Japan, Masaomi Iwamura explains the reasoning: "In Japan, a company's name value is extremely important. Big companies are respected; they have a much easier time hiring good staff and doing business. Coca-Cola was a big corporate name in America, but not in Japan, so it was crucial for us to build an organization that inspired confidence."

Instead of building lots of small, local bottlers which would have entailed great cost for the young firm, a small number of regional bottling companies were established, but not primarily with money from The Coca-Cola Company. Iwamura consulted with some of the nation's leading business executives, explaining his company's intentions and the long-term potential of its products. Precisely because these new firms would be so large and have exclusive rights to sell Coca-Cola in large regions of the country, they were attractive investments for some of the nation's most powerful companies: top defense contractor Mitsubishi Heavy Industries backed one, as did rival beverage maker Kirin Brewery; trading houses Mitsubishi Corp. and Mitsui & Co. also became big investors, as did Takanashi's old family business, Kikkoman, and the retailing giant Seibu Saison group.

The result was a national network of 17 Coca-Cola bottling companies, a very small number compared to the United States or Europe. But the backing of some of the nation's top firms gave Coca-Cola instant status in the Japanese business world. Today the group of companies that includes the bottlers and Coca-Cola Japan has annual sales of nearly ¥1 trillion (roughly $10 billion) and current profits of over $1 billion. Coca-Cola Company products hold a significant piece of the entire non-alcoholic beverage market.

Speed Bumps

Sales of Coca-Cola continued to rise along with the growth of Japan's economy. As consumer tastes began to broaden, the firm decided it was time to diversify its product line. One of the areas in which it decided to compete was the growing market for ready-to-drink coffee. In Japan, where as we have noted buying just about anything from a vending machine is considered normal, this was a natural business to get into, but to some in the United States it seemed a little crazy. However, the executives in Tokyo were convinced that they knew the local market, and they also knew they had an army of 800,000 vending machines to move a new product. So with the cooperation of the home office, the company went ahead with the project. They even named the coffee "Georgia" in honor of the parent company's home state.

Not surprisingly, it was a monster hit. You can find Georgia canned coffee—hot or cold—in every corner of Japan, and it sells so well even today that Japanese coffee makers run TV ads begging people to buy canned coffee "from a coffee company" rather than from a soft drink firm, but the ads are in vain. People trust the Georgia name even if they don't always realize who makes it, and many probably assume it *is* a coffee company. After that success, even the American head office had to admit that Japan was a special market.

The Coca-Cola story seems like a nightmare up until 1960 and then a merchandising dream thereafter. It wasn't quite that way. There were a few problems over the years, but looked at from a long-term perspective they seem more like speed bumps than obstacles. In fact, for about 30 years it seemed that Coke was invincible, that it could never lose market share.

Then in 1990 Pepsi launched a major campaign to gain acceptance in Japan. It created TV ads that were quite similar to the type the firm had used in the United States for many years, directly comparing Coke and Pepsi. This was the first serious challenge to Coca-Cola's position in the Japanese beverage market. The ads were pointed and direct and had the potential to steal away considerable market share.

In fact it was these ads that proved Pepsi's undoing at the time. They may have been effective in appealing to the younger generation that Pepsi was targeting, but their "which is better, A or B?" style was extremely unorthodox, almost offensive to many older Japanese. The problem was that this kind of comparative advertising is almost taboo in Japan. People consider it distasteful to say, "Our product is better than brand X" even if that is demonstrably true. As a result, many local TV stations decided not to run the Pepsi ads. There were rumors that Coca-Cola, a major TV advertiser, was pressuring the stations to drop the ads, and the media happily picked up the story and ran with it. But in the end it seems that at least in most cases it was the broadcasters themselves who found the ads inappropriate and asked that they be discontinued.

However, as public relations agents have argued for ages, there is no such thing as bad publicity, and the news stories brought Pepsi to the attention of many Japanese households. Pepsi's market share rose temporarily, but soon enough Coke's popularity came back and it regained its lost share.

The most recent big challenge has been on the horizon for some time. With the yen continuing to appreciate against the dollar, many companies, both foreign and Japanese, turned to importing products from abroad and selling them in Japan at far below the price of local rivals. It was only a matter of time before someone did the same with soft drinks.

In 1994, with Japanese consumers demanding lower prices, some of the big supermarket chains began to import various goods from overseas and sell them under their own labels. One of the products that grabbed a lot of attention was a no-name cola from the United States that sold in most stores for about one-fourth the price of Coke. Other colas soon appeared, and the trend has not abated. This would seem to be the kind of competition that could finally pop Coke's balloon. After all, the firm worked for years as an outsider to challenge the established order of the time, but now it has become the establishment, and the new distributor-kings (the supermarkets) are ready to unseat it.

To all of this the company's managers only smile a confident smile. Executive vice-president Suzuki explains, "For years people have said that Coca-Cola has become a huge hit in Japan, but if you look at the per capita numbers and compare them with the United States or other countries, our sales in Japan are really quite low. Why is that? One reason is the lack of competition. That's right, a *lack* of competition. When a firm has stiff competition, it struggles with all its might to raise its sales. We are not in that position in Japan. In that sense, we think this whole thing with the imported colas may prove to be beneficial . . . . Thanks to all the magazine articles about 'cola wars,' people have paid more attention to our main products than they have for some time. Look at our results for this summer (1994). In just a couple of months our cola sales jumped 50 percent compared to a year ago. Why? We think customers heard about these cheap colas, ran out to buy some, tasted them, and then decided that Coke is 'the real thing' after all. Now that they've rediscovered Coca-Cola, they're buying more than before."

Too Much Success?

Once Coca-Cola (Japan) got up and running in the 1960s, it never looked back. It grew and grew, and today the firm's single biggest problem, as Suzuki hinted, is its own success. There is no sense of crisis inside the firm, no sense of urgency, no feeling of having to learn from bitter experiences in the past. That has its good side but also its bad side, because every firm needs some stimulus to stay sharp.

Adding to this problem is the fact that there are very few employees who joined the firm in mid-career. Even more than most Japanese companies, Coca-Cola hires fresh university graduates and they tend to stay with the company for decades. In most Japanese companies, it is not uncommon for a few people of various age levels to come in from affiliated or related companies each year, bringing in management experience, market information, and other skills. Paradoxically, however, many *gaishi* firms do not do this. They want to be more Japanese than the Japanese, and the result is a staff that has surprisingly little first hand knowledge of the outside world. (We discussed the problem of how *gaishi* have overdone their "copy Japanese management practices" approach in Chapter 1.

Despite its ubiquitous products, Coca-Cola is not well known as a company even today. The firm keeps such a low profile that it is not even listed in the ranking of firms to which Japanese college students want to apply. This has the makings of a serious problem down the line, and current president Mike Hall is concerned about it. He retained McKinsey & Co. to examine the firm and see how best to invigorate its almost lackadaisical atmosphere. The full results of that new policy remain to be seen.

One sign that the company is not content to sit back and simply watch its sales grow was the hiring of a new vice-president, Masahiko Uotani, formerly vice-president of Kraft Japan. Uotani, who has worked for a number of *gaishi* firms, has experience in dealing with convenience stores, the thousands of little 24-hour shops that have sprung up from Hokkaido to Kyushu.

Thirty-five years ago Coca-Cola emphasized direct sales to small retail stores when that was not the norm; later, as its bottler network developed, it was prescient in putting its marketing muscle into vending machines. Both strategies were ahead of their time. But the rise of the corner convenience store seems to have caught the company a bit by surprise. Although Coca-Cola now holds a substantial 36 percent of Japan's overall soft-drink market, it has only 30 percent of sales in these very popular neighborhood stores. Bringing in someone like Uotani, who knows the convenience store business well, is a sign that Coke is aggressively going after that growing market.

As Suzuki says, the per capita sales ratio of Coca-Cola in Japan is still low compared to other nations, which means it has a lot of room to grow regardless of its huge market share. Coca-Cola Japan is now aiming to broaden its business base and become a total beverage company. The firm hopes to have its soft drinks, canned tea, and canned coffee lines contribute large shares to sales and profits. But other Japanese producers, specifically the big beer and food makers as well as other drink makers, are all aiming for that same market: canned coffee and tea, canned juices, sports drinks, etc. There is no doubt that the competition is getting tougher. But if the past is any guide, Coca-Cola will not only survive but positively thrive in this new market. When you hear the firm talk casually about linking its 800,000 vending machines in an online network to report real-time information on consumer preferences, it is obvious that Coca-Cola will do whatever is necessary to stay on top in Japan.

Conclusions

Nisaburo Takanashi, the "father of Coca-Cola in Japan," died as this book was being researched. But the company he worked so hard to establish has made sure that he will not be forgotten. In February 1994 The Coca-Cola Company in the United States granted $2 million to establish a Takanashi Coca-Cola Environmental Education Foundation in Japan to support evironmental education.

More than anything else, Takanashi's story—that is, the Coca-Cola story—is one of perseverance. It is too easy to assume that if a product is a hit in every other consumer culture, its success in Japan is guaranteed. It doesn't work that way, as Pepsi and a half-dozen other popular soft drinks have found out. The fact is, Coca-Cola had good management and a first-rate sales strategy to support its product, which it knew had the potential to be a hit if handled properly. Without these two key factors even the best products are left sitting on the dock or worse yet, knocking on the door, just as Coke was for so many years.

Takanashi's decade-long struggle belongs in the textbook for foreign firms trying to break into the Japanese market. Hopefully no *gaishi* company will have to endure the same ordeal that he went through, but the same kind of problems are still all too common, and the same responses (patience, perseverance, and if necessary, outside pressure) will still pay off.

CHAPTER 7

The Impossible Dream

AFLAC

You have to try harder in Japan—but the return can be worth the effort.

> John Amos, former chairman of AFLAC Inc. and a master of understatement. In 1973 his firm invested a total of $1.6 million to set up a branch in Japan. They never spent another cent on the venture. Twenty years later the Japan branch accounts for over $4.1 billion of the American company's worldwide revenues of $6 billion.

There are many success stories of foreign business in Japan, and there will certainly be many more in the years to come. But there has never been a company like AFLAC, and we doubt there ever will be another. AFLAC came to Japan, like so many other companies, with a good idea and the conviction that there was a lucrative market here waiting to be tapped. Japan had the latent demand and AFLAC had the product; combine the two and success should be a sure thing.

And like so many companies, AFLAC ran smack into a brick wall when it tried to set up in Tokyo. For a while it seemed that the little firm would get lost and disappear within the immense labyrinth of the Japanese bureaucracy long before it ever had a chance to introduce its product. At one point, even its home office felt that the government was sending it a not-so-subtle message and decided it would be better to give up. But, as in the case of Coca-Cola and a few other foreign success stories, at the very earliest stage the firm's interests in Japan were represented by a single determined individual. For this reason, we would have to say that, in the beginning at least, AFLAC's monumental success in Japan was largely due to luck—luck in finding the one person stubborn enough not to back down in the face of bureaucratic rigidity and dedicated enough not to give up when the home office said it was time to throw in the towel.

As a result of this stubborn "We won't take 'no' for an answer" attitude, AFLAC did not merely succeed in Japan—it exploded, it grew beyond all expectations, beyond any dream its founders ever had, in fact, far beyond the scale of its parent company. And in so doing, AFLAC redefined what success can mean in the Japanese market.

A Local Firm Goes International

Although AFLAC (formerly known as American Family Life Assurance Company) has become much better known in the United States in the past few years, until recently it was a relatively minor player in the U.S. insurance market and its name was not recognized in much of the country. Thanks in part to revenues from its Japanese subsidiary, that is no longer the case. However, it would be helpful to take a brief look at the firm's background before trying to understand its expansion in Japan.

AFLAC was founded in 1955 in Columbus, Georgia by lawyer John B. Amos and his two brothers, William and Paul. Their father died of cancer, which in addition to the grief it brought the family was also a great financial burden. So in 1958 the little firm started selling the world's first insurance policy to cover cancer-related expenses. It was not a big operation. Most sales were for very small policies, and they were sold one by one, door to door. Then, in 1967, the company began holding group meetings to explain the benefits of its insurance coverage. Over the next few years it shifted from selling to individuals to selling to groups, and its sales operations spread throughout the southeastern United States. In fact, these "cluster sales," as the firm called them, were so successful that only seven years after beginning this approach to marketing insurance, the firm was listed on the NYSE. Yet even with this rapid growth, AFLAC was only ranked around number 500 among America's thousands of insurance companies. Had it continued merely to expand in the United States, the firm would undoubtedly have grown and prospered, but would not likely have become one of the country's 100 biggest insurance firms.

But in 1970 founder John Amos made an overseas trip that was to change the company's future forever. As he told the story some years ago, "I went to Japan first to visit Expo 1970 in Osaka. On that trip I visited Tokyo, Osaka, Kyoto, and Kobe. I rode the bullet train and I observed the beehive of activity and production along the way. It was obvious that the standard of living was on an upward spiral and that these people, if they needed it, had the wherewithal to purchase supplemental cancer-cost insurance. I found that they did need it because the government health scheme was very limited and supplemental health insurance was unheard of in Japan at that moment in any form."

But it was not merely Amos' reading of the country's improving economic status and the lack of cancer insurance that caused him to begin thinking along bold new lines. His sharp observation of what was then a common trend in Japanese society—the wearing of white cotton masks to prevent the spread of colds—sparked the inspiration for the company's most important decision.

As Amos recalled, "It was a cold, rainy, and snowy April and I noted in every block (a number of people) in Western business suits and carrying briefcases . . . but in addition they were wearing surgical masks. I then concluded that they not only had the money to buy our product and the need to buy our product, but that they were totally health conscious and so would have the propensity to buy our product. The die was cast. We would seek to enter the Japanese market . . . ."

Of course the company did some background research. One thing it found was that Japanese people living in Hawaii had a very high awareness of cancer and bought a good deal of cancer insurance. The disease was rapidly becoming the number one killer in Japan, and the concern was obvious. As Amos noted, the need was there and the financial resources were there. Only the product was lacking. AFLAC began to think seriously about how to open up shop in Japan.

In 1971 Amos sent the comany's sales manager and executive vice-president, Walter Barton, to Tokyo to look into the possibility of tying up with a Japanese life insurance company. Barton is said to have had serious doubts about the idea: after all, why would a small firm in Columbus, Georgia want to tie up with a huge (there are no other kind) Japanese life insurer? How would they communicate and what could they possibly have to offer each other? But of course he went, and he gave it his best shot. He made the rounds of several of the top insurance companies, but it all seemed a waste of time. The Japanese firms had even greater doubts than he did. The industry colossus, Nippon Life Insurance, was already on its way to becoming the largest insurance company in the world, and its local competitors were not far behind. No one was very interested in a proposal from what they saw as a little hole-in-the-wall firm from Georgia. None of them knew anything about cancer insurance except that it was not currently approved by the Ministry of Finance, which in itself was enough to make the prospect uninteresting. Even if one of the biggest insurance companies in America had approached these firms, its response probably would have been the same: if it's already for sale in Japan, we've got a big share of it; if it's not, don't waste our time.

Today many of the insurance companies that Barton contacted act as *agents* for AFLAC, and every one of them has kicked itself a thousand times for passing up a multi-billion-dollar, once-in-a-century opportunity.

Barton made one more effort to get the job done. Since the big Japanese companies were not interested, if AFLAC wanted to get into Japan it would have to go it alone. If that was the case, it would need good people to run the Tokyo operation. Reliable consulting companies being few and far between in Tokyo, Barton contacted an American lawyer who was living in Japan, Frank H. Scorinos, to ask for advice. It was Scorinos who introduced him to a sharp, young Japanese insurance salesman named Yoshiki Otake. Otake was a hard worker, knew the Japanese insurance business well, and was looking to improve his own situation. He seemed a perfect employee for any kind of business AFLAC might want to set up in Japan.

The Right Person for the Job

Otake is a Christian, and as a young man he thought seriously of becoming a missiionary and going to Africa. In school he studied veterinary medicine, then went to the United States for two years to further those studies before returning to Japan. He gave up on becoming a minister but still wanted to do something for humanity, to find a way to help people. He decided that he should enter politics. He then became an assistant to a member of the Japanese Diet. Three years in politics showed him how little helping people had to do with a politician's work and he quit, disillusioned but not dispirited.

At the time Otake received the call from Scorinos asking him to come to his office, he was working for an American casualty insurance company—AIU (the non-life insurance side of industry giant AIG). There had been some talk of a tie-up between AIU and one of Japan's biggest insurers, Dai–Ichi Life Insurance, which had resulted in Otake being seconded to Dai–Ichi for half a year. This proved to be a valuable education in how the big Japanese life firms do business. A short while later, AIU's sister firm ALICO Japan (the life insurance side of AIG) was preparing to begin oper- ations on its own as a foreign company. Otake was asked to work on preparing the mass of documents necessary for the application. This involved both stacks of paperwork and hours of negotiations with people at the Ministry of Finance. Scorinos had heard about Otake's value to AIU, his experience at Dai–Ichi, and most im- portantly, his recent experience in dealing with MOF. If AFLAC wanted to get into the Japanese market, it would have to go through the same ordeal of application procedures and would need some- one like Otake who knew his way around. Thus Scorinos invited Otake to meet Barton that fateful day in Tokyo.

What neither of the two Americans could possibly know was that the slightly awkward fellow sitting before them with the seri- ous look and halting English would soon make AFLAC's cause in

Japan his cause, would take up that cause with an almost religious fervor, and would ultimately provide Barton's company with over $15 billion in assets, roughly *ten times* those of the parent firm.

Otake was interested in what Barton had to say particularly because he was not talking about tying up with one of the big Japanese firms, but setting up an independent office and running things efficiently. Otake had seen firsthand the incredibly old-fashioned, narrow-minded attitudes inside Japan's big life firms at that time, and he knew that tying up with any of them was likely to lead to trouble. He said as much, and Barton nodded. The executive from Columbus was tired and more than a little discouraged from making repeated presentations to the Japanese houses, only to be politely shown the door. He, too, was thinking that if the company was to do business in Japan it would have to run its own show. He knew that the 33-year-old Otake had lots of experience with AIU and ALICO as well as in doing the difficult groundwork necessary to get an insurance application through MOF. After a lengthy talk, he was ready to offer Otake the job of running the Japan operation on the spot.

"To tell the truth, I wasn't exactly sure about what I was agreeing to," recalls Otake, now chairman of AFLAC Japan and vice-chairman of AFLAC International, with a smile. "I was young, and I figured that if I made a mistake I could just go back and do something else. I also wanted to tackle something big. I wanted a challenge, and I was ready to take some risks."

Otake immediately took a pamphlet that Barton had left and went to visit MOF. At the time, life insurance in Japan was almost entirely "death insurance," so Otake's appeal for hospitalization insurance and similar benefits fell on deaf ears. The ministry's sections charged with life and non-life insurance were totally un-interested in his proposal.

Otake realized the need to prepare himself with cogent arguments rather than mere enthusiasm. He thought, "Unless I really understand something about cancer and the suffering it causes, I'll never be able to convince a bunch of officials in MOF about the need for this insurance." Fortunately, one of Otake's good friends, Izumi Hasegawa, was the president of Japan's largest medical publishing company. He introduced the young man to some of the nation's top cancer specialists. Otake began a serious study of cancer in all its forms, collecting data and researching recent health and insurance statistics.

But the research alone was not enough. Otake had to admit to himself that he was still not fully convinced of the need for special cancer insurance in Japan. Around that time Hasegawa's wife introduced him to one of her relatives whose wife had died of cancer. The woman had left a heartrending diary of her days in the hospital and the mental anguish that she and her family shared. Otake was allowed to read this diary, and it moved him as none of his research had. After coming face-to-face with the suffering of a cancer patient and seeing the toll on the family as well, Otake at last understood what the experts and the statistics could not tell him. He no longer had any doubts about the need for some kind of insurance to help alleviate the double blow of an emotional shock and a crushing financial burden that made cancer such a terrifying prospect in the 1970s.

Taking Up the Challenge

In 1972 Otake set up a new company called the International Insurance Agency Group (IAG). The firm was technically under the wing of American Family, but since AFLAC was not licensed to sell insurance in Japan, IAG operated mainly as an agent for three non-life insurance firms: AIU, Tokio Fire & Marine Insurance (part of the Mitsubishi *keiretsu*), and Yasuda Fire & Marine Insurance (part of the Fuyo group). The new company consisted of three secretaries, plus Otake and a friend, Nobuo Kawamura. We can gain some insight into the kind of team spirit and sense of mission that Otake inspired in his group by noting that two of the three secretaries were still part of the business more than 20 years later, and Kawamura is now a senior managing director of the firm.

In a short time two more key men joined, Hidefumi Matsui and Yuji Ogawa, both of whom would later become senior managers in what would evolve into AFLAC Japan. Matsui is a particularly interesting character. After graduating from university in 1968, he joined Kawasaki Steel where he was later trained in working with computers. He found a new joy in creating computer systems from scratch, for example, designing systems to monitor the process flow in a steel mill from production to shipping. It was a brand new field where the territory was not yet mapped and, unlike almost every other aspect of Japanese business, there were no superiors to show a bright young employee the "right" way to do things. Still, the number of new projects he could get his hands on and the kinds of things he could do were strictly limited. This was, after all, a major Japanese steel firm, one of the pillars of the nation's industrial growth at the time, and about as progressively minded as a government ministry.

In no time at all Matsui had discovered the joy of creating new systems and the frustrations of working for a big company. "I guess I got into really interesting work too early," he says of those years. "Pretty soon I started scanning the Help Wanteds in the Tokyo papers every day." He saw an ad for AIU, and a friend told him that working for a non-life company meant lots of free time. Free time and a certain amount of independence sounded good to someone in his position. So he broke the unwritten rule of lifelong loyalty to a single big company and jumped into the unknown.

At the time, the automatic bank transfer payment system, which is now the most common method for paying almost every monthly bill in Japan, was just coming into use. Among other things, AIU put Matsui in charge of negotiating with the banks, an experience that would serve a different company well when it came time to negotiate a different kind of arrangement with MOF. Otake met him during those AIU days and suggested that Matsui join him in a new project, IAG.

"I liked the idea of joining Otake and American Family," he remembers, "but just to be safe I called a friend at a commercial bank and had him check it out. He said the parent firm wasn't even listed in a reference book of big American companies. Any company that small probably wasn't very secure. His advice was to stay clear."

But Matsui had already seen the inside of big, secure companies and was ready for a gamble. Besides, Otake's offer was tempting—a foreign-affiliated insurance business that would be run locally by Japanese, a start-up firm that would be responsible for its own profits and its own management. Despite initial support from the parent company, it would be independent, and it would need to be designed from the ground up. Moreover, it would try to sell a product that didn't even exist in Japan.

"After leaving Kawasaki Steel I realized how much I like to build things from scratch. This is what I was doing with the computer systems at Kawasaki and then with banking operations at AIU," he says. "But I also realized there are certain advantages to a big, established firm like Kawasaki. It's an independent entity, not a crossbreed like most *gaishi* firms that can't move without orders from their home office. I liked the idea of a self-contained company, which is what Otake was proposing." He decided it was time to make another jump.

Sleepless Nights

Once IAG was set up and Otake had a small staff with which to begin operations, it was time to start preparations for the real target: filing an application with MOF to sell cancer insurance in Japan. The work actually began in 1972. Not only was it necessary to file an "Application for a License to Conduct Insurance Business in Japan," but 10 different supplementary documents had to be prepared. Even while he was still at AIU, Matsui was developing much of the strategy and the documentation that would be necessary. He'd work from 9–5 at his regular job, then spend all of his nights doing the paperwork to set up American Family in Japan. Often he slept only three hours a night.

Ogawa, who joined at around the same time, was also an AIU man. He had ten years with the firm and had been named head of claims and disbursements. But most of AIU's clients at that time were in the U.S. military or in some way related to U.S. forces in Japan. It was very much a foreign company selling insurance to foreigners. Like Matsui, he wasn't satisfied, and so, when Otake approached him he didn't spend too much time weighing his decision. But once inside IAG, Otake's shell company that would hopefully give birth to AFLAC Japan, he realized that perhaps he was going to get more than he bargained for. The preparations for filing the MOF documents were difficult and extremely time-consuming.

"We worked every day, Saturdays included, usually until 10 or 11 at night," Ogawa recalls. "Nobody took a summer vacation. The women were on the verge of tears some of the time." As 1973 dragged on and still the application wasn't ready, everyone stepped up the pace of their work. As the final papers were being prepared, Matsui's three hours of sleep per night had to be cut down.

But there was more to it than merely submitting a stack of papers to the Ministry of Finance. Much more.

Part of the problem was that MOF was genuinely worried about introducing a new form of insurance that might in some way interfere with Japan's national health insurance program which is administered by another part of the bureaucracy, the Ministry of Health and Welfare (MHW). In those days the program tried to cover all possible ills, so if MOF gave the OK to some "imported" American insurance product, it would make MHW and the national health plan look pretty foolish. While snubbing a "lesser" ministry is an everyday occurrence at MOF, the national health plan was too important an issue to play games with. The best way to preserve the integrity of the national health scheme and to deal with the annoying AFLAC issue was simply to pass the buck. Which is exactly what the MOF officials did.

Otake explains: "When we first went to the Insurance Department of the Finance Ministry, we were told to go to the Ministry of Health and Welfare. There the final judgment was to be made by consensus." In other words, MHW not only had to review the application before MOF would look at it, but had to approve it unanimously. The judgment would be handed down by MHW's Medical Affairs Bureau, which included the Public Health Bureau and Insurance Bureau. If even one official in any of these groups opposed AFLAC's application, it was dead.

So Otake went to talk to each individual bureau chief, research officer, section chief, and so on, right on down the line. He spent an enormous amount of time and energy lobbying one ministry so that it would recommend that AFLAC's proposal be given serious consideration by another ministry.

One section chief at MHW was adamantly opposed to some details in the structure of the proposed plan. Otake came back with a promise that his company had considered these objections and was already instituting change in its insurance policy. Fortunately for Otake (and millions of Japanese policyholders today), there were people in the ministry who had recently lost relatives to cancer and knew firsthand the problems involved. They helped to persuade the reluctant section chief that private insurance companies must be allowed to provide people with an opportunity to purchase supplementary insurance. Pressured by his peers, this section chief finally came around.

Just as an aside, during this long period while Otake was working to set up AFLAC in Japan, working long hours researching the intricacies of the national health plan and the domestic insurance law, and lobbying scores of bureaucrats, he received no salary. "American Family offered to pay me a regular salary, and a generous one at that," he said later, "but how could I accept it? I had no proof that we could even get a license, so I said no to their offer." While Otake tried to live on his savings, the rest of the staff did receive regular salaries, although it is doubtful if any amount of money could compensate them for the sacrifices they made in those early days.

One full year after American Family's proposal was sent to MHW it finally received that ministry's approval. Of course the approval was merely an unofficial endorsement to MOF, not a license to do business. But it was a major victory in a long, uphill battle to win government approval for a new insurance product.

The officials at MOF were genuinely surprised. MHW was the only ministry in a position to complain that some possible action by MOF would damage the national health plan, and could have easily scuttled Otake's proposal. Instead they gave it the OK after only a year of study. That meant the buck had come around again and MOF was stuck making the decision it had tried to avoid. Still, the ministry had a number of ways to kill an application without directly turning it down, and the easiest and tidiest was simply to shelve it. Which is exactly what appeared to have happened.

Regulation, MOF-Style

It is fair to ask why a relatively simple issue, in this case an application to sell cancer insurance, created such a bureaucratic logjam in Tokyo. The answer lies in understanding a little bit about the Japanese bureaucracy and the nature of the domestic insurance business.

First of all, the Japanese insurance industry is a special beast. Otake explains the background as follows: "The Japanese life insurance industry is one of the most strictly government-regulated industries in the world. It comes under the supervision of the Ministry of Finance, which derives its authority from the Insurance Business Law. The Law gives the Ministry the power to intervene in the operations of private insurance companies through the granting of approval of new products, product development benefits, expected interest rates, dividends, and sales office openings, requiring advance notice of the appointment and removal of company officers, etc. In other words, they exercise total control over every little detail of the industry. On the one hand MOF covers the industry with a network of regulation, while on the other hand it guarantees and preserves the stable existence of all the companies in the industry."

In short, MOF keeps the insurance industry on a very short, tight leash, which makes it easier to maintain stability and order in the sector. And stability and order are a bureaucrat's air and water. Unlike the United States where there are over 2,000 insurance companies, scores of which fail every year and are replaced by new ones, in Japan there are only about two dozen life insurance companies and about the same number of non-life companies. The total market is huge (in fact, twice the size of the U.S. insurance market), but the players are few, making it neat, orderly, and easy to regulate. In return for strict cooperation with the ministry, the handful of companies in the industry are guaranteed a more-or-less eternal, profitable monopoly without fear of undue competition, including the introduction of products which might threaten the stability of their business. This is precisely the kind of rigid status quo that MOF has applied to the nation's banking system, and to an extent, its stock exchanges as well. And it is precisely the kind of structure that is supposed to prevent outside elements—such as tiny American cancer insurance firms—from rocking the boat. This is what Otake and his colleagues were up against.

In the United States, for example, obtaining government approval for a new type of insurance is relatively easy because the government is not held responsible for the quality of insurance products. Unlike Japan, the United States is a free market in which consumers bear much of the burden for choosing among good and bad products and good and bad companies. The bad ones either straighten up or go out of business. This idea that the consumer knows what is good for him or her is still alien to Japanese bureaucratic thinking. However, because most U.S. firms feel that almost any approval is a simple matter if only the paperwork is done properly in the first place, they can't understand the long delays in Japan. Many a firm becomes frustrated and gives up rather than wait years for an answer. (Cynics suggest that this is one reason why the Japanese system works as it does.)

A Waiting Game

As expected, the negotiations were long and hard, much as they had been with MHW. During this process, several conditions surrounding the type of insurance AFLAC would offer were changed to bring its policies more into line with Japanese insurance practice. The company made several concessions in an effort to assuage MOF's fears that the product was too different and too risky to be allowed even a chance to fail in the open market. As with the Japanese banking system, the insurance companies are not allowed to fail publicly. There may be mergers or acquisitions, but if so MOF will have a hand in their execution; no one is allowed to go belly up and shake the public's confidence in the system. One of MOF's biggest fears had nothing to do with the intrinsic value of AFLAC's plan, but the widespread belief that it was doomed from the outset. If the ministry allowed the company to sail out into the quiet, regulated pond of the Japanese financial industry, it could not be permitted to sink suddenly and send ripples spreading outwards to upset others. Yet how could this little firm with its crazy idea about cancer insurance do anything but sink? It seemed to be a failure just waiting to happen.

And yet the Ministry of Health and Welfare, after a year of scrutiny and plentiful opportunities to kill the plan, had given it their OK. Was the MHW hoping MOF would approve it, only to watch the new company (and its new product) fail, and then wave a public finger at MOF for its inept handling of the issue? Bureaucratic chess is a complex game, and so we must assume that there were many weighty matters for the Finance Ministry officials to consider when the formal application reached them towards the end of 1973.

Of course one feature of the ministry's protection of the industries under its care is the dissemination of information that could prove useful to concerned corporations. Thus the idea that a company—for example, a foreign firm—might apply to offer a new insurance product in Japan and thus get a jump on its domestic rivals is absolutely out of the question (it would, of course, cause "confusion" in the industry). One of MOF's concerns is to show the contents of all such applications to representatives of the big insurance companies and get their reactions. Then it will study the application for some time. If it decides to grant the application, it is a sure bet that all the Japanese firms have had plenty of time to develop their own versions of the product and have submitted similar applications, all of which may be approved at the same time as the original proposal. This is simply good business sense from the standpoint of those on the inside.

Thus by the time AFLAC's application was filed, the contents were widely known. Otake and others had already spent a year lobbying the MHW and then many more months negotiating with MOF, which meant that anyone in Japan with even the slightest interest in the insurance business was well aware of the details of AFLAC's plan. This included the media. The Japanese press picked up the story of cancer insurance and decided to give the American firm's efforts to gain government approval a bit of attention. A few months after formally submitting their application, Otake's team began to read newspaper reports describing how MOF had ultimately decided in favor of the little company and that cancer insurance would definitely get the go-ahead. This was heartening news, but it was never followed by any announcement, positive or negative, from MOF. Days turned into weeks, elation dissolved into despair, and then another newspaper story would start the same tortuous process over again.

At the beginning of 1974 the nation's most respected business newspaper, the *Nihon Keizai Shimbun* (Nikkei) reported that "American Family will receive approval to start cancer insurance very shortly." Otake was overjoyed, assuming that anything he read in the august Nikkei must be true, and so had the story translated in full and sent to AFLAC headquarters in Columbus, Georgia. But January ended without a word from MOF. Nothing. February followed. Still not a peep from Kasumigaseki. Unable to endure the waiting any longer, Otake went to visit the ministry, not just once but on a number of occasions. Each time he was told, in effect, "Back off. We don't like to be pushed."

A Man Who Couldn't Quit

As the months went by the Otake's staff suffered one disappointment after another, the U.S. parent company finally sent a memo to Tokyo which said in effect, "You've all worked very hard and you've given it your best efforts, but now it's time to give up. If MOF is dragging its feet this long without any sign of approval, what they must be trying to say is that they can't give us the approval but at the same time they don't want to make a public scene by rejecting the application. They want us to forget about it. Thanks for your efforts." Some time after Otake received the memo from Georgia his funding also stopped. As far as the head office was concerned there wasn't any reason to fund an operation that was closing down.

But Otake wasn't closing down. He was just getting started. He contacted a friend at Dai–Ichi Kangyo Bank (DKB), at that time the world's largest commercial bank, and asked for a loan. It was a big request—well over a million dollars in today's terms for a company whose very existence was predicated on selling a product that did not exist and which MOF showed no signs of approving. But Otake had been in touch with DKB for a few years and relations with the bank were quite good. Of course, the bank checked out the company's standing in the business community and its prospects for future income. In those days it was commonly believed in the insurance industry that even if cancer insurance did manage to get started in Japan, it would never go anywhere. In that sense the firm's prospects did not look too good. And yet both the banking industry and the insurance industry are controlled from within the same building in Kasumigaseki. Although MOF's departments responsible for regulating banking and insurance are separate, it is not inconceivable that DKB made discreet inquiries through connections at the ministry and learned that AFLAC's application was not the dead letter it appeared to be. Whatever the case, the loan was approved.

For those readers who are not familiar with the Japanese concept of a company's "main bank," this is a good illustration of how
such a relationship develops. Old, well-established companies have
a main bank or banks from which they have been borrowing for
decades. Newer firms often find that it is in their second growth
phase when one of the dozen or so giant "city" (commercial) banks
steps in to make a crucial loan that helps the business expand
significantly. Sometimes the bank even introduces potential clients
from within its *keiretsu* (group of companies). This not only
increases the obligation felt by the borrower toward the bank, but
also helps to improve the former's business, which in turn guarantees repayment of the loans. As time goes by, the bank and the
borrower become closer, more loans are forthcoming, and the bank
may take an increasingly active role in the company's business.

Because of this early expression of faith in the AFLAC dream,
DKB became the company's main bank. Otake recalls, "Over the
years the bank not only gave us loans, but supported us in many
ways. Even after we finally got our license approval, they helped
us to get the business off the ground." In fact, DKB became one
of the first major companies to become an agent for AFLAC in
Japan and ultimately provided not just one but two of its biggest
agencies. But now we're getting ahead of ourselves.

Looking for Agents

Even before receiving MOF's approval, AFLAC Japan had begun
looking for agents to sell its new product. In Japan, where corporate size, name recognition, and product identity are everything,
the firm had three strikes against it. So the first step was to do
some PR, to make both the public and Japanese corporations
aware of cancer insurance and of AFLAC. Otake led the effort to
approach the top local newspapers and broadcasters in various
regins of Japan, as well as leading companies in each region. To
the former he pitched the importance of the company's product,
the social need for supplementary private insurance to help alleviate the financial burden of care for a cancer patient, care that
the national health insurance simply did not cover. To the latter

he gave the same basic speech with a twist: companies that signed up to represent this cancer insurance in each geographic area would get in early on a very good business opportunity that also fulfilled a real social need. They would be helping society as well as earning profits. The message had a certain appeal.

Fate stepped in once again. Just at the time Otake and his colleagues were trying to promote this idea, Japan's economy was rocked by the first major oil shock. Hundreds of big companies were forced to restructure, and Japanese industry was never quite the same afterwards. One of AFLAC Japan's earliest employees, Nobuo Kawamura, explains: "After the oil shock, Japanese companies suddenly began a rush to diversify and to split off divisions into independent subsidiaries. Many heard that there were attractive commissions to be reaped from selling cancer insurance, and a number of firms became interested in spinning off departments to act as agents."

Clearly, many companies saw AFLAC's business as one more way to deal with the new realities of the post-oil-shock business environment. Despite pretensions to a system of lifetime employment, companies had to eliminate staff by the thousands. Many were fired, either directly or indirectly, but many more were shuffled off to affiliates or to these new spin-off companies. In many cases the smaller firms simply went bankrupt, allowing excess personnel to be eliminated without being fired by the parent firm. Every company's dream, of course, was to set up a new subsidiary, send some employees there to trim its payroll, and then find that, miracle of miracles, the new company had become a profit center rather than a weight to be jettisoned. AFLAC's offer provided exactly that opportunity.

Dozens of major companies warmed to the idea, mostly because they knew they already had a captive clientele on their payrolls. Many said they would become American Family agents if the company could get a license from MOF. In fact many of these big firms were so eager to try the system that they even pressured MOF to get on with the approval. This also helps to explain why the ministry finally did the unthinkable: it not only let AFLAC into Japan, but created a special umbrella to protect it from competition with domestic insurance companies.

Selling the Product

At last, late in 1974 MOF gave its approval. It had taken about two and a half years of effort for that little piece of paper. Many years later Otake explained: "How did AFLAC manage to obtain a license? I think it may have been because at that time American Family was just a small company out in the backwoods of Georgia that didn't even rank in the top 400 insurance companies in the United States. Because of this, it was not seen as a potential rival to Japanese insurance companies. In those days the Japanese life insurance industry and the Ministry of Finance could very easily have opposed our entry into the market."

There was no more need for the little IAG operation, so it was officially merged into American Family's new Japan Branch office. To everyone's way of thinking, there was only one possible candidate for president of the new branch, the man who had made it his mission to bring AFLAC to Japan and devoted every waking hour (as well as his personal savings) to that end. But Yoshiki Otake was not interested in being "rewarded" with the presidency. He was a strategist first and foremost, and his strategy was not complete simply because the little firm had won its battles with MHW and MOF. He had much higher aims: first, to make AFLAC Japan a success—which as yet no one believed it capable of—and then to make it a winner, a major player in the Japanese insurance industry.

Knowing his penchant for planning, his close friends were not exactly shocked when Otake passed up the chance to head the new company. Nor were they surprised when he arranged to have a senior government official "descend from heaven" (*amakudari*) to fill that post. But everyone was taken aback when the head of MOF's insurance division was named to run AFLAC in Tokyo. Otake had scored another coup. Now MOF was directly connected to the little firm and vice versa. Under no circumstances could it now be allowed to fail.

But Otake wasn't finished yet. He brought in the former head of the Ministry of Health and Welfare's Insurance Bureau, plus another MOF official, and a former director of the Export–Import Bank as branch vice-presidents. Then he hired experienced managers from companies such as Tokio Marine & Fire Insurance,

Tokyo Life Insurance, Tokyo Bank, TV Tokyo, and so on to serve as department heads. Even old pal Kawamura was impressed: "He brought in people from various fields, various related companies and government agencies and instilled in all of them the need for the company to succeed. He actually gave these people a sense of responsibility and motivation in working for this little start-up company."

The next step in making the company successful was to get out and sell policies. Originally, the management had thought about doing things the way the U.S. parent did, sending its own staff out to sell the idea of cancer insurance and gradually building up a network of sales reps to do the same. But that idea was already on the back burner by the time MOF's approval came down. As we saw earlier, Otake had been going around the provinces suggesting to companies that they set up subsidiaries to sell AFLAC insurance to their own employees. With the repercussions from the oil shock still reverberating in Japanese society, companies were now lining up to win approval from AFLAC Japan to sell its insurance. The press reported that up to 40 people a day were coming to the company's offices requesting to become agents. AFLAC had only to pick and choose—and from some of the top companies in Japan.

Aside from the big companies' desire to spin off subsidiaries and lighten their payrolls, why was there so much interest in the AFLAC plan? The answer lies in the pay structure of these firms. Japanese companies pay their employees through direct bank transfers, automatically withholding taxes and insurance payments through the same system. Thus to deduct a small sum (AFLAC policies cost about $25 per month and the premiums are fixed for life at the time of purchase) from an employee's salary and transfer that fee to another firm every month requires only a single computer entry. Yet the company makes a small commission for each transaction, which means it obtains a steady income stream month after month for as long as each employee stays with the parent firm—typically 30 years or more. All this for keying in one small deduction to the payroll computer. And of course selling the policy to the employees, but that is a relatively easy matter.

Most of these firms would either set up a separate subsidiary or a new department within the main company to sell insurance.

Their own personnel departments would produce data on their employees' current insurance coverage; then the company sales-people would go around to each one offering cancer insurance. An important factor was that this was being offered *through the company*, not by some outside agent hawking insurance in the lobby. In Japan it is a rare employee who can just say no to any reasonably good product that his or her company is pushing. In this case the insurance was a very good product for a very good price and the fees were automatically deducted, so it was even easier to sign up.

In other words, each big company's employees were practically a captive market, so the income that could be generated from selling insurance policies was substantial. At the same time, having the companies collect the insurance fees rather than hiring a nationwide staff to do so was much cheaper for AFLAC. This approach helped to keep policy prices down, which helped to sell more policies.

It was an ideal system for everyone: the companies loved being able to put part of their bloated payrolls to work on something productive (and this was a very profitable business); the employees were happy to get good insurance coverage cheap; and AFLAC was the happiest of all, for it just grew and grew, gaining instant access to hundreds of thousands of employees at Japan's top com-panies, people it would have had trouble approaching even with an army of professional salespeople. Instead, AFLAC kept its own payroll slim and let its corporate agents go out and sell the products.

Japanese life insurance firms normally maintain vast armies of salespeople (the biggest firms have close to 100,000 each) to ring doorbells and try to convince people to buy insurance. AFLAC neatly bypassed both the costs and the inefficiencies of this system by having corporations sell insurance to their own staff and banks sell to their clients. Simply by eliminating the operating costs involved in using tens of thousands of salespeople, the company saved a fortune.

Monopoly

A year after obtaining a license from MOF, AFLAC hired Yoshiyuki Oda (now a director) from Yasuda Life Insurance. Oda was a pro who knew all about the business and had some specific ideas of his own. One of them turned out to be a very successful new product: a fixed monthly-deposit bank account tied to the depositor's cancer insurance policy. With this system the interest on the customer's bank account paid the insurance premium. The depositors got "free" insurance, and the banks got a terrific new service to offer their clients just at a time when they were losing depositors to the national postal savings high-interest accounts. Once again the corporate "agents" (the banks) were delighted with the system, and were only too happy to sell the product to their customers, which meant that AFLAC had little more to do than write up new policies as fast as it could and watch the money roll in.

Readers will perhaps not be too surprised to learn that today every city and regional bank throughout Japan sells AFLAC-backed insurance. That alone is a phenomenal achievement. But even more, 9 out of 10 of Japan's listed companies are also AFLAC agents. Roughly 90 percent of the firms on the Tokyo Stock Exchange sell the firm's products to their employees. Only 20 years after obtaining a license, AFLAC Japan accounts for 90 percent of all cancer insurance in Japan and 85 percent of all new contracts. If there is a *gaishi* company that has a bigger market share with a comparable sales volume, we haven't found it. In fact, there are only a small handful of foreign-backed companies that report higher annual income, and none of them has a hammerlock on its market in the way that American Family does.

The logical question is "Why?" How can a foreign firm come into the Japanese market, launch a new product, clean up big and then keep right on growing, increasing revenues without sacrificing market share? It doesn't seem possible. As we have seen again and again (e.g., the chapters on P&G or Nestle, for example), the normal pattern is for a foreign company to introduce a new product, only to have it immediately copied by Japanese rivals, get caught in a price war, and finally be squeezed out of the market or left with a much smaller share. How has AFLAC managed to maintain an almost total monopoly position for so many years?

There were several reasons. For example, we have already seen that one key to AFLAC's tremendous success was its use of the "corporate agent system" to represent its products. But that only leads back to the same question: Why didn't other Japanese insurance firms copy the same system and use their extensive corporate group connections to make it work even better?

The answer to the riddle goes back to Otake's long-term strategy. After fighting against the government bureaucracy for so long, he was determined to turn it into a powerful ally, and his strategy paid off to the tune of several billion dollars. The simple truth is that one of the most important reasons why AFLAC succeeded as it did has to do with its "godfather": the Ministry of Finance.

Consider the commission system, a common enough structure overseas, but not in Japan. Until AFLAC entered the market, all insurance salespeople were paid a salary. AFLAC was the first to introduce a commission system, and for several years it was the only company that MOF allowed to employ sales agents on a strictly commission basis.

But even this pales next to the principal reason for AFLAC's early growth during the years when we would normally expect the bigger firms to have devoured its market share. Former Chairman John Amos explained the company's unbelievable good fortune as follows: "We were granted a monopoly on the underwriting of supplemental cancer insurance for a period of three years . . . The monopoly was extended from year to year for a total of eight years. And then in the interest of an orderly market in the insurance industry, only a few of the small- to medium-sized companies with limited agency forces were allowed to compete. This was not a gratuitous favor to us but was designed—in total accord with Japanese custom—to ensure the success of our undertaking.

In other words we might say that the ministry took steps to shelter its investment.

MOF had two big worries back when it was first considering the AFLAC application: 1) that cancer insurance would hurt the national health program, and 2) that the company might be granted a license only to go bankrupt shortly thereafter in the glaring spotlight of media scrutiny. MHW took care of the first concern by reporting that it saw no conflict with the national health insurance scheme. AFLAC itself helped to alleviate the second concern by hiring ex-MOF officials and other top insurance people to watch over its development, and by setting up hundreds of corporate agency contracts throughout Japan right from the start. But MOF provided the real "insurance" for its own decision by setting up a de facto monopoly making sure that the little company would not have to compete with Japan's mammoth life insurers or anyone else for a few years. No other insurance company was able to offer cancer insurance until 1982, *eight years* after AFLAC won its license, and then only two small firms were allowed to do so. Seven more firms—none of them giant players—entered the competition in 1988, a full 14 years after AFLAC.

Fourteen years is a long time to have the market more or less to yourself. In a sense MOF gave the little American company a "patent" on cancer insurance. By the time a few other companies were beginning to offer the product, AFLAC had almost 10 *million* policies in force. This government protection, combined with AFLAC's own sales strategy, allowed the firm to grow big enough quickly enough that it no longer needed to be protected. It may be interesting to note that this is exactly the same strategy that the government used to nurture Japan's steel companies, car companies, and so on, but instead of barring foreign competition to protect domestic industry, the Ministry of Finance did the reverse.

The icing on the cake, however, was that after MOF finally did lift the firm's monopoly privileges, it gave it back something almost as valuable. Through its infamous "administrative guidance" (unofficial orders to industry), MOF put the company's use of corporate sales agencies under lock and key. In Amos's words, "Our corporate captive agency system was so successful that MOF decided that its spread to other companies would be *chaotic* for an orderly industry and thus . . . . ministerial guidance indicates that no other company may establish such a system" (italics ours).

The moral of the story? If you want to set up a company in Japan, it doesn't hurt to hire a few former top officials from whatever ministry is in charge of regulating your business to sit on your board of directors.

New Products, New Home

The AFLAC story actually goes on and on, though we only have space for a few highlights here. After 10 years of selling only cancer insurance, the Japan branch began to grow even beyond the scope of its parent's business. In that year it began to offer "Dementia Care Insurance," a first not only in Japan but in the world. With the growing awareness of Japan's aging society and the old tradition of having three or even four generations under one roof, the prospect of caring for an elderly relative became more and more of a burden. Otake's planners knew that dementia insurance was necessary and would become increasingly so, but it didn't exist. So they created it. The following year it won a Nikkei Annual Best Product Award, which helped to publicize it further. Today the company holds a 95 percent share of that market.

The firm went on to expand its policy offerings to cover other kinds of care, especially for the aged. In 1990 it introduced "Super Cancer" policies that pay as soon as cancer is diagnosed. This was a big change from the Japanese norm, where the patient is expected to pay for hospital fees, drugs, therapy, etc., and then be reimbursed later by an insurance program. The results were predictable: people signed up for new policies at a fantastic rate. One new dementia care product sold 90,000 policies in its first year. Today the firm holds 98 percent of the market for bedridden care insurance.

To celebrate its steady stream of successes, the company built its own headquarters building on the western side of Tokyo. Of course that entailed a tremendous expense, but the intangible results were more than worth it. Most *gaishi* firms, no matter how big or small, rent their office space. The message to the Japanese market should be "Japanese land prices are ridiculous." But that is not the way that local companies perceive this situation. Instead they see it as a sign of planned impermanence. Renting sends a message that says, "If things get bad, we can easily pull up stakes and get out of here," and the rapid shift of foreign company offices out of Tokyo during the recent recession seemed to prove the point. For that reason, a number of *gaishi* that want to send a very different message—"we're here, we're staying; get used to it"— decide to bite the bullet and buy their own headquarters. We have seen successful consumer products companies such as P&G, BMW, and others mentioned here take this route because they wanted an image of stability, permanence, and serious commitment to the local market. But even non-consumer businesses (e.g., Swiss Bank and Deutsche Bank) have expended huge sums to have their own highly visible buildings in downtown Tokyo. AFLAC didn't need that kind of visiblity, but it was happy to sink permanent roots in this market and to let the world know that it was in Japan to stay.

One of Otake's goals during the company's first two decades was to make it as "Japanese" as possible. Now he's rethinking that strategy. "I have worked hard to eliminate any American style or American flavor from our management," he says. "The American style of doing business is sometimes too pushy, and that only invites a negative reaction from Japanese clients.

"But in Sepember of 1993 our total capital topped ¥1 trillion ($10 billion), and our policies in force topped the 10 million mark. We've become one of the most prominent foreign firms in Japan, and it's in this situation that I've been thinking it is time to introduce a more international atmosphere to our business. Looking at Japan today, we'd have to say that it doesn't meet international standards in important areas like politics and business. Moreover, Japan's singular ways have caused increasing friction with other countries. In light of all this I am convinced that it is time for AFLAC to do what it can to promote internationalization."

As just one of those steps, in January 1994 the company added an American member to its board of directors. There are many *gaishi* that have board members sent from the home office; AFLAC Japan is a very rare case of a *gaishi* firm that operated entirely with Japanese staff for 20 years, became a huge success, and then decided to put Americans on its board.

Likewise, many *gaishi* firms have foreign secretaries. In part this is to deal with the head office, but it is also to facilitate communication with foreign customers and inquiries. But in American Family's case, its entire business in Japan is with Japanese. It is a totally domestic company and has no need whatsoever for foreign staff. Thus the hiring of two Chinese women as secretaries is all the more remarkable. It appears that these moves came simply from AFLAC Japan's dissatisfaction at Japan's slow pace of internationalization.

In June of 1993 President Otake became the chairman of the Foreign Affiliated Companies Management Association (FAMA), a group of *gaishi* that work to improve their situation in Japan and to make it easier for other foreign-affiliated firms to enter and succeed in the local market. Ironically perhaps, he has become an outspoken critic of the government bureaucracy and a vociferous champion of deregulation.

How Do You Spell Success?

AFLAC Japan accounts for roughly 82 percent of its parent company's total worldwide revenues and about 88 percent of total worldwide assets. The firm ranks number 16 out of 30 Japanese insurance firms in terms of premium income, and number 18 in terms of total assets. In terms of total declared income, AFLAC Japan ranks around number 128 out of *all* registered Japanese corporations, and number 6 among *gaishi* firms. It has accumulated more than $15 billion in total assets, and now generates annual pre-tax operating earnings of roughly $450 million. That's not bad for just 20 years of effort by a small, start-up company, especially one without a big name or a powerful parent firm to back it up. AFLAC's success in Japan is truly extraordinary, yet it shows what foreign firms are capable of if they have a good idea, good management, and dogged determination not to give up.

AFLAC succeeded in Japan by being extremely persistent (stubborn, MOF would say) and also by being extremely clever. Otake's negotiations with the ministry must have been very, very convincing for the top man in the Insurance Division to decide to head up the little venture, but his presence and that of other bureaucrats and insurance industry officials aided tremendously in convincing giant corporate clients that the firm was for real.

But perhaps the most interesting part of the AFLAC tale is how it turned two of the biggest complaints foreign firms have about the Japanese system to its advantage: bureaucratic protection of industry and the *keiretsu* system.

Almost every big *gaishi* has some kind of a run-in with the infamous bureaucracy—AFLAC certainly did. And yet when the waiting and lobbying and pleading were all over, the ministry sheltered the little American firm to an unprecedented degree, protecting it from Japanese competition. In addition, AFLAC's use of corporate agencies to sell its products turned the *keiretsu* clubbiness of Japanese industry into a money machine. For example, at an early stage the company developed a relationship with Dai–Ichi Kangyo Bank, which employs tens of thousands of people directly or indirectly. DKB has two agency subsidiaries selling American Family's policies, and between the two they have over a quarter of a million people insured. Moreover, the bank is the nucleus of an enormous *keiretsu* including other corporate giants such as the Itochu trading house, Ishikawajima–Harima Heavy Industries, Isuzu Motors, Shimizu Construction, and dozens more. The bank could easily recommend sales to these companies (if any of them were not already signed up with AFLAC) and their thousands upon thousands of subsidiaries. Thus the little insurance company from the "backwoods of Georgia" managed not only to break into the *keiretsu* system, but actually to become a member of all the big *keiretsu*. This is a remarkable, indeed, a unique achievement.

More than this, the company can honestly claim to have changed the quality of life in Japan. Not just for a few customers but for millions of people nationwide. Amway can boast that it has 1 percent of the entire population of Japan registered to sell its products (although the majority are buying without actively selling anything). American Family has over 12 percent of all Japanese households as clients, paying premiums month after month, and the numbers are still growing. No nongovernment insurance company has as large a percentage of households covered in any country in the world.

Welcome to the closed Japanese market.

CHAPTER 8

Door-to-Door Success

Amway

One of the hardest things for any foreign company to do in Japan is to set up a sales network. It takes time, money, and a great deal of effort. Hiring experienced salespeople away from other companies is difficult, yet it is essential to have native salespeople to represent your products. And once hired, they still need training in your own company's sales approach and product line. In many cases, the best shortcut is to take advantage of the *tonya* system, as we described previously. However, this also requires considerable time, effort, and skill in getting the *tonya* to represent your products. Some *gaishi* understand the power of the *tonya*, and so make the investment needed to become part of that system (e.g., Levi Strauss). Others try to go around the system entirely, investing instead in their own direct sales approach (e.g., Coca-Cola).

There is another way, however. One famous American company came to Japan less than 20 years ago and beat the system two ways: it not only bypassed the *tonya*, but also spent very little on training its sales force. Best of all it managed to attract over a million Japanese to sell its products without putting any of them on the company payroll, and then got them to recruit other people to do the same. How successful is this approach? Today close to one percent of the entire population of Japan is registered to represent this company's products, the firm is already one of the top five *gaishi*, and if it continues to grow as it has, it will soon be ranked among the top 100 firms in all of Japanese industry. Without a doubt, Amway is one of the greatest success stories of its kind.

Becoming a Distributor

The American parent company, Amway Corp., sells detergents and soaps, cosmetics, kitchen utensils, food supplements, and so on through a network of sales representatives it calls "distributors." All sales are done through these distributors, not through store outlets.

Consequently Amway does not hire salespeople, which means it does not need a huge payroll. The company exists to sell consumer products, but unlike other firms mentioned in this book, it doesn't have to worry about coordinating far-flung armies of regional sales representatives or financing their health care and pension plans. All of Amway's "distributors" are independent operators, most of them housewives who also use the products they sell. In addition, they introduce friends, neighbors, coworkers, family members, etc., to the company's product line and to the idea of buying at a discount and selling at a small profit. If asked, the majority of today's roughly one million distributors would say something like, "I was introduced to Amway by a friend in our apartment building."

Each distributor begins by buying an $80 starter kit that contains everything needed to get into business: a sales manual, a price list, a guide to most of the firm's more than 120 products, various kinds of receipts and billing forms, and an outline of the company's philosophy. Registered distributors can buy the company's products at about a 30 percent wholesale discount. They may simply want to use these goods themselves or they may choose to sell them to friends. They may even order larger volumes of the products and sell them to friends who sell them to their friends. In this way the distributors have two functions: to sell the merchandise and to serve as "sponsors"; that is, to encourage friends to become distributors. As their sales (and those of the distributors they introduced) reach a certain level, they also receive a bonus. If they raise their sales beyond another fixed level, they become a leader of a group of distributors, called a "direct distributor." In some cases, distributors buy their goods not from the company but from a direct distributor who buys directly from the company. The direct distributor handles the bonuses for the distributors in his or her group.

One indication of the company's burgeoning growth is that the number of distributors has doubled in the last five years. Of course many of these people are simply buying Amway products for themselves at a discount, but the company says that about 30 percent are real sales agents, what it calls active distributors. And in the Japanese marketing world, having 300,000 people actively representing your products to friends and neighbors, all for no salary, classifies as a stupendous success.

The average annual income for most active distributors works out to around $2,000 per year, perhaps not a huge sum, but a significant addition to a housewife's budget. For those who are more serious, the 4,000-plus direct distributors who consider Amway their main business (most of whom are also housewives), the average annual income from this business is nearly $50,000. There is also a hierarchy of direct distributors based on sales performance, with classifications like Ruby, Pearl, Emerald, and Diamond indicating one's ranking. There are over 100 direct distributors at the rank of Diamond and above, and their average annual income is an astonishing $268,000. This is the lure that keeps many new salespeople coming into the system and keeps many more on the active list year after year. Most people don't believe that they will ever have Diamond-level incomes, but the stories of others who have serve to reinforce the fundamental Amway work ethic: the more you sell, the more you make. It's completely democratic in a way that almost nothing else in Japanese society is: no one cares what school you went to or what your family name is or what kind of car you drive. Those who work hard prosper. And that concept—what used to be called the American dream—has a tremendous appeal for the Japanese.

American Dreams

The tremendous success of Amway in Japan has been a huge boost for the parent company, which began by creating its own American dream (the name comes from "American way") about 35 years ago.

The parent company started business in 1959 when two good friends, Jay Van Andel and Richard M. DeVos, were working as distributors of a California-based food supplement direct-sales company called Nutrilite. They learned direct sales from the bottom up, then went independent, initially selling household cleansers and detergents. Van Andel explained their approach something like this: "There are two ways to operate a direct sales business. One is to hire top professional salespeople; the other is to create an environment in which anyone can sell your products. We opted for the latter."

Their basic concept was to sell daily household necessities, the kinds of things that a large group of consumers wants, things that do not need to be heavily promoted. These are goods that anyone can sell with a bare minimum of sales training.

"The demand is right there waiting for you," Van Andel says, "The distributor's job is to say to the customer 'You buy certain goods all the time at the supermarket; instead, I'll personally supply you with better quality goods for the same price. And if for any reason you're not happy with them, I'll refund your money in full.'"

The pair knew their market pretty well. The idea of people with no special skills or training working their way to wealth caught on rapidly in America. By 1972 Amway had absorbed Nutrilite, and today the company has over two million distributors operating in dozens of countries worldwide, and it is still growing.

The Early Years in Japan

Amway opened for business in Japan in May of 1979. At the time, Takeshi Kure (today the company's vice-president) was looking for a job. A graduate of Cornell University's engineering department who spoke English comfortably, Kure had been working for Olivetti, but as our chapter on that firm will show, many of its good staff were heading out the door at that time, and Kure was one of them.

"I wanted to change jobs, so I went to a big placement outfit. They told me about some new American company starting up, so I went for an interview. The office was on a street lined with warehouses down in Shinagawa ward (at the time, a less than attractive part of Tokyo). I thought they must have rented this space just for the interviews. No, I was told, this was the company's headquarters." In spite of the poor first impression, Kure wound up joining the firm. On his first day at work the entire staff was assembled and everyone helped log in the money from incoming orders (the few orders already trickling in came in the mail with cash enclosed), then packed the merchandise in boxes for shipping, and then everyone went home.

Kure liked the people he met, but he knew that this wasn't a very auspicious start for a company that was hoping to be big in Japan. But Amway's system always started small, the staff was reassured. It would grow in time. Just wait and have a little faith.

Sometimes customers came to the office to pick up their merchandise in person. Kure recalls, "We were excited whenever we had a chance to talk to a distributor. We found that they were very happy with the products and we began to gain a little confidence."

The company's very first market was a logical one—the foreign community. Because the company was still unknown in Japan, it recruited *gaijin* distributors, people who had already heard of Amway back home and knew something of its reputation, and much of their marketing was aimed at friends and contacts in the foreign community. While that was a good way to bring in the first few orders, the total market potential was minuscule. What the company needed was to break out of the *gaijin* community and find some Japanese distributors.

The current head of Amway Japan's customer service division, Nobuhiro Tsuda, explains how the firm got its foothold in Japan: "We sent letters to distributors in ten foreign countries asking them to send us the names of friends in Japan. We wound up with a list of about 1,000 names."

They took the list, mapped it geographically, and organized introductory sessions throughout Japan. Then they sent out direct invitations to the people on the list, saying something like "Your friend *Jane Smith* suggested we contact you about an exciting new business opportunity. Please join us for a special introductory session on the 12th of next month . . . ."

Not surprisingly, the list included a very large number of people who had worked or studied overseas. Many of those who received invitation letters were delighted to think that coworkers, professors, or fellow students overseas were thinking of them. Rather than treating the invitations as junk mail, they saw them as a kind of "thinking of you" contact from overseas, and a fairly high percentage attended the company's introductory talks. On average, the people on the list turned out to be interesting, intelligent, and well spoken. In other words, they were an ideal group of lay salespeople with which to begin a business.

But trekking around Japan to make the presentations, explain the Amway concept, and sign up distributors was no easy task. Tsuda says, "We'd pack an 8mm movie projector to explain the business, plus our sample goods, lots of starter kits, and of course our own clothes and personal things. It came to an unbelievable amount of luggage for each of us to tote around the provinces. We'd sleep in a different town every night, leave our suits to be cleaned in one city and pick them up on our way back down the same highway. In a busy month we'd do upwards of 60 presentations. It was exhausting, and we did it for the best part of a year."

But the legwork paid off: "About 10 to 20 percent of those who came to our sessions signed up as distributors. We tried to create a friendly atmosphere, not give a hard sales pitch. We said something like, 'We want you to try our products; if you like them, we want you to show them to your family and friends.' I think we had a few thousand names by the end of the first year."

From that first group of new distributors, the word about Amway began to spread. Younger people, especially young housewives (who at the time very seldom held part-time jobs), began to join the program, and as more young people became distributors, the energy and enthusiasm that they put into promoting the company's goods spurred higher sales.

Jerry Rosenberg (now an executive at Nippon Motorola) served as marketing manager during the firm's first decade. He divides that first era into four growth periods, each lasting between two and three years. In the first period, he says, the big challenge was to make Amway's business understood and to give it a foundation from which to grow. The first distributors and first customers were largely foreigners living in and around Tokyo. The principal goods sold were mostly cleansers, detergents, and pots and pans, things that could be explained quickly and easily even to people who didn't know Amway. In the second period the main focus switched to increasing the number of Japanese distributors and broadening the product line. Nutritional supplements and cosmetics were now part of the Amway kit, and this also became a source of friction with the Japanese bureaucracy. There was a thick knot of government regulations controlling the importation and sale of products such as food supplements and cosmetics. These required special approval from the Ministry of Health and Welfare (most still do), and obtaining that approval was no easy matter.

"Vitamins and other food supplements could not be packed in containers with green tops," Rosenberg recalls, "it just wasn't allowed. The regulations were extremely detailed. Labels had to be done this way and packaging had to be done that way, and so we were told to change everything if we wanted to bring it into Japan. " In fact, cosmetics were so bound up in local regulations (many designed simply to protect Japanese makers) that the firm wound up consigning manufacture to a Japanese company rather than try to import its own. Ultimately this proved beneficial, as we will see later on, but at the time the difficulties of dealing with the bureaucracy seemed beyond comprehension.

By the third phase the number of direct distributors was growing rapidly. Amway no longer had to struggle to spread the word about its products. Also, with the addition of vitamins and cosmetics to cleansers and utensils, the company's product line was now better balanced, which also helped to improve sales.

Into and beyond the fourth stage, the company became even more solid. Today the product line has been further expanded, filling in gaps between some product categories, and both product quality and packaging have been improved.

Amway became so successful by the end of its first decade that other firms, even well-established Japanese companies, wanted to take advantage of its marketing prowess. For example, in 1988 consumer electronics maker Sharp Corp. agreed to tie up with Amway to sell one of its products, an electric induction range that heats only a metal frying pan and the food in it while remaining cool to the touch. Amway manager William Hemmer explained in an interview the following year, "Sharp had the product, but it wasn't selling well in stores. We worked with them, packaged the product, and now it's so popular we can't keep it in stock."[1]

The company went on to launch other new products based on cooperative design and development efforts with Japanese companies. Today it includes a number of such "outside" products in its catalog and several times that many firms are lined up to get Amway to consider putting their products into its formidable distribution machine.

Crisis Management

Amway's only real challenge since coming to Japan came during the late 1980s when the new Direct Sales Law was enacted. The law was a response to a rash of door-to-door selling schemes that sprang up during that decade. Some of them were legitimate, but quite a few were sheer frauds. As consumers felt increasingly vulnerable to unscrupulous salespeople working their way through residential neighborhoods, the newspapers and television were flooded with stories warning people to beware of these door-to-door hucksters. MITI drew up new regulations to severely restrict this kind of activity, passed them to the Diet (the national legislature), and they became law.

There were a number of real targets of the law. One of them was the infamous "pyramid-type" sales operation in which a small company starts a sales business by recruiting a dozen or so individuals to represent a product. They recruit others who recruit others, and if the system works well, soon thousands of people are selling the product. The advantage to the organizer is that profits flow upwards, and those at the top of the pyramid continue to receive a percentage of all sales long after they have stopped doing any work except going to the bank. Hundreds of thousands of people would be lured into these sales organizations with the idea that if they worked hard for a year or two, they could retire for life with the income they would receive from people lower down in the pyramid. Unfortunately this was true, but only for the tiny handful of people who started the program in the first

[1] Peter E. Fuchs, "Amway Leads the Way," *Business Tokyo*, November 1989; Keizaikai Co., Tokyo

place. Everyone else got less than they bargained for, and their complaints were falling hard on local politicians and the officials in MITI.

The problem was that the law "fell on the just and the unjust alike." Although Amway was nothing like the scams that the law was designed to curtail, the regulations had the potential to put a very big obstacle in the path of the company's fast-track growth in Japan. So Amway's staff began an all-out campaign to make clear that it was not part of these pyramid sales schemes and that its business was structurally different from such "get rich quick" plans. The company explained that even though it works to increase the number of distributors in its network, if those distributors do not sell a sizable amount of merchandise they will not earn bonuses. In other sales systems, once a pyramid has been constructed the people at the top are guaranteed a substantial income even if they do nothing. Amway's fundamental principle is rooted in the old Protestant work ethic: hard work yields good rewards. The idea of "do nothing and earn big money" was somebody else's American dream, not Amway's. If a high-ranking distributor does not keep working and keep selling, his or her rank will fall, and so will revenue. In other words, there is no annuity in the Amway system; work—and only work—yields profit.

Although only a newcomer in the Japanese marketplace, Amway's fast growth had given it some clout. The firm became a member of the board of directors of the Nihon Homon Hanbai Kyokai, the industry association of Japan's top direct sales companies, all of whom, like Amway, wanted the scam artists run out of the business. The firm lobbied hard to revise the law so that it would restrict the operations it was designed to restrict, but not affect legitimate firms like Amway that are clearly benefitting rather than harming the Japanese consumer. After some time, the government recognized that the Amway system is not a problem and the law was changed.

One of the big issues in the law is the problem of refunds, which were nonexistent with some of these sales schemes. The new law provided a "cooling off" period of eight days after any purchase from one of these businesses. During that period, any consumer who is not happy with the product can return it for a refund, and the company that sold it must offer such a refund. Amway pointed out that it already offers much more than an eight-day refund period for the majority of its products. This is not limited to durables such as pots and pans, but extends to consumables. "For example, if you try our cleansers or food supplements and decide you don't like them, we'll refund the entire purchase price—even if there's only a very small amount left," explains Junko Iwaki, head of the company's public relations division. "In fact, if someone becomes a distributor and later wants to quit, we'll refund the full ¥8,000 starter kit fee."

Protecting the consumer is part of the Amway philosophy, and this had a lot to do with convincing the Japanese government to revise the law on direct sales. In addition to its return and refund policies, Amway insists that its distributors observe a strict code of behavior and anyone who does not follow the rules quickly loses the right to distribute Amway products. Unlike other mass-sales systems, however, Amway also tries to protect its salespeople. For example, the firm will not allow college students to become distributors. Why not? There have been cases of Japanese college students (generally speaking, a far more naive group than their Western counterparts) who have signed up for other direct sales programs, bought huge quantities of some product, and then, when they found that they couldn't sell it, committed suicide. The company wants to prevent this kind of problem at all costs.

From the beginning Amway knew that to succeed in Japan it must be responsive to both the needs and feelings of its customers. From the time it started business, the firm set up a customer service office to handle questions, complaints, and suggestions about its products and services. In addition, the company's phone number is plainly printed on every product label so that customers will feel free to call with questions or comments. More recently, this function of responding to customer inquiries was decentralized. The firm set up eight separate customer service centers throughout Japan and staffed them with people whose only job is to respond to such calls and follow up where appropriate. At regular intervals these centers forward a summary of all questions and comments they receive to the firm's Tokyo headquarters, which translates them into English and sends them back to the home office in the United States. In this way, the entire organization, from top to bottom, is constantly made aware of Japanese consumer reactions to its products, policies, and personnel.

How to Process a Few Million Orders

One of the things that has helped Amway to grow so quickly in Japan is its distribution system. At first the firm handled all orders by mail. But with about a million distributors ordering from a selection of 120 different products, the company was in danger of drowning in its own paperwork. Most critical was the problem of time: order placement had to be speeded up so that orders could be shipped and put in customers' hands much faster. At first the company tried taking orders by facsimile instead of by mail. That helped to speed up the system, but only marginally. In 1985 Amway introduced the first automatic order entry system in the Japanese home-sales industry. It works much like the kind of systems that are used by airlines for flight reservations. People can call Amway on a push-button phone, be greeted by a computer voice, and then follow simple instructions on how to place their orders just by pushing buttons on their telephones. In this way a large number of orders can be received and inputted directly into the computer system automatically, greatly reducing the need for trained staff to keep up with the growing volume of orders. And needless to say, the system runs 24 hours a day and handles calls on Saturdays, Sundays, and holidays without charging overtime.

Once taking in all those orders was automated, the firm had to speed up the order processing at its distribution centers. Until several years ago employees had to physically examine each individual order slip, pick through a selection of 300 products, choose the right size cartons, and then pack each order. Not only was it extremely time-consuming, but it invited error and mistakes were common. Here, too, the solution was to switch to a computerized operation, so the firm codeveloped a paperless picking and packing system. In the first phase, a machine read each order slip, chose the appropriate cardboard carton for packing, and displayed the correct item number and quantity for the staff to pack and ship. Even with that system the company says it almost eliminated packing errors. But more sophisticated machines were developed, and now many orders can be entirely processed and packed automatically. Finished boxes are then divided by delivery region using bar codes and prepared for distribution.

There are two big gift-giving seasons in Japan, one at the middle of the year (called *o-chugen*) and the other at the end of the year (*o-seibo*). Amway found that many of its products were selling particularly well during these two seasons. Customers were ordering quantities of merchandise but asking to have it sent to different addresses. This was a terrific business, but first someone had to read the addresses on the order forms and input them into a computer—which in the case of Japanese addresses is no simple matter. Several years ago the company recognized that processing these gift orders was becoming a bottleneck in its efforts to improve its distribution efficiency, and developed an OCR (computerized optical character recognition) system that could read Japanese handwriting and input it as text into a computer. Just the time it saved in printing labels was a major plus for the firm.

Also, every year there is a minor panic at the firm when it comes time for distributors to renew their contracts. In the United States, Amway hires hundreds of telephone operators to handle the flood of calls, and puts on extra staff to deal with all the paperwork. In Japan today they use OCR to handle the whole thing and so can process tens of thousands of renewals in a day.

No matter how well the order-taking and distribution process is executed, it still takes some time, which is why for many years some local distributors have come directly to the distribution centers to make their purchases. Usually this business was done in cash, which meant long lines of cars in front of the centers and lots of cash transactions. In 1988 the company switched to using bank cash cards. Customers simply put their bank cards into a special machine, punch in their code numbers and the amount of their purchase, and the machine debits their bank account and transfers the correct amount to Amway's account. So far the combination of automated picking and packing and increasingly automated payments is a big hit with staff and customers alike.

Vice-President Kure adds that "the distribution centers send all order and shipping data to the U.S. headquarters. We update it every day and we do rigorous inventory control. About 25 percent of all the products we handle in Japan are made here, mostly cosmetics. But roughly 75 percent of our products (right down to the Japanese labels) are made in America. So inventory control is critical for us."

Durables + Consumables = Long-term Profit Picture

As we noted, Amway began doing business in Japan with basic household goods, like cleansers and detergents, and then expanded into kitchen utensils and other consumer durables. In fact, one of the company's all-time biggest hits was a $1,500 set of pots and pans. Of course, such consumer "durables" are more expensive, which means they have substantial profit potential for the distributors. However, they are normally buy-once items; in other words, they don't generate the same kind of repeat business as do basic household items like detergents. While selling durables is rewarding, it is unwise to depend too heavily on such products in the long term. A few years ago, the firm developed a way to get the best of both worlds—it began selling water treatment systems in Japan.

Home-use water treatment systems were not new for Amway—they had been selling in the United States for ten years. But the company had hesitated to import them because it felt that many U.S. products are not suited to the Japanese market, either due to size or consumer tastes or some such thing. Also, most Japanese felt that their water was relatively clean. But as that general perception began to change, the idea of bringing over water filtering equipment from the U.S. market became more attractive. By Amway standards, the product is a big-ticket consumer durable, but unlike pots and pans it generates repeat business through the sale of special filters. In that sense it's an ideal product—a big sale up front followed by years of repeat orders for consumables. The product was redesigned for the local market, the price was set fairly steep (around $1,500 per unit), and it was launched in 1993. In its first six months the company's distributors sold roughly $130 million in water treatment systems, and the repeat business generated by those sales is substantial. Everyone knows that if it had been introduced ten years earlier it might have been a flop; instead, by waiting until demand was on the rise, the company created a monster hit.

"For the first ten years the products we sold in Japan and those we sold in the United States were quite different," says Bert Crandell, who heads Amway Japan's marketing department.

"Gradually, though, our American products were introduced to this market in one form or another. Currently, the only things in the houseware field that are sold in America but not here are air purifiers and vacuum cleaners. Of course, we've thought about selling those two, but the Japanese consumer electronics industry is so strong that it would be difficult to differentiate our products from the array of domestic units. And if we don't make them stand out in some way, they won't sell."

Crandell goes on to talk about the need to customize products for the Japanese market:

"For example, American water and Japanese water are different, so we had to change the content of our detergents. But we kept the packaging the same. With cosmetics we changed both the products and the packaging. Cosmetics for the Japanese market had to be absolutely top quality. In fact, the cosmetics we make for this market are now being sold in both the United States and Europe." Remember, these are cosmetics that had to be developed and produced in Japan because the Ministry of Health and Welfare would not allow free imports. Now that enforced localized production has turned into an unexpected profit center.

But what about the company's still high import ratio? Amway is selling cleansers and frying pans, not BMWs or designer handbags. Is the imported image a liability? Quite the contrary. Former executive William Hemmer noted some years back, "We had a meeting with some of our distributors . . . They told us to make the 'Made in America' labels even bigger."[2]

Creating a High Profile

In April 1991 Amway Japan listed its shares on Tokyo's OTC market. For a company as big as Amway this was not unusual; what *is* unusual is that Amway in the United States is *not* listed. President Richard S. Johnson comments: "There is an all-too-common image in Japan that *gaishi* companies are happy to set up in Japan and reap profits when times are good, but as soon as things turn bad they turn tail and disappear. We wanted to show that we're different. We're here to stay. We're part of this economy. Also, because

---

[2] Fuchs, "Amway Leads the Way."

Amway operates through its distributors, our corporate 'face' is not visible. Our decision to list was influenced partly by the desire to improve our image and give the company a higher profile."

In addition to listing, Amway set up seven large regional offices outside of Tokyo as a step towards reaching out to both its distributors and customers nationwide. These are more than just business offices; they also include showrooms, places where distributors and ordinary consumers can come in, handle the company's merchandise, talk to special consultants, and see for themselves what Amway is all about. They bring Amway to life, giving both the seller and the buyer something more than just a pretty catalog and some samples to look at. For example, the Osaka regional office is downtown, easily accessible, and staffed with 15 full-time product consultants. This has a big impact on making an "invisible" company like a home-sales firm seem more visible and more real, and that has an impact on sales.

Even at the Tokyo headquarters, distributors are now invited to bring their customers in to look around and see what's going on. Every week about 30 to 50 people come in, tour the building, see the products, and see a full-time, hardworking staff operating in a clean, efficient environment. Again, this kind of simple "Come meet us, see who we are" program can have a profound effect on changing people's images of a company. More *gaishi* firms should take the hint and open themselves up to their most important advertisers, their clients.

Overcoming Internal Communication Problems

President Johnson, who joined Amway Japan in 1991 (after a career with Pepsico, R.J. Reynolds, and Nippon Tupperware), has been pushing the company to come to grips with its structural problems, such as the alienation of its head office staff and its sales force:

"Our business rests on our distributors. But too many of our employees have no contact with distributors. Our 600 employees must go out one by one and meet the distributors. Our office staff needs to find out what the distributors are thinking and what they want. We have to improve communication with our distributors."

Johnson didn't just sit in his office and make this pronouncement —he led the way. He traveled around the country, meeting with distributors at all levels, asking what they were thinking, what bothered them, and what they thought the company could do better. He listened to what he heard and put several ideas into action immediately. He encouraged Amway's office staff to accompany distributors, to find out firsthand how the business works and be able to respond to distributor suggestions and complaints from a more experienced point of view. He also increased training sessions for distributors and insisted on providing them with better explanations about the products they would represent.

One of his biggest moves was to get upper-rank distributors to pass on their experience to newer or lower-rank distributors.

"Too many people become distributors, then grow dissatisfied and give it up. Recruiting and training new distributors is inefficient. We should aim to keep more of the people who do become distributors by keeping them satisfied. Having a higher renewal rate (distributors deciding to stay on) is better for the company and it's directly connected to our profit growth, but until a few years ago we didn't pay much attention to that approach. Also, too many distributors have not been selling our whole product line, only those items that they liked or knew about. If we increase the range of items the distributors represent, we will increase both their profits and our profits as well. This is a very basic idea, but until now our efforts in that area were insufficient."

These two basic lines of thought bubbled up from the network of regional offices that were established to improve communication with the distributors. And they worked. For example, once Johnson made boosting the distributors' renewal rate a priority, the figure rose to over 70 percent, not merely the highest figure in the company's history in Japan, but the highest anywhere in Amway's worldwide network.

An Inspired Idea

One of the firm's most inspired ideas began several years ago and is something of a "three birds with one stone" project. Amway Japan wanted to continue to strengthen its image with the Japanese public. It also wanted to find something that would unite all of its legions of distributors, something to give them a common bond other than merely buying and selling Amway products. The firm also wanted to join the growing environmental consciousness that was finally beginning to spread among Japanese corporations as well as citizen groups.

"It began in the late-1980s when we provided financial aid to a research team investigating the Arctic. We appealed to Japanese citizens to wake up to the spread of pollution, to understand the importance of environmental problems and the need to preserve nature. We also helped to form groups to rescue endangered species and to do other kinds of work to preserve the environment," explains PR head Iwaki. Soon the company was selling a whole new line of goods—pencils made of recycled materials, insect repellents made from camphor wood carved in the shape of animals, and so on. The products are sold to Amway distributors and they resell them at no markup. The profits thus generated are donated to an organization called Nature Center that the company set up. The Nature Center's main job is to do research and gather information on environmental-related projects worthy of donations. In just five years the Amway team raised about $2.5 million for various environmentally concerned organizations. This process helped to unite the company's far-flung network of distributors and gave them a new sense of meaning in their work. Instead of a group of hundreds of thousands of housewives, they became a movement helping to raise funds to preserve nature. That was good for the distributors' self-image, good for the environment, and good for Amway.

Can They Keep It Up?

In its first decade in Japan, Amway's sales grew in double digits every year. That figure slowed, of course, but only in the jaws of a brutal recession. Even so, the firm realizes that it has grown too big to count on double-digit growth in the future. But 99 percent of Japan's population is still not signed up as distributors, so there is plenty of room to grow.

One of the few restrictions on the company's growth is the government. Regulations still abound, especially those connected with the Ministry of Health and Welfare. There are bureaucratic restrictions on everything connected with the vitamin business, such as the size of food supplements, labelling, packaging, and so on. Health claims are also extremely tightly controlled. For example, it is all right to say that eating carrots is good for something if there is evidence to support it, but the bureaucrats will not allow a company to say that beta carotene (a significant nutrient in carrots) is good for the same thing. Why? Because beta carotene is seen as a proto-vitamin, not a medicine, so no specific medicinal claims can be made for it, regardless of any supporting evidence. These regulations are not likely to change anytime soon.

The company had a few problems in the past with the public at large, but they were not terribly serious. In fact Amway Japan is happy to report that over a period of several years there has been no serious complaint against the firm or its products made to any of the major consumer centers around the nation. However, there was some criticism of another kind. Some critics claimed that the whole Amway system is fundamentally a negative influence on Japanese society, that it puts mercenary motives into the hearts of average housewives and injects commerce into otherwise purely social relationships among family, friends and fellow workers.

The head of the company's customer service division, Nobuhiro Tsuda, responded to this criticism simply and effectively: "All Amway is saying is that we would like people to try our products. If they like the products and think the prices are fair, we'd like these people to join us to help show the products to more people. Our business is not about selling goods to your friends; it's about introducing friends to high-quality, reasonably-priced products, and that's why we're growing so fast. Really, Amway is like a great little restaurant with low prices: when you discover it you want to tell your friends about it. If they like it, great. Maybe they'll want to tell people about it, too. That's how we grow."

It certainly seems as if a lot of people have been telling a lot of friends about it. In 1994 Amway Japan's total sales reached close to $1.6 billion and operating profit was about $400 million (and these figures are based only on the company's declared income). That ranks Amway number 3 among all *gaishi* firms in Japan. Even more astonishing is that Amway ranks number 102 out of *all* companies in Japan (as of 1994). That puts it ahead of industrial and commercial giants such as Canon, Fanuc, Kawasaki Heavy Industries, Sumitomo Corp., and Mitsui Trust & Banking, among others. And remember, the first hundred slots in Japanese business are pretty well locked up by behemoths such as Toyota, Nissan, Hitachi, and Matsushita.

In addition, like many other *gaishi*, Amway's Japanese operation turns out to be not merely profitable on its own, but also a big contributor to the company's global profit picture: roughly speaking, Amway Japan's sales comprise one-third of all Amway sales worldwide.

How did it become so successful? By following the founders' principles of starting with simple, easy-to-sell products and by putting ever-greater efforts into developing—and keeping—its distributor network. An extra bonus came with the post-1985 rise of the yen. More than three-fourths of its products still come from abroad, denominated in ever-cheaper dollars.

But perhaps Amway's most successful step of all was the decision to start up in the Japanese market in the first place. Too many companies make the mistake of believing that Japan is just like America (or just like Europe) and that if they can succeed in those markets, they can easily succeed in Japan. But quite a few make the opposite mistake—believing that what they have developed in their home market could never succeed in Japan because the culture is too different. Both of these fallacies stem from a lack of understanding of what Japan and the Japanese market is all about. To some, bringing Amway's "American dream" philosophy to Japan may have seemed culturally inappropriate. After all, many foreign observers see Japan as a highly regimented, corporate-centered society where independent action (such as selling household merchandise to friends and neighbors) is almost impossible. Yet the Japanese took to Amway and its fundamental ideas of hard work and individual success with unrestrained zeal, and the results have been enormously profitable for everyone concerned. Amway has earned its place among *gaishi* success stories and has shown once again how much potential this market holds for companies that are willing to do it right.

CHAPTER 9

Writing Its Name Large

Parker Pen

Today Parker Pen is the world's number 1 maker of writing instruments, but its origins are as humble as they come. The firm began through the handiwork of a teacher in Wisconsin toward the end of the last century. In addition to teaching, John S. Parker also repaired students' pens, and often wondered if there wasn't a way to make a better pen mechanism.

The idea of using a pen based on capillary action had already appeared in the 1880s, but there was no way to control the amount of ink that flowed, which meant that sometimes a pen would stop writing and, when the user shook it or tried to coax more ink to flow, the pen would oblige by disgorging a huge, ugly black blob.

Parker designed his own pen so that just the right amount of ink was sent to the tip ("nib") of the pen so that it would write and continue to write smoothly. When he was satisfied that his design worked well, he went into business, and in 1892 established his own company. By the 1920s Parker had become a global business, with factories operating in the United States, Canada, and England. After World War II the firm had the top share worldwide in both fountain pens and ballpoint pens. It remained a family-owned business until 1985 when it was taken over by Manpower, a leading temporary staff company.

Under its new owners, Parker's strategy changed from producing very high-quality pens to mass-marketing cheap and medium-quality pens, aiming to expand both its market share and profits. Instead, profits fell and the firm wound up losing money. Worse, the staff, many of whom had been with Parker for years and were proud of its traditional high-quality image, lost much of their enthusiasm for the business.

Some of the executives saw the combination of sliding profits and the demoralization of the company as a call to action. One of them, Jacques G. Magry, used to be a Parker salesman in England. He had worked for the company for 40 years and was very well informed about the pen business. Magry led a group of six Parker executives who engineered a leveraged buyout of the firm. He became Group Chief Executive of the reborn Parker Pen Co. and moved the firm's head office to England. There he set about restoring Parker's image and once again turning out high-quality pens, which is how the firm grew to prominence in the Japanese market.

The Word Processor of the Ancients

Although there were some Parker pens in Japan even before the war, they really began to appear during the Occupation, as officials in MacArthur's GHQ pulled them out of khaki pockets to write memos. Parker pens became yet another symbol of America during those postwar years, and so, like every other portable piece of Americana, they soon found their way to the center of the black market in Tokyo, a district called Ameyayoko-cho just south of Ueno Station (the district still exists today, although its discount merchandise is no longer illicit. Well, *most* of its merchandise . . .). In any case, Ameyayoko-cho was the place to trade and sell anything of value, especially anything obtained in one way or another from the U.S. military. (One theory about the origin of the name is that the "Amé" sound comes from "America.") Everything from GI fatigues to coffee and chocolate and Parker pens turned up along this meandering side street. The very fact that there was a market for such writing instruments in the middle of the postwar depression was a good indication of the potential consumer demand, and sometime around 1955 a Japanese importer obtained a license as a Parker sales agent. From that beginning, the firm's legitimate business in Japan grew slowly for about the next 20 years.

In 1981 a 100 percent-owned subsidiary company was set up in Japan and took over importing and wholesaling the products. But before long things began to slow. One reason was that the fountain pen, the company's mainstay product and a symbol of innovation to the prewar generation, became a victim of modernization.

It is well known that the Japanese cherish their written language, and until very recently every educated person was expected to be able to write attractively with a brush and ink. Early in this century the fountain pen became the modern substitute for the old-fashioned brush. But by the 1980s two new waves of products were making even the "modern" pen obsolete. The one which has had the greatest impact on writing in general is what the Japanese call *wa-pro,* short for "electronic word processors". One no longer needs to remember exactly how to write a complex *kanji* character, merely to recognize it and choose it from a list of several candidates presented on a screen. In many cases the "writer" need only spell out words phonetically on a keyboard and the machine can actually guess most of the correct characters to use in the communication. The result is that young Japanese today, while they can read their language easily, are far less able to write it than their parents. The rapid commercialization and diffusion of cheaper and cheaper word processors has created a society in which most college students prefer to write even a postcard with one of the new machines because they make writing Japanese so much easier.

The other product that struck a death blow to the fountain pen business was at the opposite end of the technology spectrum: the disposable ballpoint pen. These first appeared many years earlier, but by the late 1970s they were ubiquitous, reliable, and cheap — you could buy a good one for about $0.40. So, whenever the need arose to write something that was inconvenient to do on an electronic word processor, out came the throwaway plastic ballpoint. Only die-hard traditionalists clung to the expensive, old-fashioned, inconvenient fountain pen. It was during these years that Parker's business in Japan all but dried up, and this global trend was one of the reasons that Parker's new management decided to shift to an emphasis on cheap, mass-market pens in the second half of the 1970s.

Juggling Presidents

In the six short years after 1981 when the local firm was founded, Parker Pen Japan had a Chinese president, a Swiss president, and an American president. Once a company develops the image of having a revolving door on the *shacho's* office, not only do the Japanese staff have no chance to communicate effectively with the president, they lose any desire to. Why bother to build links to a person who is only keeping the chair warm until a new *shacho* arrives next year? So company morale suffered and organizational efficiency suffered more.

When Manpower took over Parker and decided to switch to a lower-market image and emphasize cheaper products, Parker Pen Japan followed orders and actually worked hard to lower its image so it could compete with the disposable pen makers. All that changed when the management buyout led to a return to the company's traditional high-quality image and its move to England. President Magry strongly supported a global localization policy. He felt that each country in Parker's international group should follow whatever policies best suited the local area it knew best. So long as the firm's long-range goals were met, many of the specifics of operating local subsidiaries were to be left to local managers.

In conjunction with instituting these new policies, the head office thought it best to bring in a new chief executive to rebuild the Japanese subsidiary. The HQ used its own connections to search for the right person, but in vain. It also advertised in the newspaper. Fifty people replied, and the field was quickly narrowed to 13:8 *gaijin*, and 5 Japanese. The outgoing president of Parker Japan felt that, based on his own experience and because the business was growing more complex, a *gaijin* president was not the right way to go. The field was narrowed again, and after a series of interviews with both the head of the Japan subsidiary and several top executives from the home office, Toshio Hayashi became the firm's fourth president.

Hayashi obviously made a very strong impression during his interviews. Even when the decision was finalized to hire him and the offer was made, he had a condition before shaking hands: "Whenever you decide something at headquarters that will affect the Japan company, I want you to discuss it with me directly." Magry liked that attitude and agreed on the spot.

Normally in Japan a contract for employment states a fixed period of time. Many *gaishi* hire presidents for 3-year terms or 4-year terms, and so on. In Hayashi's case there was no fixed period; he would work like any other employee—indefinitely—and he would be judged like any other employee: by his performance. Magry himself had only one condition: "If you want to quit, give me 18 months notice. If the company's performance turns sour and we want you to quit, you'll get the same 18 months. But unless it comes to something unforeseeable, we want you to stay on."

Why was Parker so eager to sign this new president? Because he had a variety of business experiences, including years with another *gaishi*, he was a quick learner, and he had a terrific gut understanding of how to market products in Japan.

After Hayashi graduated from Kyoto University, one of the two most prestigious schools in Japan, he joined Toyo Engineering, a joint venture founded only five years earlier by trading house Mitsui and Co. and the group's chemical company, Mitsui Toatsu. Hayashi had been studying English assiduously since college and joined Toyo Engineering with the hope of going abroad to work at a foreign plant. Unlike most Japanese his age, he wanted to work for a young company with lots of growth potential and wanted to see for himself what living overseas was like.

He stayed with Toyo for eight years, during which he spent most of his time in the firm's accounting department rather than its foreign plants. He ultimately became head of the account planning office, where he worked on multi-billion-yen loans and got some experience with international finance.

During this time the company also sent him to its Institute for International Study and Trade to learn about international economics, the trading business, and other business-related subjects. He also served as an executive in the company's union for three years and learned how to discuss management problems directly with management.

Hayashi liked working for Toyo Engineering at first, but gradually he became dissatisfied and then frustrated because, he said, the management was constantly looking to its parent firms for direction or for examples of how to do business. It seemed to have no identity of its own. Hayashi wanted something more. When he heard that Wella, the German hair products firm, was setting up a Japanese subsidiary, he arranged an introduction through a friend and joined Wella.

Up and Down With Wella

At the time, Wella was tied up with a Japanese company called Takara Belmont that made equipment for beauty salons and barber shops. Because of this direct connection to the industry, Wella had a pipeline to distribute its hair-care products to professionals, and the business was growing reasonably well. But Wella aspired to do more than sell to the trade. It wanted to expand into general retailing, something its Japanese partner was not involved in and had no interest in developing. A parting of the ways was inevitable. At first Wella tried to tie up with a foreign cosmetics firm, but the negotiations did not go smoothly, so it decided to set up a subsidiary and try to sell on its own. The new subsidiary had a German president and under him a Japanese executive who had been a director of a cosmetics *gaishi* firm that had done well in Japan. Hayashi became general secretary to the president.

After setting up the Japan company, Wella cut all its ties with Takara, even for marketing to the trade, and undertook all its own marketing and sales in Japan. This was a tough business. At this time Japanese shampoos were selling for ¥50 or ¥100, while Wella was selling for ¥700–800. It is always possible to sell quality goods at a premium in Japan, but an 800 percent premium is pushing the consumer a bit. Still, the appearance of high-grade foreign hair-care products caused a stir. They received a lot of attention from the local press, and sales rose. The German image helped, too. During the late-1970s, Wella was often cited as an example of a *gaishi* firm that had succeeded in Japan.

Unfortunately, Wella's executive operations in Japan were too much like many *gaishi*: the president was essentially the voice of the head office, not a leader in his own right. The senior Japanese executive knew a great deal about doing business in Japan but had almost no experience in international business. Hayashi, who spoke some English, wound up translating for his two superiors, who did not seem to be getting along very well, and it soon became apparent that more than their linguistic approaches were at odds. In addition, Hayashi's main job was to take care of the mountain of correspondence that came to the Japanese executives from the Wella head office and other places. Hayashi decided to redouble his efforts to study English.

He was appointed to a succession of top executive posts and then, in 1982, sent to the German head office for a year and a half. At Wella headquarters he studied marketing, manufacturing, and EDP, and also did intensive German language study. Within a short time he was able to handle much of his work in German.

But while Hayashi was studying so hard in Germany, performance at the Japan operation began to slide. Without going into great detail, suffice it to say that there were several personnel changes in the Japanese firm, and policies began to go awry. Instead of emphasizing good distribution and strategic marketing, the firm pushed sales alone. Rival products, both foreign and domestic, appeared on the shelves, and the company responded with a "hard sell" campaign. Business turned sour. Gradually, both the new college graduates who had recently been hired as well as some of the middle managers began to quit. Not all of them at first, just the good ones. Soon not even 20 percent of the first year's crop of new hires remained. As the marketing department shrank, most of the best marketing experts quit the company.

Then an even greater shock hit: for roughly five years Wella had been preparing to list on the Tokyo Stock Exchange. But at the last minute the lead underwriter for the issue recommended postponing the listing. This happened at the beginning of Japan's "bubble economy," when almost any stock could be listed and could be guaranteed to take off. For a big broker to back out of an initial public offering was serious indeed, and the rumors that inevitably circulate at such a time make a company out to be in much worse shape than it usually is. In any case, Wella was no longer attracting attention as a successful *gaishi*.

In retrospect Wella had good products and a good image, but it let its advantages slip away. Once other foreign makers and the top Japanese makers began to challenge the firm in the high end of the hair-care market, Wella's uniqueness was lost. Its marketing was inadequate and ultimately so was its management: to allow a solid brand image and an advanced market position to erode is inexcusable.

At the time Wella's performance was deteriorating, Hayashi heard that Parker Pen Japan was looking for a new president. He took a long, hard look at Wella's prospects in Japan and his own prospects at the firm. It wasn't too hard to see the handwriting on the wall, and from where Hayashi stood it seemed to be written with a fountain pen. He went for an interview at Parker. Not long after, he and President Magry were exchanging conditions for his extended tenure as *shacho.*

He found that the corporate cultures at Parker and Wella were quite different. The last year or so at Wella had been difficult for Hayashi, and soon after joining Parker he had to undergo surgery for an ulcer. Almost immediately a call came from the head office to his home, saying, "Of course, the company will pay for everything, so don't worry about that. Get some rest and get fit. We need you."

Another thing that was even more of a shock had to do with visits from the top brass overseas. In almost every *gaishi* company, when the chairman or president of the parent firm flies to Japan, with or without a retinue, the normal work schedule of the local staff goes out the window. Top executives from the home office expect to be met at the airport, escorted into Tokyo, seen to their hotel rooms, and so on. If they are accompanied by their wives, sight-seeing, shopping, and translation services must all be provided for the wives as well. Cars and interpreters must be sent to pick up the brass at their hotel and take them to meetings, and when the weekend rolls around various kinds of sight-seeing and entertainment must be planned. If many *gaishi* executives say they like their bosses but wish they'd stay in the home office, it's not hard to see why.

Imagine Hayashi's surprise when the president of Parker Pen came to Japan and all he expected was that the company would arrange a hotel room for him. It was not the company's duty to pick him up at the airport or entertain him, show him around town, or escort him to meetings. As Hayashi now says, with a trace of pride, "If we tell the president where and when our meeting will be held, we know he'll be there on time."

Changing the Natural Order of Things

Once a year Parker gathered all its country representatives for a marketing meeting at the head office. Hayashi noted that each local representative and the president of the parent firm treated each other as equals. Everyone called everyone else by their first name (utterly inconceivable in a Japanese company), and all important decisions were worked out among the relevant participants; the parent firm never simply demanded that something be done a certain way. Hayashi was impressed to see how much give-and-take there was among the various executives in Parkers global network and how much mutual respect as well.

Hayashi was grateful to discover that relations with the home office were much better than in most *gaishi*. He felt the people in England were really trying to understand his situation. But he had other problems to deal with—problems inside Parker Pen Japan. Because the previous three presidents had come and gone so quickly, most of the staff had grown accustomed to dealing with important matters on their own without informing the *shacho*. That meant the organization had developed work-arounds that left the president out of the loop.

In addition there was very poor communication at lower levels of the firm. One problem was salaries: those who had negotiated well upon entering the firm were making good salaries, but sometimes the good negotiators were neither the most talented nor most experienced people. On the other hand, some employees who were doing extremely important work were near the bottom of the pay scale. Needless to say, that situation was breeding resentment, and the lack of communication within the firm meant that resolution of the problem was impossible.

In terms of the company's business prospects, Hayashi quickly learned that the market for high-class imported pens was very rigidly structured: there were already 17 brands, with Mont Blanc at the top, followed by Parker and Cross. The top three companies alone had held 60 percent of the market for so long that people who had been in the business for years had come to assume that this ranking was natural and would never change. This is very common in Japanese business (as with the Toyota–Nissan situation), because being number 1 almost guarantees that a firm will stay number 1. The danger in this situation is that employees at lower-ranked firms soon pick up the idea of this "natural" order and the "We're number 2, We Have to Try Harder" attitude never catches on.

This was precisely the case with Parker. High-quality pens were sold at department stores and pen shops, and Mont Blanc was of course allotted more space than any other brand simply because it was number 1, Cross and Parker Pen received less display space, and the other brands were simply lined up. Parker's staff had already come to take this situation for granted, a mindset Hayashi wanted to demolish as quickly as possible.

President Hayashi gathered the entire staff at a Tokyo hotel for a day of frank discussions. He shocked some of the older employees by openly challenging many of the ideas about how the market would grow and how shares would remain as they were and whether the company's way of doing business would serve it well in the future. But that was only the beginning. After these talks, the new president brought in outside professionals to train Parker managers and set up special training programs for each employee. In total, Hayashi spent ¥100,000 (about $1,000) per employee just for this initial training phase.

Then he set about fixing the pay-scale system. Many people who had been receiving very little under the old system suddenly received substantial raises at the end of the month. Some employees got double their old salaries. Hayashi commented later, "Reforming the salary system was critical to our corporate health. Of course it increased the financial burden on the company, but it also eliminated the constant outflow of talent and the feeling that the company was falling apart. In the end, it was a cheap solution."

In addition, he improved the company's welfare benefits and reformed the severance pay system. Then, to begin to improve intra-office communication, he instituted a monthly managers' meeting and a weekly morning briefing (*chorei*), an old custom in Japanese firms in which managers gather all the staff in their departments and sections to talk about the coming week's work and to pass along information on company activities and policies. To ice the cake he organized a company-wide trip to Guam.

Hayashi explains, "Most *gaishi* firms' salary structures are disorganized and company welfare programs are quite weak compared to other Japanese firms. They offer a little more pay to entry level workers as an inducement to join a foreign company, but for workers in their 40s who are beginning to worry about the future, they seldom have much to offer. That's why you often find such high turnover at *gaishi* companies and it's one reason why these firms don't grow as they should. I tried to instill in our staff a sense of the company's reason for existing. I've also tried to give workers a sense of job security, make them feel that they have a place to work until retirement."

Together with changing his employees' consciousness, Hayashi decided their approach to work had to change. First, computerization was introduced. The firm's EDP manager was given much greater authority than before. Suddenly terminals appeared on every desk, a large part of the staff was ordered to study computer basics, and inventory and sales were being managed in real time.

Ichiro Uzawa, a company director and head of the general affairs division, was in a good position to see how computerization changed the firm: "Up until then, the inventory taking and clean-up at the end of each month was a colossal headache. People were always putting in lots of overtime. When a report had to be sent to the home office, we'd see staff putting in a week's worth of overtime to draft it. But once the computer system was up and working, we had real-time reports from each sales agent on sales quantities, money received, rebates, margins, and so on. We were suddenly able to see what was going on with our sales around the country. Where people used to do 100 hours a month of overtime, now it's almost zero. In fact, at the time we installed the system our English parent company had very few computers and they were surprised to learn that we were putting in a terminal for every worker."

Human Relations

Because of the computer system, Parker's salespeople had much less paperwork to do, and so could spend more time focusing on sales. And Parker began to pay a lot more attention to sales. In addition to its regular contacts with its wholesalers and representatives from department stores, the firm began gathering all these people together for a meeting once a year. Parker management would report on the company's performance, explain its plans for next year, and talk about what the head office was thinking and what they had under development. The company's wholesalers have a separate sales meeting where they discuss strategy and marketing together with staff from the head office. And, in order for them to gain a much fuller understanding of what the company was all about, Parker invited them to fly to England and tour both the home office and the factories.

Hayashi himself took part in the national sales meetings and, following several years of "revolving door" presidents who were seldom part of the business, made it his job to meet and chat with Parker Pen reps from all over Japan. Gradually the old complaint inside the industry—"I know the product, but I don't know anyone from Parker Pen Japan"—began to die out. Anyone involved in selling Parker pens knew the company, knew its strategy, and knew its long-term plans, all of which made it easier to represent the firm's products. This "new" company was very well received by the salespeople on whose abilities its growth would ultimately rest.

Sales manager Masatoshi Maezawa put it this way: "Hayashi always says that 'the people who sell Parker Pens for us are all employees.' He always listens carefully to what the stores have to say. Many wholesalers have told me they think 'Parker has changed.' Although we're a *gaishi* firm, our sales style is very Japanese. There aren't even any *gaijin* in the company now. Hayashi has a lot of experience working at a foreign firm, but more importantly he understands the Japanese way of thinking and doing business."

Thanks in large part to the new president's efforts, the company improved dramatically in three critical areas: internal structure, employee attitudes, and relations with the outside world. Sales representatives were now familiar with the company and were anxious to put their best efforts into moving its products. But where were the products?

Parker Pen Japan had done a tremendous job of revamping its entire organization and was functioning more smoothly than ever before. But a solid organization without good products and a good image is all dressed up with nowhere to go. So Hayashi's next task was to get rid of Parker's image as a maker of low-cost, ordinary writing instruments. His experience watching Wella's exclusive brand image deteriorate had obviously left a lasting impression: "If a foreign brand doesn't have a perceived value based on inherent quality, and also a positive image—in other words, if it doesn't have a clear reason for its existence in this market—it won't be around very long."

Japanese consumers agreed. They already seemed to be thinking, "If I want a cheap, ordinary pen, I might as well buy a Japanese brand." Rather than try to compete with the local producers in lower-end disposable pens, the obvious solution was to emphasize value-added products with style and technology not available in the local market. And this is exactly what the home office wanted to promote. The parent firm had tackled the problem of how to boost its image back to its earlier stature by resurrecting a classic fountain pen from the company's early history. This pen, known as the Duofold, was the locomotive that helped to pull Parker's image back upmarket in the United States and the United Kingdom, and Hayashi knew it was just what was needed in Japan.

The Duofold Image

The Duofold was a big, fat, bright orange fountain pen first sold back in 1921, when Parker Pen was just becoming a global enterprise. When it was remade seventy years later it was offered in black and art deco relief in addition to the original orange. Parker Pen Japan decided to make this the standard-bearer in its new campaign.

The firm's first instinct was to show off the Duofold—and the new Parker Pen Co.—on national television. But TV advertising is expensive and it hits a very general audience, which meant it was doubly inappropriate for Parker. The company thought its most effective marketing strategy for a fountain pen was through print ads in selected magazines. The firm ran a memorable series of ads featuring handsome black-and-white photo portraits of Thomas Edison, Albert Einstein, Arthur Conan Doyle, Giacomo Puccini, and others, all stating simply, "I used it" and beneath the explanatory text was a color photo of a Duofold. Effective though it was, even this print ad campaign proved too expensive for the relatively small company to cover and Hayashi had to receive financial support from the British head office. (It is important to note that the parent company recognized the potential of the Japanese market and gave Hayashi full support long before sales justified it.)

The Duofold wasn't just a cut above Parker's other pens; it was a top-of-the-line fountain pen and it went head-to-head with market leader Mont Blanc's classic models. This was an ambitious step to begin with, but Hayashi's pricing strategy was even more ambitious. Based on Mont Blanc's prices, it seemed reasonable to sell the Duofold for around ¥40,000–¥50,000. Then the marketing people had a good idea: package it together with a matching automatic pencil in a classy wooden box, and sell the package for a premium. Japanese are nothing if not extravagant gift-givers, and many a good product has commanded an outrageous price by being cleverly packaged to make an even more impressive gift. Moreover, it was 1988, the height of the bubble years, when money seemed to be no object. Surely the gift box would sell.

Then came the discussion of price: how much would the market bear? The consensus was that "¥70,000–80,000 is the absolute limit. Anything above that is crazy." Hayashi disagreed. Charge an even ¥100,000 for the set, he said. "If we're going to tell people that we're the world's best pen maker and then use all these famous people to say that we're the best, we'd better look like the best." With many inside Parker holding their breath, the $1,000 fountain pen set was launched. To the surprise of everyone but the *shacho*, sales were very solid. The Duofold was well received by stores and consumers alike. The top-end department stores even made extra space to display it.

Director Ichiro Uzawa notes, "The new policy of emphasizing top quality merchandise like the Duofold was not only good for staff morale, but it also made the stores happy. There were much bigger margins available for store owners, so they were delighted to display it. That meant our sales increased and their profits increased."

In fact over 200 stores nationwide made special display space just for the Duofold. In the past, Parker's salesmen had sporadically allowed stores some incentive money for running special campaigns, but Hayashi institutionalized it and created a system to help stores promote the company's products.

Image-Building

All of this was a big plus for Parker's sales, but the fact remained that many Japanese still thought of Mont Blanc as *the* "status pen."

During the bubble era, when the term "nouveau riche" seemed to lose any meaning, everyone from young bankers to used car dealers sported Rolexes and routinely pulled huge black Mont Blancs from inside their tailor-made suits to sign contracts; housewives used Mont Blancs to write notes in their fashionable appointment diaries, and secretaries carried them in their Louis Vuitton bags. Of course most people didn't know one pen from another in terms of construction, function, etc., but they didn't have to: there were several magazines like *Mono* (things) devoted to telling readers which names were fashionable. And Mont Blanc equalled prestige.

So for Parker to unseat Mont Blanc as number 1 it needed a terrific pen with a terrific price. With the Duofold and Hayashi's aggressive pricing strategy it had both. But it needed more. It needed publicity, it needed a sign that the company was every bit as prestigious as its French rival. And Hayashi produced that as well.

One day he heard that the owner of a small building in the heart of the Ginza district wanted to improve the image of his building. On the first floor he had a very small (170 sq. ft.) store front available, too small to use for selling most products, but just right for something like a pen company to use for displays. Through acquaintances he knew of Parker and wanted to rent them the space for a relatively reasonable sum. But what made the offer irresistible was that he would forego the usual deposit money and the gift money normally paid to a Japanese landlord when moving in. At the time, a plot of land just up the street in Ginza was the most expensive piece of real estate in the world, and deposits on enough office space to park a desk ran into several millions of dollars.

The Ginza offer was too good to pass up. Hayashi contacted the head office right away and said "We want it." In spite of the very reasonable rent, the price was still sky high as far as the managers back in England were concerned. No one could have faulted them for saying, "That much money for so little space is absolutely out of the question. Find a bigger space in a cheaper neighborhood or find anything that costs less than the gross national product of Spain and we'll consider it." But Hayashi's time spent with top management, both in London and in Tokyo, had paid off. The two sides had a good understanding of each other's position. If Hayashi thought it was important enough to ask for the money, it must be important. The reply came back: "Take it." In the summer of 1990 Parker Pen Japan's new Ginza showroom opened.

The Ginza outlet was exactly what the firm needed to round out its new image, its new attitude, and its new product line—a symbol of being counted among the best brands of the world.

Interestingly, Parker does not sell anything at the showroom. People come to see, hold, feel, and try out the company's products. They can view the company's entire line up and get answers to questions, but if they want to buy what they see, they are referred to a nearby department store or pen shop. Needless to say, this not only adds to the exclusive image of both the showroom and the product, but by not competing with its own representatives in the area, Parker reinforces its commitment to support sales through licensed dealers.

New Marketing Strategies

As part of its ongoing promotional plan, Parker Pen Japan developed a unique little booklet to explain what a fountain pen is, how it works, and why so many people like to write with one. The booklet had a big impact on Japanese buyers. Of course it helped the average person to better understand what a fountain pen is all about, but it was also fantastic PR for Parker. It showed the exceptional quality that goes into a Parker pen. Readers saw how, for example, other makers pour liquid plastic into molds to make their pen casings; Parker's Duofold is scooped out from a single acrylic bar. This makes it more resistant to heat and more resistant to shock if it is dropped. Because it is more difficult to bend or damage the casing, the ink flows all the more smoothly.

The technology shows in other ways. One of the reasons people give up using fountain pens is that they dry up and stop writing if you don't use them regularly. But the Duofold will write smoothly even if it isn't used for a long while. Parker also notes with pride that its pens, especially the Duofold, have gained worldwide acceptance. For example, there are pictures of the participants at the Toronto Summit in 1988 signing their joint statement with a Duofold, U.S. President Reagan and Soviet Premier Gorbachev signing a nuclear arms reduction treaty with a similar custom-made Parker pen, and so on.

Parker sells a broad spectrum of writing instruments in Japan, from ordinary ballpoint pens that go for $8.00 to the luxurious Duofold, one version of which lists for a little over $20,000.

"In terms of imported top-class writing instruments, there are only two firms: Mont Blanc and Parker," explains Atsuhiro Iwashita, head of the marketing section. "In terms of general purpose writing instruments, there are only two firms: Cross and Parker. In other words, we cover two major categories of products; that is our strength. No matter how well the Duofold is selling, we cannot rely only on sales of elite products. We need a balanced lineup. Right now, about 60 percent of our sales are products around the ¥10,000 ($100) level, mostly bulk orders to companies. As you might expect, ballpoint pens outsell fountain pens."

Around 1988 Parker started a new marketing drive very important to its future growth. The firm chopped one-third off the price of a ¥15,000 ($150) fountain pen with a gold nib during the period when students enter or return to college. The pen sold very well, mostly to parents buying what they saw as a quality gift that represented the traditional values of literacy and good penmanship for their college-bound offspring. After the pen had begun to sell quite well, Hayashi said to raise the price to ¥12,000. The wholesalers balked: "If you raise the price, you'll only sell about 30 percent of the stock." Hayashi's response: "For a fine fountain pen with a 14K gold nib, customers will not complain much about a slight price difference." Once again the pen was aimed at the gift market, and once again Hayashi's instincts were right. The pens sold very well. Parker became the only pen company doing "back-to-school" promotions, and in that sense had a monopoly on cultivating a new generation of buyers rather than continuing to rely only on people over 50 to buy their "old fashioned" products.

As Parker Pen Japan's string of successes became the subject of discussion at the parent company's international marketing meetings, many of Tokyo's ideas were gradually adopted for global use. For example, the Duofold's gold ring was originally smooth and flat; the Japan side suggested that one way to increase the pen's appeal was to give this gold a longitudinal, ridge-like effect, making it both more attractive and easier to hold. The Japanese staff also suggested that the nib, the pen's tip, was too flat. "When the nib is flat the pen doesn't glide as smoothly across the paper, it scratches and may get stuck," they said, and insisted on something a little rounder. The tips became rounder. Then they went a step further. Was it possible, they asked, to make a special Duofold line for the Japanese market? We know the Duofold is good and it sells well in Japan, but it's a little fat for most Japanese hands. Couldn't the company make one a little bit slimmer? Many designers at the head office were opposed to this idea, but since the Japanese side seemed to know what they were talking about, the English managers reluctantly decided to try it out. What happened? The new ¥40,000 slim Duofold sold almost as well as the old ¥50,000 one, giving the company roughly twice the income from essentially the same pen.

Director Uzawa smiles when he says, "These days, whenever the head office wants to launch a new product on the world market they come to Japan and ask our opinions first. Recently they brought several new model types here and asked us to look them over and react to them. 'What do you think of this one?' they'd say. They really value our opinions."

People always say that the Japanese consumer is one of the most difficult, hard-to-please buyers in the world. Parker Pen has taken advantage of that in its worldwide product development and marketing and it's been a big plus for their group. Just as one more example, the parent company picked up the idea of packaging the Duofold as a pen and pencil set in an expensive wooden box from the Japan operation, and it is now sold that way around the world.

Despite an unusual degree of flexibility at the parent company, it wasn't always easy for Hayashi to get the head office to understand how things work in Japan. Every time there was a committee meeting he tried to explain about the unique features of Japanese society, local customs, changing economic conditions, etc. In particular, it was difficult to make the British managers understand about the cost of Japanese real estate during the bubble years. At one point Hayashi rented a parking place in the garage under the giant Mitsui Building in western Tokyo where Parker Pen Japan has its main office. When he reported the parking fees to the parent company and asked for their understanding, the British staff could not believe the cost for a year's parking. The word got around that "Toshio's decided to buy some property in Tokyo to build a parking lot. Perhaps we should ask him about that sometime."

To improve communications between parent and offspring (a subsidiary is literally called a "child company" in Japanese), Hayashi had local newspaper articles about the company and about changing trends in the market translated and sent back to the head office—an obvious step that many *gaishi* forget to take. The result of his visits to London, his participation in several meetings with company brass, endless phone calls and faxes and newspaper clippings was that the parent company finally came around to trusting and understanding the way the Japan unit was operating. After a while, if the head office and the Tokyo office didn't see eye to eye on something, more often than not the response at the HQ was, "It Toshio feels that strongly about it, give it to him."

Becoming Number 1

When Hayashi came in as president, Parker Pen Japan's sales were about $13 million and the firm was $7 million in the red. After he arrived sales began to grow in double digits every year and the red ink disappeared. That trend continued not only through the bubble era but on into the recession, when almost every firm in every line of business was watching sales and profits fall and flat growth was considered a sign of good management. In 1993, in the pits of the recession, Parker's sales were a solid $22 million.

As the years went by and sales continued to climb, Parker Pen Japan began to close in on the most important goal of all, one that prior to Hayashi's arrival the staff had assumed was impossible: overtaking Mont Blanc. In 1992 it happened.

"In the old days Mont Blanc owned this market," says marketing man Iwashita. "Then it was Mont Blanc and our Duofold. But if you compare the two pens side by side, the Duofold is unquestionably superior. For years we chased Mont Blanc, but ultimately we overtook it."

As we noted earlier, during the bubble era it sometimes seemed as if everyone who could write had a ¥50,000 Mont Blanc, not because they needed it but because, like Louis Vuitton bags and BMWs, it was a sign of status. After the bubble collapsed, status was no longer important. Quality and value were. Mont Blanc (unlike LV and BMW) lost its position. In part, this was due to Parker's aggressive development and marketing of top-quality products. But there was more to it than that.

Mont Blanc was bought by Dunhill, which turned local operations over to its Japan subsidiary. Dunhill Japan then cancelled Mont Blanc's long-standing contract with its general sales agent in Japan. This agent was not merely a distributor, but had worked very hard to help make Mont Blanc into the status pen it became. This agent realized that Japanese like a softer feel in a fountain pen and so had added a special polishing process to the nib before releasing each pen to the market. This polishing process gave extra value to the pen. (As an indication of how important this step is, the tips of Parker's Duofold, which had to compete with the Mont Blanc, are each polished for 56 hours to obtain this "soft" feel.) When the Japanese sales agent was eliminated so was the special technique it used in polishing the nibs. And so were all the agent's hundreds of contacts at top-class stores, all of which Dunhill had to start rebuilding from the bottom up.

Cutting off its contacts with a nationwide dealer network and eliminating an agent who performed a valuable process to improve the product's value have been a big handicap for Mont Blanc. The company may regain its preeminence in the Japanese market, but that could take many years, and during that time it has effectively ceded the competition to its chief rival. Parker is making good use of the lead it has built up; it has no intention of sacrificing the number one spot.

Nor was Parker Pen able to avoid the M&A fever that began in the 1980s. When the bank that originally financed Parker Pen's management buyout decided to put its block of Parker shares on the market, the company was effectively "in play" and soon enough there were several fins visible in ever-narrowing circles around the firm. This culminated in a 1993 purchase by Gillette, the U.S.-based shaving products firm. Gillette has only two main divisions, shaving and stationery, and it wanted to bolster sales in the latter. In addition to products like Liquid Paper correction fluid, the firm already owns another famous pen company, the French firm Waterman, so buying Parker gave it double strength in that area.

Hayashi is now vice-president of Gillette Japan, struggling to compete with its old rival, Schick, which dominates the Japanese market. In terms of shaving products, Gillette has its work cut out for it; but in writing instruments it owns the top slot. Although Parker's sales are still growing steadily, Hayashi is not satisfied: "Parker Pen is number 1 in the world in writing instruments, but roughly two-thirds of all its products are sold in the United Kingdom and United States alone. That's not right. Japan makes up too small a percentage; we've got to do better."

Parker Pen Japan succeeded in large part because its parent company came to understand its way of doing business and gave it both organizational and financial support instead of arguments, demands, and complaints. Gillette is a much bigger company with far greater resources. If it manages to do as good a job with the Japan subsidiary as the former English parent did, Tokyo will gradually begin to command a bigger and bigger share of Parker's worldwide sales, and the Parker pen will remain number 1 in the field for many years to come.

CHAPTER 10

Investing in Tokyo

Salomon Bros.

Perhaps the best way to assess the impact American investment bank Salomon Brothers has had on the Tokyo financial markets is to listen to its Japanese rivals. As Salomon continues to prosper while the Japanese houses flounder, there always seem to be new grumblings, if not outright charges, about how the U.S. firm is operating "unfairly." Much of this outcry from the Japanese brokers stems from Salomon's repeated demonstrations of its expertise in various kinds of trading that the big domestic brokers are learning the hard way. Several years ago, when Salomon was first advancing into arbitrage trading of stocks and bonds, a skill with which the Japanese brokers were not yet well versed, a senior director of Nomura Securities, Japan's leading broker, snorted, "It's like exporting AIDS from Wall Street."

Salomon is regularly singled out as the bad guy, charged by its local rivals with moving or sometimes even rigging the markets. This is usually a sign that the firm has once again bested its Japanese competition, leaving bigger, older, and far more powerful Tokyo firms with little to offer their clients but lame excuses and charges that Salomon did something sneaky. As an American rival and a veteran of Tokyo's clubby brokerage system commented, "Even if some of the charges were true, for any of the Big Four brokers to say that Salomon is manipulating the market for its clients is one huge pot calling the little kettle black. They're just jealous that there's a new kid on the block and he's good and he isn't part of the old boys' club, so of course there's a lot of friction . . . ."

Another rumor that one hears constantly concerns Salomon's income in Japan. Whether it is intended as flattery or critique, the effect has certainly been to bolster the American firm's image. People regularly say that in the decade and a half that Salomon has been in Japan it has raked in over ¥1 trillion ($10 billion). CFO and accounting department chief Toshiaki Kawashima laughs, "No, it isn't that much, really only a fraction of that." And yet the same figures continue to be mentioned again and again.

One figure that did come out in the open was the salary of the firm's Japanese CEO. In a country where the average salary for the president of a major company is around $400,000, and a really top company might pay a president or chairman who has served for many years somewhere around twice that, the idea of a million-dollar salary is a nonstarter.

During the early-1990s recession, many firms were tightening executive salaries and perquisites across the board. Against this background it is easy to imagine the shock that greeted reports that Salomon's Shigeru Myojin was pulling down an annual salary of $4.7 million in 1993. Myojin, of course, would not comment on his compensation, but executives at other foreign brokers are blasé about the reports. The simple fact is that Salomon Bros. is doing well in Tokyo even during the recession, and compensating people who generate big profits is nothing unusual in the financial business. The inference, of course, is that Salomon Bros. is not a successful *gaishi*; it's a *very* successful *gaishi*.

Some Recent History

For decades the Japanese securities business has been dominated by a small group of giant firms. Among the 47 fully licensed "comprehensive" brokers, four have essentially run the market: Nomura, Daiwa, Nikko, and Yamaichi Securities. Even in Japanese they are called the "Big Four," and until a few years ago no firm, domestic or foreign, could expect any measure of success unless it cooperated with one of these big players. But times changed suddenly about five years ago when the Japanese government decided to deflate the economic "bubble" it had generated in the mid-1980s in response to the rising yen. Suddenly the Tokyo Stock Exchange (TSE), the world's richest and fastest-rising equities market, stopped its ascent like a rocket whose fuel is spent and plummeted earthward. Everyone was expecting a decline, what brokers call a "correction," in the TSE index, but no one was ready for a crash. And crash it did, setting off a ripple of financial shock waves around the world.

The subsequent recession of the early 1990s crippled the securities companies. New issues were banned by the Ministry of Finance, and both individual and corporate investors fled the market. And as if the loss of commission income, underwriting income, and other fees were not enough, there were huge public scandals dragging the Big Four brokers' names even further through the mud. As the scandals spread and the TSE sank, the biggest clients, such as Japan's mammoth life insurers and other major investing institutions, decided to put their money elsewhere. It was a new low for the securities industry. Many proud Japanese houses had to settle their accounts in the red and lay off staff.

What was happening over at Salomon Brothers? They were declaring $100 million in current profits and jealous rivals claimed they were actually booking most of their profit offshore. In good times any broker can make a profit, but during a recession most houses are lucky just to break even. Yet even in the worst recession in half a century Salomon Bros. was raking in money. No one could believe it.

Ping-Pong and *Bonenkai*

Just a few years before, no one at Salomon would have believed it either. In 1977 the U.S. investment bank decided to position itself better in the nascent Asian markets, so the parent firm set up a new subsidiary, Salomon Bros. Asia Limited—in Hong Kong.

For some time before, the company had been negotiating with the Ministry of Finance (MOF) about opening an office in Tokyo, but in true MOF style, the negotiations dragged on for years. The parent decided to open in Hong Kong (in many ways a more progressive and international market than Tokyo) and wait to see what would happen in Japan. In those days MOF did not want foreign brokers coming to Japan, in large part to protect the country's antiquated securities market. MOF knew well enough that the entry of foreign brokers into the cozy world of the Big Four brokers (and the omnipotent regulatory ministry) would change things forever. And they were right.

However, the combination of domestic and international pressures for deregulation meant that it was only a matter of time before more foreign financial companies would be allowed to open offices in Japan, and the day would come when some would actually be granted seats on the TSE. Three years after opening in Hong Kong, Salomon got the OK to open a representative office in Tokyo. This did not allow it to do business in Japan, but at least it could establish a formal presence. The firm still had its sights set on Japan and the Japanese capital market, which had been on a more or less steady uptrend since the 1950s. Salomon had hired a number of Japanese staff to work in the Hong Kong office and had already begun cultivating Japanese business in anticipation of obtaining MOF's approval to open in Tokyo.

The pace of financial deregulation slowly began to pick up, and in May of 1982, just two years after setting up the Tokyo representative office, Salomon won approval to open a Tokyo branch office. This was a major concession from MOF, for it meant the company could begin full-fledged business in Japan, though still as an outsider. A few months after the approval came through, Salomon Bros. Asia Limited closed its Hong Kong office, packed up all its staff, and moved to Japan.

This was about the time that current CFO Kawashima came over to Salomon from his previous post at Arthur Anderson. He remembers those hectic early days in the Tokyo office this way:

Before the Tokyo branch was set up, the representative office had only about five or six people. After the branch was established, there were still only about 20, maybe five *gaijin* and 15 Japanese. We rented half a floor of a modern office building near Marunouchi (the central downtown business district). But even that was much too big for our little staff. About a third of the floor space was used for storage and Ping-Pong. Come to think of it, when I look back on those days, some of my most vivid memories are of the staff playing

Ping-Pong or skating at the ice rink next door. One day we all went out skating or something and didn't come back for the rest of the day. The boss went ballistic and that was the end of our Ping-Pong tables.

Anyone who has read the best-seller *Liar's Poker* is familiar with the somewhat "relaxed" corporate culture at Salomon's in the 1970s and early 1980s. This same general feeling clearly extended to operations in the Pacific. The company's early days in Japan were a time of little business but good team-building. For example, due to its large proportion of Japanese staff, the firm opted to have the traditional Japanese end-of-the-year party, called a *bonenkai*. These are always among the most boisterous occasions at any Japanese firm, a time when managers and staff relax at large restaurants, eat, drink, and sing. All the same, as with every other aspect of life in corporate Japan, there is a protocol to be followed and certain limits on one's behavior. Significantly, even Salomon's Japanese staff seem to have adopted a more *gaijin* approach to life, and the company's *bonenkai* became occasions to remember.

Kawashima recalls, "We'd all pack into some restaurant and everybody would order whatever he wanted to eat or drink (not the way things are supposed to be done at such occasions), and we'd always go way over our budget." He winces slightly as he remembers, "We were a pretty rowdy bunch. We had to use a different restaurant every year. They didn't want us back at the old one."

Causing trouble in restaurants was the least of the firm's problems. Back in those days almost no one in the company had any real experience in the securities business. They didn't know the details of many procedures, especially those in the Japanese market. More than once someone miscalculated a sales commission, which was embarrassing enough to explain to the client, but when managers were called into MOF's offices and told not to screw up again, it was an embarrassment to the whole firm.

Salomon may have been the loudest but it wasn't the first foreign broker in Japan; in fact, it was a little late in getting into the market. By the time it arrived there were already a half-dozen U.S. securities firms operating in Japan (Merrill Lynch had been around for a couple of decades). One reason for its lack of experienced personnel was that, unlike other houses, Salomon didn't hire managers away from Japanese houses. It wanted to hire young Japanese rather than experienced personnel from the Big Four, imbue them with the Salomon way of doing things, and develop a loyal, professional staff over time. They started this ambitious program in 1984 even though the company's name was totally unknown, which made it very tough to attract new college grads. Just for comparison, these days Salomon regularly gets applications from graduates of the University of Tokyo and other elite schools.

Small Town Saloon-Keeper

MOF's Securities Bureau is extremely powerful. It effectively controls all the Japanese brokers as well as the TSE itself (nominally an independent institution). The directors of this bureau had plenty on their minds without having to worry about foreign securities firms barging into the market, demanding changes to the rules, and so on. But deregulation was in the air and the arrival of more foreign houses was just as inevitable as it was undesirable. Not surprisingly, MOF came to feel that it must be tougher on foreign firms than on Japanese companies, as the latter already knew the rules of the game and were not likely to get out of line. Although all firms are officially governed by the same Securities Law, in practice individual firms and sometimes the whole industry are regulated by unofficial, extralegal directives from MOF (the famous "administrative guidance" that we look at in several other chapters). Salomon, like any other foreign firm, was sure to need "direction," but being more successful than most, it attracted plenty of attention, including that of the Finance Ministry.

Salomon Bros. is one of the world's top investment banks. Like Japanese securities companies, it handles both brokering (buying securities on behalf of its customers) and dealing (buying on its own account in the hope of reselling at a profit). But there are two major differences. One is that foreign firms have much more experience in assuming the risks of dealing than do their Japanese rivals. The other is that big investment banks such as Salomon Bros. have a more streamlined business: for the most part, they have no individual customers; they do business with institutions, and mostly very large ones. The difference is significant. Companies like Nomura Securities must service everyone from mega-investors like Nippon Life Insurance, with one of the world's biggest portfolios, to grandmothers in Hokkaido who might buy a single stock every 10 years. That requires a huge staff to handle the retail side of the business, something firms such as Salomon can minimize. This puts the foreign newcomer in an interesting position, especially in Japan where institutional investors control three-quarters of the market.

Interestingly, MOF had never paid a great deal of attention to the brokers, domestic or foreign. The ministry's first concern always has been (and always will be) the nation's big banks. Until just a short while ago the securities industry was seen as an unsavory and unsophisticated racket more than a legitimate business. Bankers were the nation's elite servants of industry, while stockbrokers were seen as hucksters running a shell game (a not wholly inaccurate perception). For many years MOF actually worked to keep a lid on the stock business so that it would not grow very large or become a threat to the banks. Only as Japanese industry began to put on some muscle and rely less on bank lending to stay alive did the finance ministry begin to loosen the controls on the market.

One *gaijin* who has been around Japan for decades and is familiar with the way things worked in Tokyo from many years ago compares Japan to a small Old West town with a single saloon run by the local sheriff:

> There were four big card tables, each run by a different boss, and a bunch of small tables whose dealers always looked to the Big Four bosses for signals. No one was dumb enough to complain that all the games were rigged. That was understood. Instead, you played by the house rules and did the best you could. Besides, who was there to complain to anyway, since the sheriff had helped set up the system in the first place? Getting to know one of the Big Four bosses was just about the only way to get ahead. No one knew much about what went on in other towns, and no one, least of all the sheriff, wanted strangers coming in and bringing their own cards with them.

Thus when Salomon first tried to operate with a little bit of the latitude that it had in New York, it ran smack into a wall of regulations on dealing transactions, borrowing limits, etc. MOF's tacit attitude was, "That kind of fancy shuffling may be all right in New York or London or even in Hong Kong, but not in an honest establishment like this."

So the mood at Salomon Bros. in its first few years in Japan was necessarily laid back. In those days *gaishi* securities firms mostly helped foreign companies to invest in Japan and helped Japanese companies to invest overseas. Levels of investment on both sides were relatively low but business was steady, so a certain level of commissions was guaranteed. This easygoing period was an ideal time to hire new grads and bring them into the business.

It didn't last. Two major forces hit Salomon Bros., both in 1986, and catapulted it from its quiet seat on the sidelines of the Tokyo stock business into the center of the three-ring circus that the TSE was about to become.

The first was an external force, the sudden conversion of that sleepy one-saloon town into a major international financial center. It all began in the fall of 1985 with an agreement among the G–7 nations. The Plaza Accord sent the yen spiralling upward against the dollar and sent Japanese companies, which had been scoring record increases in exports to North America, into a panic. Their howls of pain reached well inside the Ministry of Finance, which was expected to respond to the imminent financial crisis in some way. Part of its answer was the creation of the now-infamous bubble economy. Interest rates were lowered, rules on stock trading and accounting procedures were relaxed, and in the words of long-time Japan expert Kenneth Courtis, chief economist for Deutsche Bank in Asia, "the government essentially opened the floodgates and pumped an ocean of liquidity into the economy. The stock-brokers were in effect MOF's agents, manning the pumps to give Japan's top corporations access to this rising tide of free cash so they could restructure and cope with the post-Plaza environment."

As Courtis often points out, MOF has always viewed the financial markets as *instruments* of policy rather than objects of policy. Thus the stock market became one of the principal tools used to rescue corporate Japan from the threat of declining exports. As the TSE took off and Tokyo became the biggest, richest market in the world, the once-dull securities business suddenly became the fastest game in town. In addition to the traditional business of domestic stocks, the soaring yen gave rise to a sudden interest in overseas markets, something Japanese investors knew next to nothing about. Thanks to the new yen/dollar rates and Japan's soaring stock prices, by the late-1980s the TSE had the highest market capitalization in the world. And MOF began to see the advantages of running the world's biggest casino instead of that small backwater Japan had been for decades.

As foreign investors and foreign capital poured into Tokyo, the ministry loosened its restrictions and allowed a few foreign brokers to become members of the TSE. Until then, all foreign brokers had to place their orders through Japanese firms, but as soon as a handful of foreign firms obtained seats on the exchange, the die was cast. The old monopolies were about to come to an end. And Salomon was among the first wave of foreign companies granted that all-important seat.

The other major force that hit Salomon in 1986 was the arrival of a new branch manager. In a company often caricatured for its tough-talking, streetwise New Yorkers, the arrival of a suave English-man, Derek C. Maughan (who has since risen to the post of chairman and CEO in Salomon Brothers Inc.) was a bit of a shock. Maughan, who had served in Britain's own finance ministry, took the old, easy-going Tokyo branch and gave it a kick in the pants. He in-sisted the company modernize, identify its targets clearly, and then do what was necessary to attain them. It was time for Salomon's in Tokyo to stop playing Ping-Pong and get into high gear.

"To do business in Japan requires a raison d'être," Maughan said. "If a company doesn't know why it's here or what it's doing, it's finished." He noted that the Tokyo markets themselves were changing, government regulations were changing, and the tech-niques of trading various kinds of securities were changing, which meant that flexibility would be one of the keys to success. Every country has regulations of one sort or another, he said; MOF isn't some impossible hurdle, just a different set of regulators and a different set of regulations to contend with. He repeated to his staff the importance of adjusting to the local situation in order to get ahead.

Maughan did more than tell people what needed to be done. He also listened carefully to the ideas of those around him, espe-cially his Japanese staff. He wanted to familiarize himself with

Japanese opinions and ways of thinking. His combination of government experience in England and a re-education at Salomon (one of the most American of American-style firms) gave him a flexible perspective from which to form strategy. But his natural inclination to understand the culture and the people around him gave Maughan a big advantage over many *gaijin* managers in Tokyo.

New York gave Maughan a great deal of leeway in running the Tokyo office. But instead of becoming a dictator or a one-man show, as so often happens with strong leaders who have lots of authority, Maughan made a huge effort to understand the thinking of his Japanese employees. He also worked hard to create an environment where both Japanese and Western employees could work together as a team.

One of the American directors of the Tokyo office said he was surprised when Maughan first told him to listen to the opinions of the Japanese staff when he was hiring new employees. "In the U.S.," he said, "if I like a candidate for a job where I do the hiring, he's in. But in Tokyo, after I gave my OK we took the candidate to meet with our senior Japanese staff. If *they* said OK, he was in."

Crazy Like a Fox

Maughan did not waste any time trying to win over grandmothers in Hokkaido. Salomon's reputation back home was built largely on its expertise in bond trading, and that is just what he aimed to do in Japan. Shortly after coming to Tokyo and getting a feel for what was—and wasn't—going on, Maughan announced that Salomon was going after the government bond underwriting business.

He might as well have said the company was going to start keeping unicorns on the roof.

Kawashima recalls, "When Maughan made that announcement, one of our managers said, 'He's lost his mind.' I had to go with him to MOF to begin negotiations to let Salomon, an American firm, underwrite Japanese government bonds. I had trouble just translating what he had to say."

It was obvious to argue that since the Japanese government bond market was so large, experienced foreign securities firms should be allowed to tender bids. But Maughan went beyond that. He proposed creating a bond loan market such as that in the United

States, trades on the day of issuance, and a number of other ideas that must have struck MOF as impudent, arrogant, and not a little bewildering. But the MOF officials also knew that the winds were shifting; simply by giving foreign brokers seats on the TSE, the inevitable internationalization of the Tokyo markets was already underway. Perhaps letting a few foreign firms (and the foreign capital they represented) into the innermost sanctum of Japanese finance was not such a bad idea after all.

Eighteen months after Maughan's "crazy" announcement, the firm won the right to underwrite Japanese government bonds.

In order to handle trading for Japan's enormous financial institutions, Salomon needed to have a sizable inventory. This required capital. Thus in January 1987 the Tokyo branch office increased its capital by 1,000 per cent to more than ¥500 million (over half a billion dollars today), becoming overnight the fifth-biggest securities company in terms of capitalization, right behind the Big 4.

The chairman of Salomon Bros. in New York boldly predicted, "We will become a leader in the Tokyo market as well," and Maughan set out to prove him right. Just a few weeks after boost-ing its capital, Salomon's Tokyo office entered a bid for mid-term (2-year) government bonds. In a stunning display of power, Salomon captured 40 percent of the total allotment. Even more significant, its ¥450 million share far exceeded market leader Nomura's ¥300 million. Salomon had walked off with the top share in the first government bond auction in which it participated. The message to the Big 4 was clear in any language: Make another seat at the table.

As a result of its successes, in October of 1988 Salomon Bros. became the only foreign securities house to become a permanent manager of the Japanese government bond syndicate. Within the next few years Salomon's share of total government bond under-writing would rise as high as 15 percent and the firm would become a prominent dealer in the secondary market.

Many observers say that one reason for Salomon's sudden rise to success in Japan is this move into the bond business. Unlike the stock business, with its complex traditions, understandings, and agreements among brokers and between brokers and clients, the bond market was of little consequence until just about the time that Salomon arrived in Japan. From about 1976 the Fukuda cabi-net issued large quantities of national bonds to cover budget deficits, and the market began to grow. In equities it was common for big institutional investors like the giant life insurance companies to distribute more-or-less fixed amounts of business to the various big brokers. If a foreign company wanted to break into that club and eat into the shares of the Big 4, there was bound to be trouble. But since bonds were a relatively new market, there were far fewer arrangements and corporate shares were not rigidly fixed.

Maughan realized that this rather undeveloped state of the Japanese government bond market was a perfect match for Salomon, whose expertise in bond trading worldwide is legendary. In that sense, his decision to target that market was not crazy, but incredibly shrewd: he knew that if MOF opened the door just a crack, Salomon could jump in and grab a meaningful slice of the business. And more important than earning profits, merely to be accepted by MOF as an underwriter meant in a sense to be a partner of the Japanese government rather than a thorn in its side. It meant that Salomon's had earned a certain amount of MOF's respect, and that was worth a lot.

Economists and Researchers

Around the time of its capital increase, Salomon's New York office sent its then-chief economist, Henry Kaufman, to Japan to give a speech. Even then Kaufman's name was well known in Japan's financial community. It was said that his forecasts could move the markets, something Japanese thought only powerful corporate forces (e.g., Nomura) could do. Bringing Kaufman to Tokyo was a stroke of PR genius. It reinforced Salomon's reputation as a force to be reckoned with in the international markets, and that in turn increased the prestige of the firm's Tokyo branch office. Kaufman's appearance in Tokyo was a visible statement that Salomon in America and Salomon in Japan were the same firm and that they expected the same kind of results and the same kind of market clout. And perhaps more than anything, it reminded Japan's big institutional investors who came to hear his speech that Salomon Bros. had something to offer them that none of their local brokers could compete with.

Jeffrey Hanna, then managing director in charge of research in Tokyo, put it this way: "Salomon can't beat a huge firm like Nomura when it comes to the number of staff covering Japanese stocks and providing information about the Japanese markets. But when it comes to information on what's happening in the global economy, particularly the United States and the various European economies and all the important markets of the world, Salomon can deliver a level of service no Japanese firm can begin to match."

One of the biggest problems for foreign securities firms in Japan is their research departments. Typically, when an analyst writes up a research report it must be sent to the company's home office in New York or London for checking. When the research division in the home office gives its approval, the report can be published. However, the head office research departments do not normally have native staff to check reports in Japanese (or Korean or Thai or any other local language), so in order to pass the firm's internal checking system, all reports must be written in English. Only after an English version of the report is approved can it be translated and sent to clients.

Consequently, Salomon's Tokyo office was writing research reports intended for Japanese clients and often originating from notes prepared in Japanese by Japanese analysts. These reports then had to be written up in English, and then the English was often rewritten by editors in Tokyo before being sent to New York, where they were proofread and content-checked and then given the OK for retranslation back into Japanese. In a bureaucratic setting this time-consuming back-and-forth paper shuffling would not cause a problem, but in the split-second world of international finance, where yesterday's news is ancient history and "real-time information" is everything, Salomon was shooting itself in the foot. Japanese investors were getting stale news. So Hanna and the Tokyo office research staff began a system of preparing timely, native-language reports especially for Japanese clients. This set the firm apart at an early stage and made it extremely attractive to large institutional investors.

Interestingly, one of the best-known names at Salomon during the high-flying days of the Tokyo market was not a trader but a researcher, economist Ron Napier. As the bubble expanded and asset values took off, TSE prices went through the roof. Foreign investors, accustomed to valuing stocks based on price/earnings ratios (PERs), all thought the TSE had gone insane. At one point the average PER in Tokyo was well over 60 (compared to 15–20 in New York), and some blue chip companies were trading at PERs of 150 or more. Japanese investors considered the price/earnings ratio all but meaningless: if everyone knew a stock was headed upward, such theoretical analysis was pointless. But foreign investors were not so intoxicated with the daily rises in equity prices and preferred to sit on their portfolios. Salomon wanted its foreign clients to see what they were missing and take advantage of some of the gains Tokyo afforded.

Enter Napier, who used to teach economics at Harvard. Napier insisted that the PER itself is an inadequate tool for evaluating stocks because it ignores the performance of the real economy underlying stock movements. He devised a system that compared a nation's long-term interest rates to its economic growth rate. Why look at long-term interest rates? Because, he said, institutional investors move in and out of the stock and bond markets depending on changes in these rates, and the markets are largely controlled by institutions rather than by individual investors. Napier expounded his system of fair stock value in 1987. Using it, he determined that the gap between America's real GNP growth and U.S. government bond yields at the time was too high, that it did not support the current state of the N.Y. stock market. In his estimation, New York was due for a serious "correction." After the infamous Black Monday crash in October of that year, Napier's own stock went up. He spent a few years in Tokyo helping to explain to overseas investors that there were fundamental structural differences between Japan and other markets and that PERs were necessarily higher in Japan. Thanks in part to his efforts, a number of Salomon's non-Japanese clients were persuaded to increase the weighting of Japanese shares in their global portfolios, and many earned huge profits during the TSE's wild, three-year rocket ride.

M&A

Maughan summed up the company's early years this way: "For its first four or five years in Tokyo, Salomon Bros. focused on acquiring staff and developing its management. In 1986 we concentrated on research and aggressive marketing. In 1988 we focused on building up the investment banking division." Investment banking comprises many different functions, but one of them, and certainly the most important one in Japan in 1988, was M&A.

Within the next several months, a wave of Japanese takeovers of U.S. and European firms would sweep around the globe, a *tsunami* of excess cash unleashed by the financial earthquake the bubble economy had created. Japanese takeovers of big American firms began long before Sony or Matsushita's purchases in Hollywood, even before Mitsubishi Estate's infamous investment in Rockefeller Center. The first buyout of real significance was that of America's Reichold Chemical by a Japanese chemical firm Dai Nippon Ink (which would go on to purchase several more U.S. companies)—a deal handled by Salomon Bros.

To support the M&A business, Salomon brought in John Schlesinger, a specialist from the New York office, in October of 1988 to run its Asian M&A division.

"For Japanese companies, the rise of the yen made it easy to buy European and American companies," Schlesinger says of that time. (It is interesting to note that this high yen was a direct result of the Plaza Accord, the international move to slow Japan's trade surplus which the officials in MOF turned to their own advantage.)

Salomon also hired a number of staff from some top Japanese companies to work with Schlesinger. Shigeki Maruyama, who joined Salomon as a vice-president, originally came from Mitsubishi Trust and Banking Co., one of the top banks in Tokyo. Mitsubishi had sent him to the University of Michigan where he obtained not only an MBA but also some insight into how the business world in the United States was changing. Soon after his return to Japan he was called by a headhunter (all headhunters in Tokyo have lists of Japanese who currently hold or are about to bring home an MBA). The phone call said that Salomon Bros. was, to borrow a phrase, looking for "a few good men." Maruyama thought about his future with Mitsubishi Trust for a long while and then decided to put his MBA to work for America's top investment bank.

In the late 1980s, information on mergers, tie-ups, and takeovers of various kinds grew from a trickle to a torrent. Every day news of seven or eight transactions or pending transactions flowed in from the United States and Europe. Suddenly companies were "in play" (i.e., up for grabs) and information networks around the world hummed with data and coded messages about who was available and who was interested. The M&A world in Tokyo seemed poised for action if only Japanese companies—who traditionally shunned takeovers, and referred to the practice as "hijacking"—were willing to get in the game.

So Schlesinger planned the strategy and Maruyama made the presentations. In the latter's words, "to take this information around to senior executives of Japanese companies, to talk to presidents and chairmen on their own terms, it is essential to have a Japanese presence . . . ." Maruyama went around from company to company to explain how this new world of M&A was taking shape and how strategic acquisitions could be of tremendous benefit to Japanese firms with long-term growth plans. He was instrumental in arranging the buyout of U.S. Semiconductor for Osaka Titanium Mfg., part of the powerful Sumitomo Metal Industries group, among other transactions. When the big M&A boom was over a few years later, the Japanese had become major players and Salomon had helped to channel their investments around the globe.

Coming into the current decade, interest in M&A waned rapidly. But even as the economic bubble collapsed, Salomon was moving its resources into another field: helping Japanese companies to raise capital. Within a short time the firm had become the market leader in helping Japanese corporations to issue bonds through medium-term note programs in the Euromarket. Also, as the value of their stock portfolios fell, Japanese banks were suddenly straining to meet new international capital adequacy requirements. Many turned to a device called Euroyen subordinated debt as a means to boost their ratios, and Salomon became the lead underwriter of this kind of debt for many of the nation's top banks.

"No one was doing Euroyen dated subordinated debt, so we practically had a monopoly on that business," says Shinji Ohyama, managing director of the investment banking division. "We also did perpetual notes (a type of instrument common in England and often issued in the Euromarkets) for Japanese banks. We were the lead manager for issues by DKB and Sakura Bank. Why did we attract so much of that business? Because Salomon has lots of experience doing this kind of work in Europe and the U.S.; we're experts in the bank capital-raising business worldwide. No one else could deliver that kind of service."

Ohyama, who used to work for Nomura, is in a good position to compare Salomon and the Big Four: "When a Big Four firm underwrites Eurobonds for a Japanese client, it usually arranges for a small Japanese credit association (*shinkin*) to buy them. Salomon, on the other hand, has close contacts with institutional investors worldwide and so can place these bonds globally. There's no reason to push them on local Japanese institutions. When a Japanese broker gets a mandate to underwrite a bond, the first thing they do is go around looking for buyers. When Salomon gets a mandate, they already know who the buyers are."

The Look of a Survivor

In 1988 one of the authors asked Derek Maughan, "Among the 80-odd *gaishi* securities firms in Japan, how many will survive?" He said, quite matter-of-factly, "Ten." Drastic as that prediction sounded, it was made while the bubble was still expanding and the TSE was rising steadily. A few years later the bubble was gone and the cold winds of recession started to blow. Stock trading commissions dried up, along with most of the brokers' fee businesses. When Salomon's current branch manager, Louis Faust, III, was asked how many firms can expect to generate reasonable returns, his stark reply was: "Five."

Yet there is no doubt in anyone's mind that whether the number is ten or five or even three, Salomon Bros. will still be there among the survivors. There are as many explanations of why Salomon has done well in Tokyo as there are theories on the future of the economy. Everyone has an answer, and everyone's answer reflects part of the whole truth.

Many of Salomon's employees—especially its Japanese staff— see the company's internal structure as one of its greatest strengths. Kawashima, who has been with the company since 1982 when the Tokyo branch was set up, looks at it this way: "Salomon is not a pyramid; it's a pretty flat organization. There's very little feeling about who's above who or who's below who. Authority and responsibility are fluid; you talk to the people you need to, and if you can make things go well, that's fine. You can go over somebody's head, talk to the branch manager, for instance, or if you can't find somebody in Tokyo with the authority you need to do something, you can call direct to New York. It happens all the time. If you did that in a Japanese company there'd be hell to pay."

Beniko Tsubaki, a vice-president in Salomon's Tokyo branch, also used to work for Nomura and is acutely aware of the differences in corporate culture. Salomon, she says, was surprisingly good at adapting to its new environment. "I remember how when the top brass came out from the U.S., whether it was the chairman or the president of the company, they joined in entertaining our big institutional clients Japanese-style. They went to Japanese restaurants, sat on *tatami* floors, and took their cue about whether it was OK to take off their jackets or not from our local Japanese staff. That sounds pretty simple, but a lot of big American companies just don't appreciate how important it is."

Salomon has structured its operations more like a Japanese company not just because it is in Tokyo but because that approach works best for its customers. In many *gaishi* firms everyone, Japanese included, has his or her own job assignment. In effect, everyone works for his or her own section on his or her own projects; no one knows much about what the person three or four desks away is doing. Even when an important client calls, he may be told "the person in charge is away on business for a week. Could you call back next week?" In Japan that is a sure way to end a client relationship. So Salomon has adopted a more Japanese-style team approach. Whether the person responsible for some project is a director or a department manager, everyone from the section chief down to the new hires has some reasonably clear idea about what that project is and what needs to be done. If the department manager is out, the section chief takes over; if the section chief is out, the next person in line takes over. One reason that Salomon did so well early on when other *gaishi* securities firms were having less success in dealing with clients had a lot to do with this team approach.

Post-Bubble Strategy

All this is not intended to portray Salomon as the perfect *gaishi* company (we've never seen one) nor as a firm untroubled by the problems in its industry. Management talks frankly about the need to cope with a much tighter business environment in the post-bubble years. CFO Kawashima says, "In 1991 and 1992 we cut expenses and examined our payroll very carefully. In fact, that's an ongoing process. Like other Japanese companies, we're taking a hard look at everything from memo paper to entertainment expenses, but also negotiating reductions in staff housing allowances and getting fewer staff sent over from America."

During the bubble days when steady expansion of sales and profits seemed likely, Salomon took a look at its office space in a building crowded with other *gaishi* financial firms in a very inconvenient part of Tokyo. At the time, the company had 600 employees and the medium-term forecast was raising that to 1,000. So in 1990 Salomon moved into a brand new building in the heart of the financial district (Nomura Securities is a tenant in the same building), where it rented a much bigger space. In fact, the company signed a lease for three full floors of this sizable building. The move was barely completed when the recession struck. Within a short time Salomon pared its staff down to around 500 and had to give up one of the floors in its new home.

This slimming of its payroll is in itself a sign of management efficiency—although Salomon is one of the most successful of all *gaishi* securities houses, it ranks fifth in terms of number of employees. A major factor has been soliciting voluntary retirements. As Faust notes, "In the fall of 1993 about 60 people left the firm. Not just the market, but the whole economy has been weak. As a result, our profits are half of what they were at the peak. We must continue to cut costs in order to preserve long-term profitability." The same comments are echoed at scores of other foreign-backed firms across Japan. Regardless of what happens to the economy in the next few years, *gaishi* firms have realized that they must be even more efficient than their Japanese competitors if they are to preserve their edge in other areas.

Conclusions

Salomon Brothers' success in Japan has been discussed at length within the local financial industry. Perhaps the best summary of its rise to prominence came from a Japanese financial writer who noted, "Salomon deals with corporations, not with individual clients. Merrill Lynch, the world's biggest securities company, has been in Tokyo for over 30 years, but it's still struggling. Salomon Bros. was in Tokyo less than 10 years and in this short time showed phenomenal growth. The reason? Corporate business. As Japanese companies grew and globalized in the 1980s, they suddenly wanted more information about what was going on in other markets. Salomon Bros., with its global network of information on bonds, equities, and corporate finance, had the right product for this market at just the right time."

Many of Salomon's big institutional clients actually developed their own global information networks, and many broke away from years of domestic investing to diversify their portfolios globally. Salomon showed them profitable opportunities in developing markets such as those in Southeast Asia where they could earn much better returns than in Tokyo. Also, many institutions have finally moved away from simple stock buying and into derivative financial products (options, futures, etc.), a broad field where Salomon has considerable know-how and has trained Japanese specialists much earlier than its domestic rivals.

In sum, much of Salomon's success derives from its consistently aggressive strategy—bringing new financial technologies to Japan and not being afraid to show up local firms by putting them to use. It also benefitted greatly from the vision and leadership of a foreign executive (Derek Maughan) as well as a host of first-rate Japanese managers. Once again, as with so many successful *gaishi* companies, the keys to success are simple: good management, good strategy, good products—and a lot of leeway from the home office to get the job done.

CHAPTER 11

"When in Rome . . ."
Nippon Olivetti

Several years ago if you'd asked most Japanese to identify Olivetti, you might be surprised to find that almost everyone knew the name. "Sure," people used to say, "It's an Italian company that makes typewriters."

Quaint though that image may be, in the computer age it's the kiss of death. In fact, Nippon Olivetti (the local company is officially called Olivetti Corp. of Japan, but we will refer to it by its more common Japanese name) has almost no share of the typewriter business in Japan, and the firm has made great efforts to change its image. Slowly but surely it has become known for a variety of business- and entertainment-linked computer equipment. It has strong ties with industrial and consumer electronics maker Toshiba (which holds 20 percent of Olivetti's stock) and also sells Toshiba-made equipment under its own brand name. All this has brought the Japan operation a yearly sales income of over $300 million, which is not bad for a "typewriter maker."

Dealing with the *Tonya*

Shortly after World War II, Olivetti branched out aggressively, building its business in fields other than typewriters. First it became a major producer of mechanical office equipment and then, as the electronics revolution emerged, the firm jumped up a level to become a comprehensive electronics maker. But long before that happened, the Italian firm was already hoping to become a global player in the business machine market, along with firms such as IBM and NCR. As its international aspirations blossomed in the late 1950s it even turned its attention to Japan, a small, relatively poor nation that was still fighting its way back from the devastation of the war. (It is interesting to remember that Italy and Japan were allies during the war, yet the former was able to rebuild its economy in a much shorter time; it must have been surprising to Japanese to see firms like Olivetti arrive in Tokyo looking much like the powerful multinationals from the United States.)

Olivetti arrived in 1961 when the Japanese economy was less than a tenth the size of that in the United States. The Ikeda Cabinet made a public promise to double Japan's GNP within a decade, but no one, not even most Japanese, believed it was possible. As a matter of fact, the Japanese economy doubled in only eight years and continued to rise at a phenomenal pace for another twenty years after that, but at the time no one in his right mind would have predicted such a future.

Yet Olivetti was branching out internationally and it wanted a foot in Japan's door. At the time, the only Italian firm with an office in Japan was the airline Alitalia, so Olivetti became the de facto head of Italian business in this unexplored market.

In a pattern that should be quite familiar by now, all of Olivetti's sales in Japan at that time were handled by a licensed sales agent. But the company knew it needed to strengthen its sales system and improve customer service. It might be the only big Italian firm in town, but when it came to office equipment, Olivetti was hardly alone. Remington, IBM, NCR, and other business machine makers were already well established here, and Olivetti was seen as a late arrival.

Olivetti's initial charge on the Japanese market was led by a talented young executive, President Carlo Alhadef. He was only 36 when he set up the firm but had already demonstrated his ability by running Olivetti's branch office in Egypt. The original team consisted of 12 Italians and 8 local staff. Total start-up capital was ¥18 million (about $50,000 in 1961 dollars).

In those days you didn't hear many complaints about the Japanese market being closed or that the local customs were unfathomable; no one was griping about the impossible distribution system or the many other obstacles to foreign business (although there were far more than there are today). Companies assumed that Japan was a very different market, with a different language and culture, and that everyone had to compete to win over customers. Getting in the door was relatively easy; earning enough profit to make the Japan operation pay for itself was a major challenge.

Nippon Olivetti's first president certainly ran into many of the same sort of problems that Western executives do today, and he tried his best to come to grips with them. The thing that he found most difficult to understand was the wholesaler (*tonya*) system. Viewed from any normal Western perspective, the *tonya* system means that at least one (and sometimes two or three) unnecessary middleman margins must ultimately be passed on to consumers or the maker has to lower its own profit margins.

"President Alhadef contacted *tonya* all over the country," recalls Tomura Takashi, formerly a director of Nippon Olivetti. "He worked very hard to understand their business. Ultimately, it took him three years to fully understand the *tonya* system. But finally he came to appreciate it. He realized that this system is hundreds of years old and he understood it has survived not because it is inefficient, but because it serves an important function. The *tonya* spread out risk and fill a variety of other roles in distributing merchandise. They are most certainly *not* unnecessary middlemen. No one loses in this system."

Of course direct sales is an excellent way to get around the old-fashioned distribution system and reach customers directly with specific products; but if your real target is to display a variety of goods at retail stores all over the nation, the *tonya* system is sometimes the most efficient approach. A company that succeeds in taking advantage of the *tonya* system can reap great rewards (as Levi Strauss discovered). By successfully using the *tonya*, a company can increase the number of retail stores it reaches by 10 to 20 times over direct marketing. Once Alhadef grasped this situation, Olivetti's indirect sales rose rapidly.

Localization

One of the biggest decisions any foreign firm must make in a local market is to what degree it should localize its operations. Many successful *gaishi* are run entirely by Japanese staff, while some have foreign chief executives, a few foreign directors, and Japanese managers. Other *gaishi* (only a few of them successful) are run exclusively by head office people, using Japanese only in clerical and sales positions.

Alhadef promoted localization right from the start. He startled people on both sides by declaring, "We cannot automatically assume that our Italian managers are the most appropriate for this market or that they should run our Japanese operation. We need local managers." The next year he hired 250 Japanese college grads and the next year 400. The idea was to bring in a lot of fresh talent and train them in the Olivetti system early on. His strategy was to remake the new employees in the Olivetti mold and to remake Nippon Olivetti in a more Japanese mold.

In the beginning the company's major products were typewriters, large-size calculators, recording-tape cash registers, etc. Olivetti's typewriters were already well known in the marketplace, but American firms such as NCR had a strong position in calculating machines and cash registers. Olivetti had a very advanced recording-tape calculating machine and sent many of its new, college-educated employees out selling these products door-to-door. At the time there were relatively few salesmen in the labor force, and the image of the door-to-door peddler was not particularly good. As a result, quite a few new employees objected to what they considered inappropriate treatment. In some ways, this may have been the beginning of worker dissatisfaction at Nippon Olivetti.

Universities and research labs ordered many of these calculating machines, and banks ordered the special model that also computed interest. Banks soon wanted devices that could record entries in savings passbooks, and orders increased even faster. Within four or five years, Olivetti had taken the top share in recording-tape calculating machines.

Olivetti's fame spread with the parent company's release of the Programmer 101 mechanical calculator. Of course, in the years that followed, advances in programmable calculating machines came one after another, but back then the device was lauded by the media as "the world's first desktop computer" and "a desktop calculating machine equal in power and function to a large computer." With the local press adding to the acclaim already given to the unit by the world media, sales in Japan took off right from the beginning.

But the fame was short-lived. This was the era when Japanese electronics companies were "borrowing" every good idea they could lay their hands on and finding ways to improve upon it. Japanese products were hard on the heels of Olivetti's star performer and, what's more, they were electronic. At this point Olivetti was behind the curve in getting with the electronics boom, and its market share in this area began to fall.

The company's major low-tech product was the one with which it had made its name, and even though its more complex machinery wasn't selling as well as hoped, the firm was selling a lot of typewriters. In 1965 it released the classic Letella Black that became a solid hit. But by that time Japanese were starting to move away from the idea that office equipment should be black, and in 1969 the firm hit the market with its "red bucket" ad campaign for a new portable typewriter that brought the color revolution to the office market. The company's new hit was called the "Valentine" and it came in bright red together with a matching case which looked like a red bucket. Unlike many previous models, it was light and easy to carry around; it could easily be carried from one office to another or even taken home.

Now that Japanese were no longer struggling and saving to buy necessities but also spending more freely on a growing variety of consumer goods, it was time to take the typewriter out of the office. So the company matched the innovative design of the Valentine with an equally original ad campaign. The new ads said that a typewriter is not merely a piece of office equipment, but a modern writing instrument like a pen or pencil. The modern generation wants a truly portable typewriter, the ads explained, because it is just as important a personal accessory as a pair of shoes or a hat.

While reliable surveys indicate there were still more Japanese wearing shoes than carrying typewriters around with them, we should never underestimate the power of creative advertising. The new image sold incredibly well and Olivetti captured 40 percent of the domestic typewriter market. In the process, its name became known nationwide. Unfortunately for Olivetti, the typewriter's days were already numbered, and the technology that would eventually replace it was precisely the field where the Italian company lagged behind major rivals: computers.

Banking on New Demand

Japanese banks have long been one of the main pillars supporting the nation's computer industry. Nowadays every big company uses computers extensively, but in the early days the biggest users were the large banks. The first real online system for a Japanese bank was set up by Mitsui Bank in 1965 (it used the system developed for keeping track of records at the Tokyo Olympics the previous year). After that, all the large commercial banks (what the Japanese call "city banks") wanted online services, and they competed with each other to install the newest, biggest, and most impressive machines, which led to an endless spiral of investment and solid growth for the computer makers.

Even in the 1960s when these systems were first appearing, the investment was substantial. Because the systems were all based on central mainframe computers supplying data to hundreds of terminals in the bank branches, the kind of partners the banks were looking for had to be strong in mainframes and related technical development.

This was bad news for Olivetti, which had given up on the idea of making big computers early on. Consequently the firm was shut out of the competition for the largest sector of the business from the beginning. This, too, had an impact on the company's fortunes in years to come. Its real fear, though, was that if it were shut out of the mainframe market it might also be shut out of the computer business altogether. Olivetti's alternate strategy was two-fold: to emphasize its strength in end-user equipment, such as terminals and peripherals, and to focus its sales efforts not on the big city banks but on the hundreds of smaller regional banks and credit associations.

The regional financial institutions have always been second-class citizens in Japan's banking world, and they are perennially behind the curve in modernization and internationalization compared to their giant rivals in Tokyo and Osaka. This proved to be an asset for Olivetti. After Mitsui's introduction of a centrally-controlled online information processing system, it took the other big banks a few years to get into the competition, and the regional banks were still not sure what an online system was all about. That gave Olivetti time to develop its own system.

In 1969, four years after Mitsui began computerizing, Nippon Olivetti announced its own information processing system, called IDP, aimed at the smaller banks. The basis of this system was an accounting machine fitted with a paper tape puncher; the data put into the machine was recorded on the paper tape, and from that tape data could be directly inputted into a central computer. The branch tapes could be sent to a bank's central processing center, and so in principle a bank had an effective, if somewhat unsophisticated, "online" system.

Olivetti made a big sales push for the small and medium-sized regional banks, selling them adding machines and simple computers and connecting them with the IDP system. The firm recommended that its clients step up to computerization, and of course this boosted IDP sales. The first IDP system was installed in a branch of Nokyo, the enormously powerful national organization of agricultural cooperatives. This branch system became the model for Nokyo nationwide, and soon enough Olivetti had captured 80 percent of Nokyo's computer-related purchases. That success plus sales to regional financial institutions kept the company's head above water for years. But it was still playing in the minor leagues.

Interestingly, it was changes in the computer market that eventually brought Olivetti into the big city banks—where it had almost given up hope of competing. In the 1980s big corporations first began to doubt the wisdom of running all their operations from centralized mainframe computers. The machines were growing too big, maintenance was becoming more and more complex, and the cost of developing mainframe software had become ridiculous. As people began to see the limits to centralized computing and information processing, there was a "downsizing" of corporate computing functions, a gradual shift towards workstations and, later, client/server systems.

For Olivetti, which had no investment in big computers but was trying hard to develop smaller, user-friendly terminals and other equipment, this was the chance it had been waiting for. The firm began working together with individual financial institutions, developing customized banking and foreign exchange systems. Through this custom-installation strategy, by responding to each institution's individual needs and designing specialized systems, Nippon Olivetti managed to get a foot in the door at many of the top city banks and trust banks, as well as the regional banks, credit associations, and Nokyo, where it got its start.

All this seemed to bode well for the company's future in the computer business. It seemed ready to expand beyond the financial sector and become a smaller but significant player in the broader corporate computer market. But this was not to be. The main problem was that even those big firms that bought Olivetti equipment needed to connect it to larger office systems and networks. Compatibility wasn't the problem; lack of a wider product line was. Ultimately, the firm didn't make its own line of office computers, so its equipment was always being connected to other makers' products. Gradually Olivetti equipment became a bit of an anomaly in the network. Japanese system managers hate having a few oddball units in an otherwise neatly integrated network, so regardless of performance, they will sooner or later lean toward replacing them with products from makers who provide complete systems.

The result was that computer sales growth, which had been expected to pick up at last and carry the firm forward, became flatter and flatter. Finally it turned downward. That coincided with growing internal problems between local staff and Italian management and frequent resignations, and soon the company's future course in Japan began to look rocky.

Clearly, it was time for a major change—of both personnel and strategy.

Matsushita Man

Nippon Olivetti's first president, Carlo Alhadef, had said, "I want Japanese to take over all ranks of management." In 1986, 25 years after the company came to Japan, it happened. The first Japanese *shacho* (president) in the company's history was Koichiro Kurita.

Kurita grew up in the Kansai region of western Japan and went to work for the top employer in Kansai, Matsushita Electric Industrial, the parent of the world's largest consumer electronics group. Matsushita sent him to the United States for two years as the first overseas executive trainee in its new plan to foster internationally-oriented businessmen. His job was to learn about American business, not in a classroom but in the field. Unlike many Japanese firms that still regularly send employees to the United States to get an MBA and then hurry them back to headquarters, Matsushita was not big on foreign schooling. The firm wanted a few of its men to live and work overseas, to get a first hand "feel" for foreign business.

Kurita got a little more feel for the business than he'd expected: "I spent two years working at Panasonic's West Coast center. During my last six months the top American salesman became sick and I had to fill in for him, visiting some of the top department stores to sell radios and so on. Back then, of course, the Panasonic name was almost unknown and 'Made in Japan' was not necessarily an asset. I didn't know what to do or what to say, but I knew I was going to give it a good try. In the end I racked up more sales than the full-time American salesman I was substituting for. In fact, I even got some of the stores' staff to take a training course in how to sell Panasonic products."

The stimulation of selling in the big, open American market must have gotten into Kurita's blood. Much to his own surprise, he seemed to be a natural-born salesman. After a year in Japan for executive training, he was back in America. He started in 1968, successively moving from one position to another, building a reputation that would spread throughout Matsushita's entire North American organization. He served with distinction as office manager in Miami, general manager in Puerto Rico, Boston, and Toronto, and then as general manager of the U.S. Office Products Division. Within a short time Kurita was known as a turnaround specialist, someone who could go into a local sales office that seemed to have gone dry, and before long bring in a gusher of black ink.

Yet his real fame was still to come—as the brains behind the Japanese electronics giant's assault on a new sector of the American market.

From the late 1970s on, Matsushita tried to break away from its image as a household electronics and appliance maker. One sector it emphasized was office equipment, and by the 1980s this had become a major thrust of the company's strategy. Kurita was the man in charge in the United States. At one point he had to develop a complete sales and marketing strategy for Matsushita's entire line of office equipment and carry it out nationwide. Just as one example, within two years of implementing his plan the company had grabbed a 10 percent overall share of the electronic typewriter market. The story of his success has been regularly used as an example inside Matsushita's management committee, and he became something of a legend within the firm's executive ranks.

In 1984 Kurita took a course at the Harvard Business School, and while there he met the vice-president in charge of personnel for an Italian company that was one of Matsushita's rivals in the office equipment sector. The next year he happened to visit Italy, and while he was there he followed up his Harvard friend's invitation to stop by at Olivetti's head office. Although he didn't know it at the time, he had exactly the qualities that Olivetti was looking for to get its Japan operation back on track: a Japanese executive who also understood corporate cultures outside of Japan, a salesman's salesman, a market strategist, and, best of all, a turnaround specialist whose forte was the office equipment business.

The offer came a short while later. How would Kurita like to give up being a subordinate for Matsushita and become a CEO for Olivetti, give up America and return to Japan? Under normal circumstances a rising star at a prestigious firm such as Matsushita would not have been quick to leave. But just by chance Olivetti's timing happened to be perfect.

"Right around the time I was in contact with Olivetti, things began to change suddenly in my personal life," Kurita confides. "I guess I was devoting too much time to business and my wife decided to leave me. I was shaken and I knew it was a crossroads in my life. I finally decided to start it all over, to change my lifestyle, change my job, change where I was living, the people I knew, everything all at once. I had already received a bunch of offers from other companies in America, but suddenly I wanted something different. I wanted a job that would be stimulating and enjoyable. It turned out that my ideas and Olivetti's corporate culture were a good match, so I said OK.

"I didn't waste any time; I told the people at Matsushita right out. They were stunned. Finally, I persuaded them that I wanted a challenge, I wanted to try something new, and I think they understood. Matsushita and Olivetti have had a very close relationship because Matsushita is a parts supplier to Olivetti. So instead of just saying 'goodbye,' I said 'We've got a lot of business to do together; please help me,' and even today I'm on close terms with a lot of executives at Matsushita."

The Key to Restructuring: Personnel Policies

Kurita was 45 when he took over the top spot at Nippon Olivetti, quite young to be *shacho* of an important firm by Japanese standards, but ready to do what was necessary to save that firm. His instructions from the Italian head office were simple: "Build a new Nippon Olivetti."

It took a few months for him to get a feel for his new surroundings, and when he did he wasn't too happy. "The truth is, the company was in terrible shape. Most of the talented staff between the ages of about 25 and 35 had already left or were on their way out to other firms. The firm's stock of promising candidates for middle management positions was dwindling. Profits were deteriorating and market clout in Japan was already weak. The company was nothing but a mass of problems."

But what surprised Kurita more than these big problems were the little things that seemed to have gone wrong inside the company. How was it possible, he wondered, that they didn't use a *ringisho*? This is one of the most fundamental elements of any Japanese company, a simple, one-page form that circulates among managers whenever an important decision is made; each manager puts his seal in red ink in the appropriate box to indicate his approval. In many cases it is just a formality, but it is an essential element of team building. It is a visible manifestation of agreement within the managerial levels of a firm and helps to solidify agreement when disparate opinions need to be unified. Nippon Olivetti, he found, didn't even have a *ringisho*, so Kurita had to start by drafting one. That was his only easy task.

Next came the most crucial stage of his internal reorganization: the personnel system. First he headhunted several managers from other companies, filling the hole in middle management. In 1987 he reinstated a policy of hiring new college graduates, bringing new blood back into the firm on a regular basis and hopefully building managerial talent for the future. Then in a dramatic move to increase staff motivation and loyalty, he significantly increased salary levels across the board and changed the salary system so that employees could boost their paychecks more through performance-based rewards than they could through the traditional seniority-system-based pay increases.

The reasoning behind this shift in personnel policies was to instill in all employees the idea that their contributions were directly related to the company's profits. Thus, he switched from a very Japanese personnel approach where everyone is evaluated by age and position and everyone at the same level essentially rises through the ranks together, to a meritocracy where each person's accomplishments are clear and people are judged on performance. In addition, staff evaluations were made a two-way street: employees now had to take the responsibility for looking objectively at their own performance and talking it over with their supervisors and with company officials.

Kurita's approach to personnel may not seem terribly radical to most Western readers, but in Japan it was the human resources policy equivalent of the industrial revolution. Here's how someone with years of experience working for a Japanese company explains the normal state of affairs even today: "In Japanese companies there is always an overwhelming sense of the 'inequality of equality.' That is, people with no ability get paid the same as people with tremendous ability. Every year your salary automatically goes up, which means the whole system is skewed to older workers, and so the young guys with real talent and motivation are treated worse. In this kind of system, no matter how hard you work you know that everyone must be regarded as equal, so talented young employees lose their drive very quickly."

And contrary to the image still popular overseas in which Japanese corporate employees are all pulling together, working 110 percent to make their company stronger, most young workers quickly learn that the system rewards longevity, not talent. The purpose of the system is to create an environment of job security, but the inevitable result is widespread mediocrity. Sooner or later every employee catches on to the idea that whether or not he works hard or works well makes very little difference. Pay scales do vary, but not tremendously, and promotions have traditionally been tied to age, not performance.

Kurita knew well enough how Japanese companies work and how a person who "gets along well" at the office is usually valued far more than someone with good ideas. He had also spent enough time working in America to know that a little carrot-and-stick motivation can work wonders for turning around a sleepy company.

How did the staff react to losing the comfortable arrangement they'd known for years? Predictably, those with talent welcomed such a system and felt better about the company because of the change; the ones with less talent realized immediately that it was time to put down the newspaper and get back to work because a cold wind was starting to blow. Those who expected to draw a paycheck until retirement for doing nothing began looking for the Exit door, and the firm's total staff dropped from 1,380 to 1,080 in three years without any firings. By instituting this new personnel system, the company eliminated a lot of "dead wood" and did so without having to put up a fortune in severance pay. Rather than weakening the firm as the previous attrition had, these resignations gave the company more leeway to increase salaries and other inducements for employees who were ready to work.

Oriental Desk

Since its founding, Nippon Olivetti's approach to business was simply to manufacture products in Italy and sell them in Japan. But Kurita had other ideas about that, too.

First he insisted that the head office in Italy establish an Oriental Desk in the product development division. The idea was to produce goods that were more in tune with the needs of the Japanese market (a theme we have seen at many other successful *gaishi*), and in a sense to bring the Italian head office and the Japan office closer together.

"You can't just make whatever looks good in Italy and assume it will sell in Japan," Kurita says. "The market doesn't work that way."

For example, it is often said that one of the main reasons why Olivetti started with a good reputation in the Japanese business machine market but then failed to become a contender in the computer market was because it didn't have local production facilities and so tried to sell Italian-made products as they were. Because the firm lacked a local product development group, the single most critical factor for expanding computer sales—a Japanese-language operating system—was developed very late. This painful experience provided a good lesson for the new Oriental Desk.

In fact, Kurita started pushing the head office to "send us products aimed at the Japanese market" early on. At first the reply from HQ was usually something like, "Sell 20,000 units of what you've got and then we can talk about doing something for the Japanese market." But after many tries Kurita finally succeeded in getting his point across. And in part the head office must have decided to back up the bet they made when they hired Kurita in the first place. One of the maxims for running a successful *gaishi* is "hire good people and give them plenty of support." Many companies do the first part but not the second, and Olivetti may be said to have been guilty on that score. But in 1993 everything changed.

In the autumn of that year, Olivetti finally announced what the Japan office had been waiting for—and then some: 11 new lines of equipment with a total of 32 new models. In Tokyo, most of the attention went to an extremely stylish, compact notebook computer designed by Mario Bellini. The unit weighed less than three pounds, its batteries ran for 3 to 6 hours, it had built-in sound recording capability, could handle Japanese software, and retailed for a reasonable price in Tokyo. Best of all from the sales point of view, the machine came wrapped in a very stylish leather cover. With the Olivetti name and Bellini design, it was a natural for young Japanese women who needed a sophisticated computer but saw no reason why it had to look like a black brick. Analysts noted that had it come out five years earlier, at the peak of the bubble economy, it probably would have sold out as fast as it could be delivered to stores.

Kurita wanted to advertise it heavily, but with the company still in its recovery phase the ad budget was not up to the kind of campaign he had in mind. Then a long-overdue stroke of good luck hit the firm: a well-known Japanese computer magazine did an entire special issue on Olivetti. The thrust of the report was: "From here on, the differences in features between one maker's laptop computer and another will grow less and less noticeable. As that trend progresses, makers will increasingly have to compete on the basis of design—and when it comes to design, it's hard to beat Olivetti."

The effect of this review together with the appearance of so many new products was an enormous shot in the arm for company morale. It quickly revamped its PC sales division and inaugurated a mail-order sales business to supplement normal sales channels. In the meantime, the little leather-covered notebook became a minor hit among younger buyers. Olivetti was back.

Scoring Big with Sports Equipment

President Kurita's first strategic move was to shore up the firm's reputation in basic computer and system technology, where it had already established an identity years before. Then he turned his attention to new fields in an effort to expand into new lines of business where the competition was less cutthroat but the potential rewards were high. Kurita is something of a sports nut, so he used his familiarity with various sports and leisure businesses as a springboard for new ideas which would position the company in high-growth sports-related niche markets.

One of the first ventures was bowling, a sport which is now enjoying a huge new wave of popularity in Japan. At most bowling alleys in or around the cities on a Saturday or Sunday these days, you need to wait in line to get a lane. One reason for this boom is that bowling has been "rediscovered" by young Japanese. Another reason is Nippon Olivetti.

Until recently bowling alleys had a pretty old-fashioned image, certainly not the kind of place where young people would go to have a good time. Olivetti changed that image by modernizing the lanes, bringing basic computer and display technology into a field that last encountered automation when pin boys were replaced with machines half a century ago.

Olivetti introduced a system in which the number of pins knocked down is automatically calculated and the score is immediately displayed for the bowler to see. The display also shows the remaining pins in an easy-to-read diagram and can display a replay of the last throw for those who wish to improve (or relive) their unique approach to good form. By electronically eliminating the bother of scorekeeping and showing the remaining pins at a glance, the system makes bowling easier and more fun.

Many alleys have already installed this system and more are doing so as old lanes are modernized. And Nippon Olivetti holds the top share in this field.

Olivetti systems are also being installed in ski lifts to check tickets. Not long ago a trial system was tested at Shiga Kogen (a major ski resort) with dramatic results. At many Japanese resorts different companies operate the lifts and the resort management must count how many people rode on which lift. With the Olivetti system, skiers attach a special ticket containing an IC chip to their sleeves, and an electronic device at the lift entrance automatically counts the number of people who entered. The same ticket keeps track of rental skis, poles, boots, etc., making it a big hit with resort operators. All signs are that the system will spread to dozens of ski slopes within the next few years.

What about golf? Many sports equipment firms feel that any product they can successfully market to the amateur golf industry is like having a license to print money. No one knows if there really are more driving ranges than post offices in Japan, but it certainly seems that way. Golf addicts (which include 95 percent of the population over the age of six) can be found at 6 in the morning or 11:30 at night lined up in double- and triple-decker practice ranges, swinging away at buckets of balls.

Olivetti decided to modify its bowling system and go after this driving range business. With the new system, the avid linkster can watch instant replays of his or her form after every shot. Moreover, the display system monitors the flight of the ball and provides useful information for improving your swing. Needless to say, these are not inexpensive systems, but initial tests indicate that the driving ranges are enthusiastic about installing them. Precisely because there are so many practice ranges, the owners desperately need some value-added function to differentiate their service from the one next door. Once again Olivetti looks well positioned to sell these systems nationwide within the next few years.

Communicating with the Head Office

There were many cases in Nippon Olivetti's history where the Italian way of thinking and the Japanese way of thinking collided. As Kurita puts it, "You know, I was in America for a long time; I'm used to the American style of negotiating. But things are a little different with an Italian firm." For instance, there was the matter of advertising. The Italian side said, "When you've sold X thousand units, we'll put up some ad money." The Japanese side responded, "We need ad money in order to sell. Advertising money comes before sales, not after."

A more significant case concerned the company's relations with Nokyo, the giant organization of agricultural cooperatives. As we saw earlier, when the big banks introduced large-scale computers one after another, Olivetti was left out in the cold, having withdrawn from the mainframe market. But because it had such strong business relations with Nokyo, Olivetti was able to develop its expertise in terminals and peripherals and get a foot in the door at small and medium-sized banks that were just beginning to computerize.

But when profits from the Nokyo business started to dry up, the head office recommended loosening ties to that group. Kurita recalls: "In 1986 an exec came out from Italy, examined our margins with some of our biggest customers, and said we should cut our trading with Nokyo. I opposed that. In Japan, once you develop a solid trust relationship with a big company, you don't break it. On the contrary, you do everything possible to keep it. It takes about four years to build up a solid customer relationship and more to keep it healthy. I kept telling the head office that the trust relationship is an important asset beyond any immediate profit or loss. It took a long time to explain that and get the head office to understand and accept it."

Kurita concludes, "Whether a *gaishi* firm succeeds or not has a lot to do with how well the parent company understands the local company's situation. You can't overemphasize how important it is to understand Japanese culture and the Japanese market in order to do business successfully here."

Conclusion

Kurita played a big role in turning around Nippon Olivetti, a firm with a long history in Japan but one that was on the skids for a number of years. The parent company essentially made a life-or-death bet on the future of the firm when they brought in the turnaround artist from Matsushita. Had he not been able to deliver the kind of management expertise they needed, it is quite likely the company would have had to withdraw from the Japanese market. Instead, after only three years of restructuring, Nippon Olivetti's overall performance rose significantly and it is once again being cited as an example of a *gaishi* firm that has overcome past difficulties to "make it" in Japan.

The keys to Kurita's success were simple:

- He sought quality staff.

- He changed the company's internal personnel system to motivate both existing workers and new hires.

- He pushed the parent company to reconsider its commitment to Japan, to produce new products for an important local market.

Along the way, these new policies strengthened the company's identity and improved its image with everyone from prospective employees to its clients and suppliers. Kurita himself has been the sparkplug that has fired up Nippon Olivetti's engine. He took the experience he gained in America of going around to offices where sales were nonexistent and turning those branches into top-sellers and transplanted both that enthusiasm and those sales techniques into a new team of young salesmen in Japan. Undoubtedly the single biggest factor in Olivetti's turnaround in Japan has been the injection of a smart, tough, experienced chief executive.

CHAPTER 12

A Success Story in the Making

Nobelpharma Japan

This is a book of success stories, examples of foreign companies that have already made it in Japan and are now looking to further growth. In that regard, this firm may not belong on the list. However, we thought it would be interesting to look at a small firm with an unknown product that has struggled hard to make it in Japan and is now on the brink of success. The firm has had to contend with all the usual obstacles (bureaucratic regulations, difficult distribution and sales routes, etc.) as well as many problems that are common to *gaishi* operating in Japan, such as unstable management, lack of product awareness, and so on. In addition, Nobelpharma Japan is quite different from P&G, Coke, BMW, and most of our other examples in that its most significant product is not a typical consumer item, but rather a medical prosthesis whose effectiveness must first be "sold" to the Japanese medical profession and then, through their recommendations, requested by patients. It makes trying to sell left-hand-drive Cadillacs in Tokyo look easy by comparison.

A Million Patients

Nobelpharma is a Swedish company, part of the corporate group whose founder was the legendary Alfred Nobel, inventor of dynamite and the originator of the Nobel Prizes. Nobelpharma's principal business is in manufacturing dental implants as support for artificial teeth. This may seem a hard concept to grasp at first, but it is really not very technical. For a variety of reasons—accidents, disease, old age, etc.—people may sometimes lose a large number of teeth. Where several teeth are completely missing there is no support for conventional crowns or bridgework. Use of dentures is sometimes possible, but not always the most desirable option.

To respond to such situations, Nobelpharma has developed a system which involves surgical installation of titanium implants into the patient's jaw bone, then uses this implant as a foundation for artificial roots to which false teeth can be attached securely.

The problem with attempting to implant metal in human bone is that the two materials do not normally have an affinity for one another, hence the use of pins and bolts to attach metal prostheses in hip, leg, and other kinds of surgery. The rule is that metal can be a good brace, a supplement or a replacement for human bone, but it is generally something that the bone regards as a foreign substance and resists no matter how long the two are together.

There is one exception, however, and it was discovered quite by accident in Nobelpharma's home country. In 1952, Dr. Per–Ingvar Branemark of Goteborg University tried attaching an element made of titanium to an animal's leg bone, and then after some time he tried to remove it to examine the results. To his surprise, the metal and the bone seemed to have merged in some way. It was almost impossible to separate them. Because the very idea of metal and bone forming a natural bond went against established science at the time, Dr. Branemark knew that he had stumbled onto something with profound implications.

The next step was to see if the same phenomenon held true with human bones, and Dr. Branemark soon discovered that indeed, titanium and human bone seemed to like each other in a most unusual way. For some reason the body did not reject the metal as foreign material, and no inflammation developed as a result of the implantation of titanium. His conclusions were simple: unlike other metals, titanium bonds with bone naturally (a process he called *osseo integration*), and the longer the two remain in contact, the stronger the bond becomes.

After more than a decade of research and testing, Dr. Branemark encountered a patient who had lost all his teeth in a traumatic accident. The question was raised: Would it be possible to build a metallic foundation in a human jaw bone and then attach artificial teeth to that base?

Dr. Branemark assembled a team of surgical specialists, implanted an artificial base in the patient's jaw, and then attached artificial teeth to this secure base. The surgery was completely successful. For more than 30 years that first dental patient has been living a normal life with what are essentially titanium roots extending from artificial teeth into his jaw. This was the beginning of what has come to be known as the Branemark System for implanting artificial teeth, and it is the basis of Nobelpharma's business.

Is this a highly specialized technique that can only be done at a few major hospitals? Hardly. In fact, while the technique is difficult and does require both special training and facilities, it is spreading rapidly. Already over one million people around the world have had this surgery, with nearly one-third of them using the Branemark System, and the pace is quickening. Within the next five years it is expected that there will be a million Branemark System patients. Therein lies a large potential market, and one that is bound to expand as the years go by and the process becomes even more common.

Selling the System

Nobelpharma makes and sells the titanium implants and other components for the Branemark System and imports them to Japan. More than this, however, the firm proselytizes the Branemark System and helps to train dentists and other medical professionals in the techniques necessary to apply it. In 1986 the Swedish parent firm set up a subsidiary, Nobelpharma Japan, to handle this business.

Noriko Hornmark is a Japanese married to a prominent local Swedish business consultant, Nils Hornmark. Both she and her husband have at different times served as Nobelpharma Japan's top executive. When we asked her about the company's history, she explained as follows:

"Nobelpharma set up a company in the United States in 1983, and the next target on their list was Japan. My husband knew the president of Nobelpharma in Sweden and so he came to be consulted about the prospects of entering the Japanese market. In 1985 the company ran seminars here in Japan to introduce the Branemark System. I was asked to help out as a translator. In 1986 Nobelpharma Japan was set up and applied to the Ministry of Health and Welfare for permission to sell its products. Of course, it always takes a long time to get ministry approval for anything new. In the meantime, the company wanted to become active in Japan. My husband became president and I became the sales manager."

Noriko herself is an interesting person. She studied at a well-known nursing school in Tokyo, then traveled abroad on a Fulbright fellowship. After returning to Japan and her nursing school, she decided that she wanted to do something non-medical, so around 1980 she formed a company with a Swedish friend to import foods. The next five years were spent learning about the difficulties of managing even a small company. Then when she was asked to help out with the Branemark System seminars, her medical background and Swedish language ability were both assets.

Like many *gaishi* start-ups, Nobelpharma Japan began without even its own office, simply renting some office space from a group affiliate in Tokyo. Noriko Hornmark soon became a Branemark System evangelist. She still says, "It's a marvelous system. Nobelpharma isn't selling the hardware—the implants themselves—but the software, the whole system." Since she believed so strongly in the product, she was determined to put together a specialized sales team.

"Because of the system," she explains, "we didn't use dealers. It had to be sold directly. But our clients are professionals—dentists and professors at major dental universities—so the salespeople must be professionals, too. People who cannot confidently discuss the details of the system with dentists will not do, and when it comes to the surgery itself, those who cannot also assist the dentist and help with the procedure are likewise no good to us."

As a result, Hornmark hired many nurses with surgical experience. Also, because much of the documentation is in English, she looked for people with English ability. "We looked for people with all these qualifications, and it turned out that very few men fit the bill, so most of the staff I hired were women." This proved to be a big asset for the firm because many of these women were extremely talented, but it also proved a liability, as we shall see shortly.

Attracting the Dentists

Most of Japan's approximately 70,000 dentists run small, one-man offices with just a hygienist and a secretary. However, the Branemark System requires not merely a dentist, but a dental surgeon as well as a radiologist to work as a team. For a solitary dentist to try to implement the system is quite demanding. In addition, one important factor in the Branemark System is the need for absolute hygiene—the procedure is surgical, and like other forms of surgery, it is essential to prevent germs or bacteria from infecting the patient through the exposed areas. Thus the dentist must have a special "clean area" available to perform the surgery. The system also requires two surgical procedures a few months apart to complete the process.

Clearly, this is not something that even a majority of these 70,000 dentists are going to want to explore. It requires special equipment and special training. Considering that dentists are already near the pinnacle of both social status and income in Japanese society, it might seem as if there is little incentive to try this new, complicated system.

But Noriko Hornmark thinks differently: "I've spent a lot of time with Japanese medical people. I can tell you, by far the great majority of them are thinking primarily of helping their patients, not about money. They want to provide the best therapy possible for their patients . . . .

"However, it is not necessary to sell the Branemark System to all the dentists in Japan, only a small fraction. The system requires special study. Those who don't want to make that commitment are better off not to have anything to do with the system. Nobelpharma would prefer to work with a small percentage of dentists who really want to learn the system thoroughly."

The company's initial strategy was to invite specialists to come to Japan from Sweden. Nobelpharma organized seminars for 30-odd universities, and on three or four occasions they sent Japanese dentists to Sweden to study the system. Since the firm still hadn't received MHW approval for its technique and products, Japanese dentists couldn't do actual implants on patients in Japan. However, by going abroad they had an opportunity to participate in such surgery and so could properly evaluate the process.

In 1987 the MHW finally gave Nobelpharma Japan the official OK to import and sell its system. In 1988 the little firm moved to its own offices in a more prestigious part of town and began sales.

The medical fraternity in Japan is relatively small and close-knit for a country with a population half that of the United States. For a foreign company to succeed with any medical-related product, whether pharmaceuticals or medical equipment, two hurdles must be cleared: the MHW and the opinion makers of the medical establishment. Nobelpharma managed to clear the first, but the second required more than patience. It required strategy.

The company reasoned that it needed the cooperation of the two most influential universities in the field, Nippon Dental University and Tokyo Dental College, which together train a large number of Japan's top dentists. The effort proved to be an uphill battle, however.

For one thing, there was competition. Some time before Nobelpharma began operating in Japan, electronics maker and ceramics specialist Kyocera Corp. had developed artificial teeth made of ceramics and man-made sapphire. Kyocera had been urging Japanese dentists to try these products just as Nobelpharma now hoped to do.

There was another problem as well: cost. The surgery and the implanting of expensive metals is not covered by Japan's national health insurance. In Japan today, using the Branemark System to treat a whole jaw costs between $13,000–$30,000, all of which must be borne by the patient. Critics are quick to point out that you can buy a rather nice car for the price of putting some artificial teeth in your mouth.

The main reason why Kyocera's and other ceramic products are still widely used is cost. In some cases their price is only about 10 percent that of the Branemark System. Although Nobelpharma says the Kyocera artificial teeth often fail within three to five years (while its method is nearly permanent), the affordability of the rival products is a major attraction.

Of course the fact that titanium is particularly useful in this process has not escaped anyone's attention, and Kyocera among others has begun to offer products using titanium in addition to ceramics and artificial gems. In America, for example, there are a number of companies copying the Branemark System, and some Japanese companies are now importing those products. However, there is little historical data on most of these products; most do not have extensive clinical records to back up their claims.

And this was the root of the biggest problem. As a result of some lower-quality products and a lack of training, the number of problem cases involving implants has increased. Some patients who have been injured or suffered through faulty implants have actually sued their dentists (which in Japan, where legal recourse is almost never used and where the medical profession is held in unimaginably high esteem, is a shocking statement). When these implants resulted in a number of tragic experiences for both dentists and their patients, many professionals simply decided to stay far away from the whole nasty business. Thus, the subject of artificial teeth and bone implants had already acquired a decidedly negative image among Japanese dentists.

It was into this atmosphere of powerful mistrust that Nobelpharma had to venture in order to sell its products.

The firm's salespeople spent months explaining to their target "buyers" at the two big dental universities that its products were very different and clearly superior to what had been available in Japan previously. They pointed out that unlike many of the cheaper copycat systems, Nobelpharma's had been clinically tested for decades. Before Nobelpharma ever began operations in Japan, it had already been well received for over 20 years around the world, including in America (which is seen in Japan as the benchmark of advanced medicine). After much persuasion the two big universities agreed to cooperate. Nobelpharma arranged for each university to hold 4-day seminars a few times a year (to explain the technique) and to develop a basic course in the Branemark System for their students. Today, Nobelpharma Japan only sells its products and services to dentists who have taken one of these courses or something similar.

Revolving Presidents

Unfortunately, like quite a number of *gaishi*, Nobelpharma's difficulties in Japan were internal as well as external. For a small firm such as this, having a tight, smoothly functioning management team is essential. There must be clear direction from the CEO at the top and a stable network of salespeople to carry out the president's vision (BMW is a good example of how well this can work). Instead, Nobelpharma Japan seemed to have a revolving door in its president's office. In addition, many of its key salespeople left during the early stages of the firm's growth, and the company's strategy was naturally influenced by these changes.

As we noted, the first president of the Japan operation was the consultant who was asked to help bring the firm into this market. But Nils Hornmark was happy being a consultant and did not want to give up all his other work in order to run a company. As the burden of heading this growing firm (with its growing problems) began to swell, Hornmark stepped down. He was replaced in 1988 by another Swede chosen by the head office. But here the parent company made a classic tactical error, choosing a man who knew nothing about Japan, the local market, or the language. Worse yet, he was brought in from outside the parent firm, so he also lacked any background in the firm's products and philosophy. The brevity of his reign was a foregone conclusion. Less than a year after taking office, he resigned.

The third president was the former head of Nobelpharma Canada. He knew nothing of Japan but at least he knew the products well and, unlike his immediate predecessor, he had considerable management experience. He remained at the helm for 3 years, and during that time the company's performance gradually began to pick up. But this executive had already been away from his home for four years while stationed in Canada; after another three years in Japan, he was anxious to get back home. He, too, stepped down, and Nobelpharma Japan was once again without a leader.

Now the parent company tried a new approach: rather than simply sending someone to Japan to run the company, it discussed the situation with its twenty or so Japanese employees. Who did they feel was best qualified to run the company? Early in 1992 a decision was reached and a popular new president was named: Noriko Hornmark. She had a medical background, she was fanatically devoted to the products, she was something of a business-woman (she had run her small import business), she understood Japan, and she was bilingual. Her selection seemed the perfect answer for both the Japan operation and the parent company.

Problems with Female Workers

The advent of the second President Hornmark at Nobelpharma Japan did not eliminate the company's problems, however. This time the source of the difficulties was not the management but the staff. As we noted, when Noriko Hornmark had earlier served as sales manager she had staffed her sales and marketing team with people who had a medical background, were familiar with clinical testing procedures, and could read English. That limited most of her hiring to former nurses, and so the company's sales staff were de facto mostly women.

It is important to note that the results of this policy were both good and bad, and that Nobelpharma's experience is not at all unique. Quite the contrary, it provides a valuable lesson for all firms trying to do business in Japan today.

Obviously this is not the place to discuss in detail the problems of sexism in Japanese society, but it is a fact that despite some effective PR about equal opportunity (and a toothless law to guarantee the same) very few Japanese companies have ever considered women workers as valuable employees. The result is that women are almost never given important jobs (there are barely a handful of women directors among the more than 2,000 companies listed on the Tokyo Stock Exchange), and even lower-level managerial positions are routinely given to a man even when there is a woman employee available with years more experience in the same department. More overt forms of abuse are not uncommon.

Most Japanese men feel that the majority of Japanese women cannot handle the rigors of the corporate world, and they assume that all women really want to do is to get married and have children, so a career is only a kind of hobby before marriage. When these same men become managers at *gaishi* firms, they bring with them these attitudes. However, all but the most famous *gaishi* usually find that they cannot attract the very best Japanese male employees, so to one extent or another they have no choice but to accept qualified female workers. (A quick glance at the rosters of some of the top foreign banks and securities houses will testify to the numbers of Japanese women working in responsible positions there.) And yet many of these companies discover that Japanese women, once given responsibility and meaningful work, are every bit as talented as their male counterparts and in many cases more highly motivated.

Nobelpharma certainly found this to be true. The former nurses and others whom Noriko Hornmark hired worked very hard to promote the company and the Branemark System, and they are largely responsible for the firm's early successes.

But there is another side to dealing with female employees in Japan.

In most Japanese companies when there is some kind of trouble or something happens that deeply bothers the staff, the male employees will openly complain and, one way or another, the problem will be resolved; female workers, on the other hand, tend to keep their complaints to themselves and try their best to put up with whatever is causing the problem. In large part this probably stems from Japanese society's emphasis on *gaman* (endurance) as a prime virtue of womanhood. Whatever the reason, the job situation seldom improves of its own accord, while the women's willingness to endure the unendurable sooner or later wears thin. The result is that female employees often resign, and often quite suddenly.

Both the resignation and the way it is handled create problems for the company. A majority of Japanese men still expect to remain with a company for many, many years. Women, of course, have not been given the same expectations of long-term employment and so are understandably more willing to consider resigning if the job situation becomes uncomfortable. When it comes to that, a man will usually announce his resignation a few months in advance so as to pave the way for the transition after his departure. Quite often, however, female employees simply *gaman* as long as they can and then abruptly announce one day "I'm quitting." Within the next day or two there is simply an empty desk. Because they have built up so much resentment toward the company, they are far less concerned about what problems their sudden departure will cause.

Foreign companies are still hiring large numbers of Japanese female workers and giving them responsible work. Those firms that take proper advantage of the high quality and high levels of motivation of Japanese women are to be commended (although too many still pay women workers less than male staff doing the same job). But if *gaishi* firms do not understand the problems and typical psychological patterns associated with female employees, they are in for a lot of trouble.

This was certainly the experience of Nobelpharma. Many hardworking women helped the company to grow and to make important contacts among the medical profession. The problem was that they didn't stay in the company for very long. For various reasons many quit suddenly. Consequently, Noriko Hornmark turned the positions of sales manager and manager of the Osaka regional operation over to men and then she gradually increased the number of male employees. Yet even this did not solve the sales-team's problems.

The salesmen who came on board were mostly men who had worked for pharmaceutical companies or sold other medical-related products. To them, sales technique meant simply providing more "customer service." Prices were naturally something to be discounted. This did not sit well with President Hornmark, who had decreed that Nobelpharma's system was a quality product and not to be discounted.

The salesmen were also burdened with a social mindset common in Japan. As we have noted, doctors and dentists are still held in very high esteem by Japanese society. Salesmen who have worked for Japanese drug firms are accustomed to thinking of themselves as socially inferior to their clients. They feel that doctors are somehow born a few ranks above everyone else, and a doctor (or dentist) who also happens to be a university professor should be treated with even greater deference. Thus the role of the lowly salesmen is not to bother these doctors too much, but to make himself useful by wining and dining them at company expense.

At least the ex-nurses who had worked for the company before were well acquainted with the medical profession and could speak to the dentists—however lofty their positions at important universities—with some degree of professional expertise. This was one of the factors in their success in winning over reluctant dentists, despite their lack of real sales experience. Their replacements, the professional salesmen, were not well equipped to speak to dentists: they had no medical background, no license of any kind, and certainly could not assist in surgical procedures.

And so even as Nobelpharma's products and training began to make headway in Japan, its sales team was not prepared to market them effectively.

The Electrolux Story

It was fortunate that Nobelpharma had found someone like Noriko Hornmark who had a medical background, understood the products, and could talk to Japanese dentists intelligently. She helped the company immeasurably during a critical period in its growth. Still, Noriko was not trained as a businesswoman; her only management experience had come from her small import company. In some ways, she admitted, she was out of her depth managing a real business. There were also policy disputes with the head office, and for a number of reasons she, too, decided to step down. Thus, less than two years after hiring president number 4, Nobelpharma Japan found itself talking to president number 5.

Gunnar Kniberg took over from Hornmark in January 1994, and he is now turning Nobelpharma into the kind of firm that will soon be cited as a typical "successful *gaishi.*" Kniberg is no stranger to Japan or to corporate turnarounds. He came to Japan several years ago and, against all odds, turned a local subsidiary of Sweden's famed Electrolux into a thriving business. As a matter of fact, a brief look at Electrolux's story may also be useful in observing different paths to success for foreign firms.

In 1967 after graduating from business school in Sweden, Kniberg went to work as export manager for a Swedish foods company that was selling in Japan. In 1969 he moved to Electrolux, and a year later, at age 28, became head of its Asian operations.

After a year of negotiations with trading giant Mitsui & Co., Kniberg helped to establish a joint-venture company, Nihon Electrolux System Co. (NESCO), to pursue the company's interests in the Japanese market. As part of this venture, Mitsui people were sent to Sweden to learn about Electrolux products and the parent firm's executives in Sweden made several trips to Japan.

In 1973 Kniberg went a step further, setting up a Far East representative office for Electrolux in Tokyo. In reality it was nothing more than Kniberg, his wife, and his Japanese secretary working out of a small rental space, for the company's Japan presence aside from NESCO was minuscule.

Kniberg worked hard for two years, learned a little about the local culture and market, and in 1975 set up a new subsidiary company, Electrolux Japan. He served concurrently as vice-president of the NESCO joint venture and as president of the new subsidiary.

Until that point, Electrolux's business in Japan was mainly done through sales agents, and the latter's main success was in selling refrigerators to Japanese department stores. Annual sales at the time were roughly ¥4 million (about $15,000 at that time). In other words, its sales agents were not exactly turning Electrolux into a corporate giant. Consequently, Kniberg had to build Electrolux Japan up from a virtual zero base.

As with Levi Strauss and other companies we have looked at here, the firm's biggest problem was deciding how best to cope with the Japanese distribution system. Getting your products into established Japanese distribution channels is difficult, and even if you do, there is no guarantee that they will sell. The major Electrolux product in Japan was a large-size home vacuum cleaner, a product that competed head-to-head with the rapidly rising power of the Japanese electronics makers. Companies like Matsushita (Panasonic), Hitachi, Sanyo, and Toshiba were already capturing the domestic appliance market with a torrent of new goods.

Japanese-made products such as washing machines, steam irons, and vacuum cleaners were not terribly cheap, but at least they had trusted brand names and they were backed by good service from local shops. The big Swedish-made vacuum cleaners were unknown, they were not widely distributed, and who knew if anyone would service them when they broke down? Worst of all, because the yen was relatively low compared to other currencies, the Electrolux products became more expensive than they would have been otherwise. The young Kniberg had his work cut out for him.

The only advantage Electrolux could brag of was a critical one in the eyes of the Japanese consumer—quality. Its concept was quite different from the simple vacuum cleaners sold by domestic rivals. The Electrolux system included a vacuum, carpet shampoo, power nozzle, and other components, making it a complete floor-care system. This helped to justify its price, which was 10 times that of ordinary Japanese vacuum cleaners. The company was convinced that if housewives saw the system in action they would be persuaded. Kniberg's decision was simple: he had to get around the distribution system and go straight to the consumer. And so the firm began a massive telephone canvassing campaign to arrange appointments for demonstrations of its unique product. Over a period of 20 years Electrolux representatives telephoned 8 million households, the first time a telephone campaign had ever been done on such a scale in Japan.

Needless to say, many Japanese firms (and not a few foreign "experts") said the whole idea was foolish. After all, Japanese housewives wanted to shop in familiar stores where they could see familiar name brands. No one would want to buy a more expensive foreign product from an unknown company, and even if they did, who would ever let salespeople from some strange foreign firm into their homes to do demonstrations?

The answer was, "a million Japanese housewives." The demonstrations were almost like entertainment—people invited friends and neighbors over to watch. And what they saw was convincing. The Swedish product was dramatically superior to any of its Japanese competitors, and the built-in quality was obvious to housewives looking for durability. It took a lot of time and a lot of effort, but Kniberg and Electrolux got around the distribution system by winning over customers in person. Gradually sales began to climb. In that same 20-year period, Electrolux performed 1.3 million product demonstrations and sold a total of 250,000 systems. So much for the experts.

By 1990 Electrolux Japan was doing well enough that it no longer needed the partnership with Mitsui & Co. that had once been its entree into this market. Electrolux announced that it wanted to withdraw from the JV, and Mitsui bought the outstanding shares in NESCO.

Electrolux Japan showed that a company with a good product, a good marketing idea, and unwavering determination can not only break into this tight market but can sometimes do the impossible, like selling electrical appliances to the Japanese.

In time the parent firm began talking about bringing Kniberg home again. They wanted to promote him to a post at the head office, perhaps a senior vice-president or something, but nothing they could offer could compare to running the entire Japan operation and supervising most of Asia. Generous and well intentioned though the company's offers might be, they seemed somehow a step down. He decided it was time to move on.

Perhaps the truth of the story lies beyond mere titles and job descriptions. Kniberg, like so many executives who spend more than five years or so in Asia, may have succumbed to the lure of living and working in a very different culture. Many people who spend two years or less in Japan can't wait to get back home again, but those who come to terms with being a stranger in a strange land for as long as Kniberg did are not likely to rush back home at the first opportunity. This, too, is something that parent companies often misjudge in dealing with staff they have sent to Asia. Managers who spend too little time don't know enough about the local culture to be effective; those who spend more time may discover that the new environment offers both work-related challenges and rewards as well as lifestyle and cultural attractions that can easily rival anything available back home. Whatever it is about Asia, and Japan in particular, a significant number of foreign executives don't want to return when their term is up.

Time to Move

In Kniberg's case the roots were starting to show. Clearly it was not another job offer that kept him in Tokyo. For three years he stayed on without a company affiliation, working as commercial counselor at the Swedish embassy, helping his countrymen to get started and to improve their business in Japan. Spiritually rewarding as this must have been, he was probably pleased in 1993 when the word came from Nobelpharma that it was looking for a new president to run its Japan operation. After meetings in Sweden with the parent company brass and a close examination of the firm's products and potential, he signed on.

His predecessor, Noriko Hornmark, had emphasized promoting the Branemark System to specialists—dentists, professors and students of dentistry, and others in the medical profession with a direct interest in the technique. If they became supporters, she believed, they would ultimately promote the system to their patients and reduce the need for marketing efforts. Kniberg saw things differently.

Kniberg believes that in the Japanese market alone there is tremendous latent potential. Over 10,000 patients have been successfully treated already with the firm's products. However, very few potential customers are as yet aware of the Branemark System, and so the demand for it is still largely dormant. Even if they hear about this kind of system, most people have no basis from which to evaluate it against its cheaper imitators. Thus, while promoting the system to the dental profession was still critical, it was also necessary to begin a long-term program of more general public relations.

Kniberg looked at Nobelpharma Japan and saw a good product, a solid potential market, and the beginnings of successful distribution. (A few thousand dentists had already taken the special training necessary to work with the Branemark System.) What the company needed was professional management and a much broader approach to marketing.

Kniberg invited Dr. Branemark to come to Japan and organized a large medical conference in his honor. In addition, he ran a seminar at the Swedish embassy in Tokyo. The focus of these sessions was of course on disseminating information about the Branemark System, but not merely for dental applications. The conference and the seminar opened up all sorts of new possibilities to the Japanese medical profession, as the same basic system can be applied to other kinds of implants. Dr. Branemark showed how the system has been used successfully outside Japan in various types of reconstructive surgery. For example, the system can be used to implant a titanium base in the facial bones, then apply artificial skin in layers over it and create artificial noses and ears so realistic that they seem completely natural. The Branemark System has helped people whose faces were horribly disfigured after cancer surgery to look normal once again. It is no exaggeration to say that this technique has dramatically improved patients' lives.

Currently Dr. Branemark is working on applying the technique to arm and leg prostheses, making artificial limbs that are connected to real bone and work more naturally than current devices. One project involves people with advanced rheumatism who cannot even bend their fingers. By careful use of the system in surgical implants, patients have regained the use of their hands.

All these and many other projects are still under testing at hospitals around the world, but so far the results have been very promising.

The Nobelpharma-sponsored conference and seminar were very well attended, not only by dentists but by various surgeons and specialists. As the Japanese doctors heard about this ongoing research, the respect for the Branemark System and its official sponsor in Japan grew enormously. Kniberg's first step to broadening the appeal of the company's products was a success.

From here on the firm will continue to promote its system to the medical—not just dental—profession and will move toward making the system better known among prospective users. As has been often noted, Japanese insist on quality in whatever they buy. As the advantages of the Branemark System become better known, both to doctors and patients, the demand is sure to increase at an even faster pace. The first signs of that are already appearing. Within a short time Nobelpharma Japan will find itself included among the ranks of small *gaishi* companies that have come to Japan, fought against both domestic and foreign competition, overcome mistrust and lack of interest in their intended market, survived internal reorganizations, and come out on top, examples of how a company can succeed given a good product and good management.

Afterword: Some Notes from the Top

Gunnar Kniberg has spent many years in Japan, built one *gaishi* from nothing into a highly profitable business, and is now turning a second one into a thriving concern. One reason for his success is his experience in the local market and understanding of Japanese trends. Here are a few comments for other *gaishi* managers:

> Recently Japanese firms have started moving away from the old lifetime employment system. Japanese workers are becoming somewhat mobile. If young people join a firm and then stay in that company all their lives it becomes a burden for the firm. Just look at all the companies trying to get rid of their glut of middle-aged workers now. Many of these are talented people, and many can be well employed by *gaishi*.
>
> In Japan, personnel costs are high, consumer costs are high, and land and office rents are high. Companies that aren't prepared to take a long-term view are never going to get anywhere.

One of his most apt comments pertains to the closed nature of Japanese society. Kniberg notes that while there is discrimination, it is not specifically anti-foreign discrimination; it is often just as applicable to small or new Japanese firms as it is to foreign-owned companies. But, he says, firms that have good products and a will to win are on track to get a piece of one of the most lucrative consumer markets in the world:

> The whole Japanese system is designed to help insiders and set up obstacles for outsiders, so the only solution is to become an insider. A *gaishi* firm that comes to Japan with a good idea, one that has not already been taken up by a domestic company, and makes a serious commitment to this market will be well received. You can become an insider. You can succeed here.

CHAPTER 13

If at First You Don't Succeed

Nestlé

"We are often cited as an example of a successful foreign firm operating in Japan, but aside from one product—soluble instant coffee—we haven't really made great efforts to promote our business. For several years even Nescafé was not a big plus for us. Of course we know the dangers of relying on the contributions of only one product, so for some time we've been stepping up our efforts to sell a wider range of products, including chocolate, pet foods, and mineral water. We want the firm to grow and to grow in a more balanced fashion," explains President Hans J. Klett, of Nestlé Japan Limited.

Many Western readers may suspect that Klett, who has headed the firm since October 1992, is being unduly modest. After all, Nestlé is the world's largest food and beverage group, and the Swiss-based giant is one of the most familiar brand names around the world. Millions of children grew up eating Nestlé's chocolate or drinking Nestlé's chocolate-flavored milk drinks, and many adults are big consumers of other Nestlé products, such as Perrier mineral water.

Both of Nestlé's major products, chocolate and coffee, were known in Japan before the war and both were catapulted to popularity in the years afterwards. Moreover, Nestlé products have had over a century in Japan to build their reputation (and the company has been in Japan for 80 years, far longer than most *gaishi*). Surely this is one powerful firm that had a head start on other *gaishi*, had popular products to sell, and should have grown like crazy, putting out one hit after another.

And the company wishes it had. In fact, while the Nestlé story in Japan is quite a long one, it is a tale of innumerable trials and errors leading to its ultimate success.

A Long History

Nestlé has been in Japan almost as long as any *gaishi*. The parent firm was founded in Switzerland by Henri Nestlé in 1866, just a year before Japan overthrew the last shogun and marched into the modern age. In 1905 a merger with Anglo–Swiss Condensed Milk produced the company we know today as Nestlé S.A. Although its products were imported into Japan in the late nineteenth century, the company set up here early in the present century. As early as 1908 we can already find the firm's products listed in an advertising pamphlet distributed by Meidi-ya, a famous Yokohama-based importer of foreign goods that was backed by the Mitsubishi combine (and is still well known today). Although primarily a dairy products business, Nestlé had begun selling chocolate in Japan from early on. It opened its first branch office in Yokohama in 1913, one year before Japan's oldest chocolate-maker, Morinaga & Co. At the time, chocolate was not seen as a very lucrative enterprise. It was a delicacy, a gourmet product for the well-to-do, not a product for mass consumption the way it is today. So the company kept its focus on other lines. In 1922 the firm moved its Japan branch from Yokohama, the main city for foreign business, to Kobe, the second major port frequented by foreign traders. Kobe had a large *gaijin* community and a more Continental atmosphere as opposed to Yokohama's distinctly American and British ambience.

As early as 1915, just two years after setting up the Yokohama branch, the parent firm had planned to tie up with a Japanese company for local production of dairy products such as condensed milk. Had it done so, Nestlé's history in Japan would have been very different. As it was, the negotiations failed and the parent firm decided to set up a local subsidiary and build its own factories.

In 1937 the parent company developed a tremendous new product, something that changed modern lifestyles forever and probably had a greater impact on corporate productivity than either the assembly line or just-in-time production. It was called soluble instant coffee. The product became a huge hit in the United States, especially during the war years that followed. In fact, most Japanese first saw "instant coffee" after the war, when the Nestlé product was standard military issue for the American Occupation forces. Soon instant coffee along with dozens of other imported goods found its way to the black markets like the famous Ameyayoko-cho (discussed in chapter 9).

Executives from the Swiss parent started including Japan on Far East survey trips, and by the 1950s were convinced that the company had a big future in Japan. They were surprised to see quantities of Nescafé selling in Ameyayoko-cho and took this as a sign that it was time to produce locally. Until that time, the company had operated with a dual structure: a sales operation, Nestlé Japan, and separate manufacturing facilities. The decision was made to merge these operations and to move toward a single, unified company identity. Henceforth, Nestlé Japan would produce and sell its own products and try to build a stronger reputation in this expanding market.

The company's big break came in the early sixties. In 1960, government regulations governing the importation of coffee beans were liberalized, and the following year restrictions on importing soluble instant coffee were also relaxed. Although an application still had to be filed and ministry approval was still officially required, coffee could be freely imported. The significance of this change is visible in the company's performance record: in its 1962 term alone, Nestlé Japan's sales jumped 3.6 times over the previous year. The reason that the government began taking these first steps toward market opening was the very healthy expansion of the economy. (For more background, see chapter 6.) Over the next few years the nation's GNP would double and personal income levels would soar. As families bought their own houses, cars, washing machines, and air conditioners (things undreamed of just a decade or so before), life styles changed dramatically. Some of those changes began to happen in the kitchen. Nescafé jars appeared on Japanese breakfast tables as hurried husbands dashed out the door to catch the 6:05 train. The media focused on instant coffee as one of the three instant food trends (along with instant ramen noodles and instant curried rice) that were destined to become long-term hits and signalled changes in the Japanese diet.

Looking at the huge jump in sales figures, it was clear to Nestlé executives that instant coffee, not chocolate or condensed milk, was going to be the company's big *dorubako* (moneymaker) for some time to come. And so in 1961 the firm also began its first major promotional campaign. The company did something unusual: it took its products on the road; not even in Tokyo but out in the provinces. A caravan of VW buses with the Nestlé logo painted on their sides travelled the countryside, visiting local distributors and small stores in ordinary little towns in every prefecture. This promotion gave potential vendors and distributors throughout Japan a chance to "see the company's face." The response was very positive, so the following year the Kobe headquarters decided to concentrate on the one area where it was still weak: Tokyo. It stepped up advertising and local promotion efforts and soon became the top seller in the critical Tokyo market.

Tonya Power

Today Nescafé-brand products hold 70 percent of the market for instant coffee. One key to this remarkable success was Nestlé's decision to rely on local distribution channels. Instead of investing huge sums to develop its own distribution network, the firm left it in the hands of the regional *tonya* (wholesalers).

The first- and second-level *tonya* are very thorough: they check products very carefully, and if they think the merchandise will sell, they distribute it to every nook and corner of Japan. There may be those who would criticize the firm for using the same marketing routes as its rivals instead of developing its own, but we disagree. Nestlé knew that it had a first-rate product, but its rivals were using a first-rate distribution system. To try to compete with the latter would have driven up Nestlé's costs tremendously. Instead, Nestlé took advantage of that system and trusted the quality of its products to win in the marketplace.

These days every big store and all discount stores and super-markets use a sales technique called mass display: piling up dozens or even hundreds of the same product to create an eye-catching mountain of goods that no shopper can miss. But it was Nestlé that first introduced that technique to Japan. Early on the company saw that the nation's fledgling supermarkets were going to grow—together with the economy and consumer affluence—and would spread throughout the country. Based on its experience in Western markets, Nestlé knew how very effective these super-markets could be in moving large quantities of a product and, through their sales displays, convincing consumers that one brand was the "standard" against which others must compete. Nestlé was one of the first big makers to take full advantage of the supermarkets; it even developed competitions among different stores to come up with the most effective display for its products and awarded cash prizes to the winners.

As its strategy of effective mass distribution via the *tonya* and effective mass sales through the supermarkets continued to de-velop, the company began to concentrate on advertising to a mass audience as well. The first Nestlé TV commercial had run back in the watershed year of 1961, and from then on the firm invested heavily in advertising. It developed a striking series of TV spots for its instant coffee, many of which are memorable even 20 years later. In addition, Nestlé sponsored sporting events, concerts, and a variety of other cultural events. Nestlé worked hard to become a household name in Japan and then worked harder to make sure it stayed that way.

Learning about the Local Market— the Hard Way

Although the parent company is a highly diversified foods business, Nestlé Japan was becoming a one-product company, a situation its managers knew was an invitation to trouble. So various efforts were made to diversify into other areas. It would have been nice for the firm if everything had gone as smoothly as the coffee business, but it didn't.

One major effort that in the end proved to be an expensive learning experience was the company's entry into the cereal business. Breakfast cereals are a huge market in North America, but in Japan rice, not Rice Crispies, has been on the breakfast table for roughly 2,000 years. Even today the majority of Japanese eat grilled fish, warm rice (often with dried seaweed), and perhaps a fresh or hard-boiled egg in the morning. Until quite recently, sugar-coated corn flakes and cold milk did not strike many Japanese as either an appetizing or healthy way to start their day. Add to that the fact that a number of Japanese cannot metabolize milk very well and you have what marketing people would call "a couple of minor obstacles" to overcome.

Even so, the American cereal giant Kellogg, which had a much larger stake in that business than Nestlé, was determined to sway the eating habits of a nation. At the time Nestlé was planning its entry into the cereal market in the mid-1980s, Kellogg had been hard at work for over 20 years trying almost single-handedly to turn the Japanese diet toward a new course. Although the progress had been slow, the American company was beginning to see some reward for all its efforts. In the early 1980s, the cereal market was worth about ¥8 billion (about $80 million), and Kellogg had cornered roughly an 80 percent share.

Nestlé believed that the market would grow much faster than in the past, but it also knew that cereal was still a relatively small business and dominated by one firm. If the company's market entry was not handled well, it would simply be lost in Kellogg's shadow.

According to the company's manager of cereal product planning at the time, "We did not just jump into the cereal market. We looked at several research studies that showed that Japanese breakfasts were unsatisfactory before making our decision. We also looked at positive market research data from Europe and Southeast Asia before we decided to go ahead in Japan."

All the same, the company had an uphill battle ahead of it. Not only do Japanese not like to eat cereal for breakfast, but the common image of Western cereals was as a midday snack for young children. So when Nestlé launched its products in 1987, it aimed them at the children's market.

The first battle proved to be with its own head office. As the same product planning manager explained, "The Nestlé name is used prominently on coffee and chocolate, but not much on other packaging. When we said we wanted to use the name on breakfast cereals, the Swiss parent was not happy. It took some time, but eventually we persuaded them."

Then there was the problem of taste. People brought up on rice-based meals and flavorings such as *miso* (soy) and sesame are not likely to be attracted to the kind of sweet, crunchy cereals popular abroad. To create a taste that the Japanese palate would like, the firm experimented with *miso* flavorings and other ways to appeal to the Japanese palate. This problem was largely solved by a health food boom that grew in the late 1980s, which not only shifted the emphasis to different tastes but also made "natural" cereals an option for health-conscious adults. By 1988 the firm was bringing out cereals using barley (a flavor to which the Japanese were accustomed) with names such as "Fitness" and "Bran-Rich."

The company promoted the high fiber content of these new cereals and their importance in contributing to a balanced diet, and within a short time these new products had become best sellers. By 1988 Nestlé had grabbed an astounding 35 percent share of the adult diet cereal market. Its next target was the all-important family market. It decided to stay with the healthy theme. As the cereal product manager recalls, "Many Japanese feel that they don't eat enough vegetables, so that seemed a good way to go. We tried all sorts of ideas but settled on a few key items that were important for health but also popular with Japanese consumers, such as carrots, spinach, and pumpkins. We had to enhance the colors a little bit—naturally, of course—but what we developed was a healthy cereal that included vegetables. Then, to differentiate our cereals from the competition, we developed a special manufacturing process so that when you poured on milk they didn't get all soggy, but stayed crisp and crunchy."

Then, to prevent any embarrassment to a product bearing the Nestlé name, the firm did even more market research. Just before releasing its new vegetable-based cereal, it tested the product on 200 typical households. Of that group, 82 percent said they liked it and nearly 70 percent said they would buy it as a breakfast food for the whole family. That was all the marketing people needed to know. In March 1989, Nestlé released *Yasai Taimu* (Vegetable Time).

Winning and Losing a Market

Developing a new product turned out to be easier than selling it, however. The problem was Nestlé's own salesmen who were fundamentally oriented toward instant coffee, the company's proven winner.

"Whenever we'd put out something new, they'd try to push for a little while, then they'd go right back to selling Nescafé. That's what they know best."

So, to get *Yasai Taimu* and other new products out into the market, a special sales team was put together. In a more dramatic step, the cereal product planner moved his desk into the sales department and took personal responsibility for part of the sales campaign.

"When you're doing sales, you get input from the marketplace every day. And when you go to stores in person and the store manager has an idea, instead of having to say, 'I'll bring that up with the people at the head office later on and we'll see what we can do,' you can make the decision on the spot." For example, when the supermarket chain Daimaru Peacock had its thirtieth anniversary sale, they asked some of the food companies to help out. The product manager immediately arranged to have "30th Anniversary" imprinted on boxes of certain products that were 30 percent bigger than normal. Also, where in the past every request had to go through the company headquarters in Kobe and then to the processing plant, he was able to send orders directly to the plant.

After much effort, *Yasai Taimu* became a big hit, ultimately ranking number 2 among all cereals in Japan, right behind market-leader Kellogg's top brand.

Although the Japanese cereal business had been growing at a slow but steady pace for many years, Nestlé got into the market at the right time with the right kind of products, and the business started to boom. Supermarkets, which had all but ignored the product, began putting in cereal corners. Kellogg responded by launching its own new products and marketing them heavily, which gave the cereal sector an even bigger boost. In 1986, the total market grew to a substantial ¥14 billion, but within three years it had doubled to ¥30 billion. Suddenly the cereal market had become a viable business in Japan.

And that was the problem. As in other sectors of Japanese industry, the food sector includes a number of giant domestic firms with enormous clout in the market. These companies, which had been content to focus on snacks, instant noodles, or frozen foods rather than waste time on something as unimportant as breakfast cereals, suddenly woke up to the profits they were missing. They saw the market double, and then double again, and they also saw that two big *gaishi* firms were running the show. Pulling out the old tried-and-true Japanese playbook, the big food companies shifted to a "me-too" offense. With their huge production capacity and distribution muscle, the short-term result was predictable: in no time at all the market was crowded with look-alike cereals and domestic brands were elbowing the two *gaishi* intruders off the shelves. Going back to the standard playbook (which, though it has been around for decades and should have been memorized long ago by every *gaishi* executive, always seems to catch foreigners off guard), once the competition heated up on the shelves, the big Japanese food makers began slashing prices. What had been a crisp, lucrative market turned soggy almost overnight, and in 1991 Nestlé said "Enough," and withdrew from the business it had helped to create.

Many inside the firm wondered why it had given up so easily, but management knew the outcome of a protracted price war. Sure, Nestlé could stick it out, for years if necessary, while all the makers battled it out. In the end Nestlé might well be one of the few remaining players. But what would it have accomplished? Spending vast quantities of time, money, and human resources on a business venture only makes sense if its profitability justifies the investment. But even after the price war was finished it would be hard to make margins in the cereal business attractive again, leaving the firm with a large share of a relatively unprofitable market.

Of course there were those who wanted to continue the battle, but the top brass said no, it made better sense to pull out earlier rather than later. Nestlé had learned a basic lesson about doing business in Japan: if you have a good idea, a dozen local firms will copy it well enough that you'll be in a price war before you know it. The only way to win is to have proprietary technology you can protect, or to stay two steps ahead in developing and refining your product so that rivals can never fully catch up. Nestlé could follow neither path in the cereal business, and so its withdrawal was ultimately inevitable.

Three Misses: It's All in the Timing

Like any successful company trying to diversify, Nestlé introduced a variety of new products to the Japanese market. Some worked and some didn't, but unlike many other *gaishi*, the company learned from its mistakes and stayed the course. Chocolate was perhaps the biggest initial failure. Chocolate products are very important to the Nestlé group, accounting for about 15 percent of all sales worldwide in 1993. And so back in 1972 Nestlé Japan began importing chocolate bars. Initially the Japan side wanted to make the chocolate locally but the technical staff in Switzerland said that Japanese technology could not guarantee Nestlé quality levels, so management decided that imports were the way to go. Of course the cases of chocolate bars were imported by ship, and on a long voyage the taste of chocolate changes slightly (making it difficult to guarantee Nestlé's quality levels). But even if they had made the product in Japan, the effort was doomed. Problems with distribution, pricing, market targets, and just about everything else plagued the business from the start. Inside the firm the chocolate fiasco is seen as an example of how a *gaishi* firm can stumble if it does not plan carefully. In the end, Nestlé withdrew from this market for several years and then made a comeback.

Let's take a quick look at the company's problems.

Chocolate candy in Japan is traditionally handled through confectionery stores and cake shops. Nestlé tried to sell principally through supermarkets, just as they had done in Europe and were already doing with coffee in Japan. Back in the 1970s the supermarkets were still small and not well organized. This misjudgment in distribution hurt the firm badly. Then there was pricing. In the West, a large portion of chocolate sales go to adults, who will pay higher prices for more upmarket brands (Godiva, etc.). But in Japan the market has been aimed almost exclusively at young children. In other words, if a product isn't cheap it won't sell. Of course, because Nestlé was importing, it had to pay both for the cost of production and for shipping, so it couldn't sell at low prices.

It is also possible to repackage ordinary chocolate and sell it as super-premium (a few Japanese brands have tried it and gotten away with it), but the chocolate must be in small, expensive-looking balls or bite-size pieces in a fancy wrapping. Nestlé's product was plain old bar chocolate, and no matter how you wrapped it, it didn't look expensive enough to the Japanese eye. In fact, the bars that Nestlé was importing were actually too big for Japanese tastes, so between the size and the high price, the product was not suited to the local market.

The firm realized that it had made a few mistakes in getting started in the chocolate business in Japan. It tried to get around the import problems by consigning production to Lotte (a local candy maker), but even then things still didn't go well. Nestlé pulled out of that tie-up about five years later. They tried it once again in the late 1980s, when all sorts of markets were growing, spending was on the rise, and almost anything Western was likely to be popular. (This was the same time that the cereal business was starting to take off.) This time the products were modified for the Japanese market and the timing was good. The business slowly gained ground, and today, after much effort, chocolate has become one of the firm's growth areas.

Another product that missed its market by a few years was yogurt. About 15 years ago Nestlé introduced a ready-to-eat fruit yogurt. Today there are so many such products on store shelves that it's difficult to tell them apart, but back then they were very rare. Japanese consumer demand was close to zero and, because it was fresh, the product had a very short shelf life. Any product that consumers didn't want and store owners had to replace every week was on the critical list from the very beginning. Once again Nestlé realized the difficulties it was up against and withdrew from this market as well.

In our examination of Coca-Cola we talk about the importance of the canned coffee business in Japan. Today the market for canned coffee from vending machines alone is worth somewhere around $5 billion, so a firm like Nestlé, whose image is already closely tied to coffee, should have been well positioned to take a leading role. Needless to say, a large share of a multi-billion-dollar market would have been a solid boost to the firm's bottom line. Yet even though Nestlé did develop both a line of canned coffee products and its own coffee products for vending machines (making both hot and iced coffee in cups in the same machine), it was a late entry and so had much less impact. Sales are likely to keep increasing over the years, but Coke's tremendous lead in this area looks impossible to overtake. Once again the firm has a good product, but market timing was a problem.

Going Native

Although Nestlé had been in Japan for many decades, it had not completely localized its business until fairly recently. In many ways it still looked and felt like a *gaishi* firm. There were not a few instances where product development was driven by the company's home office rather than by local needs. Like so many *gaishi*, the firm used to operate on the assumption that if something was selling well in Europe and the United States it would sell well in Japan. The whole attitude toward localized operations changed significantly after 1977 when Heinz J. Sinniger arrived to take over as president of Nestlé Japan.

Sinniger had experience doing sales and marketing in Thailand, Hong Kong, and Malaysia, then was named president of the firm's subsidiary in the Philippines before coming to Japan, so he knew about the special needs of Asian markets. After studying the situation in Japan for a while, he began a thorough localization program in 1979.

Yet even he was surprised by Japanese consumers: "The first thing I learned in Japan was that if the label on a jar of Nescafé was slightly torn the item would be returned. Japanese consumers insist on exceptional quality. They always expect things to be just right, and they always want the best . . ."

As a result of ongoing policies over the past 15 years, today Nestlé is highly localized, even compared to some of the most advanced *gaishi* firms. For example, many *gaishi* companies continue to write job titles in the Japanese phonetic alphabet, so that an important executive's business card may say something like "Maaketingu Manejaa." Nestlé opted to use standard Japanese hierarchical job titles (*bucho, kacho,* etc.), which makes both clients and employees feel more at ease. The firm also provides housing loans for employees, just like a big Japanese company. Every day begins with a short speech (*chorei*) from the head of each division, who discusses the day's work, immediate goals, upcoming events, etc. And though Swiss companies traditionally dislike unions, Nestlé Japan has a union. This is perhaps the ultimate sign of how localized the company has become. (Many readers may be wondering if the firm hasn't gone a little *too* far, but company unions in Japan are quite common and often prove to be beneficial in achieving management's goals. They are rarely confrontational or aggressive.) In addition, the company has a softball tournament, sports day (*undokai*), summer holiday (*O-bon yasumi*), and in other ways looks and acts like a Japanese firm.

But perhaps the most important aspect of localization is product development. When the company considered a new product or a new flavor, Sinniger always said, "Ask Mrs. Watanabe." He explained: "'Mrs. Watanabe' is just my way of saying 'the average Japanese housewife.' Whether I like a new product or not has no bearing on whether it will sell in Japan. The final judgment is always made by Japanese consumers, and I want our people to remember that."

Cold Coffee

As we saw earlier, Nescafé has been Nestlé's top earner for some time. But until several years ago it was not a dependable source of revenue year-round. Understandably, sales of instant coffee drop off in the summertime. Summers in Japan's big cities are long, hot, and steamy. Who wants to be mixing drinks with boiling water in July? But as demand drops, production drops, which means that factory utilization rates drop, and this puts a strain on overall costs. So the company needed to find a way to sell its instant coffee in the summers as well.

Of course one kind of coffee does sell pretty well during the summer—iced coffee. Coffee shops throughout the nation sell large quantities of the stuff all through the hot months; in the Osaka area there's even a special name for it (*reiko*). This became the inspiration for Nestlé's first assault on this market. The company decided to switch from selling instant hot coffee to instant iced coffee in the summertime. Of course it was the same coffee, but the company thought that if it could be packaged differently and marketed as instant iced coffee, there might be a way to perk up sales during the "down" months from June through early September.

Fortunately one of its main brands was well suited to this idea (something in the manufacturing process for Nescafé produces coffee crystals with a greater surface area and a greater water absorption rate that helps it to dissolve faster). In 1972 the firm tried test-marketing Nescafé Excella as instant iced coffee. The results were good, so it took the product national the next year. But test markets aren't always reliable. The product didn't go. One problem was that the combination of cold water and ice just wasn't dissolving the coffee powder as fast as it should. The firm needed a simpler, faster way to assure that the mixture dissolved smoothly. So it began selling Nescafé together with a tall mixing bottle. The consumer simply had to measure out the right amount, add water and ice, and shake. The coffee dissolved better and the process was so fast it put the "instant" back in instant coffee. At last the company thought it had a good-tasting, foolproof iced coffee.

But again the firm had failed to reckon with the fickle Japanese market. Shaking the mix created bubbles, actually a lot of bubbles in the bottle. The resultant mix didn't *look* cold, and some customers said the foam on the top turned them off. Nestlé decided that the only really foolproof approach to create a new coffee-drinking fashion was to eliminate the mixing step as well. So in 1986 it began a new summer theme campaign, selling ready-made Nescafé iced coffee in glass containers. This was simplicity itself: consumers could just take the attractive containers home and put them right into their refrigerators. At last Nestlé had a summertime hit on its hands.

Several years ago, the firm's summer coffee sales were less than 50 percent of winter levels. Nowadays, summer sales are equal to about 85 percent of winter sales and are still growing. This is a tremendous achievement considering all the colas, beers, and other cold drinks competing for the summer yen. As a former coffee-product planning manager put it, "When the whole campaign started many years ago, we just wanted to get people to drink their Nescafé in the summer; then we wanted them to buy Nescafé in the summer; now we just want them to buy more."

He added, "The biggest advantage of the iced coffee campaign is this: In the past, the supermarkets used to pull our merchandise from display areas when the winter season ended. Now they have something to display all year round, which means we hold onto shelf and floor space for new product campaigns and events, and that is very important to us."

Was it a lot of trouble developing these products just for the local market? Absolutely. Was it worth all the effort? Absolutely. After it caught on in Japan, the company decided to take instant iced coffee overseas, and is now selling it in the United States, England, Mexico, and a number of other countries.

Diversification

Going into the 1990s Nestlé began to expand its markets. First, it repackaged its old standby. Coffee was promoted in aluminum cans, paper cartons, etc. Then in 1993 the firm introduced two new kinds of instant coffee: instant *cappuccino* and instant *café au lait*. But what it really needed were new products, not merely variations on a theme.

In 1993 the parent company bought French mineral water giant, Source Perrier, and thereby acquired several new brand names. In 1994 Nestlé Japan introduced a new line, Valvert mineral water, entering a market already overflowing with competing brands. President Hans Klett is confident that the market still has considerable room for growth: "In France and Germany, people drink an average of 100 liters of mineral water per person. In the U.S. they drink about 40 liters. In Japan the figure is only 4 liters. This is a huge potential market."

Another big step was to reinforce the chocolate business. In 1988 Nestlé bought British chocolate-maker Rowntree Mackintosh, which already had a tie-up with a Japanese firm, confectionery maker Fujiya, which was licensed to sell its products in Japan.

Nestlé talked to Fujiya and the two firms came to an understanding. In 1989 they set up a new joint venture firm, Nestlé Mackintosh K.K., which took over sales of Rowntree Mackintosh chocolates. Two years later a local Nestlé plant began producing Rowntree Mackintosh's top seller, Kit Kat chocolate, and soon the JV was handling all procurement, production, and sales of confectionery items. Within a few years sales were double what they were before the JV took over.

Nestlé Makcintosh President Hiroshi Hasegawa points out that the firm had to change the flavor of some of its products to suit Japanese tastes, so the Japanese versions taste different from Rowntree Mackintosh products overseas. Moreover, some products had to be repackaged—not with Japanese writing so much as with a different approach to packaging.

Masahiko Uotani, formerly with Jacobs Suchard (one of the top chocolate makers in Europe) and now vice-president of Coca-Cola Japan, explains why:

> In Japan, 70 percent of chocolate purchases are impulse buying, so packaging is very important. Japanese consumers choose many products simply on the basis of packaging. They feel a company naturally puts great effort into its packaging and does everything possible to appeal to consumers on looks alone. This is one way Japanese judge the quality of what's inside the package. But most American and European companies think it's crazy to invest a lot of time or money in packaging; instead, you put your investment into the products themselves. I remember when I tried to convince the Jacobs Suchard executives of this truth, I took them around to a *kaiseki* (a very traditional and refined form of Japanese cuisine) restaurant and other places where they could see how important form is to Japanese aesthetics, how much we judge food by the way it looks. They finally came to understand that in Japan form comes first, otherwise no one will taste what is inside.

The results of Nestlé's efforts to adapt its products to the local market testify to the success of its strategy. "In five years our sales have doubled," Hasegawa says with pride. "That is unprecedented growth in this sector. In 1989–90 import tariffs on chocolate fell from 35 percent to 10 percent and all sorts of foreign-brand chocolates began to appear in Japan. But within a short time almost all of them disappeared while we continue to grow."

Charles Ireland was originally with Rowntree Mackintosh and is now vice-president of the Japanese joint venture: "Kit Kat has become a leading chocolate product in Japan. Nestlé has a lot of other chocolate products it could introduce here, but we have to be careful. Just because something sells overseas, we can't assume

it'll sell in Japan. Jacobs Suchard's "Milka" is a top-selling chocolate in Europe, but it failed in Japan and had to be withdrawn.
Nestlé is very strong in bar chocolate overseas, but in Japan the
bar chocolate market is not all that big."

Feline Gourmets

Another step in the company's diversification was to develop its
pet food business. In 1985 the parent firm bought American food-
maker Carnation, which owned Friskies pet foods. The question
was: Could it sell well in Japan? Until the 1980s, 85 percent of
Japanese gave their pets leftover table scraps, and only 15 percent
bought special pet food. Then, as affluence continued to rise, so
did the demand for pet food. However, all cat food sold in Japan
(including Friskies) was the standard dry or wet type. Nestlé
became the first to sell what the market calls "premium" wet cat
food (canned Friskies costs four-to-five times as much as the dry
cereal type). When people in the industry heard that the company
was going to try to sell premium wet-type cat food, the response
was "You're crazy," "It'll never sell," and "Friskies is making a big
mistake." But the bubble era brought with it a wave of gourmet
foods, and before long quality pet food became a trend—one that
outlasted the bubble economy.

To get a paw-hold in this "gourmet" market, a few changes
were necessary. What the firm was selling in America as "Fancy
Feast" became "Mon Petit" in Japan. But more than the name
needed a makeover. In the United States cats are assumed to like
meat-based dishes, so beef, liver, and chicken bases are common.
In Japan (and in fact throughout the Orient), cats are thought of
as fish-eaters.

Toshihiro Mannami, president of Friskies K.K., explains, "In
America it is commonly thought that cat food should be based on
meat, but we Japanese think differently. To respond to that market
image, we had our cat food made from a fish base. Do cats like it?
Let me put it this way—it has done so well in Japan that we are
preparing to launch the same kind of product in the U.S. market."

Mon Petit grew in double digits annually, and the company
ultimately captured 60 percent of the premium wet cat-food market. Nestlé was fairly satisfied with its success in this area and had

no great desire to diversify further into the dog food business. After all, dog food is mostly cereal and there is no big advantage to making wet-type canned foods. But Japanese pet shops wanted to sell both dog and cat food, and the company soon felt the pressure to be seen as a comprehensive pet food maker. Now in addition to cat food, the firm has a whole new line of dog food, and sales just keep growing.

Changing Organizational Strategy and More

Nestlé also changed its organizational strategy to keep pace with this diversification of its product line. The firm now appoints a unit manager for each product field, someone who has full authority and responsibility for a specific product type. President Klett comments, "Our administrative division was getting bigger and bigger as we tried to cover an expanding business. By adopting the unit management system we have started to simplify our management structure. We are training people at the local level now and are pleased with the results."

Giving young employees responsibility for an important sector of the firm's product line has proved to be a big success. The new system is expected not only to streamline the company's management, but to help motivate these younger employees by giving them a more central role in the firm's operations.

Many *gaishi* would be delighted to find themselves in Nestle's place today, and many would be enjoying the fruits of that success. But Nestlé expects its future in Japan to be at least as long as its past, and is working as hard as ever in an effort to increase sales and profits. For example, it already holds a 70 percent share of the soluble instant coffee market. Is Nestlé satisfied? Not at all. It continues to support an aggressive advertising campaign, now aimed at improving the company's image. The Nestlé name is still not well enough known, they feel, so TV commercials for its number 1 product prominently feature the company name. Nescafé's market share may increase and it may not, but the company is getting a corporate identity boost by using ads for an already famous product to remind consumers of the company behind it.

This PR campaign should have positive effects on sales of the whole range of products bearing the Nestlé name.

As the years have gone by—and with them, many bitter experiences—Nestlé has learned a good deal about how to create and support a hit in this market. It has taken a very Japanese approach to selling its products. Marketing, advertising, and sales support all served to back up the stores that handle the company's products. Nestlé took a comprehensive, professional approach to its business years before most *gaishi* were thinking along such lines.

In its early growth years, the firm built up a reputation for instant coffee and was known almost exclusively for that one product. Its efforts to diversify were not always rewarded, and the company suffered a number of setbacks with various products. Ultimately, though, its business as a whole was growing and it was not about to give up on what was obviously a very lucrative consumer market. Nestlé stuck it out and learned from its failures as well as its hits. As a result, it finally achieved the kind of success that foreign observers assumed it had had from the beginning.

This is a good lesson for foreign companies. The Japanese market is constantly changing, more so now than ever. Companies that 1) have a fundamentally good product, 2) are willing to refine it and change it to suit local needs, and 3) are also willing to change their distribution or marketing strategy when necessary, can expect to find substantial rewards. Success doesn't always come in the first year or in the first five, but firms like Nestlé that have an important product category that has not yet succeeded in Japan and are willing to keep trying will sooner or later get what they're after.

══════CHAPTER 14══════

An Eye for
Opportunity

Alcon

Recession? What recession?

"Our sales have grown 1,000 percent in the past seven years. Before too long we hope to surpass Japan's top eye medicine company," says an obviously proud President Kunihiko Iwata of Alcon Japan Ltd. The Japanese firm is a subsidiary of Alcon Laboratories, a leading U.S. pharmaceutical maker specializing in eye-care products. Its main lines include medicines for the treatment of glaucoma and other diseases of the eye, cleaning agents for contact lenses, intraocular implants, and ophthalmic surgical instruments.

Now the subsidiary is going after the Japanese eye-care market in a big way. Fiscal 1993 sales jumped 60 percent year-to-year, and that was on top of a hefty 30 percent rise the year before. Nor were these figures anomalous. The company seems destined for even more double-digit growth in years to come.

But success hasn't come overnight. Despite the firm's current high-growth record, for many years prior to Iwata's arrival the company was just getting by. Sales growth was sluggish and the firm just couldn't seem to get a solid foothold in the market. Alcon Japan was like many *gaishi* in Japan, not losing but not gaining, a classic example of the maxim that good products without good management go to waste. In a sense, the parent rescued it by installing a new president, and under his leadership the subsidiary turned around dramatically.

This is a good illustration of a problem we have pointed to repeatedly: finding the right kind of managers, whether home-country natives, other expats, or Japanese nationals, to push a *gaishi* to its full potential. Before we look at Alcon Japan's business, let's take a quick look at the man who transformed the firm from an also-ran to a winner in just four years.

America Beckons

Iwata grew up in Japan's early post-war years and was, like many of his generation, fascinated by America. By the late-1950s, though, many college students were rebelling against the U.S. government's complete domination of Japanese foreign policy and America's continued use of Japan as a military base. This culminated in major riots surrounding the 1960 signing of the US–Japan Security Treaty. From that time on, it was less fashionable to worship things American—except of course, jazz, blue jeans, and James Dean. Thus it was a fairly radical move for a teenager like Iwata to apply to a U.S. university. At the time, overseas travel and spending were limited by the government. Almost the only Japanese students travelling abroad were on Fulbright scholarships. But Iwata knew what he wanted: to see a U.S. campus and find out what America was really like.

All students who wanted to study abroad had to take a special exam administered by the Foreign Ministry. If they failed to pass it, they were not given permission to leave Japan. Iwata crammed for this test and managed to clear it. He somehow persuaded his parents that his visit to the land of the giant, long-nosed, white-bread-eating foreigners was not the end of the world, and set off to enroll in the University of Wisconsin.

In order to study abroad, Iwata had been going to a special English language school. However, like many Japanese even today, when he got to America he found that what his textbooks taught bore little relation to how people really communicated. His English

was incomprehensible to Americans and theirs even less compre-
hensible to him. Yet his biggest problem wasn't the language; it
was cash. His family was not rich and could not afford to send him
much to live on. Even if they could, Japan was still a poor country
and the exchange rate (¥360 to the dollar) made it difficult to buy
greenbacks. Moreover, the Ministry of Finance was very strict
about how much money could be moved out of the country.

Foreign students studying in the United States were not allowed
to hold jobs, but Iwata somehow didn't hear about that rule. He
worked cleaning the university kitchens and toilets and doing all
sorts of menial jobs that other students didn't want to do, and he
saved his wages. During a summer break he teamed up with a
Chinese friend whom he had met at school and went to New York
City; they rented a dirt-cheap apartment and washed dishes in a
Japanese restaurant to stay alive for the summer. In a pattern that
became all too familiar at American universities in later years, the
young Japanese student also studied like a maniac and by his
sophomore year had won a full-tuition scholarship.

Upon graduation he planned to return to Japan, but was immediately offered a job in a large U.S. electronics company. He signed
up, only to find the firm in the middle of a bitter labor struggle
that looked ready to turn violent any day. Gun-toting private
security guards were everywhere. In a sense, this was Iwata's first
introduction to the differences between Japanese and American
corporate life. He left the tension-filled atmosphere of the electronics firm and returned, not to Japan, but to the peaceful life of
the university. Though still unsure of his English, he studied to
be a CPA, working nights and weekends to pay his tuition. In the
end he passed all his tests with flying colors.

New degree in hand, he went to work for the Oscar Mayer meat
company. He was selected to be part of the company's management training program, in which two or three promising candidates
each year were given six months of special training to turn them
into managers. But this was not the "safe" world of the university
campus. There were no classrooms at Oscar Mayer, and the prospective managers were not being trained from textbooks. The
candidates were passed around within the company and made to
take on real work in a variety of jobs. At one point the young
Japanese wound up in a procurement section, negotiating pork

prices with Midwest farmers. At another posting he found himself working until the middle of each night cleaning pig stalls prior to early-morning FDA inspections. He worked a stint as a supervisor of a unionized production line, and as a salesman in Chicago.

The training was very strict. There were constant checks on his work and no special privileges or special pay. If any manager in any of the sections he was assigned to complained about his work, his pay could be docked. It was a stark contrast to business styles in Japan, and it made a big impression on Iwata.

An Impressive Career

He stayed at Oscar Mayer for nine years, rising slowly but surely toward top management. He became one of the firm's negotiators in its ongoing struggle to restructure its Japanese partner, Prima Meat Packers, Ltd. (a.k.a. Prima Ham). Oscar Mayer had tied up with Prima Ham in 1972, acquiring 25 percent of the latter's equity. Prima Ham sold Oscar Mayer products in Japan, but despite the capital participation, the American firm had no say in Prima's management. As Japan changed its regulations on foreign ownership of domestic companies, Oscar Mayer increased its stake, but was still not happy with the performance of its Japanese partner. It wanted to shake up the management, which was effectively controlled by the company's main trading house, Itochu Corp. (then known abroad as C. Itoh & Co.). Even Prima Ham's president was from Itochu and the trader had far too much influence on the company for Oscar Mayer's liking.

Although he had left Japan right after graduating from high school and learned all about business in America, Iwata knew instinctively that you don't go head-to-head with a big company like Itochu if there is any way to avoid it. Instead, a more subtle, indirect approach can prove much more effective. So at Iwata's suggestion, Oscar Mayer went not to Itochu, but to Dai–Ichi Kangyo Bank, Prima Ham's main bank, and negotiated for a restructuring of the management. DKB interceded, as planned, and arranged to have the president of Prima Ham take early retirement. Thanks to Iwata's strategy, the restructuring could begin in earnest.

But Iwata never got a chance to carry it through or to push for a successful conclusion, as Oscar Mayer was bought out by General

Foods. Iwata found himself sitting on the transition committees that were deciding how General Foods should best take advantage of its new acquisition. The General Foods executives were impressed with Iwata's knowledge and his natural talent for strategic thinking. Rather than asking him to come on board as a member of the Oscar Mayer management, he was asked to become an executive of General Foods itself.

It was a very tempting offer, and so he went to work at General Foods' offices in New York. But he had seen big company life at Oscar Mayer and he had heard mixed reports about the state of management at General Foods at that time. He decided that he wanted something different, something with more direct responsibility, even if it was a bit out of the ordinary.

He found it. Alcon Laboratories was looking for a new area controller for Canada, the Far East, and Australia. Iwata thought it sounded like the kind of thing he was looking for, and Alcon acquired much more than what it was looking for.

From JV to Independence

Alcon started in Japan in 1973 by establishing a 50/50 joint venture with Teijin, a synthetic fiber company with a long history. Teijin was just beginning to diversify away from its main line of business. It had already set up a JV with Volvo to sell cars, and was expanding into a variety of other unrelated fields as well. But Teijin's diversification seemed a little *too* diverse for the American eye-care specialist, and so in 1978 Alcon bought out the other half of the business from its partner, and from that point on the firm had a 100 percent-owned subsidiary in Japan.

One of the old-timers recalls, "Back then, Teijin and Alcon were in adjacent buildings. A fellow named Ono, who was first with Itochu America and then with Teijin, became a director of Teijin Alcon, and after the JV was dissolved he became president of the new firm, Alcon Japan. Our total staff was only eight people. President Ono had to type all his own letters and he always had a mountain of papers on his desk."

Over the next two years Alcon Japan tried hard to expand its business, but found it difficult to make significant progress. Something was definitely wrong. The products were good, though more expensive than the competition's, and not sufficiently diversified to meet the needs of the market. The staff were loyal and hard-working, but the executive "spark plug" was missing.

In 1980, Shigeko Nakazawa came over from Teijin and served for three years as head of Alcon's Analytical Research office. She remembers:

> "President Ono invited me to join the company, and I thought seriously about it. My boss at Teijin was very much against it and he tried hard to persuade me not to change jobs, but Teijin is no place for a woman to accomplish much . . . so I moved. I found that, including me, there were only 13 people in all of Alcon. I was hired to do research but there was no lab and no equipment. As far as I could see the firm was strapped for cash and there was no way to buy equipment for us.

When Nakazawa graduated from university in 1957, it was extremely rare for a woman even to want to go to a four-year college, much less to graduate with a specialty in science. Fortunately for her, that period also saw tremendous growth in Japanese industry, and almost every manufacturing company decided that it needed a research center. If it already had one then it probably needed another. The result was a surge of hiring over the next several years, placing engineers and researchers of various backgrounds in jobs that did not exist only a few years before. Nakazawa joined Teijin just when it was expanding from fibers into chemicals and pharmaceuticals. The company established a special medical-products related research center, and she found herself doing analysis on eye medications.

> At Teijin there was a section and a department for everything. It's a big company, very well organized, with a clear-cut division of labor and special staff to handle every function. When I got to Alcon I was in shock at first. The company was so small that anything you didn't do yourself simply didn't get done—planning, filing, requisitions, office work, everything. It was an education, believe me.

Indeed, at Alcon everyone had to help each other as well as trying to handle their own jobs. Another former employee remembers helping Nakazawa to prepare stacks of paperwork on application documents for new medications. Is this kind of situation abnormal? Not at all. With the exception of the very largest companies, almost all *gaishi* start this way: the first office in Japan is usually very small, understaffed, and incredibly busy. And yet, our interviews show that for many people—even the supposedly organization-dependent Japanese—this crazy, no-one-knows-exactly-what-we're-doing start-up phase is a paradoxically satisfying time. Scores of managers at dozens of firms report the same thing: the early days were hectic, usually short of cash and personnel, but those difficulties gave rise to a sense of teamwork and belonging that no big, comfortable Japanese firm could rival.

Growing Pains

Another American eye-care firm, Coopervision, had also gained a foothold in the Japanese market, but rather than do it from scratch and cope with the many problems that Alcon was struggling with, it took a common shortcut: it acquired a Japanese company. The Japanese firm it bought was called Takada Machinery (the firm made optometric and ophthalmic equipment), and for a while the newly acquired Japanese unit was known as Takada Coopervision. Then, in 1989, Alcon Japan's parent company bought Coopervision.

While the acquisition made a lot of sense in the two companies' home market, in Japan the Alcon operation was much smaller than that of Takada Coopervision. Over the years Alcon had built up its staff to a total of about 40—quite an achievement compared to a few years before—but Coopervision had over 120 people in Japan, so the merger of the Japanese units proved a challenge.

Fortunately, Alcon had just moved to much larger quarters, so absorbing the Coopervision staff was slightly less of a headache than it might have been. For an American firm to deal with such a big change would probably have required a year of planning, perhaps moving to an even bigger building, setting up separate offices for all the managers, buying various sizes of executive desks and other furniture "appropriate" to people in responsible positions, and so on. Because of the flexible, open-room look of a Japanese office, and because people are accustomed to working in cramped spaces anyway, adding more staff meant only adding new partitions inside the office. In Japan most executives other than the company president expect to sit right beside the rest of the employees in a big room. And in many companies the president's desk is just in one corner of the same room with the rest of the staff. It may look unbearable to the Western eye, but the results are often surprising.

The real problems in a Japanese merger have to do with attitudes, not desk space. Because employees tend to be very loyal to the companies they work for, an acquisition requires a transfer of loyalty which is sometimes very difficult to accomplish. Moreover, Japanese firms each have what is called a *shafu*, a certain style or way of operating that the employees (and sometimes other firms in the same industry) recognize as part of its identity. Simply selling the company's stock to a new owner does not eliminate this *shafu*. Thus, the result of the multiple mergers that produced the new Alcon Japan was not one but three companies—and three *shafu*—under one roof: Alcon, Coopervision, and Takada Machinery.

Although they were now only one company on paper, in fact there were three styles of working, three salary schedules, three different sets of expectations about what work entailed, how to do it, when to take holidays, etc. As one employee remembered it, "Some of our new divisions were just parts of other companies, and they still operated just as if they were other companies."

All of these disparate elements had to be merged if Alcon was going to become an effective force in the Japanese market. There are numerous cases of mergers that have taken 20 years or more to "digest" (Dai–Ichi Kangyo Bank is a well-known example), and Alcon could not afford that kind of delay in getting its business running.

But the biggest problem the firm faced was a lack of leadership. A former manager recalls, "Yes, of course we had a president, but he didn't have real control over the operation," and other staff echo her comment. A Japanese firm that is internally fragmented and lacks the necessary leadership to pull it together is not merely at a disadvantage compared to its rivals—it is in serious trouble.

Fortunately, at least one new arrival at Alcon Japan knew that this was a crisis waiting to happen and had some very clear ideas about what to do to correct it.

Iwata had become the area controller for the U.S. parent company back in 1985. He came to Japan in 1988, the year before the

Coopervision buyout, as the new sales and marketing director. Although new to the Japan operation, Iwata could see right away that things were not going well (the firm was already awash in red ink) and that leadership would be the single most important factor in rescuing the company. Shortly thereafter, in 1990, Iwata was made president of the Japan subsidiary.

There Are Going to Be a Few Changes Around Here

Iwata says:

> When I joined Alcon Japan, I started in sales. I showed up at the office every day at 8 because that's what I felt was normal for people doing sales. But a lot of the staff and most of the executives never appeared before 10. When I asked one of the managers about the casual starting time, his response was, "I had a lot of entertaining to do last night; I can't always get in early." Of course in a Japanese company, entertaining clients is an important part of a manager's work. But at that time Alcon didn't have all that much entertaining to do, certainly not enough to keep most of the executive staff out late every night.

The truth was that the whole place was just taking life easy. There were people on the payroll who did nothing all day. Nobody wanted to push too hard, and the person who held ultimate responsibility for cracking the whip—the president—wasn't in control of anything. So when Iwata took over, it was necessary to restructure the whole thing.

Restructuring was easier said than done. The sales staff looked like a rag-tag bunch of guys on a permanent lunch break. All the company rules needed to be unified, and all the accounting procedures and flows of money within the firm had to be standardized. Most of all, Alcon Japan needed a single, common identity, a *shafu* that both its old and new staff could identify with. That meant bulldozing the "three companies under one roof" mentality. Even the old Alcon Japan identity had to go; it was time to create a whole new company from the shambles of what had come before.

The most important job was to change the company's "face," the image its representatives presented to the world every day. That meant shaping up a gang of easygoing guys in casual clothes into a professional, hardworking sales team. It wasn't easy.

The Iwata reign began with a shocker—he told the salesmen to check in for work at a specific time and not to check out before a specific time. No more come-in-when-you-feel-like-it, or "I sort of overslept" nonsense. Step two was appearance. Many of the salesmen wore whatever they liked on sales calls, old blazers with brightly checked pants, jaunty ties, or something equally sporty and informal. In Japan not even a used-car salesman dresses this way. The stereotyped image of millions of Japanese businessmen all wearing exactly the same blue suit is an exaggeration—but relatively speaking, not very much of an exaggeration. Especially for salesmen, who must make a good impression even before they open their mouths, a dark suit, sober tie, and shined shoes are a must. And for a salesman whose work included talking to doctors (the Japanese equivalent of a streetsweeper addressing a Lord of the Realm), the very idea of looking less than presentable is an insult and a surefire way to kill sales. Iwata ordered his team to wear smart-looking suits, cut their hair, and clean up their acts.

But what he really wanted from his salesmen was something more important than just a new image. He wanted them to have confidence in themselves and in the products they represented. Alcon Japan had never trained its employees in how to sell, how to look at a market or how to price their products. Iwata discovered that the sales staff had no idea how to position a product on the market, so they simply discounted prices as much as necessary to make a sale. Iwata set out to change all that.

One key move was to send promising salesmen to the United States for training. There the Japanese were shocked to see American salespeople talking to doctors almost as equals. Doctors may be highly respected in American society, but that does not mean that they are aware of all the new products available in their particular field. Moreover, they are not above listening to presentations from medical and pharmaceutical salespeople. The latter don't need to push their products, but work by explaining their merits. In a sense, pharmaceutical salespeople are an extension of the medical profession.

In Japan all salespeople, including those in medical or pharmaceutical sales, hold a rather low social position, while any doctor, however young or inexperienced, has a kind of unquestioned status unknown in the West since the early part of this century. Does anyone remember the days when suing a doctor would have been unthinkable and asking for a "second opinion" would have been close to blasphemy? That is Japan today. Japanese salesman are taught to be servile and obsequious and to constantly show deference to the *Sensei* (as doctors are addressed). Yet here were these American salespeople chatting with senior hospital staff as if they were practically friends. This, probably more than any sales techniques the Japanese picked up in the States, made a lasting impression on them, which is just what Iwata intended.

Alcon Japan's salesmen were made to go on rounds with their American counterparts, and in doing so they saw a whole different approach to their business. They learned to have confidence in the company's products, to be knowledgeable about those products, and to provide the doctors they talked to with something useful— information. In short, despite all the language difficulties those short trips to America taught the Japanese salesmen confidence, pride, and some effective sales techniques.

Until that time there had been nothing in Alcon Japan like a sales incentive, so Iwata instituted a sales bonus system. Those whose performance surpassed a certain target were rewarded. The idea was that the company was working hard to back up its salesmen and it wanted the salesmen to work just as hard to help the company. Hard work would yield immediate rewards (still not a common approach in Japanese companies). On top of that, salespeople who consistently performed well were given raises.

At first the newly attired, newly motivated sales team went around to university hospitals trying to make contacts. But the past several years of weak management and weaker sales efforts had left their mark. At first no one wanted to talk to them. They kept at it, and gradually they began to make inroads. Then the company pitched in, holding a series of seminars for doctors and university professors at which the firm's products could also be explained in detail. Amazingly, the company's new look and new attitude began to pay off earlier than anyone, even Iwata, had dared to imagine. After only a little over a year under the new system, Alcon Japan jumped from a nonentity in the field to grab close to 30 percent of its first target market. This huge success gave the salesmen greater confidence and spurred them to even greater efforts.

The company was also lucky in that its second start in Japan happened to coincide with a move at the parent firm to expand its overseas operations. Alcon's head office became more committed to developing its international business and willing to invest in new products, new staff, and new manufacturing facilities. The company's management back in Texas saw this as a good opportunity to make significant progress in the Japanese market—something it had long wanted to achieve.

The next big project was to convince the Japanese medical profession of Alcon's sincerity and reliability. That meant some serious PR was needed, which in turn meant that the full support of the U.S. parent was critical. And the home office came through in a number of ways. For example, every year a committee of the Alcon Research Institute composed of leading ophthalmologists from around the world presents an Alcon Award to the most outstanding doctor in the field of ophthalmology worldwide. The award carries a $100,000 check and a good deal of prestige in the medical fraternity. A number of Japanese doctors began to be nominated for the award, which got the company's name known in just the right way in Japan. When Alcon Japan heard that some ophthalmologists wanted to go to underdeveloped countries to do charity work in local hospitals, a few calls were made, and a short time later Alcon Japan was able to donate vital medical products and sent one of its employees to act as an assistant to this group. Through these and many other means, the Alcon name was reinforced in the Japanese market and the company's image was polished.

Teaching the Home Office about Japan

One of the important factors in the success of that in-house corporate identity/PR operation was the understanding and cooperation of the parent firm. But it is never easy for a Japanese subsidiary, especially one with Japanese management, to convince an overseas parent of the importance of giving it unwavering support.

Iwata realized early on that one of his most difficult jobs was going to be getting the home office to understand the Japanese market. In order to achieve that, he and the head office jointly established a series of "Japan focus meetings" that ran for two and a half years. Once every three months, Alcon's top people were called together, along with top staff in the HQ's international and R&D departments, to meet with Iwata and his top managers to discuss the Japan situation and to consider the subsidiary's future strategy.

The meetings were held alternately in the United States and Japan. When they were in Japan, Iwata chose a meeting spot with a view of a Japanese garden or some other traditional scene that would help to change the participants' mental framework. At these sessions he tried to emphasize the importance of having non-Japanese managers understand the Japanese way of doing things. If a company thinks only in terms of its own market perspective, of what works well and what makes sense in the American market or the European market, but it doesn't really grasp the fundamentals of the Japanese market, the odds are that its products will never be truly successful in Japan.

To win in Japan, Iwata said, it is essential to commit to the market in a big way, and that usually means a big investment in terms of capital. Sometimes it means investing in things that are simply not justifiable by Western standards. As an example, he noted that a company needs to have memberships in some of the nation's better country clubs and invite clients and others connected with their business to play golf. In Japan, where a single golf club membership can run close to a million dollars, and green fees *for members* can be $300 each, this is a very serious proposition. But as Iwata explained, golf is less of a sport and more of a high-level networking tool in Japan. Any firm that is not willing to make a serious commitment to doing business the local way, no matter how much that might require in terms of money, time, and effort, is headed for something less than stellar success.

In short, he said, for the firm to succeed in Japan it would need understanding and it would need support, and both of these would be difficult at first for the home office and other offices to accept. But if the company did succeed in Japan, the contribution to Alcon's global profit picture would be substantial and would surely repay that commitment handsomely.

When executives from the home office came to Japan, Iwata also arranged dinners with leading doctors at universities and hospitals so that the home office people could get a better understanding of their customers and important Japanese clients could see the commitment Alcon was making to the market. One important point that many *gaishi* overlook on such visits is to go over a number of basic policy matters before going out to dinner. Iwata knew how critical it was that what he said to clients and what the head office brass said sound the same. It is very important for Japanese clients to feel that talking to the president of the local subsidiary is the same as talking to the president of the parent company. It is vital to build "face" for the CEO of the Japan unit by showing that he has the full support of the home office—even if this requires papering over a few cracks in ongoing intracompany policy debates.

Gradually, Iwata's internal reforms and his program to build better relations with the home office began to show effects. Alcon Japan's sales and profit figures began to rise substantially, and just as he had promised, the firm began to contribute to consolidated sales. About 30–40 percent of the Alcon group's global sales come from outside the United States. When Iwata took over in 1990 the Japan operation was in the red. Three years later it was the top foreign company in the group, leading in both sales and profit.

Bureaucratic Myopia

One of Alcon's biggest product lines is solutions for cleaning and storing contact lenses. Yet these goods were not originally available in Japan. The problem? Bureaucratic myopia.

"Contact lens cleaners and storage solutions were regarded by the Ministry of Health and Welfare as 'miscellaneous' goods," explains Iwata. "The thinking about such products in Japan is still far behind that in the United States and Europe."

MHW worried, among other things, about allowing these chemical-based products into Japan. While chemical sterilization of soft contact lenses is commonplace in the West, in Japan lenses have always been boiled. Alcon tried to show that its internal company standards are extremely high and that the products are quite safe. Iwata adds: "Clinical tests show that chemically cleaning soft contact lenses is a better approach. We think MHW understands that and we should receive permission to sell our products shortly."

Although it can be highly frustrating at times, executives such as Iwata have little choice but to be patient in dealing with the ministry and move ahead at its pace. Fighting the bureaucracy is not usually the way to further your company's progress in Japan, as the following story about two other firms in Alcon's field illustrates.

Some years ago the MHW approved the sale of disposable contact lenses in Japan. The acknowledged leaders in this field were two American firms, Bausch and Lomb and Johnson and Johnson, and both were quick to bring their products to the Japanese market. Although there were no problems with any of the lenses in the clinical tests submitted to the MHW, the ministry was still worried about what might happen if several "me-too" firms jumped into the field. In a move typical of Japanese bureaucratic thinking, it privately instructed the two big American makers to "go slow." In other words, the government effectively ordered private corporations to avoid large-scale ad campaigns and to try to keep their products from selling too quickly. The ostensible reason was the need to verify the safety of the new products, but it is difficult to imagine the ministry having allowed them into the market unless it was already fully satisfied as to their safety. Of course the command to move slowly at first was not a formal, written order, but was handled through *gyosei shido*, Japan's infamous "administrative guidance."

This administrative guidance is deservedly famous worldwide, but most managers associate it with the Ministry of International Trade and Industry (MITI), which exerted enormous influence over the nation's major industries from the 1950s to the 1970s without ever issuing orders. The ministry simply called executives of certain companies to its offices and told them what it wanted to see done. While MITI's power to get away with that has long since faded, the same attitude pervades most of the bureaucracy, and most ministries continue to give unofficial "instructions" to the industries they regulate. And until fairly recently, no firm in its right mind thumbed its nose at the ministry that regulated its business.

With this background it is easy to see that ministries feel empowered to do as they like and on occasion to give orders to private sector companies as if the government officials were their real board of directors.

Consider the Swiss drug company Sandoz. This world-renowned pharmaceutical firm had sold a weight-reducing drug in Europe and America for more than 10 years. Still, the MHW kept it out of Japan for several years with the argument that "fatness is not a disease." Sandoz submitted all the required forms and presented reams of clinical study reports, but all to no avail. To win approval in Japan the company had to limit its stated efficacy to cases of extreme obesity.

The executives of Sandoz may very well have thought that the ministry's arbitrary handling of the issue was nothing short of scandalous. Once again the Japanese consumer was being denied products that were readily available all over the world. Some people inside Sandoz might even have enjoyed discussing the case with the Japanese press, but no one ever did. Why not? Because MHW officials ordered Sandoz not to talk to the media; not about the drug or the problems with its approval.

Of course there are overweight people in Japan, and when the "diet drug" finally appeared on the market some Japanese newspapers and magazines naturally picked up the story on their own. The same day that the first story appeared, a senior official at MHW got on the phone to Sandoz executives in Tokyo and angrily accused them of deliberately organizing a publicity campaign.

No doubt, after such a long wait to get into one of the world's most lucrative markets, Sandoz would have liked to do some publicity for its product, but the truth was that the firm was too afraid of upsetting officials at MHW. It had other drugs awaiting approval, and there is no way of knowing what the ministry's retaliation might be. So the firm stayed away from the press and after that first call put a company-wide ban on comments about its products.

Obviously, any company making health-related products must obtain MHW approval to sell in Japan, and that means dealing with *gyosei shido.* Firms that do not understand its implications or are not willing to bow to this sometimes absurd system will unquestionably suffer. Thus, Iwata's approach for Alcon—do things by the book and don't fight the government—may seem conservative, or even (to some foreign managers) weak, but ultimately it makes good sense. You *can* fight city hall, and you may even win. But the odds are stacked against you, and if you lose, you lose big. Even *gaishi* that went up against the bureaucracy, such as Coca-Cola and American Family Life Assurance, succeeded not by *fighting* with the bureaucracy but by playing its game so relentlessly and so tirelessly that they ultimately won the approvals they sought.

There is a lot of criticism these days that regulations at the Ministry of Health and Welfare are too severe and need to be relaxed. The ministry even took the first steps to unravel the net of regulations that binds the drug industry. Executives of foreign drug firms who have been in Japan for a long time say that compared to the previous decade there has been visible change, although it is sometimes very slow. The problem is that recently the U.S. Food and Drug Administration has become stricter in its own regulations and in restrictions governing product safety and possible side effects of medications. The merits of this policy aside, when the MHW saw the United States (which was already far more progressive than Japan in this area) moving in a conservative direction, it allowed the pace of its reforms to slide from foot-dragging to glacial.

Smoke Doesn't Get in Your Eyes

Alcon Japan has a number of interesting products either already in use or in its pipeline. Sales of intraocular lenses have proved very successful. The intraocular lens is a man-made lens fitted over the retina of a patient with advanced cataracts. Needless to say, it cannot duplicate the sophisticated focusing operations that the human eye performs constantly; the intraocular lens has a fixed focal length. However, it provides sight to those who have lost it due to disease, and by wearing glasses the patient can adjust his or her vision to various distances. The Japanese national health insurance plan has accepted the implantation of intraocular lenses as an approved medical treatment, and the availability of insurance coverage has been a big boost to sales.

Another interesting product which holds great promise is Alcon's new glaucoma medicine. The top-selling drug for the relief of glaucoma in Japan is licensed from an American pharmaceutical firm. Because glaucoma results in a build-up of pressure in the eye, this drug acts to lower the patient's blood pressure. But some side effects have been noted. For example, the drop in blood pressure puts a heavy burden on the heart. There have even been extreme cases in which death has resulted. Already these problems have begun to come to light abroad, and the future of the currently imported drug is unclear. Alcon's new medicine, on the other hand, has no side effects, which is one reason why it is being so widely anticipated.

One of Alcon Japan's most interesting products is not a chemical or medicine at all, but a new tool for eye surgery. Using the firm's exima laser to make tiny incisions in the human eye, it is actually possible to correct nearsightedness and astigmatism. The parent company in the United States invested in a venture business to speed development of this special laser equipment. So far there have been less than 100 units of the device sold worldwide, but that number could surge rapidly, especially if it gains approval for widespread use in Japan.

The technique is now being used in Europe, Southeast Asia, Australia, the Middle East, South America, and Canada. In Japan it is currently in clinical testing but should be given ministry approval very soon. One unit of this machine will sell for hundreds of thousands of dollars, so the implications for Alcon Japan's business are staggering.

The problem is that despite the very specialized nature of this technology, there are already rivals in the field. Canon Inc. is importing a different kind of exima laser developed by another American venture company. It uses a different technique than Alcon's laser and the market price is only around $300,000–$400,000, which makes it cheaper as well. Some in the industry say that it may be difficult to introduce a more expensive product into this market.

That concern does not extend to the president's office. Iwata is confident that Alcon Japan's laser is significantly different in more than just price. He says the beam does not cut at the same angle as Canon's device and that in various respects it is "easier on the patient." In fact, in many ways Iwata is quite optimistic, both for the industry and for his company's business: "Human beings receive about 80 percent of our information through our eyes. These days heart transplants have become common, but you cannot transplant an eye, because eyes are directly connected to the brain's nervous system. As Japan's population continues to age, the entire eye-care business, that is, Alcon's business, is sure to grow. I have no doubt of it."

Of course that's just what we'd expect a president to say. But does he really think the firm can keep turning in solid growth numbers over the next few years, despite the lingering recession and increased competition? The answer to that question may surprise even his own staff.

Japan's top eye-care company is Santen Pharmaceutical, which chalks up annual sales of roughly $500 million. According to Iwata, Alcon, with sales of roughly $100 million, is going to catch up to number 1 and pass it in the coming years.

"Many of Santen's products are licensed from foreign and Japanese firms. The company has so far limited its development of in-house products. In other words, its business rests on having a stream of good foreign products and a good sales force." A look at Alcon's sales shows that the contribution from some of its most promising new products has yet to appear. As these products come on stream, the firm's sales figures should climb impressively, and the idea of catching up to Santen Pharmaceutical may soon seem a natural next step rather than an impossible dream.

Conclusions

When Iwata took over the helm of Alcon Japan in 1990 it had only a dozen sloppy, untrained salesmen. Today the firm has well over 240 employees, almost half of them are in sales, and the sales force is a trained, efficient, professional team. The keys to this overnight transformation of the company were inspired leadership and good strategy, plus steady support from the U.S. headquarters. Without the parent company's strong commitment to the Japanese market, the local firm would never have been able to grow as it has.

In only five years a small *gaishi* firm turned from total chaos into a successful dynamo. It digested a large merger, re-created its own identity, and began making a very substantial contribution to its group's worldwide revenues. But to hear its top executive talk about the future, the company is just getting started. Alcon Japan may be a success story today, but it seems to be on the verge of becoming a much bigger success story just a few years down the road.

CHAPTER 15

Drinking in Success
United Distillers

Probably every Japanese old enough to read knows the names of whiskies such as Johnnie Walker, Bells, White Horse, Old Parr, Dewars, Haig, and Black & White, and most are equally familiar with I.W. Harper bourbon, Gordon's gin, and Guinness stout. Yet not one Japanese in a hundred could name the company behind all these famous brands, as well as dozens more, nor would anyone even recognize them as products belonging to a single company.

The reason that such famous brands are known throughout Japan but the company that sells them is completely unknown has to do with corporate policies established long ago. Even today as United Distillers Japan (UDJ) works to develop a more unified business strategy for its scores of liquor brands, the company itself is still lost in the shadow of its own familiar labels.

Until just a decade or two ago, most British distillers were relatively small, independent concerns. It was only in that period, as hard liquor became increasingly unfashionable in America (the world's largest liquor market), that the industry as a whole fell on hard times. In 1977 a group of six Scotch-whisky makers banded together to form Distiller's Company Ltd. (DCL). The group included the makers of Johnnie Walker, Dewars, White Horse, Old Parr, Haig, and Black & White, all major brands. DCL was acquired in a huge buyout in 1985 by Guinness plc, which only the year before had bought rights to another famous Scotch whisky, Bell's.

As a result of the buyout, one division of Guinness came to be called United Distillers. Other results were more problematic. The company's chairman retired amid a storm of controversy, there was some messy litigation, and Guinness went through some top management shake-ups. The new team decided to jettison some other recent acquisitions but hold onto the company's beer and spirits businesses, which would become its central core once again.

They sold off over a dozen companies and split the Guinness "group" into three corporate parts handling beer, spirits, and distribution. One of these firms was Guinness Beer Worldwide and another was called United Distillers. The whole group came to be known as United Distillers Group (UDG).

UDG also took steps to improve global distribution of its products. One big step was to cut connections with hundreds of distributor organizations. Whereas in the past the group controlled the distribution of only about 25 percent of its products, after the buyout and restructuring it raised that level to 75 percent Then came a tie-up with another liquor group, France's Moet–Hennessy. Another step was the purchase of Schenley in the United States, which was the sole local agent for Dewars, the top-selling Scotch in America, and also controlled the I.W. Harper brand. Little by little, UDG was growing into a worldwide liquor-trading powerhouse with a royal flush in Scotch whiskies. What it needed to further its goals as a comprehensive liquor manufacturer and·distributor was to penetrate and capture a large share of a potentially huge but relatively untapped market: Japan.

Protecting Domestic Drinkers from Imported Liquor

Considering that the Japanese have a well-deserved reputation as dedicated drinkers, and whisky and other liquors have been popular here for over 100 years, why was the vast potential of the Japanese market still largely untapped by Western distillers as late as the 1980s? The answer has to do with the retail cost of the products. While good whisky, brandy, and wine are not cheap in the West, neither are they ferociously expensive. Makers from around the world compete openly for regional tastes and pocket-books. There were imports in Japan, but the only brands that were within the reach of the average drinker were all Japanese.

Japan applied both a specific tax (*juryozei*) and an ad valorum tax (*jukazei*) on imported liquor. The latter was accomplished in part through a system which classified liquors into three ranks: "special class," the top grade, then "first class," and "second class." Liquor taxes were based on this structure, i.e., "special class" products, such as high-end whiskies, brandies, and even *sake* were taxed at a high rate, while "second class" drinks got off very lightly. Japan's regional *sake* makers were famous for declaring that their modest home brews were only second-class beverages, not worthy of being called first class much less special. This tax dodge fooled no one, and *sake* connoisseurs used to prize the delicious but under-taxed "second class" products of the better *sake*-producing regions. But foreign producers did not have this luxury. Almost all imported whisky and brandy was automatically labelled "special class" regardless of quality.

Thus not only did makers have to pay shipping charges to deliver their product to Japan, but once landed the liquor was assessed with a whopping tax rate. Add to that the profit margins of multiple distributors and the result was shelf prices that made the most ordinary Scotch whisky look like a collector's item. As late as 1988 a 12-year-old blended Scotch might easily sell for over ¥10,000 ($100 in today's terms)—not the kind of price that would encourage the average worker to pick up a few bottles on the way home.

Needless to say, this high tax on imports was not an accident. The system was designed to nurture and then indefinitely protect the Japanese liquor industry. As in so many other areas, the government's position was, "Why should Japanese consumers be given the opportunity to buy foreign products (i.e., send scarce capital overseas) when they could be buying domestic products and supporting the local economy?" This kind of thinking was extremely effective when the industries in question were small, under-capitalized, and needed protection, even from each other. Moreover, it made sense for all those many years when Japan ran a trade deficit with the rest of the world. But as the decades went by and companies like Suntory Ltd. (the nation's largest distiller) and Kirin Breweries (the top beer-maker) turned into muscle-bound conglomerates and Japan's deficit turned into an embarrassingly large trade surplus, the idea of protecting domestic industry could no longer be justified.

The area most hurt by the system was not the United States but the EC, whose high-grade whiskies, brandies, and wines were prime targets of the Japanese tax agents. It was the many EC-produced spirits that were hit for inordinately high value taxes. Largely at the urging of the British government, the EC brought the problem of Japan's blatantly discriminatory liquor tax before the General Agreement on Tariffs and Trade (GATT) and demanded a ruling. In 1987, GATT's executive committee ruled in favor of the EC complaint. GATT recognized the Japanese system as a means of protecting local industry at the expense of imports and a clear violation of international trading practices. As a result, in 1989 Japan's National Tax Administration Agency announced sweeping revisions of the liquor tax. The three classes of alcohol were abolished, as was the distinction between *juryozei* and *jukazei*; thereafter all liquors were assessed only with a specific tax.

One interesting case involved *shochu*—a Japanese neutral spirit something like vodka—that traditionally had been popular in the western part of Japan and with blue-collar workers everywhere because of its extremely low price. In the mid-1980s urban college students "discovered" the old drink and it suddenly became fashionable. The media talked about a "*shochu* boom" and all the big distillers jumped into the arena with new products. Of course the "boom" was entirely due to the fact that the nation's college students saw *shochu* as the cheapest high you could buy in a bottle. And the low price stemmed from the absurdly low tax rate applied to *shochu*, essentially as a favor to that part of the distilling industry. (In fact, the tax rate was so low that Japan's beer makers complained publicly that their sales suffered in comparison.) After the revision, however, the tax rate on *shochu* rose by 75 percent and the "*shochu* boom" (purported to reflect a fundamental change in the tastes of Japanese young people) disappeared almost overnight.

As a result, liquor prices came tumbling down. Johnnie Walker Black Label, which used to sell for ¥10,000, dropped by ¥2,000 from the tax break and another ¥2,000 from the effects of the yen appreciation. The result was premium whisky selling for 40 percent off. Parallel imports skirted the normal distribution routes and brought prices down even further. An ordinary bottle of Scotch whisky soon fell to the ¥2,500–¥3,000 range, which put it fairly close to the price of Japanese whiskies, making direct taste comparisons meaningful for the first time. Since the most popular Japanese whiskies of the time were best suited for stripping paint off an old desk, this was a big victory for the imported brands.

Japanese traditionally defended the taste of their local brews by saying that they only drank whisky mixed heavily with water (the infamous *mizuwari* known to every foreigner who has ever entertained or been entertained by a group of Japanese businessmen). However, when those same drinks were made with real Scotch whisky, the difference in taste was all too apparent. Just as with foreign cars, foreign clothing, foreign accessories, and dozens of other products, once the price was brought within the range of the best domestically-produced goods, and the products were made more readily available, Japanese consumers decided that they liked the foreign products better (which is just what the government and industry had feared all along). As with BMWs and Louis Vuitton bags, many people decided that they preferred the quality of real Scotch whisky to the domestic concoctions, and an imported liquor boom began—which, unlike the *shochu* boom, has continued for years and really has led to a gradual shift in the tastes of Japanese consumers.

This of course put great pressure on the Japanese liquor companies. Industry king Suntory is perhaps the best example. Suntory is not only Japan's biggest liquor producer, but at that time it was also Japan's biggest liquor importer. Much of what it imported was bought in bulk. All the big Japanese liquor firms imported foreign wine by the barrel, not the bottle, mixed as much as 95 percent with as little as 5 percent domestic wine and sold the resulting product as "domestically-produced." As the tax on foreign wine also dropped, foreign shippers began to look more seriously at the Japanese market, and Japanese consumers began to look more seriously at French, Italian, and Californian wines.

Whisky was much the same. Suntory imported foreign whisky and blended it with its own products to produce some of its better grade brands. After the liquor tax reform consumers could buy straight Scotch whisky in the bottle for about the same price as Suntory's mega-popular brand, "Old." While "Old" made a passable *mizuwari*, its taste was no match for any of the readily available Scotches. Moreover, Suntory also operated as an importer and distributor of certain foreign brands. It invested considerable time and money to promote brands such as I.W. Harper. But control of Harper's importing and marketing now shifted to a new affiliate of the UDG group which we will discuss in a moment. Then Haig scotch, Ancient Age bourbon, and Martell cognac also slipped out of Suntory's grasp. The Japanese giant felt a looming sense of crisis and took a radical step for the proud old firm: it tied up with a foreign maker. Suntory bought a minority interest in Britain's Allied Lyons plc, which owned Canadian Club, Ballantine's, Courvoisier, and other well-known labels, and Japanese marketing rights to these brands shifted to Suntory. The import battle was on.

Foreign Studies

When Britain's United Distillers Group decided to expand its operations in the Japanese market, its strategy was to set up a local subsidiary, United Distillers Japan (UDJ), to control importing and distribution. The man they chose to head that operation is largely responsible for the success UDJ has achieved, and his story deserves a bit of explanation.

Shunji Noritomi was born to a Japanese government official serving in Taiwan (still a Japanese colony at the time) and came to Japan when he was in elementary school. After graduating from university he joined Toyo Rayon (now Toray Industries), a well-established maker of synthetic fibers. After the war his father became involved in the export business, and this, combined with his foreign birth, helped to convince Noritomi that Japan was on the verge of a much more international age than it had yet known. He developed a craving to study overseas—a near impossibility in the early postwar days.

Only a short time after joining Toyo Rayon he became head of the firm's export division and was soon sent overseas for a month on business. When Toray later formed a joint venture with a larger and more famous American firm, it was Noritomi who was put in charge of business related to the JV, Toray–DuPont. From then on he went to the United States every year. He encountered American management styles, he saw the awesome growth of American business, and his desire to study overseas increased.

Toray had an overseas study program for employees, but people as busy as Noritomi never seemed to be in line for it. Moreover, it was a program for people under 30, and he was already at the ceiling when he asked to be allowed to go abroad to study. He would not take advantage of the company-sponsored program, he said, but asked only for permission to take a leave of absence from work; he would travel and study on his own without using any of the firm's funds.

When his supervisor heard this he was understandably taken aback. There weren't a lot of Japanese who wanted to go overseas in the first place, and almost none who would sacrifice their salaries to do it. This young man was so eager to go that he would give up his salary and spend what little savings he had to do it. Clearly this Noritomi was an unusual fellow. The supervisor told him to go study overseas but to do it at full salary. Noritomi's father was impressed with the company's generosity but warned his son to remember that the future is always uncertain. It would be better not to have such an obligation to repay, his father advised, and Noritomi duly explained this concern to his supervisor. The latter replied, "Go abroad, study hard, and don't worry about any obligations to the company."

So in 1967 Noritomi packed up and set off alone to study overseas.

At that time it was very difficult for an individual to apply to a foreign university. Sponsorship was necessary, and since one of Noritomi's professors had studied in England, he recommended him to the local chapter of the British Council. With a letter of recommendation in hand from the Council, he was able to apply to a few specific British institutions and was admitted to the University of Lancaster.

He found Britain a fascinating if different kind of place, but had little time to explore it. He was enrolled in a special MBA program which condensed the normal two-year course into one year of intensive study. Although the course was full of foreign students it was anything but relaxed for their benefit. There was a test every three months, and those who could not pass were dropped from the class. Noritomi watched as his classmates disappeared one by one, and that gave him all the more motivation to study hard. He lost over 22 pounds during that year, but he passed his tests.

As the end of his term neared he was, in the British university tradition, expected to consult with his professors. "What will you do after graduation?" he was asked, and he duly replied, "Return to my company." "What a pity," came the reply. "Why don't we introduce you to a good firm here?"

He remembered how his boss at Toray had said "don't worry about any obligations to the company." Of course he felt a strong obligation to the firm anyway, but he also felt a growing sense of connection with Britain and the culture into which he had been so kindly received. One of his professors introduced him to Gillette, which was looking eagerly at the potential of the Japanese market. Gillette liked him, he liked the company, and he soon began his new career as an employee of a foreign firm.

Career Moves

Gillette sent him to Canada for half a year to get acquainted with the business, and then to Japan to its just-established subsidiary, as a marketing manager. He combined his working experience at Toray with the textbook lessons from his MBA studies in England and quickly became known as a good manager. After five years with Gillette he was sent to another overseas post, part of the company's normal routine for the career development of its managers. He chose Australia, where he spent a year and a half as a marketing manager.

Then word came from Japan: "We need you back here." In his absence much of his work in setting up human networks and arranging distribution channels had been undone, staff he had trained were leaving the company, and he felt as if he didn't know where to begin to set things right again. Both time and good staff had been lost, and Noritomi knew that this can be a much more critical problem for a *gaishi* than for a company in its home market.

While he was growing more despondent over the setbacks at Gillette's Japan operation, he got a call from someone at the giant Canadian distiller Seagram asking if he would be willing to consider a career change. The timing was right, although as he admitted later it was an odd switch for someone whose limit is two *mizuwaris*. He made the move into the liquor industry, a step which would soon lead him to UDJ.

In 1972 Seagram had set up a 50/50 joint venture with Kirin Breweries, called Kirin–Seagram Ltd. The president of the JV came from Kirin, the vice-president from Seagram's. But the American vice-president who had helped set up the business was approaching retirement age and the firm was looking for someone to replace him. Noritomi was the man they wanted: a native Japanese who had both studied and worked abroad as well as managing at a *gaishi* in Japan.

The president of Seagram in the United States turned out to be unusually well informed about Japan. He had lived in the country for about ten years right after the war, spoke the language fluently, and understood Japanese business as few foreigners did. His plan was to hire Noritomi and move him into the company's top spot (the vice-presidency) at Kirin–Seagram. But he knew better than simply to appoint Noritomi to the job.

"In Japan if a young man suddenly shoots to the top it always causes problems with those around him," he said. "But if he starts at the top it makes matters much worse. Why don't you start as a *kacho* (section manager) and we'll move you up from there?" So at age 38 Noritomi joined Kirin–Seagram as a *kacho*.

Within a short time, the Seagram president's plan became reality and Noritomi took over as vice-president of the joint venture. The CEO of the JV was the third president installed by Kirin in 11 years, a man in his sixties. The difference in their ages was like that between a father and son.

"If the vice-president had been a *gaijin*, I think the difference in ages would not have been a problem—everyone knows that foreign managers tend to be younger. But because I was Japanese, the president couldn't help but feel uncomfortable. Partly because of this, I really threw myself into the work." And there was plenty to do.

Number Two Blues

When Noritomi joined the company it imported Chivas Regal, which always did well in the Japanese market, but it produced only a single whisky of its own, called Robert Brown. Noritomi took charge of developing new products one after another. The Japanese whisky market is pretty well dominated by one firm: Suntory. Noritomi's strategy was to create a Kirin–Seagram product to match every entry in Suntory's whisky lineup. Under his direction the firm put out "Emblem," a slightly better-grade whisky to compete with Suntory's very popular "Reserve," and "Crescent," an even more upmarket brand to compete with the more prestigious Suntory "Royal."

These successes were followed by newer, more youth-oriented products which were completely original, not responses to market niches Suntory had already carved out. The JV started to grow and various new products (with names like NEWS and Boston Club) began to give the firm a larger chunk of shelf space in the average Japanese liquor store.

However, as time went by Kirin and Seagram began to have diverging views about strategy and how best to position the company for the future. The home office president who had hired and supported Noritomi was now retired. With the JV structured as it was, Noritomi realized that he had already risen as far as he could ever go: not being from Kirin, he could never become president, and being permanent VP to a constant succession of old men sliding down from Kirin prior to retirement did not seem the best way to put his now considerable executive skills to work.

As he was reflecting on his growing dissatisfaction with the Kirin-Seagram job, he got a well-timed call from a headhunter. Britain's UDG was setting up a Japan subsidiary (that would become UDJ) and they needed a capable *shacho*. Was he interested in the president's position? From his work in the past few years he knew only too well what a powerhouse of top-name brands UDG represented. That product line plus the chance to take full responsibility for running a company was a combination too good to pass up.

Radical Surgery

"At the time, UDG was wrapped up in the after-effects of the DCL buyout and was too busy trying to restructure itself to have a clear strategy for Japan. The company obviously had a lot of excellent brand names, and I thought that with the right approach it could do very well here," he said years later. Indeed, UDJ was just a vague notion back at the home office. Noritomi was getting in on the ground floor of the Japan operation; in fact, there wasn't even a ground floor yet. As president of the new company he naturally rated a private office in a prestigious area of downtown Tokyo. This he got. Unfortunately the office was a little more private than he expected: UDJ was a one-room rental. Total employees: one. No secretary, no assistants, nobody. President Noritomi had to answer the phone, answer the mail, deal with a flood of inquiries and requests from the head office, and in his spare time go hunt for some permanent quarters for the company to expand into.

UDJ's strength lay in its array of top name brands. But at the same time, this diversity of good products was also its weakness. It couldn't tout all its brands as number 1; it couldn't even promote them all as best in their category because it had so many rival products in the same category. Another big problem was that each brand had a different agent in Japan and a different strategy.

Consequently, Noritomi's first major task as president of UDJ was to deal with the firm's 33 import agents. This group had to be drastically slimmed down, which meant that contracts had to be cut—a delicate process even in the West, but a very touchy matter in Japan, where long-term relations are taken as a matter of course. Yet Noritomi knew that surgery was necessary. In the end he cut the 33 agents down to just three primary distributors.

One was a three-way joint venture which combined the British and French tie-up partners UDG and Moet/Hennessy, plus Hong Kong-based trading house Jardine Mathiesson. The three each put up capital for the Japanese JV, which was called Jardine Wines & Spirits. Jardine Mathiesson already handled Moet champagne and Hennessy cognac as well as UDG's White Horse brand Scotch. The firm had a good reputation and had showed good results for both Moet/Hennessy and UDG products, so putting together a more formal association of the three groups was almost a natural outcome. Jardine Wines & Spirits then took over names such as I.W. Harper and Gordon's gin in addition to Jardine's previous brands.

Another distributor was a top Japanese liquor wholesaler, Nihon Shurui Hanbai, which had handled importing and sales of Bells whisky. It was assigned rights to Haig (previously handled by Suntory) and Vat 69 (previously sold through Kyowa Hakko, an industrial chemicals company that also makes popular brands of *shochu*).

Black & White whisky, another UDG/UDJ product, was previously handled by Black & White Japan, a 100 percent-owned subsidiary of the Kanematsu trading house. It ultimately came to be imported by UDJ and sold by Jardine Wines & Spirits.

The company also set up a new firm as its most important distribution operation in Japan, a 100 percent-owned subsidiary called UDJ International Liquor Marketing Limited (UDJ–ILM). This firm was charged with representing some of UDJ's best brands, including Johnnie Walker, Dewars, and Old Parr.

Cutting agents and cutting staff was tough. For example, the president of Old Parr Japan was also the chairman of the Japan Scotland Society and very influential in the local liquor business. But when the shake-up came he wasn't even made a director of UDJ–ILM. Many of the agents had been handling the same brands for years and felt that they were responsible for whatever success those brands had achieved. Noritomi had to face some angry sales agents. Some even demanded compensation for being cut off abruptly.

Backed by four lawyers (a sign that Noritomi had picked up more than an MBA in his years overseas), he handled the negotiations in a friendly but firm manner. The agents had to be dealt with. "Our home office had decided that it was time to take greater control of the sales and promotion of our own brands. I believed that this was a good policy decision, and it was my job to carry it out," he said later. Noritomi knew full well that the agents were sore because they had been raking in money on some of these products and did not want to let them go without a fight.

"Of course there were problems and some people will always complain, but to those who demanded compensation I could only say 'you have handled these brands for so many years and have made substantial profits all along. Now the time has come to give it up.'"

Time to Rethink Strategy

Noritomi would have surely lost both his sanity and his health had he tried to do all this alone. Even as he was beginning to hire an office staff to relieve his burden, he turned for advice on market strategy to someone he'd met while working for Kirin–Seagram. Shigetada Wakasugi ran a small consultancy called Marketing Investment and he became Noritomi's all-around backup and co-strategist.

One thing that helped with the paring down of agents and the strategy that followed was a survey that Noritomi and Wakasugi commissioned. The research was designed to assess current consumer reactions to some top UDG brands. There were exhaustive studies of tastes and packaging. Blind taste testings were held, the results tabulated, and then sent back to the home office. Among many other things, they discovered that Johnnie Walker, the world's top-selling brand of Scotch whisky and formerly one of the most prestigious brands in Japan, had lost a lot of its status.

Wakasugi notes, "There was a flood of parallel imports that knocked the whisky's shelf price down substantially and that hurt the image. Moreover, the sales agents were doing nothing to reverse the situation. They had no new ad campaigns and no strategy of any kind to deal with changing circumstances."

Clearly, damage control was necessary. UDJ responded by changing both the Johnnie Walker label and the logo, and playing up its image as the world's leading Scotch. A new series of ads was developed using some of the world's top photographers, and the product was given a more modern image. Then to deal with the parallel importers and to reestablish the high-quality image at the same time, they created a new whisky: Johnnie Walker Gold Label. Gold was a rank above Black Label, and it made its debut in the summer of 1990 (the end of the "bubble" era) for an eyebrow-raising price of ¥10,000.

"This was a special product aimed just at the Japanese market and made especially for UDJ," explains Takao Nakata, a director of Tokyu Agency International Inc., which handles UDJ's advertising. "The company created a 15-year-old whisky that was not available through other channels, only through UDJ. That way it cut out the parallel imports completely. Johnnie Walker has a rather smoky flavor, but for Gold Label they adjusted the blend, making it milder and smoother, the way Japanese like it. The main target was the gift market, with sales aimed primarily at finer department stores and clubs. Johnnie Walker Gold should become a mainstay in the company's lineup within a few years."

After just a short period of revamping the Johnnie Walker image and issuing Gold Label, total sales of Johnnie Walker whiskies doubled.

Another one of the firm's big products in Japan is Old Parr, which has cultivated an image of tradition as an "old time" Scotch whisky. But the survey revealed that to many consumers it was considered a drink for old timers. That is, the whisky (whose brand name refers to a Methuselah-like figure) was seen as something for more elderly drinkers to savor as they remembered the good old days. Apparently this was not a new phenomenon, for long before the survey was conducted Old Parr's former agent had tried desperately to change the product's image and appeal to a younger crowd. One of the tactics had been TV spots featuring heavy metal music, and that combined with an image as staid as that of Old Parr had managed to turn off young and old consumers alike.

UDJ took a different approach, determined to preserve the product's traditional image but still appeal to younger drinkers. The firm developed a series of ads based on the catch phrase "Leaders still drink Old Parr" which set out to show that the whisky was the choice of Japan's leaders decade after decade. In other words, it was traditional but not "old," something that each successive generation rediscovered as one of life's pleasures. The company used a variety of historical figures to make its point, including Tomomi Iwakura, one of the leading figures in the late-nineteenth century Meiji government who brought Old Parr back from his journeys to Europe; another was former Prime Minister Shigeru Yoshida, who helped to shape the growth of postwar Japan and was a devoted Old Parr tippler. In Japan you can almost always improve both image and sales by raising prices, and in the bubble economy that was even more true. So in 1989 a new, high-end product hit the stands, Old Parr Superior, selling for a cool ¥15,000 ($150) per bottle. Old Parr soon reestablished itself as a choice whisky, and sales continued to grow.

Although the firm's main line was and still is Scotch whisky, a field in which it holds the majority of top name brands, Noritomi realized that American bourbon had a great deal of potential in the Japanese market. The firm owned I.W. Harper, but in the past the bourbon's marketing had been erratic. In the late-1980s and early 1990s, however, bourbon suddenly caught on with college-age Japanese and sales took off. The whole market doubled in less than three years. The problem was that, like the *shochu* boom, bourbon might be a fad that came and went. It is difficult to rely only on college students to make a product a long-term success.

Of course, part of the appeal of bourbon was its rough, "country" image, which all the other makers were playing on heavily in their advertising (cowboys, rodeos, even Ry Cooder playing slide guitar and sipping bourbon in one TV spot). Harper took a different approach and tried to reach out to a wider audience. That meant losing its faded-blue-jeans-and-dusty-boots image. The company developed a whole line of flashy, uptempo TV ads featuring young male dancers in top hats and tails shot against the lights of a city at night. Suddenly the whole bourbon image was transformed from dirty Western bars to sophisticated Manhattan skylines and Harper stood out from all its rivals like a silk scarf in a bunkhouse.

Two Jobs

After carefully studying the results of the survey, President Noritomi chose some of the best of UDJ's more than 120 brands to be represented by the new distributorship, UDJ–ILM. This was to be the firm's top distributor and so was given control of many of UDJ's most important products, including Johnnie Walker, Old Parr, Dewars, President, and Gordon's gin (which was acquired from Jardine Wines & Spirits in 1990) among other top brands.

In fact, after Noritomi had overseen the development of a successful new marketing strategy for UDJ, the head office asked him to become more involved in UDJ–ILM. For a while he served concurrently as president of UDJ and as chairman of the distributor. One might have thought that running a giant *gaishi* liquor firm trying to win a large share of the Japanese market would have been responsibility enough, and that Noritomi would have little energy left even for the less-demanding role of chairman of the distributor. However, this was a man who originally came to UDJ from Seagram because he wanted more responsibility, more challenges. And so after much consideration, he decided not only to keep up the president's responsibilities at UDJ but to move into the hot seat at UDJ–ILM as well. Today he serves as president of both firms.

Aiming for Number 1

As we have noted, until recently the Japanese hard-liquor market was a one-man show dominated largely by Suntory. The company imported various liquors from abroad, both to mix with its own products and to sell under its own labels. In addition to various kinds of Suntory whisky, brandy, wine, and beer, the firm also sold its own brands of gin, vodka, and other spirits. But with the revision of the liquor tax system and the continuing growth in the domestic beer market (where Suntory is the weakest of the four big players), the situation began to change. Blending foreign wines and whiskies to make "domestic" products is no longer as good a business when foreign originals are available at every corner liquor store and consumers are more willing to experiment with unknown brands with strange foreign labels.

Suntory must now compete with a host of determined rivals and must do so without the protection of the old tax structure. Consequently it has, as we noted earlier, turned into a big importer itself and even tied up with one of UDJ's rivals in the United Kingdom. Even Suntory Old, the firm's biggest moneymaker just a decade ago, has seen sales drop to less than one-third of their peak level. Although still a formidable adversary, Suntory no longer looks invincible.

As Wakasugi points out, "The world's top-selling brand of Scotch whisky is Johnnie Walker, which sells about 8 million cases a year. But at its peak Suntory's domestic brand "Old" sold 11 million cases. The really amazing thing is that Suntory accomplished this incredible feat by selling in only one country. You could buy Suntory Old anywhere. It seemed as if everyone drank it. It was like a symbol of Japan's homogeneous society. But times have changed; these days people don't go out drinking with people from their company as much as before, and when they do go drinking they are far more likely to order different things instead of all the same *mizuwari*. As a result, sales of Old have dropped precipitously. The challenge for UDJ has been to decide how best to respond to this situation."

Many foreign liquor makers have tried to grab a piece of the Japanese market. But most companies had one or two potential hit products to offer; few had a broad product range to appeal to all segments of the market. Suntory and UDJ both have a full product range, and that has made their battle all the more significant. For example, UDJ is obviously strong in top-end brands, particularly in whisky, but it also has less expensive products such as Haig whisky to aim at supermarket shoppers and the not-so-casual drinker. With a full lineup of well over 100 brands, covering Scotch, bourbon, gin, and other liquors and liqueurs, UDJ is well positioned to take on Suntory at every level.

Today UDJ and President Noritomi have a new goal, one that would have been a joke just a few years ago and a lunatic fantasy back when he was sitting in his little one-man office: beat Suntory. "We have so many good products and a solid organization. Overtaking Suntory is no pipe dream."

The Family Relationship

Unlike many *gaishi* firms, relations between UDJ and its parent company are quite good. The British group UDG took an active approach to boosting sales in Japan by establishing UDJ. It invested time and money to make its local subsidiary into a solid company with good management and a clear strategy. But the parent firm was also wise enough to realize that it does not fully understand Japanese tastes or the Japanese distribution system, and so it is far more effective (and efficient) to leave decisions about the local market to local pros. Like every *gaishi* in Japan there have been misunderstandings, but thanks in large part to Wakasugi's efforts the two companies are closer than ever.

"The parent firm still believes that it has good products and so, if we simply advertise them well, those products should sell," says Wakasugi. "The important point to remember is that Japan is overflowing with good products. Just bringing a good product into Japan and saying, 'Well, here it is' won't get you anywhere. The key to success in this field is to develop efficient distribution and build up a sales force that can sell."

Wakasugi has made it something of a personal crusade to get the home office staff to understand Japan, Japanese culture, and Japanese people. To this end he has summarized and translated into English over a dozen books on Japanese culture (including Nagami Kishi's *Studies of Gaishi Businesses* about why certain *gaishi* succeed while others fail) and sent these translations back to England. "The people at our head office are also trying very hard to understand Japan, and I have to give them a lot of credit for that," he says.

Weathering the Recession

UDJ has of course suffered from the impact of the recession. "The bubble collapse has meant a big drop in the bar and club business in places like Ginza and Akasaka where whisky and other liquors are purchased in large volumes," Noritomi says. "However, although this impact has resulted in broad sales declines at other firms, UDJ's sales have been more or less flat."

Noritomi credits the bubble itself with cushioning UDJ from the shock of the recession: "We did our planning in the middle of the bubble period and we released new products during that time. In that sense we captured some of the bubble energy before things began to turn downward. For instance, we released Old Parr Superior and Johnnie Walker Gold back when consumers were still spending heavily. Many of our rivals brought their new products to market too late and caught the recession full in the face."

Even so, for a company that has been enjoying double-digit sales growth for years, the recent softening of the market has been difficult. Noritomi believes that reasonable prices and high quality are the keys to attracting business today. "During the bubble period a lot of Japanese felt that they were rich," he says. "If they found quality goods with obvious value they bought them regardless of the price. It was a good experience in some ways. Now consumers are watching their wallets much more carefully." Indeed, liquor discount shops are opening almost daily across the country. Is the head of UDJ worried? "Today's consumers won't just run out and buy something because it's cheap. That is a fallacy . . . ." In other words, discounters may be rife, but the public still wants name brands they can trust. Companies that provide consistent quality and realistic prices will not only survive the recession but prosper in its wake.

Conclusion

In just a short time UDJ grew from one man in a small office to a firm with 250 employees that generates $500 million a year in sales. Today it accounts for over 50 percent of all the Scotch whisky that comes into Japan and is planning to increase its share of that business. As a result of this success, the president is often asked, especially by other firms in Britain, if it is a good idea to copy UDJ's approach to the Japanese market. Noritomi replies with a definitive "No." He says Japan is not the kind of simple market where a foreign company can come in, copy another company's way of doing business, and expect to achieve success. It doesn't work that way.

But he points out, " . . . recent statistics show that on average each household in Japan has roughly $130,000 in savings. That says a lot for future consumer spending patterns. The bubble may be gone, but the idea that one should buy things of quality and undeniable value has taken firm root in the Japanese mind."

==========CHAPTER 16==========

Delivering on its Promise

DHL

In the 1960s a new business was born in the United States. It seems that shipping concerns sometimes found that their cargoes had arrived in foreign ports and were ready to be unloaded but the documents necessary to pick up the merchandise were not yet in hand. So a private air express service appeared to carry, among other things, bills of lading and other documents. The company, which used commercial air carriers and built its reputation on quick, efficient service, took as its name the initials of its three founders—Dalsey, Hillblom, and Lynn.

At first the firm transported bills of lading and other papers between San Francisco, Los Angeles, and Honolulu. Shortly after it started up, the company hired a young American of Japanese descent. Kenneth D. Sato was excited about joining DHL because it meant he could travel to Hawaii, an idea that appealed to him at the time. What he found instead was that he flew to Hawaii, ran around delivering shipments to customers, and then had to fly back the same day. After a few dozen such trips he realized that what had looked like a working vacation in paradise was really a gruelling schedule.

315

But he stuck it out, and so did the little start-up. Word about DHL's fast, reliable service began to spread. Customers in Hawaii began asking if the firm could make deliveries in Guam, the Philippines, even as far as Japan. Before Sato knew it Hawaii looked like his own back yard as he spent more and more time on the road. A new company, DHL International, was established in Hong Kong to service this expanding Asian business.

One-Man Show

In 1972 the company decided that it needed a Japan office. Sato was sent to Tokyo's only international airport at the time, Haneda, to set up that office. Only two months later Sato was opening another office in downtown Tokyo. He had the impressive title of president of the Japan subsidiary of DHL International, but, like many other *gaishi* startups, it was a one-man office. Sato alone was in charge of sales, accounting, deliveries, answering the phone, everything. Yet that was easy compared to trying to do business with his name in 1970s Japan.

Sato was of Japanese ancestry, what the Japanese call a *sansei*, meaning his grandparents emigrated from Japan. Like many *sansei* on the West Coast, he did not speak a word of Japanese. Being a *gaijin* doing business in Japan is hard enough, but having a Japanese name and a Japanese face and not actually being Japanese is much worse. To the Japanese such a person is practically a walking disgrace.

(It is ironic how often foreign firms choose employees with Japanese or even Chinese ancestry to send to Japan, as if their heritage will somehow give them some kind of natural bond with the people they meet. In fact just the opposite is true, and most non-Japanese in such a situation can't wait to get out of the country. Likewise, ABCs—American-born Chinese—are viewed very differently from "real" Chinese when they are sent to China and as neither American nor Chinese if sent to Japan. The results can be painful.)

In those days business in and out of Japan was still largely connected with shipping companies (SeaLand, SeaTrain, US Lines, etc.), although now the firm carried more cargo as well as shipments of documents. Through its work for these shippers the company came into contact with the banks that handled their accounts (Citibank became an early client) as well as the big Japanese trading companies that at that time still made their living by importing and exporting goods to and from Japan.

But aside from the *shosha* (trading firms), Sato's office made very little progress breaking into the Japanese market. Not only was his company small and unknown, but it was out of the question for most businessmen to deal with a person of Japanese ancestry who did not speak Japanese. Sato got smart and hired two native salesmen and kept trying. For the next three years DHL's Japan office had a grand total of three employees, but little by little the business grew. Still it was almost entirely foreign companies that were asking to have goods delivered to Japan.

Because there was no staff to handle the increase in incoming shipments, Sato and his two assistants wound up spending every day making deliveries by themselves. For example, Sato might pick up bunches of documents from a shipping company's office down in Kobe and bring them up to Tokyo, then hop a plane to Osaka and take a bus into the city to make more deliveries, then take a train back to Kobe. This kind of thing went on every day. Often he had well over 200 pounds of shipments to transport, so even though hiring a taxi to move his cargo cost more than the delivery charges would cover, he had no choice. Besides, he knew that the firm's most important customers had to be served properly, regardless of his office's profit or loss. When funds didn't arrive from the United States on time, he would withdraw money from his own account to make up the difference. In short, he gave everything he had to making sure that the Tokyo office provided the best possible service to DHL customers. In retrospect, Sato had more Japanese blood in him than the local business community gave him credit for.

Finally the company began to break through into the local business world, mostly as a result of Sato's Herculean efforts. One episode in particular helped to spread the word about this new, "total service" delivery firm.

One Saturday morning a section manager (*kacho*) from a Japanese company came running into DHL's Tokyo office. His firm had a very important meeting scheduled for Monday morning, but some crucial documents were still sitting in Seattle. Was there anything DHL could do? Sato got on the phone and made arrangements to have the documents put on a flight that would reach Haneda Airport by Sunday evening. He drove out to the airport himself, picked them up, and delivered them to the *kacho's* house in suburban Tokyo late Sunday night. The next morning when the meeting opened, the *kacho* told everyone present how a very diligent fellow from an American company had personally taken charge of the delivery of the documents on the table before them. This incident was not rare for Sato and DHL, while stories of this kind of service from an American company were quite rare. The Japanese were impressed, and word about DHL's service began to spread and sales at the Tokyo office doubled, and then doubled again.

The company weathered the rough years of the first oil shock and then kept on growing. In 1979 the Tokyo office was incorporated as DHL Japan. Sato was promoted to general manager of all Asian business and another *sansei* took over as president of the Japan company.

The company kept on growing for years. Total sales in 1978 were ¥460 million; one year later they were ¥1 billion, a year later ¥1.9 billion, a year later ¥3.5 billion, and a year later ¥6 billion.

But as the 1980s unfolded, DHL Japan's business reached a turning point. The worldwide DHL network covered 150 countries and was growing rapidly. But rivals were not sitting idly by watching this sudden growth. Firms like Federal Express and UPS, which were much larger than DHL within the United States, began to shift their emphasis to international routes.

DHL had grown by responding to growing demand from its customers. But the company did not continue to respond to all its users' needs as it should, and just at this time when rivals were charging into its market, sales growth slowed. The Japanese company that had grown at such a torrential pace was suddenly becoming complacent, out of touch with its customers. Worse, it was totally unaware of the disparity between its internal belief in its total domination of the local market and the changing reality outside its walls. The head of the firm was specifically headhunted from a famous electronics maker to take charge of the company's continued expansion in Japan. But the new president did little to shake up the firm. Instead, the situation grew ever more dire.

A few years later DHL Japan was saved, not by the handpicked *shacho,* but by another man who joined the firm during this troubled period.

Leaving Home Without It

Shinichi Momose knew something about *gaishi.* He had started his career at Olivetti Corp. of Japan (whose rise and fall and subsequent rise we profiled previously), where he worked for 15 years. "Olivetti in Japan has an extremely good in-house training program and as a result, produced a number of good managers who later spread out to a variety of companies. Many of my coworkers there left Olivetti eventually and took jobs in other computer or electronics firms, but I couldn't see myself selling products for a company that had been a rival in the past, so I looked for something completely different." He found it in American electric tool-maker Black & Decker, where he worked for six more years. Then he joined American Express as a director. Amex turned out to be quite an experience, a good lesson for Momose, and an object lesson for other *gaishi.*

At the time Momose arrived, almost all the executives of the company's Japan office were Americans. Very few Japanese were allowed into the decision-making process. Not surprisingly, many of the policy decisions did not suit the Japanese market at all, and business did not go well. As a result, the parent firm began changing the top management fairly often. The incoming foreign executives, wanting to produce some immediate results to show the home office that they were more competent than their predecessors, made faster decisions, with even less input from the Japanese staff, and the results were all too predictable. Basically the company had done well in the United States and in most other parts of the world, so it assumed that it could do well in Japan by following the same strategy that had made Amex a household name elsewhere. There was very little thought about adapting to the local market.

It is wrong to put all the blame on the foreign management, however. A large part of the problem lay in the Japanese staff themselves—Amex didn't acquire particularly talented local managers in the first place, so even when the American executives wanted to work together with their Japanese counterparts, they were surprised to find them indecisive and unsure of themselves. The foreign managers were puzzled that the shrewd, hard-working Japanese businessmen they had heard so much about seemed dull and a bit confused; the Americans' reaction was simply to bypass the local managers and do things on their own. Of course the Japanese could see that the Americans not only outnumbered them but were running the show without much outside input, so they shrugged their shoulders and said, "Let them run it any way they please." Sadly, this led to bad feelings all around, a completely unmotivated Japanese contingent, and worst of all, the creation of an American Express operation that was less and less suited to the market it was trying to capture.

It may seem odd that a firm as big and prestigious as Amex did not attract top-notch Japanese talent from the beginning, but this situation was not at all unusual just a few years ago. The vast majority of Japanese executives are, by definition, men in their late-forties or fifties and sixties, and most of this group is about as internationally-minded as a frog in a well. Those who joined *gaishi* firms usually did so because they could not get jobs in first-rate Japanese firms or because of some problem in their old company which necessitated a job change. (We should note that there are exceptions—extremely talented individuals who for one reason or another joined foreign companies early on, became good managers, and ultimately found themselves at the head of a *gaishi* operation in Japan. In fact, most of the success stories collected in these pages feature just such individuals. However, they are a distinct minority among Japanese businessmen.)

In many *gaishi* like Amex, the first round of hiring brought in the kind of people who killed enthusiasm among their subordinates, and precluded the development inside the company of some bright young fellow who might turn things around. These do-nothing managers often treated their underlings so badly that the most talented ones left early on. Some managers would simply pass all the work they received from their American superiors on down to their subordinates and tell them to take care of it. If things went well the manager took the credit; if not, he could always say that he was doing the best he could but his witless subordinates held him back.

Needless to say, this situation is not unique to Japan, but its appearance at a *gaishi* firm is like the beginning of a cancer that spreads quickly and saps the strength of the organization. Talented people become frustrated and quit, while mediocre managers spend most of their time trying to find ways to protect their jobs.

This was the atmosphere in which Momose found himself. He discovered very quickly that the commission paid by vendors such as stores and restaurants for each use of an Amex card was higher than that for other cards available in Japan. As a matter of fact, if the average Japanese consumer stopped to chat with a store owner when he or she went to pay a bill, showed him a bunch of credit cards and asked which one to use, a lot of them would say, "Any one except American Express." Momose knew that the Amex card was still new to the Japanese and had no special aura, so if there was any reason to use another card, people would do so. He told his American bosses about his findings and pointed out that, at least for a while, the firm should try to make its commissions the same as those of other card companies. The strategy was never carried out.

Momose found there were a few people such as himself on the Japanese side who had ideas about how to make the company better. Having worked for *gaishi* before and being good at presenting arguments logically (not usually a Japanese strong point), the new director soon became a conduit for a number of suggestions from the Japanese staff to the American management. But most of the suggestions were in vain. The company's management had decided on its course and planned to stick to it. Pretty soon the few talented Japanese remaining in the firm stopped offering suggestions: after all, the Americans obviously had their own ideas about running the company, so why bother?

The company did all sorts of promotion campaigns, but they were generally brought over from America by American managers, or sometimes based on ideas from an American consultant living in Japan. From a Japanese point of view most of them were way off the mark.

One classic example of the right strategy in the wrong country was a campaign to refund the price of any goods purchased with the Amex card that were accidentally broken. There was a whole series of warm, family-like TV commercials for this kind of "purchase insurance." But every time the Japanese staff at Amex saw those ads they winced and changed the channel. Traditionally, Japanese don't like to complain about things, at least not publicly.

Recently many U.S. mail-order firms that have "100 percent satisfaction guaranteed" policies have been surprised by the low rate of returns or exchanges from Japanese customers, and they usually assume that this means their products are exactly what the customer wanted. Nothing could be further from the truth. Japanese assume that a business will bend over backwards to make sure that any goods or services it delivers are absolutely correct in every detail. (Remember the story about Apple dealers returning whole computers, unused, to the head office because the shrink-wrapping on the manuals wasn't neat.) Once something has been purchased, if there is anything wrong with it, most Japanese will not demand a refund; they will simply stop buying from that company and tell all their friends never to deal with it.

In fact, the common perception in Japan is that the only kind of people who do make frequent complaints about defective merchandise, poor service, and so on are either *yakuza* gangsters or the mentally deranged. Thus as far as Amex's employees were concerned, the company's campaign served only to encourage the wrong kind of people to sign up for an American Express card.

The Emperor's New Clothes

About the time that Momose was thinking about moving on, he was invited to meet with the management of DHL Japan. He thought it would just be a short chat, nothing like a real job interview, and walked in cold. He wound up face-to-face with DHL's Asian regional manager and Far East regional manager for a three-hour interview.

Far East Regional Director John Kerr remembers, "When I asked him, 'Who do you think should get top priority in a company: customers, employees, or stockholders?' he immediately replied, 'Customers.' That's when I knew we saw things the same way. It was 1985 and the competition was starting to heat up. DHL needed somebody who would really push customer service above all else, and I thought right then about hiring Momose."

Of course it wasn't just his attitude toward customer service; Momose had an impressive record at a number of *gaishi* firms, and his interview made a good resume look all the better. Before he knew it he was signing a contract to become DHL Japan's new sales manager.

When Momose came on board, the company had just instituted a price increase that brought howls of complaint from customers and caused more than a few to switch carriers. Even an outsider like Momose could see that trouble was brewing. When he asked who had ordered the price increase, everyone said the Hong Kong office had demanded it over the objections of the Japan company president. That went against everything Momose had been told about DHL's policy of localization.

Momose noted that all the DHL Japan employees he talked to mouthed the same platitudes, things like "Our service is the best" and "Our customers trust us." This was more than just company pride; there was a devout belief that the firm was and always would be number 1, as if its competitors were no threat at all. While such a positive attitude was reassuring, much of what Momose saw was not. The new price increase was obviously causing dissatisfaction among customers, yet everyone he talked to seemed to think that DHL customers were loyal forever. Something was very wrong here.

Having barely joined the firm, Momose was technically in a period of training and not supposed to take up any executive responsibilities. But what he saw around him started alarm bells ringing and he decided to do something about it. He commissioned an outside firm to conduct a "shipment test," that is, an objective comparison of services offered by different package delivery companies under the same conditions. In this case, identical packages were shipped between two points using different carriers, and everything from price to speed to staff attitudes were rated.

The results were shocking. In comparison with its rivals in the industry, DHL Japan provided the worst level of service at the highest prices. The truth was, Japanese customers continued to use DHL only because it was the first company in the business and so had a longer history. As is still common in Japan, they were reluctant to switch to a newer company and so kept using DHL but complaining loudly. Momose knew that the time would come soon when some little event would prove to be the last straw, and the whole bunch would run to Federal Express or one of the others. The recent price hike could be just that last straw.

To Momose what was needed was not higher prices but a complete review of costs and a new system of increasing profits without raising prices. In addition, the whole customer service approach had to be rebuilt from the bottom up.

He took the results of the survey and his own conclusions to the president, who was just about to leave for Hong Kong for the semi-annual meeting of DHL International chief executives. The president asked Momose to come along and present his findings. The meeting in Hong Kong was normally confined to company presidents, and the appearance of a mere sales manager, even as an observer (which is how Momose was admitted), was something extraordinary. But as the results of his report were presented, they quickly became the focus of the meeting. Until then, reports from Japan to DHL International headquarters had all been pretty much the same as the reassuring platitudes Momose heard when he first joined the company: everything is going well, customers love us, our service is tops. His objective study of the company's deteriorating services and attitudes was like a live electric cable whipping around under the conference table.

"The survey showed that as far as customers are concerned there is very little difference between any of the companies. In this situation, when DHL raises its prices it immediately sets itself apart from other carriers—in a negative way. The result is customer dissatisfaction." After years of assuming all was well in Japan, here was this stranger telling them that service was rotten and customers were unhappy.

Momose said that much of the problem seemed to stem from the Hong Kong office telling the Japan office how to run its business. The Hong Kong executives replied that this was not at all the case. In fact, the Japan office was often asked for reactions or ideas, but seldom offered anything constructive and seemed reluctant to make decisions. After a while the Hong Kong office would become frustrated and make whatever decision seemed best. The price hike was a case in point: Japan had said it needed higher profit levels, Hong Kong had asked how they would achieve that, and no reply ever came. Finally the Hong Kong side proposed a number of possible solutions and the Japan president chose the price hike. Hong Kong agreed that the price hike was inappropriate considering the new information about conditions in Japan and gave the OK to roll it back.

Momose suddenly realized that the real problem wasn't the overbearing attitude of the Hong Kong office but a lack of leadership in Tokyo.

As soon as he got back to Japan, Momose started getting calls from the regional manager in Hong Kong. He was asked his opinion on all sorts of matters pertaining to company business. Having worked in *gaishi* firms all his life, Momose knew well enough what happens to managers who stick their noses where they don't belong, so he always replied, "That is outside the scope of my authority." But the calls kept coming and the people in Hong Kong were very persistent. Momose had obviously made an impression as that rarity among Japanese executives, someone who got things done and done right and wasn't afraid to speak his mind even if it meant ruffling a few feathers. Which is why his attempts to beg off with "that's not my department" were repeatedly brushed aside.

Finally he gave in and started answering the questions he was asked. From that time on, the regional controllers in Hong Kong began bypassing the president's office and talking directly with Momose about anything important relating to the Japan operation. He hadn't been in the firm one full year, yet he was already functioning as the de facto CEO.

But what about that Japan president? Wasn't he a guy hand picked from a top-notch company and brought in to head DHL precisely because he understood international business? It may seem odd to many readers that such a person would not be an effective manager. A short explanation of sorts is in order.

Most Executives Have Never Used a Computer

In most Western companies, executives are assumed to be extremely bright, often aggressive, and always well informed. The executive who doesn't have a clear grasp of what's going on in his or her company is in line for retirement, voluntary or otherwise, and many a junior VP has been astonished to discover that a white-haired CEO can describe in detail operations in some distant division that the young veep has yet to visit. Executives are expected to be decision makers. That means they require information and the ability to analyze it quickly and make correct decisions.

This whole concept is alien to Japanese business. Most managers are not chosen for any kind of skill or aptitude; they are promoted as a result of age and selected for the choice posts on the board of directors (there being few if any outside directors) on the basis of their ability to get along with others. The law of seniority is inviolate: older men are managers; younger ones do the dirty work. In many if not most Japanese companies, becoming a manager is viewed as a kind of reward for working hard in your youth: you don't have to work so hard as a manager because your subordinates do all the work. When there is an executive meeting, the various *bucho* and *kacho* appear with thick reports carefully prepared by their subordinates and simply read them. No one expects them to understand their contents in any great detail. If questions arise, a subordinate can always be called upon to answer them.

This attitude continues right up to the top levels of many companies. Even at a board of directors meeting, if a director were to be asked a specific question requiring a specific answer, it would be considered perfectly normal for him to put his hand out and wait for the appropriate document to be passed forward by an assistant sitting slightly behind him. Even when Japanese company presidents negotiate with their counterparts from other companies they rely to a very large extent on help from well-informed assistants.

In short, the real work of any senior executive, and especially the president, of a Japanese company is human networking. This all comes back to the fundamental nature of Japanese business, which can be grossly simplified but easily understood by the old saw "It's not what you know but who you know that counts." A lowly *kacho* knows all the people in his group; a *bucho* knows the *kacho* beneath him, plus many of their subordinates, plus the other *bucho* in the company, and a few key people on the outside. As you go up the ladder, the directors know not only the various *bucho* in the company but many important people at banks, companies in the same industry and in other industries, ministry officials, politicians, etc. The top of the ladder is the president, or *shacho,* and his role seldom has much to do with decision making. His prime responsibility is to be acquainted with influential politicians, bureaucrats, business leaders, and others whose opinions or actions may somehow impact his company. He is, if you will, the apex of the social networking function of a Japanese organization.

It may come as something of a shock to Western executives to learn that the vast majority of Japanese middle managers do not have the faintest idea how to use even an ordinary personal computer. Most senior managers are in the same boat. They have no idea how to write a report, prepare a presentation, etc. Information management is left to subordinates, and decision making is left to groups of indecisive individuals who spend inordinate amounts of time discussing every possible aspect of a proposal in the hope of avoiding a mistake.

All of this works well enough (though some might argue the point) in a Japanese firm. The problem begins when a foreign firm starts headhunting Japanese managers. They may find some Mr. K. who went to a good university, then into a good company, where he rose to a management position. Maybe he even lived overseas or worked for a foreign firm for a few years, and he currently holds an impressive title at a reputable company. They lure him away from his firm with the offer of a directorship or even the presidency of a *gaishi* company. The honeymoon then lasts about a year until it becomes obvious to everyone that the guy is bright, personable, knows a lot of people, and is totally incompetent to fill the position that he was hired for. He is cut off from his old staff who used to do everything for him and now must do things on his own.

In some cases this kind of executive throws himself into the social aspects of his job with unrestrained zeal: he entertains people from the head office day after day when they come to visit and does everything possible to keep them from spending much time with others in the company. He polishes his English, he chats on the phone a lot, and he tries to establish warm relations with his superiors in the home office. But when it comes right down to whether he is managing his subsidiary well, making incisive decisions, and staying on top of what is happening in his firm, the truth is that some of his secretaries could probably manage better than he does.

In passing we should note that these are not "incompetents" in the objective sense, any more than a Western executive suddenly dropped into a Japanese company could be called "incompetent" for cancelling an unimportant committee meeting in order to devote more time to finishing a vital company project. Both executives are simply fish out of water, people who have spent their lives preparing for one set of corporate expectations only to find that they are suddenly being judged on their ability to perform according to an entirely different—and baffling—set of criteria.

In other words, we are not saying that hiring a senior Japanese executive from a good company is a quick route to trouble—only that expecting him to act like an American CEO may often prove disappointing. However, the successful Japanese executive has a wealth of contacts and knowledge that can be extremely useful for a *gaishi* firm. Thus the real message is not "Beware of incompetent Japanese executives" so much as "Beware of what you *do* with Japanese executives." Placed in the right position, even the most "incompetent" by your criteria may prove invaluable to your firm in other respects.

Takashi Kurisaka, head of the Japan branch of executive search firm Egon Zender, sums up the situation: "Two-thirds of the so-called 'elite' managers at Japan's big companies are totally unfit to become managers or directors at *gaishi* firms." While his point is right on target, the fact remains that a lot of *gaishi* firms continue to hire Japanese with good credentials without stopping to think, "This guy is very well thought of in a Japanese firm, and he gets along well in a Japanese company, but what will happen when he makes the jump to our firm?" The result is a lot of supposedly elite but in fact unsatisfactory executives holding key positions at some very good foreign companies in Japan.

DHL Japan was a basically good firm that had acquired a highly respected executive from a world-famous Japanese company to be its president, but discovered too late that he was not what they were looking for.

Motivation Makes the Difference

After returning from the meeting in Hong Kong, Momose knew that his top priority was going to be finding a way to reform DHL Japan. The question was "How?" The staff still clung to the old image of DHL as "Number 1—the customer's choice." In order to improve service as drastically as was necessary, it was essential to snap them out of their laid-back, self-satisfied reverie and wake them up to the crisis already enveloping the firm.

Of course, Momose was the new sales manager. He could simply order the staff to become more attentive to customer needs, increase efficiency, and so on. But that would have little effect. Moreover, if he began by criticizing the firm he would be regarded as a newcomer and so, despite his title, someone who really didn't understand how prestigious and well-loved DHL was in Japan.

He began by gathering every manager with any kind of title, in other words almost everyone who had been in the firm for more than a few years, in a general meeting and showing them the results of the survey in a cool, objective manner. He asked them, "If you were a customer, would you want to do business with a company like this?" The managers smiled. Of course their new sales manager was making some kind of joke. He was from a credit card company or something, right? Maybe that's the way they do things over there . . .

But Momose wasn't smiling. Gradually the smiles and chuckles around the room disappeared, faces slowly began turning pale, and the managers turned to each other as if for reassurance that this report could not possibly be true. After several minutes, as the message began to sink in, they looked at Momose with expressions of desperation. It was clear that they cared about DHL and they had carried that "We're Number 1" image with enormous pride. Now that pride was shattered. What could they do?

Momose had some pretty good ideas of what he thought needed to be done. He knew that as their superior he could instruct them to put those changes into effect. And he knew that if he did so their basic attitudes and ways of looking at their work, their customers, and their company would never change. He said to them, "I've only just arrived here. I don't know the answer; I only know that we're in big trouble. But you people know this company inside-out. I will leave it to you. I want you to break up into project teams and talk among yourselves right now. Come up with a plan that will make DHL Japan *really* number one. And find a way to do it without spending a lot of money."

And that's just what they did. The group split up and talked most of the night. Momose joined some of the discussions, adding advice or comments, but mostly listening to see what kind of approach they wanted to take. He also took time to interview each person one by one, to sound out ideas that might never come out before a group of their peers, and probe problem areas that others were not yet aware of. Before the night was out the group had produced a full report on how to reform the company.

For example, it came to light that DHL Japan only picked up in the mornings, putting shipments on outgoing flights that day. But many customers wanted to be able to send shipments later in the day and still know that they were on a plane that night rather than the next day. After much discussion, the staff admitted that there were some inefficiencies with pick-ups and collection routes. Eliminating those problems would immediately yield visibly better service—two pick-ups a day—with the same number of workers and minimal extra cost.

All sorts of other ideas developed, most related to eliminating waste and inefficiency. For example, just one small item, the order slips used on parcels, turned into big savings. Instead of having them printed by the same printer the firm had always used, the company did something unusual—it opened the job up to competitive bidding. Momose found that the same slips could be printed for ¥5 (about 5 cents) less per unit—and DHL went through at least 20 million slips per year.

In addition, Momose took a hard look at the staff itself. Because the company had grown so fast, there were quite a few men who had reached management positions simply by virtue of being with the company for a certain number of years. Upon closer inspection it was clear that there were a number of people who had no aptitude as managers and were getting by only because the general state of affairs inside the firm meant that efficiency was no criterion by which to judge anyone.

Momose looked at the ranks of managers and decided there was hardly a *bucho* in the firm who was worth his salary. He began hiring people from outside the firm to take over some jobs and did something unbelievably radical for a Japanese company: he demoted some managers. In one extreme case a director of the company was demoted to *kacho*. He resigned rather than bear the humiliation.

Momose sums up the situation at this turning point in DHL Japan's history: "As far as our customers were concerned, the biggest immediate problem was the price hike. That was easy to deal with—we rolled it back. But another big problem was that we were perceived in Japan as a foreign firm—cold, insensitive to customer needs, that sort of thing. Our response was to appeal to our customers by adopting Japanese-style management, by improving our service dramatically, and other such steps."

Momose found that there were only ten people in charge of sales. DHL is a service business, and unlike manufacturing, you can't replace service smiles with robots. So he increased that number to 130 and kept them conscious of the importance of paying attention to customer needs. He also cancelled a contract with a *gaishi* advertising agency that the home office had designated for them to use, and replaced it with a Japanese agency. He instituted a sweeping program of computerization, not just in the back offices but in cargo collection, management, and distribution as well. This not only saved labor but cut costs and eliminated most of the mistakes in shipping.

But there was one more important change to be made, and Momose didn't make it.

Japanese companies' identity within industry has nothing to do with their products, but with the people who lead them. This does not contradict our previous comments that presidents are often not decision makers. As we noted, presidents are there to be the "face" of the company, a symbol of the firm. Whether that symbol is also a good CEO or not is a very different matter. Throughout DHL's years in Japan it had developed a very strong image for its service but its management was unknown. The company had no "face," no real identity for the heads of other companies to relate to. The solution for this was obvious, even to Momose's superiors, and so he lost his job as sales manager. From the day Momose was named president, everyone in Japanese business knew precisely "who" DHL was in Japan. His face was the company's face. He became a visible symbol of the firm and his word was accepted as company policy. That was the kind of reassurance that many corporate clients had been looking for, and the results began to appear on the bottom line.

Profit Center

As we noted earlier, DHL Japan's sales took off in the late 1970s and early 1980s, then stagnated. Momose came on board in the mid-1980s and soon thereafter took over as president. From that time on, sales jumped close to 20 percent per year. In 1990, total sales hit ¥15 billion, a new record for the company. That put the Japan office behind only the United States and Britain among all of the 210-plus countries in which DHL operated. More importantly, the Japan operation made the largest contribution to group profits of any firm in the entire global organization.

Like other *gaishi* we have examined here, the company also decided to build its own headquarters building in Tokyo. Momose admits, "Yes, it was very expensive, but viewed over the long term it was a good move and ultimately cheaper than paying Tokyo's high rents forever." Normally when a subsidiary invests $100 million in a new headquarters the parent will help share the burden, either by increasing the subsidiary's capital or in some other way helping to finance the project. But profit-leader DHL Japan raised the capital it needed for the new building entirely on its own, a fact which did not go unnoticed among the rest of the group.

The worldwide DHL organization is divided into two parts: DHL Corp. in the United States and DHL International, now based in Brussels. Clearly the success of the Japan operation was one reason behind the 1990 decision of two major Japanese companies, Japan Air Lines and trading house Nissho Iwai, to join with German carrier Lufthansa in a capital participation in DHL International.

"DHL is currently the number 1 company in the international air express field, and in terms of cargo originating from Japan we hold a 30 percent share on a value basis, which also makes us number 1 in that market," says Momose. "But the competition is becoming fierce. Federal Express purchased cargo airline Flying Tiger and is putting a lot of effort into the international end of its business. In addition, UPS and other firms are also fighting for bigger pieces of the market. Both Federal Express and UPS own their own aircraft, and both operate on a bigger scale than DHL in the U.S. domestic market. It was with an eye to the growing competition from these two firms that the company decided to tie up with Lufthansa, JAL, and Nissho Iwai."

Conclusion

The recession has slowed the local firm's profits and pushed sales growth slightly into negative figures, but with much of Japanese industry watching sales drop in double digits, DHL's decline is almost worthy of applause. The increased competition has forced prices down throughout the business, which cuts deeper into profits. Momose has forbidden his staff to cut prices further just to bring in business and bolster the numbers. Of course the firm could cut prices and show a respectable growth in sales, but sooner or later that strategy would come back to haunt them. In the same way it could cut costs much further than it has, but not without impairing the level of service needed to maintain its reputation.

"There are a lot of articles in the papers and magazines these days about Japanese companies slashing costs. Naturally our home office wonders why we don't cut back further. But Japanese firms have lots of room to cut costs. Slimming down is relatively easy for them. Most *gaishi* don't have that luxury."

On the contrary, Momose has had to make hard decisions about how to keep the company out front. Despite the negative sales figures, in 1994 he ordered the purchase of a sophisticated new sorting system. Few companies would make such a substantial investment in the middle of a recession and particularly not at a time when the home office was looking for evidence of cost cutting. But Momose knew that the equipment would increase productivity, which would ultimately be both economical and would contribute to better service.

As this book goes to print, the "Heisei recession" looks about to end, and DHL's strategy seems to be right on target. It was the first international air-express firm in Japan and has built up a very solid reputation which its rivals have not yet matched. As long as it keeps its service standards up and controls costs, the company looks sure to take off again as soon as the overall business climate improves.

What about those rivals snapping at its tailfeathers? Momose's response is telling: "Federal Express is the one we have to watch out for. It could be a fearsome competitor in Japan. But so far the local management has been taking orders from its American parent rather than acting on its own. As long as they don't adopt a more realistic strategy for this market, I don't see them closing the gap with us."

A Few Notes to Firms Hoping to Find Success

In the previous chapters we have seen how a number of different companies responded to the challenges of doing business in Japan. In every case these companies found ways to overcome a myriad of difficulties, both internal and external, and join the ranks of those who have "made it" in Japan. No doubt companies that follow will have some of the same problems and some unique ones as well, but those who learn to avoid others' mistakes and remain forever dissatisfied with their current level of performance will sooner or later find themselves referred to by their Japanese rivals as yet another "successful *gaishi.*"

Before we close, let us offer a few more general words of advice.

On Dealing with the Bureaucracy

Perhaps the one thing that will have made the greatest impression on readers, and a very negative impression at that, is the apparent difficulty of coping with the Japanese bureaucracy. We saw how Coca-Cola was kept out of Japan for years and then, once allowed to sell here, only under such strict conditions that it could never

335

make much of a profit. We saw AFLAC's Japan office go to great lengths to have its proposed insurance policy approved by two different ministries. In both cases, and a few others mentioned here, the impression has no doubt arisen that the Japanese bureaucracy exists only to keep foreign companies out of Japan or to limit their activities in such a way that they do not become a threat to domestic firms.

We would like to make clear that this is not the case today. True, in years past certain elements of the bureaucracy (particularly the Ministry of Finance and the Ministry of International Trade and Industry) behaved in such a way that foreign executives could be forgiven for believing that government officials went through special training to learn how to make life difficult for *gaishi*. There were both legal problems (tariffs, etc.) and extra-legal problems (the archly conservative, protectionist bureaucratic mindset). But from about 1960 onward, very slowly but surely the legal problems began to disappear. By the late-1980s many of the regulations that had hobbled foreign business were gone and the pace of liberalization was finally picking up. Today the situation is still improving and it should continue to do so for some time to come. As for the bureaucratic mentality, it too is changing, though perhaps at a slower pace; but all the same it is not what it was in the 1960s.

Needless to say, senior Japanese officials tend to be old-fashioned and more than a little narrow-minded. Critics say that the bureaucrats don't want to accept responsibility for any kind of problem that might ever crop up with any new product or service, so if they see even the possibility of a problem occurring several years hence, they will refuse an application. Moreover they will automatically turn down anything they don't understand, which may cover a lot of new ideas from abroad. To be fair, however, we must also note that the ministry officials are not simply being mean. Many if not most of them honestly believe that it is their duty to guard the Japanese public from what they see as dangerous, improper, or immoral merchandise, services, etc. The ministries exist, they believe, to protect the national welfare—a concept of federal intervention in the smallest aspects of private citizens' lives that is alien to a nation like the United States.

Unfortunately this sometimes results in a foreign firm with a good idea having to wait years to set up in Japan. But if a firm is willing to stay the course, as the Japanese representatives of both

Coca-Cola and AFLAC did, even the conservative bureaucrats can ultimately be persuaded to see things another way. Often they can provide real help to a company trying to get established in Japan, and in some cases they may even offer unexpected benefits to such firms. When we talked with executives of Coca-Cola in preparation for this book, they emphasized that the bureaucracy was not their real problem all those years ago, but rather the special interest groups that were demanding that the government do something to protect them from Coca-Cola. In fact the company says the bureaucrats have in many ways proved helpful to them. And as we noted in the AFLAC chapter, one of the keys to that firm's success was the protection it received from the Ministry of Finance after its application was finally approved.

The lesson to be learned is that, despite all outward appearances, the Japanese bureaucracy is not the Immovable Object it sometimes appears to be. Especially when it meets a truly Irresistible Force, such as the single-minded representatives of these two companies many years ago, or a foreign firm today that just won't give up, the bureaucracy can move, it can bend, and in the end it *can* be extremely helpful.

Our advice to *gaishi* coming into or expanding operations in Japan: Don't assume that the bureaucracy is there to give you a hard time; learn how to deal with it correctly and you may be one of the many firms that discover just how much times have changed.

A Touch of Humility Doesn't Hurt

Gaishi constantly forget that being big at home doesn't mean a whole lot in Japan and that Japanese consumers often don't know their company from a hole in the ground. When you talk to distributors or bankers, when you go to hire new staff, when you deal with the business community at large, you should constantly remind yourself that not many people know who you are, no matter how important or globally high-profile you may think your company is. If you are used to getting the red carpet treatment in other countries it may be difficult for you to be humble and patient, but in the long run it will pay off. Always start from the assumption that your company is nothing in Japan and begin from there. Even if you think the guy across the table must know a good deal about a firm as famous as yours, you can do credit to your listener (as well as to yourself) by being modest about your own firm and its accomplishments. In Japan, that is simply good manners.

For example, many a Japanese executive meeting you abroad might introduce himself by saying something like, "I'm with Mitsubishi Heavy Industries. We build ships and things," as if his firm were a small twinkle in the firmament of Japanese industry. So don't feel foolish to introduce yourself in Japan, regardless of the size of your company, by saying something like, "I'm with a company called Ford. We make cars . . ." At the very least, a little practice in humility will serve you well in Japan.

One of the biggest pitfalls that *gaishi* seem to leap into with depressing regularity derives from this lack of "perspective"; that is, the attitude best summed up as "we do things this way everywhere else in the world and it works just fine, so we're going to do it that way here, too." This inflexible attitude (particularly common in American companies but by no means limited to them) may stem from nothing more than a belief in efficiency: what works well for us in 26 other countries is undoubtedly the most effective, consistent, and therefore efficient system to try in Japan. And in the end it just might be. But too many companies simply insist on doing business "their way" without first checking to see if that is going to work well in Japan or whether it will be perceived as arrogance by their clients, insensitivity by their employees, and so on.

There is a famous story about NTT, one of the world's largest corporations. Years ago it was under considerable pressure from the Japanese government (its real boss) to purchase foreign, preferably American, telecommunications equipment to ease trade friction. NTT was well aware of the superb reputation of equipment made by its American namesake, and the decision was quickly made to buy from AT&T if at all possible. NTT planned to buy a certain kind of exchange equipment and install it in every telephone office throughout Japan. In short, it was a huge order. The only problem was that the U.S.-made equipment was physically a bit larger than the Japanese equipment it would be replacing. Since these exchange boxes would be installed nationwide, making sure the equipment would fit into a certain allocated space that was the same in thousands of offices was quite important. NTT asked AT&T if it could repackage the same equipment in a slightly smaller case. The AT&T representative replied to the effect that his company had installed the same equipment all over the world. Why should they change it just for Japan? If it didn't fit, NTT should make more space to accommodate it.

Not surprisingly, the NTT executives were more worried about the attitude problem than the size problem. In the end they bought the equipment they needed and installed it in thousands of offices nationwide—but they bought it from Northern Telecom.

Beware of Consultants

One of the areas in which *gaishi* are usually at a disadvantage compared with Japanese rivals is in their total number of staff. *Gaishi* companies are usually limited in terms of office space and the amount of available personnel. It is perfectly natural that they have come to depend in many areas on certain kinds of outside "professionals" such as research companies, consultants, and headhunters. Unfortunately, many of these firms are not very good.

Many of the "corporate service" companies that grew up in Tokyo, for example, became well known in their field more or less by default—often they were the "only game in town." The few *gaijin*-oriented firms that were active decades ago were popular more because of their friendly faces and sympatico business styles than their demonstrable results. Over the years, *gaijin*-oriented (and usually *gaijin*-run) consulting firms have supplied their clients with a staggering amount of poor advice and they have misread the Japanese market in such a way as to cost their clients handsome sums.

It is only natural for *gaijin* executives to turn to *gaijin* consultants or foreign-based consulting companies. Just look at Japanese companies operating overseas—*gaishi* in reverse. When almost any kind of service is needed their first reaction is to look for a Japanese company, however good or bad, to handle it. They feel better having another Japanese to talk to even if they know nothing about the company. In fact most Japanese firms will pass up an opportunity to deal with a well-known, first-rate domestic firm right next door to bring in a Japanese company from across town that they know absolutely nothing about. More or less the same can be said about *gaishi* firms in Japan.

Sadly there have been too many cases in which a foreign company in trouble turned to a foreign consultant for advice and, thanks to that advice, found itself in even deeper trouble. A certain European airline was having problems with its excessive payroll, but no matter what kind of restructuring plan it put forward, the local union resisted and tensions continued to grow. The airline called in a foreign consultant who claimed to be an expert on such matters. "Leave everything to me," he said confidently. He studied the situation, then recommended that the company divide the cooperative employees from the uncooperative, separating them by pay scale and job evaluations. It sounded good to the airline at first, but the advice proved tragically misguided. First, it was technically illegal, breaking the company's wage agreement with its workers, and, secondly, it put the union in an even more defensive stance. The union demanded that all salaries, which had previously been paid by bank transfer, must be paid to each employee in cash. Then the union sued the company for breach of the labor law and won a total victory. What about the consultant who caused this firm so much grief and financial loss? He took his fee and went on to work for the next big *gaishi* client. He is still active in Tokyo today, has a number of famous corporations for clients, and has caused more trouble for them than we could put in this book. All the same, his office is bigger and nicer than the presidents of many of the companies for whom he contracts, he's written books about his work, and he still has a steady stream of business.

Many readers unfamiliar with Tokyo must wonder how this can be. In New York or London or Paris the word would be out overnight and consultants like this would be practically out of business. But not in Tokyo. The reason is that *gaishi* want to do business with *gaishi*; they want to see a *gaijin* face, someone they can trust. People think that anyone who's been in Japan a few years and speaks more Japanese than they do is to be trusted. If he calls himself an expert he must be an expert. After all, he does this for a living. If he wasn't any good he wouldn't still be around, would he?

Our advice: Beware of the easily-impressed-*gaijin* syndrome. Remember: Experience Does Not Equal Expertise.

Do not assume any relationship between the number of years someone has been in Japan and that person's knowledge of the country's customs, language, business practices, etc. There are hundreds of *gaijin* who have lived in Japan for 20 years or more and don't speak enough Japanese to find their way to a bathroom, much less advise anyone on how to solve delicate personnel problems. As a matter of fact, when it comes to difficult questions such as problems with a company labor union, there are very few really capable Japanese consultants. Good foreign consultants? We haven't met one yet.

The other side of the coin is Japanese consultants who speak fluent English. They seem to mix the best of both worlds. Very few of them are independent; they usually work for one of the big foreign consulting firms and so appear even more trustworthy. Some of them are every bit as good as they appear to be, but they are a minority. Most are not much better than their *gaijin* counterparts. The reason is that the majority of consulting firms look for the same kind of Japanese employees: slick, smooth-talking individuals with good English, and preferably an MBA or another advanced degree from a U.S. university. They are very reassuring to talk to and their resumés look great. But the problem with such people is exactly the same as with Japanese executives who have spent a long time overseas. A consultant who has spent years in the United States getting a Ph.D. from Harvard or somewhere is probably better qualified to talk about American business than Japanese business. He has missed many of the crucial years when his peers were learning about the inner workings of Japanese companies, and he has missed out on building the *jinmyaku* that is necessary to solve certain problems. He sees Japan not from his experience in working with Japanese firms, but as a case study from a textbook combined with a lot of hearsay. Big consulting firms are full of these young men (and women), and the *gaishi* manager who hires them should be prepared to take their advice with more than a few grains of salt. Worse, some of the biggest and most famous consulting companies don't hesitate to stick a client for a few million dollars for the privilege of offering them bad advice neatly printed and bound in a nice-looking folder. Then they say goodbye and leave the client to clean up the mess. Some of the most famous Japanese consultants working for big foreign firms are notorious for this.

Once again, there are good firms out there and good individuals even at some ordinary firms. But there are far too many would-be experts and outright hustlers who see the lucrative *gaishi* market as an easy meal ticket. A well-financed corporate client who assumes that anyone who has a book or two to his name, or a plush down-town office, or platoons of bright young research associates *must* be trustworthy is about to be taken to the cleaners. And the fact that most clients don't know when they're getting bad advice (and pay for it even when they do) makes this business especially attractive to the wrong kind of people.

. . . And While You're at It, Beware of Headhunters

Sad to say, a lot of headhunting firms aren't much better. A foreign executive who's been in Japan for a few years, has some contacts, and knows a little about how the system works, will seldom resort to calling a headhunter. Not only are their fees ridiculous, but they all bring in the same kind of people. It doesn't matter much which firm you use because they've all got similar lists of every Japanese with an MBA. Of course as we've noted, an MBA is totally worthless inside Japan (except to foreign personnel man-agers who don't know better) and except in rare cases indicates a *lack* of experience. Most headhunters refer the kind of people they think corporations like to have around the office: sharp-looking men and women who perform well in interviews, speak reasonably good English (or whatever language is required), and seem alert and interesting. In some cases these might be the kind of people you want, but not very often. Some of the best people you could find as managers for your local business are probably terrible dressers, come across rather poorly in an interview, and can't say much more than hello in English. But they are extremely bright, can usually read and understand foreign languages with no prob-lem, have hands-on experience in major companies, and are firmly plugged into important human networks. Moreover these people are loyal and hard working, not likely to pick up and leave when the same headhunter calls them back two years later with a better offer from one of his new clients.

Headhunters are salesmen, not advisors. Their job is to sell you what you want (or what they think you want), not to show you what you need.

And don't think the problem is limited to lower-level employees or middle managers. Tokyo is full of Japanese presidents of *gaishi* firms who are just older versions of the smooth-talking young MBAs. A quick look at their resumes usually turns up a similar pattern: senior executive at half a dozen or more *gaishi* over a period of many years. A little more research usually shows that in almost every case the company was in worse shape after they were hired than before, and some digging will almost always show that they left rather hurriedly from each post. But do *gaishi* examine the background of their new CEOs? Not often. "He speaks good English, he dresses well, he looks good—for a Japanese— and besides, he was vice-president of Japan–American Widget for two years and then president of ABC Bank's Tokyo branch for a few years. We're lucky to be able to snatch him away."

Just like the consultants and the headhunters, these professional *gaishi shacho* feed off the ignorance (and the poor communication) of the foreign community in Japan. But Japanese companies know who many of these men are, and when your firm hires one, its reputation suffers as a result. If your company has already made a good name for itself, your Japanese clients, suppliers, bankers, etc., may say to themselves, "If we wait two or three years, that *shacho* will move on to another firm, and then we might want to talk to this company again."

The bottom line is this: There are some very good people in the job market in Tokyo, but there are also a lot of good-looking phonies. Don't trust a headhunter's opinion and don't trust only your own gut instincts. When it comes time to hire people for important positions in your firm, get a trusted Japanese manager or two to interview the candidates separately and then talk over their reactions thoroughly before you make any decisions.

A Tip for Structuring Top Management at a *Gaishi*

Here is our recommendation for establishing a successful management structure that will satisfy the needs of both the home office and the Japan subsidiary: have not one but two senior executives in Japan, one a representative from the home office (the real CEO) and one a Japanese (the COO). The important point to remember is not to do as some *gaishi* have done and make the CEO the president. Instead, install your home office chief executive as chairman of the local firm, and the senior Japanese exec as president.

Why is this particular structure so important?

In Japan the chairman (*kaicho*) of a company is certainly an important figure and often in the business spotlight, but he is seldom the firm's chief executive. The real power in a corporation is almost always held by the president, or *shacho*. While this is somewhat different from management policy at many Western firms, it provides an ideal situation for a foreign firm trying to communicate with two different cultures. By installing a Japanese executive as president, you give him or her considerable prestige, respect, and, most of all, the ability to get things done. Inside the company it may be an open secret that the chairman is the real CEO, but to Japanese outside the firm the home-country chairman appears to be something of a figurehead. Providing you have good communication between these two executives, this can work to your advantage.

The foreign chairman's role is to act as liaison with company headquarters, international divisions, and other foreign organizations. The Japanese president is responsible for overseeing hiring and personnel policies, relations with clients, suppliers, banks, government ministries, etc. In other words, the *shacho* acts just like any other *shacho* and takes care of all normal executive responsibilities, while the *kaicho's* role is hardly visible to the outside world. An added advantage of this system is that there is no need for the chairman to learn every nuance of Japanese society, customs, language, and so on. That's what the *shacho* is there for.

If you look for a highly qualified Japanese executive to serve as president, someone who can run a company efficiently and responsibly, there are many good candidates. But if you look for someone who combines both functions, who can run a Japanese company well and deal with local problems, and who is also comfortable back at your home office, can fly back for top-level meetings, make presentations in English, etc., you will discover that there are very few good people around. And if you find one, you probably shouldn't be paying whatever he asks.

Thus the only practical solution is "duplex management," a foreign chairman and a Japanese president. It should be obvious to anyone who studies Japanese business for a week or two that calling the *gaijin* "president" and the Japanese "vice-president" or "executive assistant" or "special advisor to the president" or anything else is a huge mistake, yet it is one that countless foreign firms continue to make. Japanese companies instinctively direct their attention to the *shacho,* and anyone below the rank of *shacho* is considered relatively unimportant. If your top local manager is called vice-president, no one will talk to him because they will assume he has no final authority about anything. The only way to give your Japanese executive the power and respect that is essential to get the job done is to confer the title of *shacho,* and the only way to ensure the same respect for the home office representative is to use the title of *kaicho.*

This "duplex" system should give your firm the flexibility to operate smoothly both inside and outside Japan.

Conclusion

In closing, we would like to reiterate that there are still plenty of problems for *gaishi* operating in Japan. No one is saying that setting up a business here is easy nor that becoming successful in this market is a simple proposition. In addition to all the potential problems connected with regulations, personnel systems, consumer preferences, distribution channels, and so on, there is the totally unpredictable. For example, P&G and Nestlé both suffered considerable damage to corporate facilities in the Kobe earthquake in January 1995, as did a number of other foreign firms. And yet despite all the problems, *gaishi* continue to grab larger and larger segments of the Japanese markets, and Japanese firms continue to look for foreign products to import or license and call their own. There is no lack of demand for foreign goods and services.

Japan is an affluent and expanding market—in many ways one of the most attractive markets in the world. *Gaishi* succeed not by attacking this market or its peculiarities, but almost always by becoming part of it. Many segments of Japanese business are still largely "insiders' clubs": a few big firms run those markets and limit outsiders to insignificant pieces of the pie. Where *gaishi* have made the biggest successes they have often done so by working patiently to become insiders themselves. Is it difficult to adapt to changing markets here? Not really. Firms that listen carefully to consumers and distributors find out what to do. Once they become successful and their brand names are well known, *gaishi* can go from being outsiders to insiders in much the same way as did P&G, Coca-Cola, and several others. These firms have become among the biggest players in their respective markets and as such are able to profit from the same kind of advantages as their leading Japanese rivals. If there is a single basic strategy for success here, this is it in a nutshell.

We earnestly hope that by studying the successes and failures of the companies in this book other firms will be better prepared to take advantage of the opportunities that are waiting for them in Japan.

Index

Adaptation, of product, 26–27
Administrative guidance (gyosei shido), 289
AFLAC (formerly American Family Life Assurance Company), 129–55, 290, 336–37
After-care policy, 3
AIG, 133
Air express service, 315–33
AIU, 133, 135, 136
Alcon Japan Ltd., 275–93
Alcon Laboratories, 275, 279
Alcon Research Institute, 286
Alhadef, Carlo, 220, 221, 226
ALICO, 133
Alitalia, 220
Allied Lyons plc, 300
Amakudari, 22–23, 146
American Express, 319
American Family, 135
Amos, John B., 129, 130, 150
Amos, Paul, 130
Amos, William, 130
Amway, 157–75
Apple Computer, 4
Arthur Anderson, 202
Artzt, Ed, 100
Asahi Denka Kogyo (ADK), 90

ASI Market Research (Japan), 26
AT&T, 338
Audi, 79

Barton, Walter, 132
Bausch and Lomb, 289
Baxter International, 21
Bellini, Mario, 232
Biculturalism, 48
Big Three auto maker, 70
Big Four, 200, 202, 204, 209, 214
Big Two (Toyota and Nissan), 74
Black & Decker, 319
Black & White Japan, 306
Black market, 56
BMW (Bayerische Motoren Werke A.G.), 5, 6, 28, 69–87, 195
Borden, 4
Brand recognition, 37
Branemark, Per-Ingvar, Dr., 238
Branemark System, 239
Breakfast cereal, 260–61
Bubble economy (era), 41, 51–54, 87, 191, 195, 196, 211–13, 308
Bucho, 14, 21
Buitoni, 26–27
Bureaucracy, in Japan, 113–16

C. Itoh & Co. *See* Itochu Corp.
Cancer insurance. *See* AFLAC.
Canon Inc., 174, 292
Carnation, 271
Chappell, John, 47–49
Christian Lacroix, 66–67
Chrysler, 70
Coca-Cola Export Corporation
    (CCEC), 109, 113, 118
Coca-Cola (Japan) Co. Ltd., 4, 28,
    105–28, 157, 265, 270, 290, 335,
    337
Commission system, in insurance
    sales, 150
Consumer durable, 169–70
Coopervision, 281–82
Corporate headquarters
    BMW, 84
    DHL, 331–332
    Parker Pen, 191–92
    Procter and Gamble, 101
    Salomon, 217
Corporate identity, in Japan, 5–6
Counterfeit manufacturer, 64–65
Courtis, Kenneth, 206
Crandell, Bert, 169
Credit association (shinkin), 215
Cross, 185, 186, 193

Dai Nippon Ink, 213
Dai-Ichi Kangyo Bank (DKB), 143,
    154, 278, 282
Daiichi Kogyo Seiyaku (DKS), 90
Dai-Ichi Life Insurance, 133
Daimaru Peacock, 262
Daimler-Benz, 75
Daio Paper, 94
Daiwa, 200
Daiya Sangyo, 29
Dalsey, Hillblom, and Lynn, 315
Dental implant, 237–54
Deutsche Bank, 152, 206
DeVos, Richard M., 160
DHL, 315–33
DHL Corp., 332
DHL International, 332
Diet, 111–13, 119, 133, 164

Digital Equipment Corp. Japan, 85
Direct sales, 157–75
    Nihon Homon Hanbai Kyokai,
        165
Direct Sales Law, 164
Discount, from department store, 63
DistillerUs Company Ltd. (DCL),
    295
Distribution channel, 27–29,
    115–16
Distribution system, 250
    Amway, 167–68
    Nippon Olivetti, 221
Distributor, for Amway, 158–59
Diversification, of product line, 124
DKB, 214
Dunhill, 196

Egon Zender, 328
Electrolux, 28, 248
Elsing, Peter, 89
English skill, 14–15, 18–21
Equal opportunity, in Japan, 245–48
Euroyen subordinated debt, 214
Executive, role of, 326–28
Export-Import Bank, 146
Eye care product, 275–93

Fanuc, 174
Faust, Louis, III, 215
Federal Express, 318, 323, 332
Fields, George, 26
Financial deregulation, 202
Fincher, David, 46
Flying Tiger, 332
Food and Drug Administration,
    U.S., 291
Ford, 70
Foreign Affiliated Companies
    Management Association
    (FAMA), 153
Friskies K.K., 271
Fujiya, 269
Fuyo group, 135

Gaiatsu, 114
Gaishi securities firm, 206

General Agreement on Tariffs and
Trade (GATT),298
General Foods, 278–79
Gift giving season, 168
Gillette Japan, 28, 196, 302
Giorgio Armani, 41
GM, 6, 70
Gorbachev, Soviet Premier, 192
Guinness Beer Worldwide, 296
Guinness plc., 296

Hall, Mike, 127
Hamawaki, Yoji, 71, 72, 74, 79, 82,
83
Hankyu, 59
Hanna, Jeffrey, 210
Harajuku, 41
Hasegawa, Hiroshi, 270
Hasegawa, Izumi, 134
Hata, Gojiro, 53, 57, 67
Hayashi, Toshio, 180, 186, 191, 193
Headhunting firm, 342–43
Headquarters. *See* Corporate
headquarters.
Hemmer, William, 163, 170
Hirazuka Distibution Center, 32
Hitachi, 175, 249
Home sales industry, 157–75
Honda, 71
Hornmark, Nils, 239, 244
Hornmark, Noriko, 239–40, 244–45

IBM, 43, 220
Ijiri, Tokio, 93, 97
Image, in Japan, 3–5
Information dissemination, by
ministry, 142
Insurance Business Law, 140
Insurance company, 129–55
Insurance Department, Finance
Ministry, 138
International Insurance Agency
Group (IAG), 135, 136
Inventory control, 168
Investment banking, 199–218
Ireland, Charles, 270
Iron triangle, 116

Ishikawajima-Harima Heavy
Industries, 155
Isuzu Motors, 155
Itochu America, 279
Itochu Corp, 278
Itochu Shoji (C. Itoh & Co.), 90, 155
Iwaki, Junko, 166, 173
Iwakura, Tomomi, 308
Iwamura, Masaomi, 123
Iwashita, Atsuhiro, 193
Iwata, Kunihiko, 275, 276, 282–84,
293
Izuzu, 70

Jacobs Suchard, 270, 271
Japan Air Lines, 332
Jardine Mathiesson, 305
Jardine Wines & Spirits, 305
Jinmyaku, 15–17, 21–25
Johnson and Johnson, 289
Johnson, Richard S., 170
Joint venture (JV), 90–91

Kacho, 14, 303, 318
Kanematsu, 306
Kao Corp, 89, 94, 96, 97
Kaomi Shoten, 107
Katakana, 2
Kaufman, Henry, 210
Kawamura, Nobuo, 135, 145, 147
Kawasaki America, 72
Kawasaki Heavy Industries (KHI),
71, 72, 73, 174
Kawasaki Steel, 135, 137
Kawashima, Toshiaki, 200, 202, 208,
215
Keio, 59
Keiretsu system, 59, 107, 144, 154
Kellogg, 260, 262
Kerr, John, 322
Kikkoman, 107, 123
Kirin Breweries, 123, 298, 303
Kirin-Seagram Ltd., 303
Kishi, Nagami, 311
Klett, Hans J., 255, 269, 272
Kniberg, Gunnar, 248
Koami Shoten, 109

Komatsu, Manpo, 21–22
Kravitz, Lennie, 46
Kure, Takeshi, 160, 168
Kurisaka, Takashi, 328
Kurita, Koichiro, 226
Kuwabara, Shizue, 61
Kyocera Corp., 242
Kyowa Hakko, 305

Lee, 36
Levi Strauss Japan K.K., 28, 31–49,
    121, 157, 221, 249
Liar's Poker, 203
Lifetime employment, 8, 145
Lion Corp, 89, 96
Liquor
    industry, 295–313
    tax, 297
L.L. Bean, 5, 41
Localization, 222–24, 267
Loewe, 66–67
Lotte, 265
Louis Vuitton, 5, 6, 51–67, 191, 195
Lufthansa, 332

Macintosh, 4
Maezawa, Masatoshi, 188
Magry, Jacques G., 178, 180
Management, in Japan, 6–14
Mannami, Toshihiro, 271
Manpower, 178, 180
Market identity, 5–6
Marketing Investment, 307
Maruyama, Shigeki, 213
Matsui, Hidefumi, 135
Matsushita (Panasonic), 227, 249
Matsushita Elecric Industrial, 175,
    213, 226–28, 236
Maughan, Derek C., 207, 215
Max Factor, 101
Mazda, 70
MBA, status of, 15–21, 213
McKinsey & Co., 24, 127
Meidi-ya, 256
Mercedes, 74, 79
Merrill Lynch, 203, 217

Ministry of Agriculture, Forests, and
    Fisheries (MAFF), 112, 115,
    119
Ministry of Finance (MOF), 93, 109,
    132, 136, 138, 141, 143, 201,
    205, 277, 336
    administrative guidance, 151
    Securities Bureau, 204
Ministry of Health and Welfare
    (MHW), 21–22, 138, 141, 163,
    170, 173, 240, 288–89, 290, 291
    Insurance Bureau, 146
    Medical Affairs Bureau, 138
Ministry of International Trade and
    Industry (MITI), 24, 92, 109,
    112, 118, 164, 289, 336
Ministry system, 110–11, 137–39
Mission, 12
Mitsubishi Corp., 36, 70, 123
    keiretsu, 135
Mitsubishi Heavy Industries, 123
Mitsubishi Trust and Banking Co.,
    213, 256
Mitsui and Co., 123, 181, 248, 250
Mitsui Toatsu, 181
Mitsui Trust & Banking, 174,
    224–25
Mitsukoshi, 59
Mitsuwa Soap, 90
Moet-Hennessy, 296, 305
Momose, Shinichi, 319–33
Mont Blanc, 29, 185, 186, 193, 196,
Morgan Stanley, 6
Morinaga & Co., 256
Motivation, 11–13
Myojin, Shigeru, 200

Nakata, Takao, 307
Nakazawa, Shigeko, 280–81
Napier, Ron, 211
National legislature. *See* Diet.
Nawa, Hideaki, 121
NCR, 220, 222
Nestle, Henri, 256
Nestle Japan Limited, 255–73
Nestle Mackintosh K.K., 269
Nestle S.A., 256

Nihon Electrolux System Co. (NESCO), 248–51
Nihon Homon Hanbai Kyokai, 165
Nihon Keizai Shimbun (Nikkei), 142
Nihon P&G, 94–95
Nihon Shurui Hanbai, 305
Nikko, 200
Nippon Life Insurance, 132, 205
Nippon Motorola, 162
Nippon Olivetti (Olivetti Corp. of Japan), 219–36, 319
Nippon Sun Home, 90
Nippon Tupperware, 171
Nissan Motors, 56, 83, 87, 175, 185
Nissho Iwai, 332
Nobel, Alfred, 238
Nobelpharma Japan, 237–54
Noda Shoyu, 107. *See* Kikkoman.
Nokyo, 235
Nomura Securities, 199, 200, 205, 209, 214, 217
Noritomi, Shunji, 300, 301, 306, 312
Northern Telecom, 339
NTT, 338–39
Nutrilite, 160

Occupation, U.S. Military, 113, 178, 257
Oda, Yoshiyuki, 148
Odakyu, 59
Office equipment, 219–36
Ogawa, Yuji, 135
Ohki, Masafumi, 35, 41
Ohyama, Shinji, 214
Oil crisis, 91–94, 145, 318
Oishi, Takeshi, 53, 62
Olivetti Corp. of Japan. *See* Nippon Olivetti.
Omae, Kenichi, 24
Operating style (shafu), 282, 283
Osaka Titanium Mfg., 214
Oscar Mayer, 277
Otake, Yoshiki, 132, 133

P&G Sun Home, 90
Panasonic (Matsushita), 227, 249
Parker, John S., 177

Parker Pen, 177–97
Pay scale, in Japan, 8
Peat, Marwick, Mitchell, 57, 62
Pepsico, 171
Pepsi-Cola, 4, 118, 120–22, 124
Personal connection, 15–17
Plaza Accord, 206
Political pressure, 112–14. *See also* Gaiatsu.
Porsche, 79
Post-bubble strategy, 216–17
Prima Meat Packers, Ltd. (Prima Ham), 278
Procter and Gamble Far East, Inc. (P&G), 5, 6, 89–103, 152

Quality control, 42–44

Ralph Lauren, 41
Reagan, Ronald, U.S. President, 192
Recession (early 1990s), 53, 87, 89, 201, 215, 312, 333
Reichold Chemical, 213
Remington, 220
Revlon, 102
Richter, Siegfried, Dr., 85, 86
Ringisho, 229
R.J. Reynolds, 171
Rolex, 191
Rosenberg, Jerry, 162
Rowntree Mackintosh, 269

Saab, 79
Sakura Bank, 214
Sales agent, 28
Salomon Bros., 6, 24, 25, 199–218
Salomon Bros. Asia Limited, 201–202
Sandoz, 290
Santen Pharmaceutical, 293
Sanyo, 249
Sato, Kenneth D., 315–19
Sawallisch, Walter, 80
Schenley, 296
Schick, 28, 196
Schlesinger, John, 213
Scorinos, Frank H., 132, 133

Seagram, 302
Securities industry, 205
Securities Law, 204
Seibu Saison, 59, 60, 123
Seiko, Hattori, 28
Seniority system, 8
Shacho, 21, 180, 184, 226, 304
Sharp Corp., 163
Shimizu Construction, 155
Shoten, Koami, 118
Sinniger, Heinz J., 266
Sony, 21, 213
Source Perrier, 269
Sterling Drug Co., 91
Studies of Gaishi Businesses, 311
Sumitomo Corp., 174
Sumitomo Metal Industries, 214
Suntory Ltd., 298–300, 310
Super 301, 103
Suzuki, Roy, 120, 125, 126
Swiss Bank, 152

Takada Coopervision, 281–82
Takada Machinery, 281–82
Takanashi Coca-Cola Environmental
    Education Foundation, 128
Takanashi, Nisaburo, 107–8, 110, 128
Takara Belmont, 182
Takashi, Tomura, 221
Takashimaya, 59, 60
Tanaka, Hajime, 39
Tanegashima, Tsutomu, 76–78, 80
Teijin, 279
Teijin Alcon, 279
Tokio Marine & Fire Insurance, 135,
    146–47
Tokyo Bank, 147
Tokyo Beverage K.K., 116, 118
Tokyo Coca-Cola Bottling Co., 116,
    122
Tokyo Life Insurance, 147
Tokyo Stock Exchange (TSE), 149,
    201, 206, 207, 209, 245
Tokyu, 59
Tokyu Agency International Inc., 307
Tonya (wholesaler), 28, 44, 107, 115,
    157, 258–59
Toray Industries, 300

Toray-DuPont, 300
Toshiba, 219, 249
Toyo Engineering, 181
Toyo Rayon. *See* Toray Industries.
Toyobo, 36
Toyota, 38, 83, 87, 175, 185
Tsubaki, Beniko, 216
Tsuda, Nobuhiro, 161, 174
TV Tokyo, 147

UDJ International Liquor Marketing
    Limited (UDJ-ILM), 28, 304,
    306, 309
Unicharm, 94, 97
United Distillers, 296
United Distillers Group (UDG),
    296, 300, 304, 305
United Distillers Japan (UDJ),
    295–313
University of Tokyo, 16
Uotani, Masahiko, 127, 270
UPS, 318, 332
U.S. Semiconductor, 214
U.S.-Japan Security Treaty, 119
Uzawa, Ichiro, 187, 190, 194

Van Andel, Jay, 160
Vending machine, 122, 124
Veuve Cliquot, 66–67
Volkswagen, 28
Volvo, 74, 79, 279
Vuitton, Gaston, 55
Vuitton, Georges, 55
Vuitton, Louis, 54

Wada, Heisuke, 32
Wakasugi, Shigetada, 307, 310, 311
Waterman, 196
Wella, 182, 188
Wholesaler system (tonya), 221. *See
    also* Tonya.

Yamaha, 72
Yamaichi Securities, 200
Yanase, 28
Yasuda Fire & Marine Insurance, 135
Yasuda Life Insurance, 148
Yoshida, Shigeru, 308

About the Authors

Nagami Kishi is recognized internationally as an authority on cross-cultural management in Japan. He is the President of Human & Industry Research Co., Ltd. (H&IR), a Tokyo-based consulting firm specializing in human resource policy. A former NHK-TV journalist assigned to cover international business and economics, Mr. Kishi is a frequent speaker on topics relating to international business, the founder and Secretary-General of an organization for international companies doing business in Japan, and a contributor to business magazines on HK issues. Prior to his affiliation with H&IR, Mr. Kishi was General Manager of Far East Research for Prudential-Bache Securities and Managing Editor of *Business Tokyo* magazine. He has authored nine books (in Japanese), on business, culture, and economics.

Author **David Russell** is a business journalist living in Tokyo. Fluent in Japanese, he has led seminars for Japanese people doing business abroad, been an Editor for a major Japanese securities firm, edited a weekly for *Nihon Keizai Shimbun*, and served as Editor-in-Chief of *Business Tokyo* magazine. Mr. Russell is currently Managing Editor for Toyo Keizai's *Tokyo Business Today* magazine. He is the co-author, with Kenichi Miyashita, of the award-winning book, *Keiretsu: Inside the Hidden Japanese Conglomerates* (McGraw-Hill, 1994).

The authors may be contacted at:

Trans-Pacific Productions
Sun-T Bldg., 6th Floor Taishido 1-12-25
Setagaya-ku, Tokyo 125
FAX [813] 5430-0302

TITLES OF INTEREST IN
BUSINESS AND INTERNATIONAL BUSINESS

HOW TO CREATE HIGH-IMPACT BUSINESS PRESENTATIONS, by Joyce Kupsh and Pat Graves
EFFECTIVE BUSINESS DECISION MAKING, by William F. O'Dell
HOW TO GET PEOPLE TO DO THINGS YOUR WAY, by J. Robert Parkinson
HANDBOOK FOR MEMO WRITING, by L. Sue Baugh
HANDBOOK FOR BUSINESS WRITING, by L. Sue Baugh, Maridell Fryar, and David A. Thomas
HANDBOOK FOR PROOFREADING, by Laura Killen Anderson
HANDBOOK FOR TECHNICAL WRITING, James Shelton
HOW TO BE AN EFFECTIVE SPEAKER, by Christina Stuart
FORMAL MEETINGS, by Alice N. Pohl
COMMITTEES AND BOARDS, by Alice N. Pohl
MEETINGS: RULES AND PROCEDURES, by Alice N. Pohl
BIG MEETINGS, BIG RESULTS, by Tom McMahon
HOW TO GET THE MOST OUT OF TRADE SHOWS, by Steve Miller
HOW TO GET THE MOST OUT OF SALES MEETINGS, by James Dance
A BASIC GUIDE TO EXPORTING, by U.S. Department of Commerce
A BASIC GUIDE TO IMPORTING, by U.S. Customs Service
CULTURE CLASH, by Ned Seelye and Alan Seelye-James
DOING BUSINESS IN RUSSIA, by ALM Consulting, Frere Chomeley Bischoff; and KPMG Peat Marwick
THE GLOBAL MARKETING IMPERATIVE, by Michael Czinkota, Ilkka Ronkainen and John Tarrant
THE INTERNATIONAL BUSINESS BOOK, by Vincent Guy and John Matlock
INTERNATIONAL BUSINESS CULTURE SERIES, by Peggy Kenna and Sondra Lacy
INTERNATIONAL HERALD TRIBUNE: DOING BUSINESS IN TODAY'S WESTERN EUROPE, by Alan Tillier
INTERNATIONAL HERALD TRIBUNE: GUIDE TO EUROPE, by Alan Tillier and Roger Beardwood
INTERNATIONAL HERALD TRIBUNE: GUIDE TO BUSINESS TRAVEL IN ASIA, by Robert K. McCabe
DOING BUSINESS WITH CHINA
MARKETING TO CHINA, by Xu Bai-Yi
THE JAPANESE INFLUENCE ON AMERICA, by Boye De Mente
JAPANESE ETIQUETTE & ETHICS IN BUSINESS, by Boye De Mente
CHINESE ETIQUETTE & ETHICS IN BUSINESS, by Boye De Mente
KOREAN ETIQUETTE & ETHICS IN BUSINESS, by Boye De Mente

For further information or a current catalog, write:
NTC Business Books
a division of NTC Publishing Group
4255 West Touhy Avenue
Lincolnwood, Illinois 60646–1975

DATE DUE

DEMCO, INC. 38-2931